Library of New Testament Studies

668

Formerly the Journal for the Study of the New Testament Supplement series

Editor
Chris Keith

Editorial Board
Dale C. Allison, Lynn H. Cohick, R. Alan Culpepper, Craig A. Evans,
Jennifer Eyl, Robert Fowler, Simon J. Gathercole, Juan Hernández Jr.,
John S. Kloppenborg, Michael Labahn, Matthew V. Novenson,
Love L. Sechrest, Robert Wall, Catrin H. Williams,
Brittany E. Wilson

Paul, The Apostle of Obedience

Reading Obedience in Romans

Jason A. Myers

LONDON • NEW YORK • OXFORD • NEW DELHI • SYDNEY

T&T CLARK
Bloomsbury Publishing Plc
50 Bedford Square, London, WC1B 3DP, UK
1385 Broadway, New York, NY 10018, USA
29 Earlsfort Terrace, Dublin 2, Ireland

BLOOMSBURY, T&T CLARK, and the T&T Clark logo are trademarks of
Bloomsbury Publishing Plc

First published in Great Britain 2023
Paperback edition published 2024

Copyright © Jason A. Myers, 2023, 2024

Jason A. Myers has asserted his right under the Copyright, Designs and
Patents Act, 1988, to be identified as Author of this work.

For legal purposes the Acknowledgments on p. xii constitute an
extension of this copyright page.

All rights reserved. No part of this publication may be reproduced or transmitted in
any form or by any means, electronic or mechanical, including photocopying,
recording, or any information storage or retrieval system, without prior
permission in writing from the publishers.

Bloomsbury Publishing Plc does not have any control over, or responsibility for, any
third-party websites referred to or in this book. All internet addresses given in this
book were correct at the time of going to press. The author and publisher regret any
inconvenience caused if addresses have changed or sites have ceased to exist, but
can accept no responsibility for any such changes.

A catalogue record for this book is available from the British Library.

Library of Congress Cataloging-in-Publication Data

Names: Myers, Jason A., 1984– author.
Title: Paul, the apostle of obedience : reading obedience in Romans / Jason A. Myers.
Description: London ; New York : T&T CLARK, 2022. | Series: Library of New
Testament studies, 2513-8790 ; 668 | Includes bibliographical references and index. |
Summary: "This book situates Paul's phrase "the obedience of faith" in its
Greco-Roman context and then traces obedience as a theme through
Romans"–Provided by publisher.
Identifiers: LCCN 2022011484 (print) | LCCN 2022011485 (ebook) |
ISBN 9780567705839 (hardback) | ISBN 9780567705877 (paperback) |
ISBN 9780567705846 (pdf) | ISBN 9780567705860 (epub)
Subjects: LCSH: Bible. Romans–Criticism, interpretation, etc. |
Obedience–Biblical teaching. | Greek literature–History and criticism. |
Latin literature–History and criticism.
Classification: LCC BS2665.6.O26 M94 2022 (print) | LCC BS2665.6.O26 (ebook) |
DDC 227/.106–dc23/eng/20220525
LC record available at https://lccn.loc.gov/2022011484
LC ebook record available at https://lccn.loc.gov/2022011485

ISBN: HB: 978-0-5677-0583-9
PB: 978-0-5677-0587-7
ePDF: 978-0-5677-0584-6
ePUB: 978-0-5677-0586-0

Series: Library of New Testament Studies, volume 668
ISSN 2513-8790

Typeset by Newgen KnowledgeWorks Pvt. Ltd., Chennai, India

To find out more about our authors and books visit www.bloomsbury.com
and sign up for our newsletters.

Dedicated to
My wife Lisa
and our children Augustine and Phoebe

Contents

Preface		x
Acknowledgments		xii
List of Abbreviations		xiii
1	Introduction	1
	Common Approaches	3
	The Missional Approach	3
	The Exegetical Approach	5
	Key Works on Obedience	8
	Recent Works on Obedience in Paul	11
	Purpose of the Study	13
2	Reading Romans Rhetorically	15
	The Rhetorical Situation	15
	The Rhetorical Situation at Rome	16
	Reading Romans as a Roman: The Ideal Audience	17
	Reading Romans against Rome? A Note on Anti-Imperial Readings	19
3	Obedience in Greek Literature	29
	Terms of the Study	29
	Polybius: The Foundations of Obedience in Empire	31
	Polybius on Obedience	40
	Dionysius of Halicarnassus and the Rhetoric of Obedience	40
	Dionysius of Halicarnassus's Perspective on Obedience	45
	Cassius Dio on Obedience	46
	Dio and the Theme of Obedience	57
	Select Examples from Other Greek Authors	58
	Strabo and the Geography of Obedience	58
	Perspectives on Obedience in Greek Literature	60
4	Obedience in Latin Literature	63
	Livy and the Foundations of Obedience	63
	Livy on the Importance of Obedience	70

	Tacitus: Obedience in the Aftermath of Chaos	70
	Reflections on Obedience in Tacitus	80
	Perspectives on Obedience in Latin Literature	81
5	Philosophizing on Obedience	83
	Obedience in Aristotle	84
	Obedience in Epictetus	87
	Obedience in Plutarch	90
	Obedience in Cicero	94
	Obedience in Seneca the Younger	99
	Philosophical Reflections on Obedience	101
6	Sculpting Obedience	103
	The *Res Gestae*	104
	Examples of Obedience in Inscriptions and Monuments	106
	The Pisan Decrees of 2 and 4 CE	107
	The Oath to the Emperor	108
	Examples of Obedience in the Campus Martius	110
	The Impact of Images on a Roman Audience	114
7	Reading Obedience from the Margins: Rom. 1:1-12 and 15:14–16:23	115
	The Species of Rhetoric	116
	A Rhetorical Outline of Romans	117
	The Exordium	117
	The Peroratio	119
	The Exordium: Introduction and the First Appeal to Obedience (1:1-12)	120
	The Peroratio: Final Appeal to Obedience and Final Greetings (15:14–16:27)	124
	Conclusion on Rhetorical Bookends	128
8	Reading Obedience in the Argumentation in Romans	129
	The Propositio: Thesis Statement (1:16-17)	129
	The First Proof: A Diatribe on Gentile Disobedience (1:18-32)	130
	The Disobedience of Both Jew and Gentile (2:1-16)	131
	Jewish Disobedience (2:17-29)	134
	Jew and Gentile under Sin's Sway (3:1-20)	136
	Abraham: The Father of the Gentiles (4:1-25)	139
	The Second Proof: 5:1–8:39	142
	No Longer Obedient to Sin and Death (6:1-23)	147
	The Dilemma of Obedience and Disobedience (7:1-25)	151
	Obedience by Grace via the Power of the Spirit (8:1-39)	153

The Third Proof: 9:1–11:36	158
The Tragedy of Israel's Disobedience (9:1-29)	160
The Failure to Exercise Obedience (9:30–10:21)	161
Israel's Disobedience Is Not Final (11:1-36)	167
The Fourth Proof: (12:1–15:13)	171
The Obedience of Faith at Ground Level (12:1–13:15)	172
The Historical Situation: The Golden Age of Nero	177
The Obedience of Faith toward One Another (14:1–15:13)	185
9 Conclusion	191
Tracing Obedience through Romans	191
Common Themes	193
Appendix	197
Bibliography	199
Subject Index	223
Index of Modern Authors	229
Index of Biblical and Other Ancient Sources	231

Preface

This book represents a revision of my doctoral thesis accepted by Asbury Theological Seminary in 2015. I wish to thank Dr. Chris Keith who read and accepted my work for publication in the Library of New Testament Studies, and Sarah Blake, the commissioning editor who helped see this project to completion. My earnest appreciation also goes to the entire team at Bloomsbury Publishing for their editorial work.

I would like to express my appreciation and gratitude to those who helped, in numerous ways, to bring this work to completion. First, I would like to thank my *doktorvater*, Ben Witherington III, who read the various stages of this dissertation with a critical eye to the large and small issues: from correcting various errors to the bigger issues of asking penetrating questions and improving the overall quality of the work. Dr. Witherington has proved the most apt guide to nurture me through this process. He has been nothing but gracious to me in the guiding of this work to completion. I am thankful for his friendship and guidance not only over my doctoral work but also for a friendship that has extended well beyond our program.

Second, I'd also like to thank my second reader, Dr. Craig S. Keener. On professional and personal levels, Dr. Keener has been enthusiastic in his support of me and this work. He has offered much personal encouragement during this process at critical stages. His friendship has proved essential to my success in this endeavor.

Third, my study of the New Testament began at Cedarville University (2007) and continued at Grand Rapids Theological Seminary (2010). Both Dr. Chris Miller and Dr. Gary Meadors have invested much time and energy in preparing me for doctoral work. Dr. Chris Miller first introduced me to the fascinating study of Paul in the fall of 2005, and that excitement has continued to this book. His friendship and encouragement were integral to the development of this project over the years. Likewise Dr. Gary Meadors with his critical eye and passion for scholarship of the highest caliber was a formative experience in graduate school and was an essential part of preparing me for doctoral work. Under his critical watch, my research skills were developed and grown and the fruit of which is found in this work.

Fourth, the support of family and friends through this process has been a constant source of joy. Without friends, too many aspects of this journey would have been unbearable. At various points, Philip Richardson, Tad Blacketer, Jason Jackson, and Chad Foster have provided the encouragement, prayers, and reality checks that I've needed to bring this journey to a joyous conclusion.

I'd also like to extend appreciation to Tyndale House in Cambridge, UK, where research for this work began in June 2014. The resources there saved me valuable time in writing the literature review and without their help this process would only have taken much longer. The warm community welcome and scholarly interaction provided an enjoyable context to begin my work.

Finally, none of this, from graduate school to my doctoral program, would have been possible without the unending support of my wife, Lisa Myers. She has shared so much of the burden of doctoral work with much faithfulness. She has been a constant source of encouragement and support through this long and arduous process. She faithfully stands behind each and every accomplishment that I've done. I lovingly dedicate this work to her and to our children.

Jason A. Myers
Greensboro, North Carolina, 2022

Acknowledgments

All translations were taken from one of the following sources:

1. The Perseus Digital Library (http://www.perseus.tufts.edu/)
2. The Loeb Digital Library

Abbreviations

Aristotle

Cael.	De Caleo (On the Heavens)
Rhet.	Rhetoric
Pol.	Politics
Eth. nic.	Nichomachean Ethics
Meta.	Metaphysics
[*Mag. mor.*]	Magna Moralia
Soph. elench.	De Sophisticis Elenchis (On Sophistical Refutations)
Top.	Topica (Topics)
Virt. vit.	Virtues and Vices

Augustus

RG	Res Gestae

Cassius Dio

R. H.	Roman History

Cicero

Att.	Letters to Atticus
Caecin.	For Aulus Caecina
Clu.	For Aulus Cluentius
De Rep.	On the Republic
Div.	De Divinatione
Ep. Brut.	Letters to Brutus
Fam.	Letters to his Friends
Fat.	De Fato
Inv.	On Invention
Leg.	De Legibus
Nat. d.	de Natura Deorum
Off.	De Officiis
Parad.	Paradoxa Stoicorum
Phil.	Philippics
Prov. cons.	On the Consular Provinces
Rab. Perd.	For Rabirius on a Charge of Treason

Resp.

Sest.	For Sestius
Tusc.	Tusculan Disputations

Demosthenes *Meg*

On the Accession of Alexander

Aristog.	Against Aristogiton 1
Boeot.	Against Boeotus
[Macart.]	Against Macartatus
[Olymp.]	Against Olympiodorus
[Poly.]	Against Polycles
[Theocr.]	Against Theocrines

Diodorus Siculus

The Library of History

Dionysius of Halicarnassus

Ant. Rom.	The Roman Antiquities

Epictetus

Diatr.	Discourses
Disc.	Discourses
Ench.	Enchiridion

Herodotus

Hist.	Histories

Homer

Il.	The Illiad
Od.	The Odyssey

Livy

Hist.	History of Rome

Plato

Rep.	Republic

Plutarch

[Apoph. lac.]	Sayings of the Spartans

Adul. amic.	How to tell a Flatterer from a Friend
Aem.	Aemilius Paullus
Ages.	Agesilaus
Amat.	Amatorius
Ant.	Antonius
[Apoph. lac.]	Apophthegmata Laconica
Arat.	Aratus
Arist.	Aristeides
Art.	Artaxerxes
Caes.	Caesar
Cam.	Camillus
Cato. Maj.	Marcus Cato
Cat. Min.	Cato Minor
Cic.	Cicero
Coheb. ira	On Controlling Anger
Comp. Ag. Cleom. cum Ti. Gracch	Comparison of Agis and Cleomenes and the Gracchi
Comp. Eum. Sert	Comparison of Sertorius and Eumenes
Comp. Lys. Num.	Comparison of Lycurgus and Numa
Cor.	Caius Marcius Coriolanus
De Auditu	On Listening to Lectures
Demetr.	Demetrius
Dion	Dion
Fab.	Fabius Maximus
Flam.	Titus Flamininus
Fort. Rom.	On The Fortune of the Romans
Frat. amor.	On Brotherly Love
Galb.	Galba
Garr.	On Talkativeness
Gen. Socr.	On the Genius of Socrates
Inim. util	De Capienda ex Inimicis Utilitate
Inst. Lac.	The Ancient Customs of the Spartans
Liv.	Parallel Lives
Luc.	Life of Lucullus
Lyc.	Lycurgus
Mar.	Caius Marius
Marc.	Marcellus
Mor.	Moralia
Num.	Numa
Oth.	Otho
Pel.	Pelopidas
Per.	Pericles
Phoc.	Phocion

Phil.	Philopoemen
Pomp.	Pompey

Praec. ger. rei publ.

Publ.	Publicola
Rom.	Romulus
Sert.	Sertorius
Sol.	Solon
Sull.	Sulla
Ti. C. Graech.	Tiberius Gracchus
Tim.	Timoleon
Tu. san.	De tuned sanitate praecepta
Comm. not.	On Stoic Self-Contradiction
[Reg. imp. apophth.]	Regum et imperatorum apophthegmata
Her. mal.	On The Bravery of Women
Princ. iner.	Ad principem ineruditum
Quaest conv.	Quaestionum Convivalium
Quaest. plat.	Quaestiones Platonicae
Quaest. rom.	Quaestiones Romanae
Sera	On the Delays of the Divine Vengeance
Virt. mor.	On Moral Virtue
Vit. pud.	De vitioso pudore

Polybius

Hist.	Histories

Seneca the Younger

Ben.	de Beneficiis
Clem.	de Clementia
de. Const.	de Constantia
de. Prov.	de Providentia
Ep.	Epistulae
Ira.	de Ira
Nat.	Quaestiones naturales
[Octavia]	Octavia
Tranq.	de Tranquilitate Animi
Vit. beat.	de Vita Beata

Strabo

Geo.	Geography

Tacitus

Hist.   The Histories
Ann.   The Annals

Thucydides

Hist.   History of the Peloponnesian War

Virgil's

Georg.   Georgics

Xenophon

Ages.   Agesilaus
Anab.   Anabasis
Apol.   Apology
Cry.   Cyropaedia
Hell.   Hellenica
Mem.   Memorabilia
Oec.   Economics

1

Introduction

In Paul's monumental letter to the Romans, we encounter an idea central to his role as an Apostle and his theological program: obedience. This idea has suffered continual neglect, yet attention to this theme offers an intriguing angle into the mission and purpose of Paul. In Rom. 1:5, he unequivocally states that his apostleship is for the *obedience* of the nations. At the onset, one is struck by the apparent contradiction of such a connection between Paul and obedience. Isn't this the apostle of grace? Is not Paul the triumphant hero of the reformation who disparages works and prioritizes belief? What are we to make of such a startling claim that obedience forms a central plank in the imagination of Paul's vocation and in one of his most important letters?

Such is the purpose of this monograph to reconsider the meaning and context of the phrase "the obedience of faith" (ὑπακοὴν πίστεως) and the theme of obedience in Romans. By investigating how obedience language functioned within the Greco-Roman world, particularly in the discourse of the Roman Empire, it will allow us to more fully understand how some in Paul's audience may have understood the language of obedience. This will also have the further corollary of illumining Paul's purpose(s) in Romans.[1] Second, this work hopes to draw further attention to obedience as a recurring theme of Romans. Paul's use of obedience language, both at the beginning (1:5 *exordium*) and end (15:18 *peroratio*) of Romans, serves as rhetorical bookends and signals a theme that runs throughout the letter. Fresh light is shed on the phrase "the obedience of faith" by studying the Greco-Roman use of obedience language during the empire—and in particular, that it shows that this phrase would not have seemed odd or alien to the Gentile Christians in Rome. Attention to the way obedience language functioned in Greco-Roman contexts will help us understand how Gentiles in Paul's audience may have heard the terms and images relating to obedience.

Much of the work in understanding the obedience language in Romans has been almost exclusively limited to the Hebrew scriptures and Second Temple literature.[2] One

---

[1] The purpose(s) of Romans is a notoriously problematic issue. Cf Karl P. Donfried, ed. *The Romans Debate: Revised and Expanded Edition* (Peabody: Hendrickson, 1991); A. J. Guerra, *Romans and the Apologetic Tradition: The Purpose, Genre, and Audience of Paul's Letters* (New York: Cambridge University Press, 1995); A. J. M. Wedderburn, *The Reasons for Romans* (Edinburgh: T&T Clark, 1988); A. Andrew Das, *Solving the Romans Debate* (Minneapolis: Fortress, 2007); Richard N. Longenecker, *Introducing Romans: Critical Issues in Paul's Most Famous Letter* (Grand Rapids: Eerdmans, 2011).

[2] A helpful example of this approach for Romans as a whole is *Reading Romans in Context: Paul and Second Temple Judaism*, ed. Ben Blackwell, John K. Goodrich, and Jason Maston (Grand Rapids: Zondervan, 2015).

understands such an emphasis as important for understanding what Paul means by the ὑπακοὴν πίστεως.³ However, an understanding of the Greco-Roman background is equally important for grasping how some of his non-Jewish audience would have been familiar with the concept of obedience. It is surprising, given the attention to the historical situation of the letter to the Romans, that an understanding of the Greco-Roman background of obedience has not been pursued.⁴ It seems no one has asked the obvious question, "How would those in Rome understand a call to obedience?"

One purpose, therefore, of this work is to investigate the sociohistorical dimension of the obedience language from the particular viewpoint of the Gentiles in the Roman audience to bring added nuance to Paul's call for obedience in Rom. 1:5.⁵ In Romans, such avenues have been pursued by Peter Oakes who attempts a reading of Romans 12 from "ground level."⁶ Both the works of Peter Oakes and Peter Lampe show that a historically informed reading of Romans offers fruitful avenues for understanding the letter within a first-century Greco-Roman context.

What is meant by a "Gentile reading?" Drawing on the work of Peter Oakes, we may imagine Romans being heard by such persons as a slave, a freed person, a poor stoneworker, or a migrant worker.⁷ How might certain sections of Romans sound to them? What images or contexts might Paul's argument evoke? Awareness of how Gentiles like these might have understood the images and language of obedience will open up fuller avenues for understanding Romans.

A few examples of obedience language from Greco-Roman literature will suffice before a fuller treatment is undertaken later in the project. In the *Aeneid*, Virgil

---

³ Examples of works rooted in the Jewish literature are: Glen N. Davies, *Faith and Obedience in Romans: A Study in Romans 1-4* (Sheffield: Sheffield Academic, 1990); Don B. Garlington, *The Obedience of Faith: A Pauline Phrase in Historical Context* (Tübingen: J. C. B. Mohr (Paul Siebeck), 1991); James C. Miller, *The Obedience of Faith: The Eschatological People of God, and the Purpose of Romans* (Atlanta: SBL, 2000). As Karl Donfried has recently stated, "By stressing the Jewishness of Paul one must not deny the validity of the Greco-Roman context for Paul's apostolic activity" as one who "interacts with the pagan culture in partnership." Karl Donfried, "Paul's Jewish Matrix: The Scope and Nature of the Contributions," in *Paul's Jewish Matrix* (ed. Thomas G. Casey and Justin Taylor, Rome: Gregorian & Biblical Press, 2011), 48. See also his edited work: Karl P. Donfried and Peter Richardson, eds., *Judaism and Christianity in First-Century Rome* (Grand Rapids: Eerdmans, 1998).
⁴ One thinks of historically oriented works such as Peter Lampe, *From Paul to Valentinus: Christians at Rome in the First Two Centuries* (Minneapolis: Fortress, 2003). A more recent work on Paul is Neil Elliott and Mark Reasoner, *Documents and Images for the Study of Paul* (Minneapolis: Fortress, 2011). Although even in this work, little attention is given to the obedience language. As Edward W. Said has importantly noted, "Texts are tied to circumstances and to politics large and small, and these require attention and criticism ... We cannot deal with the literature of the periphery without also attending to the literature of the metropolitan centers." Cf. Edward Said, *Culture and Imperialism* (New York: Vintage, 1994), 318.
⁵ The task of my work is very similar to some recent treatments of the Pauline letters. See Joseph H. Hellerman, *Reconstructing Honor in Roman Philippi: Carmen Christi as Cursus Pudorum* (New York: Cambridge University Press, 2005); James R. Harrison, *Paul and the Imperial Authorities at Thessalonica and Rome: A Study in the Conflict of Ideology* (Tübingen: Mohr Siebeck, 2011).
⁶ Cf. Peter Oakes, *Reading Romans in Pompeii: Paul's Letter at Ground Level* (Minneapolis: Fortress, 2009). Oakes's work focuses on four hearers of Romans from various social types. This understanding of Romans from the viewpoint of nonelite first-century people aims to show how Romans might have been understood by a diverse audience in Rome, attempting to understand how Romans would sound "to people at ground level" (179).
⁷ Oakes, *Reading Romans*, xii.

poetically remarks, "But, Rome, it is thine alone, with awful sway, to rule mankind, and make the world obey" (*Aen*, 6.852). Likewise, Polybius states, "The Roman conquest, on the other hand, was not partial. Nearly the whole inhabited world was reduced by them to obedience (ὑπήκοος): and they left behind them an empire not to be paralleled in the past or rivaled in the future" (*Hist.*, 1.2.3). These references are a small sampling of the substantial evidence of obedience language within the Roman Empire. Before we look at the historical evidence, a survey of the previous scholarship on Paul's obedience language is needed to situate this project.

Common Approaches

Paul's obedience language is primarily understood in one of two approaches. The first avenue is what I will call the *missional* strategy. This approach focuses on Paul's calling and/or missional activity. Obedience is understood within the framework of Paul's self-understanding of his task and vocation. The most common treatment is the ethical treatments of Paul's obedience language that attempt to understand obedience within Paul's theological scope and aim for his congregation(s) or the larger enterprise of early Christianity. Usually, this approach is not concerned with historical referents for obedience language.

A second approach is what I will call the exegetical approach. This approach seeks to interpret the phrase in light of its grammatical features and then place the terms within an appropriate historical background. This avenue attempts to understand Paul's language of obedience within Romans and situate Paul's language within its appropriate contexts, such as Second Temple Judaism as is often the case, but rarely, against a Greco-Roman background.

Such an approach is not inaccurate; rather, the lacuna that remains is an understanding of Paul's obedience language within its Greco-Roman context. Naturally many of the commentaries fall within this second category. This study falls into this latter approach as well. How does each approach specifically treat obedience language? The following section will outline a few of the main contributions and the weaknesses that this work seeks to address.

The Missional Approach

Quite often Rom. 1:5 is treated within monographs that discuss Paul's person—either his call (Gal. 1, Rom. 1, etc.) or within a description of his missionary strategy.[8] These

---

[8] William Paul Bowers, "Studies in Paul's Understanding of His Mission" (PhD dissertation, Cambridge University, 1976), 84; Ksenija Magda, *Paul's Territoriality and Mission Strategy: Searching for the Geographical Awareness Paradigm behind Romans* (Tübingen: Mohr Siebeck, 2009); likewise, Larry Hurtado also notes, "It is clear from his letters that Paul understood his calling as requiring him to make obedience to the gospel of Jesus Christ the sole condition of the salvation of Gentiles and of their admission as fully fledged participants in the Christian movement." "Paul's Christology," in *The Cambridge Companion to St. Paul* (ed. James D. G.

types of treatments appear in works concerned with Romans and Pauline theology.⁹ Obedience is often left in the theological abstract, as no attention is given to the meaning of obedience. Thus this approach lacks what the exegetical approach provides.

Such an example is found in the work of Peter T. O'Brien who after surveying Paul's gospel and mission regards Rom. 1:5 as the "totality of Paul's missionary endeavors" and expresses the "purpose of Paul's missionary labours."[10] Following Don Garlington's influential work (see later), O'Brien states that the meaning of ὑπακοή πίστις is "unique to the whole of pre-Christian literature."[11] Statements like this are problematic as they are only half-true. Certainly, Paul's combination of ὑπακοή and πίστις is unique. However, such a statement entirely neglects the Greek and Roman literature where both terms appear frequently, often near one another in various passages in the literature of the Greco-Roman world as will be highlighted later on in this work. By arguing that this phrase is not found within pre-Christian literature, such statements have essentially closed off research for the terms involved, primarily ὑπακοή. What remains to be undertaken is an investigation of the obedience language within the Greco-Roman world.

As mentioned above, within the missional approach, many investigations of obedience language focus on Pauline ethics. One of the strongest ethical treatments of Paul's obedience language is provided by Michael J. Gorman in his work *Cruciformity: Paul's Narrative Spirituality of the Cross*.[12] Similar to the works cited above, Gorman views obedience as part of Paul's apostleship. Gorman rightly identifies the thematic nature of obedience and the connection between Rom. 1:5 and Rom. 5:19 where obedience reoccurs with the obedience of Jesus. Gorman draws out the ethical ramifications to show that participation in the life of Christ (by baptism) "is a life of obedience."[13]

Dunn, Cambridge: Cambridge University Press, 2003), 189. Sandra Hack Polaski, *Paul and the Discourse of Power* (Sheffield: Sheffield Academic Press, 1999); Michael D. Barram, *Mission and Moral Reflection in Paul* (New York: Peter Lang, 2006), 80–2; David G. Peterson, "Maturity: The Goal of the Mission," in *The Gospel to the Nations: Perspectives on Paul's Mission* (ed. Peter Bolt and Mark Thompson, Downers Grove: IVP, 2000), 185–204. A unique angle is approached by Joshua Jipp who understand the obedience in Rom. 1:5 as owning to Christ as a Davidic king. Although this approach is helpful for the political implications, it is rooted in a Second Temple understanding of the nature of obedience. See Joshua Jipp, *Christ Is King: Paul's Royal Ideology* (Minneapolis: Fortress, 2015), 178–9.

[9] For example, the work of Terence L. Donaldson, *Paul and the Gentiles: Remapping the Apostle's Convictional World* (Minneapolis: Fortress, 1997). Donaldson falls within this category of missional approaches, even though his work is not focused on Romans in particular (see pages 81, 100, 183, 342, 360, 361). Cf. J. Christiaan Beker, *Paul the Apostle: The Triumph of God in Life and Thought* (Philadelphia: Fortress, 1980), 128.

[10] Peter T. O'Brien, *Gospel and Mission in the Writings of Paul: An Exegetical and Theological Analysis* (Grand Rapids: Baker, 1995), 32–3.

[11] O'Brien, *Gospel and Mission*, 59.

[12] Michael J. Gorman, *Cruciformity: Paul's Narrative Spirituality of the Cross* (Grand Rapids: Eerdmans, 2001). Also, Michael J. Gorman, "What Did Paul Think God Is Doing about What's Wrong?," in *The New Cambridge Companion to St. Paul* (ed. Bruce W. Longenecker, New York: Cambridge University Press, 2020), 205.

[13] Gorman, *Cruciformity*, 32. Cf. John M. G. Barclay, *Obeying the Truth: Paul's Ethics in Galatians* (Minneapolis: Fortress, 1991), 226–7. He identifies this trend within the study of Pauline ethics when he notes,

> One of the most important theological concerns underlying much Pauline scholarship has been the desire to contrast Paul with a "Pelagian" theology of self-achieved salvation and

Gorman also rightly connects Rom. 1:5 and 5:9 and stresses that "to share in Christ's faith is to share in his obedience ... accepting Christ's death not merely as the *source* of salvation but as the *pattern* of faith/obedience."[14] He rightly notes that this is reemphasized in Rom. 6:17 where the Roman congregation is praised by Paul for being "obedient from the heart to the form of teaching to which you were entrusted." Gorman concludes, "Obedience is not an option for Paul, not even a good supplement to faith. ... The Gospel is not merely to be *believed*, but *obeyed*."[15]

What does all this mean for Paul's moral formation of his communities is that the Roman audience is now released from their former obedience to their passions to presently obey the gospel.[16] Gorman's work raises important questions when he notes that the obedience of Paul's audience is transferred from their former passions to gospel obedience. The primary question is "transferred from who?" or "transferred from where?" Was the obedience previously offered similar to or different from the obedience Paul expected? One detects a former area of obedience that is now replaced by gospel obedience.

The Exegetical Approach

The exegetical approach utilizes the primary source literature to understand Paul's obedience language within the matrix of his contemporaries. Such an approach is common and necessary but at stages vastly *underdetermined*. In the following section, I show there is much agreement with the previous works on obedience. The one qualification to the agreement with this approach is that there remains the need to situate the language of obedience within the matrix of the original audience. This necessitates an investigation of the literature of the Roman Empire, which remains entirely lacking in many works.[17] As stated previously, there are not many monographs on the topic of obedience, and much of this approach is exemplified in commentaries on Romans.

> to distinguish his thought from all forms of "synergism." Not only has this contributed to a serious misrepresentation of Judaism, as if it were concerned with man achieving his own salvation; it has also led to many embarrassed attempts to explain the significance Paul attaches to his moral imperatives, which mostly conclude that Paul saw Christian works as "evidence" for salvation rather than "instrumental" in it.

> His conclusion, although directed toward Galatians is particularly apt and he even references Rom. 1:5: "It is this *constant interplay* between the grace of God and the work of the believer ... which make's Paul's ethics of particular interest. It accords with his complex understanding of faith as response, reception, trust, decision, and obedience (cf. Rom 1.5; 10.16, etc.)."

[14] Gorman, *Cruciformity*, 133.
[15] Gorman, *Cruciformity*, 133. He goes on to note that "obedience and faith are essentially synonymous" citing Rom. 10:14; 16 as evidence.
[16] A point of fundamental agreement with Barclay, *Obeying the Truth*. Gorman cites him, *Cruciformity*, 134n.30.
[17] One of the striking absences of a discussion of the primary source literature is provided by David R. Wallace in his work, *The Gospel of God: Romans as Paul's Aeneid* (Eugene: Pickwick, 2008). One would anticipate that in a treatment arguing that Paul's message countered the "symbolism and message of the *Aeneid* and its salvific promise for Rome," (xiii) we would find a comparison of obedience language, as obedience appears in both Rom. 1:5 and throughout the *Aeneid*. Yet, no

The most common strategy in commentaries on Romans for 1:5 and the "obedience of faith" is neglect.[18] If in exceptional circumstances, it does receive a comment, it often receives only a brief grammatical treatment before the authors move on to the more pressing concern of the thesis statement (1:16-17).[19] Such laconic treatments of the "obedience of faith" are found frequently in the commentaries that focus on either the Christological formulation of 1:1-4 or discuss Paul's "call" in light of his mission to the Gentiles.[20] When Rom. 1:5 receives extended treatment, it often entails the nature of Paul's apostleship and very rarely refers to the content of that mission to the Gentiles—the ὑπακοή πίστις. Exceptions to this standard practice are rare.

---

discussion of obedience takes place within this work. This is surprising, and a bit disappointing, in a work seeking to offer such a comparison.

[18] Entirely missing a treatment of the phrase is Neil Elliott, *The Rhetoric of Romans: Argumentative Constraint and Strategy and Paul's Dialogue with Judaism* (Minneapolis: Fortress, 1990); Hendrikus Boers, *The Justification of the Gentiles: Paul's Letters to the Galatians and Romans* (Peabody: Hendrickson, 1994); Giorgio Agamben, *The Time That Remains: A Commentary on the Letter to the Romans*, trans. Patricia Dailey (Stanford: Stanford University Press, 2005); Sylvia C. Keesmaat, "Reading Romans in the Capital of the Empire," in *Reading Paul's Letter to the Romans* (ed. Jerry L. Sumney, Atlanta: SBL, 2012), 47–64; Mary O'Brien, "The 'Obedience of Faith' in Paul's Letter to the Romans" (paper presented at the international meeting of the SBL, Vienna, Austria, July 10, 2014), 1–12. Ms. O'Brien graciously provided a full copy of her paper for use in my work. One wonders if this is tied to the theological programs in operation in more traditional readings of Romans that misconstrue the Protestant emphasis on *faith alone*. Certainly the New Perspective on Paul readings and Paul within Judaism readings would provide a more appreciative context for obedience. For a recent treatment of these readings see Ben Witherington III and Jason A. Myers, *Voices and Views on Paul: Exploring Scholarly Trends* (Downers Grove: IVP, 2020).

[19] See George H. Parke-Taylor, "A Note on 'Εἰς Ὑπακοὴν Πίστεως' in Romans I.5 and Xvi. 26," *Expository Times* 55 (1943–4): 305–6; Ernest Best, *The Letter of Paul to the Romans* (Cambridge: Cambridge University Press, 1967), 1; Karl Barth, *The Epistle to the Romans*, trans., E. C. Hoskyns (Oxford: Oxford University Press, 1968), 31–2; Ernst Käsemann, *Commentary on Romans* (Grand Rapids: Eerdmans, 1980), 14–15; Paul J. Achtemeier, *Romans* (Louisville: Westminster John Knox, 1985), 32; C. K. Barrett, *The Epistle to the Romans: Revised Edition* (Peabody: Hendrickson, 1991), 22–3; Joseph A. Fitzmyer, *Romans* (New York: Doubleday, 1993), 237–8; Peter Stuhlmacher, *Paul's Letter to the Romans: A Commentary*, trans., S. J. Hafemann (Louisville: Westminster John Knox, 1994), 19–20; Stanley K. Stowers, *A Rereading of Romans: Justice, Jews, and Gentiles* (New Haven: Yale University Press, 1997), 43–4; Thomas R. Schreiner, *Romans* (Grand Rapids: Baker, 1998), 34–5; Christopher Bryan, *A Preface to Romans: Notes on the Epistle in Its Literary and Cultural Setting* (New York: Oxford University Press, 2000), 62; Luke Timothy Johnson, *Reading Romans: A Literary and Theological Commentary* (Macon: Smyth & Helwys, 2001), 23–4; Charles H. Talbert, *Romans* (Macon: Smyth & Helwys, 2002), 33; Phillip F. Esler, *Conflict and Identity in Romans: The Social Setting of Paul's Letter* (Minneapolis: Fortress, 2003), 137; Ben Witherington, *Paul's Letter to the Romans: A Socio-Rhetorical Commentary* (Grand Rapids: Eerdmans, 2004), 34–5; Leander E. Keck, *Romans* (Nashville: Abingdon, 2005), 45–6; Thomas H. Tobin, *Paul's Rhetoric in Its Contexts: The Argument of Romans* (Grand Rapids: Baker, 2005), 49; Craig S. Keener, *Romans* (Eugene: Cascade, 2009), 21; Udo Schnelle, *The Letter to the Romans* (Leuven: Peeters, 2009); Frank J. Matera, *Romans* (Grand Rapids: Baker, 2010), 30–1; Arland J. Hultgren, *Paul's Letter to the Romans: A Commentary* (Grand Rapids: Eerdmans, 2011), 50; Hermen C. Waetjen, *The Letter to the Romans: Salvation as Justice and the Deconstruction of the Law* (Sheffield: Sheffield Academic, 2011), 45.

[20] For example, Donaldson, *Paul and the Gentiles*; Francis Watson, *Paul, Judaism, and the Gentiles: Beyond the New Perspective* (Grand Rapids: Eerdmans, 2007).

The few commentators who note the importance of the phrase/theme do so without demonstration of the evidence.[21] Robert Jewett comes closest to our purposes in raising awareness of obedience in the larger Greco-Roman world by providing a *single* example. He notes, "Paul's expression addresses a central feature of the honor system in the Greco-Roman world, because obedience carried the 'stigma' of slavery and even the Emperor preferred to phrase his directives 'as suggestions and advice.'"[22]

N. T. Wright is also one of a few exemplary commentators who draw attention to the recurring theme of obedience, yet without discussing the social context of obedience.[23] Wright briefly highlights the recurrent theme of obedience throughout the letter to the Romans in his unpublished doctoral dissertation in 1980. He states, "Rom 1.5 and 1.16-17 are programmatic statements of this outworking of Paul's Christological gospel, which thus holds together Rom. 2 and 8 with 3-4, 9-10."[24] Nevertheless, this theme of obedience is not pursued further.

He offers further comments in his 2002 commentary on Romans, noting

> a more prominent theme in Romans than elsewhere in the NT ... It serves as a shorthand both for the total work of Jesus the Messiah, over against that of Adam (5:19), and the sphere or realm into which, or under the rule of which, Christians come through Baptism (6:12-17). Paul can again use it as a summary of that which he seeks to bring about among the nations (15:18; cf. 16:19) and in a concluding formula that closely echoes this opening one.[25]

He rightly notes that the obedience language is connected to Romans 5 and 6 and connects the phrases at the beginning and end of the book. However, given the limits of the commentary, Wright is only briefly able to discuss the theme of obedience in

---

[21] Here we include works that give more attention than most to the phrase but still fall short of understanding its thematic element and/or situating the phrase in the Roman sources. See James D. G. Dunn, *Romans*, 2 vols. (Dallas: Word, 1988), 1:17-18; G. Segalla, "L' 'Obbedienza Di Fede' (Rm 1,5; 16,26) Tema Della Lettera Ai Romani?," *Rivista Biblica* 36 (1988): 329-42; Douglas J. Moo, *The Epistle to the Romans* (Grand Rapids: Eerdmans, 1996), 50n.67; Haacker, *Der Brief Des Paulus an Die Römer*, 29; Katherine Grieb, *The Story of Romans: A Narrative Defense of God's Righteousness* (Louisville: Westminster John Knox, 2002), xix, 3, 102; Brendan Byrne, *Romans* (Collegeville: Liturgical, 2007), 40; Colin G. Kruse, *Paul's Letter to the Romans* (Grand Rapids: Eerdmans, 2012), 50-3.

[22] Robert Jewett, *Romans: A Commentary* (Minneapolis: Fortress, 2007), 108-11. "Cicero placed duty to officials under the rubric of 'respect': 'The duty of respect requires us to reverence and cherish those outstanding because of age or wisdom, or office, or any other claim to prestige'" (Cicero, *Inv.* 2.66). However in the footnote he shows that he is primarily relying on Lendon's work. Although Jewett is primarily relying on the work of J. E. Lendon, he nevertheless highlights an impetus for further research into the primary source literature for further investigation of this topic.

[23] Also C. E. B. Cranfield, *The Epistle to the Romans: A Critical and Exegetical Commentary*, 2 vols. (Edinburgh: T&T Clark, 1980). Although Cranfield only mentions 1.8; 10.16; 11.23, 30-31; 15:18; Dunn, *Romans*, 17-18; Witherington, *Romans*, 33-6.

[24] N. T. Wright, "The Messiah and the People of God: A Study in Pauline Theology with Particular Reference to the Argument of the Epistle to the Romans" (PhD dissertation, Oxford University, 1980), iii.

[25] N. T. Wright, "Romans," in *The New Interpreter's Bible: Acts—1 Corinthians* (ed. Leander Keck, Nashville: Abingdon, 2002), 420. Contra A. B. du Toit, "Faith and Obedience in Paul," *Neot* 25 (1991): 65-74. du Toit fails to grasp the significance when he states, "Coming back to Romans 1:5 it would be too bold to assert that the phrase ... is programmatic for the whole of Romans" (69).

Romans. Further, no attention is devoted to the primary sources as a background for obedience.

Wright's *Paul and the Faithfulness of God*, however, takes a more detailed approach to the phrase.[26] Wright comes close to the purpose of this work in his discussion of the cross. After noting that crucifixion was the punishment of choice by the Romans, Wright remarks, "Their rulers have now been defeated through his death, and *they and their people can be summoned to 'faithful obedience'*" (italics mine).[27] The idea inherent here is the transfer of obedience from one ruler to another. The people who were once obedient to Rome are now obedient to Jesus, the gospel, and faith. Sadly, Wright moves on to other pressing matters and does not investigate further the implications of such obedience language.[28] What is interesting is that Wright's statement raises the inherent political implications of such a transfer of obedience. Still, there remains a marked silence on what exactly the ramifications of such a transfer might be. Further, Wright's statements assume, rather implicitly, that obedience is something that Rome demanded or even sought. My work will provide a context for how obedience may have been understood within the Greco-Roman world with specific examples.

Key Works on Obedience

Moving away from the commentaries, a few monographs have been devoted to the topic of obedience.[29] First, we might mention the works bearing the title "obedience of faith," such as one of the earliest treatments by Paul S. Minear in his 1971 work entitled, *The Obedience of Faith: The Purposes of Paul in the Epistle to the Romans*.[30] Paul Minear's title is misleading. Properly speaking, he emphasizes the different factions that make up the Roman community(s) and how these disparate groups shape the ongoing argument in Romans. Minear takes the introduction and ending chapters of Romans as the key to understanding each major section of Romans. As such, the "obedience of faith" language gets little to no attention in his work, with the key verse of Rom. 1:5 only mentioned three times.[31] Minear gives no attention to the meaning of the phrase or to how the phrase finds its place within the overall argument. His contribution lacks a thorough analysis of the "obedience of faith" language that connects the initial and ending repetition of the phrase with the entirety of the letter, as well as a social context for the term.

---

[26] N. T. Wright, *Paul and the Faithfulness of God*, 2 vols. (Minneapolis: Fortress, 2013), 367, 383, 405, 685, 843, 911, 916, 944, 1066, 1421.

[27] Wright, *PFG*, 2:911.

[28] Wright connects obedience language to the *Kyrios* language, which he notes from Rom. 1:5 onward that this refers to the "sovereign rule of the Messiah … in charge of the nations" (*PFG*, 2:1066).

[29] One might also include dissertations, such as the more social scientific-oriented work of Ben Holdsworth, "Reading Romans in Rome: A Reception of Romans in the Roman Context of Ethnicity and Faith" (PhD dissertation, Durham University, 2009).

[30] Paul S. Minear, *The Obedience of Faith: The Purposes of Paul in the Epistle to the Romans* (Naperville: SCM, 1971), 1.

[31] Minear, *The Obedience of Faith*, 1.37, 41.

Introduction 9

The most focused and influential treatment of Rom. 1:5 and the obedience of faith comes from Don Garlington in his work, *The Obedience of Faith*.[32] Garlington sets out to place this phrase within its historical context. Building on the work of O. Michael, Garlington understands this phrase as a Pauline creation that functions both antithetically and polemically against Paul's opponent(s) in Rome.[33] Garlington attempts to place this phrase within its historical context to better understand "the nature of the controversy between Paul and his counterparts."[34]

The essential groundwork for understanding the two principle parts of the phrase lies in their Hebraic background; Garlington sets this out with clarity and brevity. Garlington summarizes his thesis as an understanding of the phrase, which was for Paul "fundamentally significant for his missionary message" and one that "represented the sum and substance of the apostle's commission from the risen Christ."[35] The phase not only sufficed to summarize the missionary endeavors of Paul but also functioned as a polemical tool to differentiate his message from that of his "opponents." Within Romans, the phrase is to be understood as one of the "recurring ideas" in highlighting that the "law of God must *now* (i.e. in the eschatological present) be fulfilled on the level demanded by the 'obedience of faith' rather than by Jewish nationalistic self-definition."[36]

Another critique is that several of Garlington's phrases such as "Pauline creation," a "unique phrase," or arguing that the phrase "does not occur before Paul" are quite unhelpful. As mentioned above, although the explicit combination of the two terms in a genitive construction does not appear before Paul, this is not nearly the entire story. The terms "obedience" and "faith" do appear frequently in Greco-Roman literature as the subsequent sections of this work show. Further, just because the words do not appear together does not mean that the concept is unique. For example, the genitive construction *pistis Christou* is also unique to Paul and does not occur before Pauline usage. However, this does not mean that we should neglect to study the concept of

---

[32] Garlington, *The Obedience of Faith*. See also Davies, *Faith and Obedience in Romans*. Very similar to Garlington's work is the work of Miller, *The Obedience of Faith*, although Miller attempts a broader treatment of "obedience" within Romans. As it relates to defining "obedience," Miller only notes, "The noun 'obedience' (ὑπακοή) was not a common term in the New Testament era, probably becoming established through Christian usage" (Miller, *The Obedience of Faith*, 8). This statement is only partially true. A search for the noun will certainly turn up only a few hits on TLG; however, a search of the adjectival form returns with a plethora of references.

[33] Garlington, *The Obedience of Faith*, 1. Similarly compare with James M. Scott, *Paul and the Nations: The Old Testament and Jewish Background of Paul's Mission to the Nations with Special Reference to the Destination of Galatians* (Tübingen: J.C.B. Mohr (Paul Siebeck), 1995).

[34] Garlington, *The Obedience of Faith*, 4. Similar issues arise with Mark D. Nanos, *The Mystery of Romans: The Jewish Context of Paul's Letter* (Minneapolis: Fortress, 1996), 218-38. He offers the tantalizing thesis that the "obedience of faith" language used in Rom. 1:5 refers to the requirements of the apostolic decree in Acts 15. Although considerable arguments are put forth to prove his point, in the end there does not appear to be enough evidence to prove Nanos's case. One wonders that if the "obedience of faith" is equal to the Acts 15 apostolic decree, then why are there not more syntactical or textual links with the language of Acts 15 to indicate this background? See also Michael Theobald, *Der Römerbrief*, vol. 1 (Stuttgart: Katholisches Bibelwerk, 1992). On the issue of Acts 15 see Ben Witherington, "Not So Idle Thoughts about Eidoluthuton," *TynB* 44 (1993): 237-54.

[35] Garlington, *The Obedience of Faith*, 14.

[36] Garlington, *The Obedience of Faith*, 14.

πίστις in Greco-Roman literature because we don't find faith linked to Jesus Christ. Similarly, to state that the phrase "obedience of faith" is unique has no bearing on the study of both concepts in the related Greco-Roman literature.

One further limitation in Garlington is that he only undertakes a study of the phrase within its immediate context of 1:1-8. This is somewhat offset by his subsequent work that traces the phrase through Romans, but oddly only through chapter 7.[37] It is obvious that there remains room to offer a reading different from the one he offers of Rom. 1–7, and also to extend this study to the rest of Romans. Indeed, it is odd that one can conclude Paul's view of obedience or the law without a discussion of Rom. 8:1-4 and Rom. 10:4. Further, as much as he has offset the weaknesses of Minear by rooting the phrase in its Hebraic background, space remains to situate the term within Greco-Roman literature in light of how a Gentile audience may have been familiar with obedience language.

Cynthia Kittredge's work, *Community and Authority: The Rhetoric of Obedience in the Pauline Tradition*, is the publication of her 1996 Harvard dissertation of the same title.[38] In this work, Kittredge defines the language of obedience as those discourses in Paul's letters to churches that refer to obeying and submitting, and that "this language of obedience depends upon … social relationships."[39] Kittredge shows how obedience language not only occurs within relationships but also constructs social relations. Obedience is essentially a social term found in certain social contexts of the early Christian symbolic universe, such as marital relations, parent–child relationships, and slavery. For Kittredge, obedience language is situated in the social environment of the "kyriarchical family" whereby the early Christians sought to understand their new identity from within the existing social framework of the surrounding culture.

The primary aim of Kittredge's work is to understand Paul's obedience language within its historical and rhetorical contexts. The conclusion of her study of the two terms, ὑπακούω (to obey) and ὑποτάσσω (to submit), shows that there is substantial overlap between them in the works of Greek authors. Further, as this work shows, her exploration of both terms indicates that the terms for obedience occur in military, political, philosophical, and domestic subjugation.[40] Kittredge shows that both ὑπακούω and ὑποτάσσω are within the same semantic field of obedience. She then applies her conclusions to Philippians and Ephesians.

Much is to be commended in Kittredge's work. First, she is one of the few who attempt to situate Paul's obedience language within its Greco-Roman context. She rightly shows how such a background illuminates Paul's discourses. A few issues differentiate Kittredge's work from my own. Primarily, the focus of her work is on Philippians and Ephesians, although her conclusions are helpful for Romans especially for the implications of ὑποτάσσω in Rom. 13:1. More so, instead of focusing on ὑποτάσσω, my contribution to the semantic field of obedience will be to show the

---

[37] Don Garlington, *Faith, Obedience, and Perseverance: Aspects of Paul's Letter to the Romans* (Eugene: Wipf & Stock, 2009).
[38] Cynthia Briggs Kittredge, *Community and Authority: The Rhetoric of Obedience in the Pauline Tradition* (Harrisburg: Trinity Press International, 1998).
[39] Kittredge, *Community and Authority*, 5.
[40] Kittredge, *Community and Authority*, 50.

importance of the verb πειθώ (to persuade) and its cognates for an understanding of obedience alongside ὑπακούω and its cognates.

Recent Works on Obedience in Paul

Although obedience has not been a central theme of recent works, the topic of faith and therefore allegiance or loyalty has found renewed interest in the past several years as seen in the publication of key texts.[41] These works deal tangentially with the concept of obedience but do not address it primarily. What is fascinating about these proposals is how neatly they fit within a Pauline understanding of obedience. It is refreshing to see this issue being taken seriously once again. My main critique of these works is that one ought to press on to a full-throated defense of Pauline obedience to which these books give adequate foundations for pursuing.

The landmark study of Teresa Morgan, *Roman Faith and Christian Faith*, on the topic of faith in the Greco-Roman world is an invaluable contribution to our understanding of faith (*pistes/fides*).[42] She has offered a penetrating analysis of the ways that this language operated in the Roman world and within Early Christian discourse. Her conclusion is that trust forms the bedrock of faith language in the ancient world. The overlap between the Greek and Latin concepts is, in her words, part of an "extensive cultural *koinē*" where these terms functioned in similar ways across the linguistic and geographic landscapes.[43] In the domains of law, religion, and philosophy, similar aims and understandings emerge of these important terms. She argues persuasively that these terms are found in the social domains of family members, master/slave, client/patron, as well as militias, political, and legal contexts. Trust is the essential meaning of these terms, and as such, she demonstrates that these terms are the "basic building blocks of societies."[44] Disagreement arises on her interpretation of Paul's use of faith language, where she argues that Paul "virtually redefine *pisits* as a divine-human relationship without intra-human analogue."[45] Positively, her study bears out many similarities to this work; although the semantic terms differ, my work should be seen as analogous and in agreement with the broad understanding of obedience language in the Roman Empire. Although her study is immensely helpful, it might not appreciate the role of faith toward one another that Paul seeks to imbue in his communities. As will be argued in Chapter 8 (pp. 286–96), Paul expects the obedience of faith to be exercised toward one another in the Roman communities. The model of divine faithfulness then expresses itself in concrete acts of obedience toward other members.

---

[41] John Barclay, *Paul and the Gift* (Grand Rapids: Eerdmans, 2015), 449, 460–1, 492; Matthew Bates, *Salvation by Allegiance Alone: Rethinking Faith, Works, and the Gospel of Jesus the King* (Grand Rapids: Baker, 2017); Nijay K. Gupta, *Paul and the Language of Faith* (Grand Rapids: Eerdmans, 2020). Ironically, the mention of Rom. 1:5 is entirely lacking from Sylvia C. Keesmaat and Brian J. Walsh, *Romans Disarmed: Resisting Empire, Demanding Justice* (Grand Rapids: Brazos, 2019).

[42] Teresa Morgan, *Roman Faith and Christian Faith: Pistis and Fides in the Early Roman Empire and Early Churches* (New York: Oxford University Press, 2015).

[43] Morgan, *Roman Faith*, 27.

[44] Morgan, *Roman Faith*, 75.

[45] Morgan, *Roman Faith*, 306.

Nijay Gupta has published one of the most recent full-length treatments of "faith" language in Paul. Although his work does not directly engage with the obedience of faith, his conclusions on faith language are important for this study. He rightly notes that it would be going past the evidence to equate faith with obedience, although related to the concept, and cites Rom. 1:5 as an example. Gupta points out, "If obedience is fully active, then obeying πίστις is 'preobedience.' It is faith that dovetails with obedience."[46] This fits nicely with the Greco-Roman evidence from forthcoming chapters where entering into faith/loyalty to Rome leads to obedience. Both are distinguished from one another in the primary sources of ancient literature so that they are not synonymous with one another but very closely related in thought and practice. Gupta's work argues the relevant points from the "faith" side of the obedience of faith in this argument. Whereas his study was directed toward faith language, the obedience piece was beyond his scope, but this work would fill out and in many ways cohere with the portrait he constructs from the Pauline evidence.

In the newer treatments of faith as fidelity language, Matthew Bates has offered a helpful treatise on the nature of salvation as allegiance. While primarily focusing on faith as loyalty, Rom. 1:5 does make an important appearance. Bates argues that the phrase should be understood as "embodied loyalty" or in a longer definition "the practical obedience characteristic of allegiance to a king" or what I have termed, "enacted allegiance."[47] Bates's work rightly touches on the political notions of the term obedience and allegiance that the primary evidence bears out repeatedly. There is much agreement with the main conclusions of Bates's work. This work more fully builds out the case among the Greco-Roman sources for understanding the obedience of faith as enacted allegiance.

In a nod to the more missional approaches sketched out above, the landmark study of John Barclay, *Paul and the Gift*, also situates obedience within the mission of Paul.[48] Barclay notes, "Paul is perpetually conscious of the incongruity of grace as fit to the ungodly and disobedient; but his goal is not their continuing disobedience, but 'the obedience of faith' (1:5)."[49] This approach sees obedience as part of Paul's overall aims for the community in Rome. Barclay rightly emphasizes that Romans is written to a community and is "wholly relevant to the believers in Rome" and that Paul "writes to the believers *as Gentiles* (italics original)."[50] However, taking these elements into account, Barclay does not substantially develop just *how* these Gentiles—to whom the discourse is *wholly* relevant—might understand this pattern of life they are called into. To use his phrase, what *incongruities* might a group of Roman Gentiles find? A group

---

[46] Gupta, *Paul and the Language of Faith*, 178.
[47] Bates, *Salvation by Allegiance Alone*, 86.
[48] Barclay, *Paul and the Gift*. Also, Paula Fredriksen, *Paul: The Pagan's Apostle* (New Haven: Yale University Press, 2017), 120.
[49] Barclay, *Paul and the Gift*, 492.
[50] Barclay, *Paul and the Gift*, 458. Also Matthew Thiessen, *Paul and the Gentile Problem* (New York: Oxford University Press, 2016), 44–5. Contra Beverly Roberts Gaventa who argues, "It is unclear whether Paul means that the audience itself is made up of gentiles or that its members live among the gentiles." See Beverly Roberts Gaventa, *When in Romans: An Invitation to Linger with the Gospel According to Paul* (Grand Rapids: Baker, 2016), 5.

that was previously obedient to the Romans but now is exercising allegiance to Jesus Christ? These questions remain to be answered.

Scot McKnight has also offered an intriguing reading of Romans by prompting readers to read Romans *backward*.[51] Sensitive to the literary nature of Romans, McKnight is key to detect how the latter themes in the letter are woven in and throughout the discourse as a whole. Such a concern rightly positions McKnight to detect the way obedience functions in the letter. Although falling within the missional approach, he notes that Paul's mission of the obedience of faith "must be connected especially to Romans 14–15."[52] By acknowledging these bookends to the discourse, it allows him to detect references to obedience in other major sections (i.e., 6:12-17), but still the other major sections of Romans are left unillumined by a connection to obedience. Likewise, there is no attempt to root this obedience language in the first-century world.

Purpose of the Study

First, this work aims to situate Paul's obedience language within the broader Greco-Roman literary and epigraphic environment to produce a fuller understanding of ὑπακοή. As the literature review has shown, much of the discussion of Paul's obedience language, if not neglected entirely, has been oriented around Jewish literature. Again, this is not so much a problem as it is a one-sided deficiency. This neglect is all the more surprising, because in a letter *to* Rome, the Roman sources have not had an influential role in understanding ὑπακοή πίστις. Situating the obedience language within the Greco-Roman literature provides a fuller understanding of obedience in the world of Paul and his audience. To date, very little attention has been directed to this area; and, therefore, there remain several fruitful areas for investigation, primarily in the Greco-Roman historians and philosophers, that offer numerous examples of how obedience functioned in the Greco-Roman world.

Second, past studies of Romans have failed to give adequate attention to a central theme of obedience as a thematic concern of the entire letter. Therefore, the second task of this project will be to argue that obedience is a central theme of Romans and to trace the obedience language through the letter to show its recurrent nature. For example, a quick survey shows that obedience is, in fact, a pervasive theme. It is found in Rom. 1:5; 2:8, 14-15, 25, 27; 3:23, 31; 4:1-8, 15; 5:14, 19; 6:12-17; 7; 8:4, 13; 10:16-17, 21; 13:8-10; 15:18; 16:19, 26.[53] Some of these references are more explicit than others, and some I will attempt to argue later on in the work.[54] However, even if the study

---

[51] Scot McKnight, *Reading Romans Backwards: A Gospel of Peace in the Midst of Empire* (Waco: Baylor University Press, 2019).
[52] McKnight, *Reading Romans*, 94.
[53] This includes the inverse of the obedience language—disobedience.
[54] These passages include the language concerning fulfillment of the law—Rom. 2:14-15, the character of Abraham—Rom 4:1-15, and any references to slavery language also entail a discussion of obedience, and Rom. 8:1-4. One could also make the case for the language concerning sin/transgression/death amounting to the term "disobedience" but for now the latter terms fall outside the limits of this research.

is limited to the most explicit references, the theme of obedience occurs throughout Romans. To repeat the main focus of the monograph: fresh light is shed on the phrase "the obedience of faith" by studying the Greco-Roman use of the obedience language during the empire; and in particular, it shows that this phrase would not have seemed odd or alien to the Gentile Christians in Rome.[55]

In conclusion, it is helpful to see how obedience language once set within its context will assist in a more robust understanding of obedience in Romans. Anticipating our argument, we may note the following. Obedience formed the main part of Paul's theological and practical mission with his work in Rome as reflected by its usage in Romans. Theologically, obedience functions as an identity marker of God's people both past and present. Obedience also functions as an eschatological marker of the inbreaking of God's kingdom reign and rule as signified in the prophets by the inclusion of the Gentiles into the people of God.[56] Pragmatically, obedience language serves Paul's purposes for constructing communal life that reflects the righteousness of God as creatures of God's new creation in Jesus Christ. Obedience, far from being ancillary to Paul's modus operandi, is central to the life of Paul's communities and the outworking of the gospel of God for the world.

---

[55] Stanley Porter acknowledges this: "The Gospel that Paul introduces in 1.1-5 leads not just to forgiveness and justification but to obedience among the nations (1.5) and the salvation Paul mentions in Rom 1:16 is unpacked not merely in the first four chapters of that letter, but in the letter as a whole." See Stanley Porter, "Paul's Theology of the Gospel," in *Paul as Missionary: Identity, Activity, Theology, and Practice* (ed. Trevor J. Burke and Brian S. Rosner, Edinburgh: T&T Clark, 2011), 186. However, his article is bent toward a different purpose than the one here.

[56] See Seyoon Kim, "Paul as an Eschatological Herald," in *Paul as Missionary: Identity, Activity, Theology, and Practice* (ed. Trevor J. Burke and Brian S. Rosner, Edinburgh: T&T Clark, 2011), 9–24.

2

Reading Romans Rhetorically

The Rhetorical Situation

The rhetorical persuasion in a text is irreducibly connected to the social context of the author and his relationship with the community.[1] A keen awareness of this involves the identification of the situation of Paul and the community, the events, as well as the problems that surround those situations.[2] We may begin by analyzing Paul's role as rhetor and his rhetorical task in Romans through the issues raised in the *exordium*.[3] We will then move to the rhetorical situation in Rome and its bearing on Paul's rhetorical task.

At the forefront, my argument is that one of Paul's purposes, as indicated by the *exordium* in 1:1-15 and supplemented by the *peroratio* in 15:14-33, is that obedience is central to his purpose(s) in Romans, especially in bringing the Roman communities under his authority to make it possible to move west to Spain.[4] The similarities between the *exordium* and the *peroratio* indicate that Paul's purpose in writing to and visiting Rome includes the topic of obedience.[5]

---

[1] Research on the relationship between the rhetoric and the situation began with the work of L. Bitzer, "The Rhetorical Situation," *PR* 1 (1968): 1-18. Further research has taken up his claims, with modifications. Cf. A. Brinton, "Situation in the Theory of Rhetoric," *PR* 14 (1981): 234-48; George A. Kennedy, *New Testament Interpretation through Rhetorical Criticism* (Chapel Hill: University of North Carolina, 1984), 35-6; David E. Aune, *The Westminster Dictionary of New Testament and Early Christianity Literature and Rhetoric* (Louisville: Westminster John Knox, 2003), 422-5.

[2] Various commentaries provide the helpful background; see Ben Witherington, *Paul's Letter to the Romans: A Socio-Rhetorical Commentary* (Grand Rapids: Eerdmans, 2004), 7-16; James D. G. Dunn, *Romans* (Dallas: Word, 1988), 1:xxxix-liv; Richard N. Longenecker, *Introducing Romans: Critical Issues in Paul's Most Famous Letter* (Grand Rapids: Eerdmans, 2011). Cf. the pertinent sections in Karl P. Donfried, *The Romans Debate: Revised and Expanded Edition* (Peabody: Hendrickson, 1991). For a sociohistorical description, see Karl P. Donfried and Peter Richardson, eds., *Judaism and Christianity in First-Century Rome* (Grand Rapids: Eerdmans, 1998); Peter Lampe, *From Paul to Valentinus: Christians at Rome in the First Two Centuries* (Minneapolis: Fortress, 2003), 19-66.

[3] Kennedy, *New Testament Interpretation*, 35-6.

[4] Along with Jewett, I view Rom. 1:1-15 as part of the *exordium*. See Robert Jewett, *Romans: A Commentary* (Minneapolis: Fortress, 2007), 95-6.

[5] On the relationship between the *exordium* and the *perorations* see Wilhelm Wuellner, "Paul's Rhetoric of Argumentation in Romans: An Alternative to the Donfried-Karris Debate over Romans," in *The Romans Debate: Revised and Expanded Edition* (ed. Karl P. Donfried, Peabody: Hendrickson, 1991), 135-6. Also supported by N. T. Wright, "Romans and the Theology of Paul," in *Pauline Theology* (ed. David M. Hay and E. Elizabeth Johnson, Minneapolis: Fortress, 1995), 30-67; Robert Jewett,

The current situation is not as simple as that of Paul merely writing and visiting Rome before traveling to Spain. Paul's absence has caused a new problem for him to address. As Karl Barth noted, "In him a void becomes visible."[6] The *exordium* and the *narratio* is Paul's attempt to persuade the communities at Rome of his previous intentions of visiting. Paul must overcome the distrust of the Roman communities to enlist them for his purpose of getting to Spain. From Paul's perspective, this is one of his rhetorical exigencies.

Another issue that Paul faces is that he did not found this community. Contrary to Melanie Thurén's opinion, however, Paul was not merely desiring more power in an "ecclesiastical no-man's land."[7] Rather, one of Paul's exigencies was establishing communication with the Roman community(s). Paul functions as an outsider with this community, and the a priori task is to establish contact in a heightened honor-shame context in which he starts in the negative.

The Rhetorical Situation at Rome

The situation between Paul and the Roman communities is only half of the reality that Paul encounters in Rome. The situation in Rome is also fraught with its difficulties. Indeed, one of the primary problems in Rome is not only the community's relationship with Paul but also their relationship with one another. Rom. 12–15 bears witness to the fraying fabric of these Roman communities. The problems in Rome derive from their historical exigencies, such as the return to Rome of the Jewish groups exiled by Claudius in 54–55 CE.[8] The Jews have returned to primarily Gentile-dominated congregations and are seeking to reclaim their old status and, possibly, their previous positions. They are met with contempt by the Gentile members of those congregations if they are not meeting separately. This recent arrival by the Jews, combined with a high degree of Roman imperialism and anti-Jewish sentiment, creates some of the problems encountered in the Roman churches.

Both Paul's exigencies in writing and the problems occurring in Rome shape his rhetorical task and tact. Paul's pragmatic concern is to get funding for a Spanish mission (Rom. 1:8-15; 15:23-33); however, to do this, he needs a united, obedient community at Rome—which is currently in a state of disarray (Rom. 12–15). Paul's rhetorical task in writing the main section of Romans (Rom. 1:1–11:36) is to achieve the unity he desires in those churches to secure their strong support.

"Ecumenical Theology for the Sake of Mission: Romans 1:1–17 + 15:14–16:24," in *Pauline Theology* (ed. David M. Hay and E. Elizabeth Johnson, Minneapolis: Fortress, 1995), 89–108. Cf. Lauri Thurén, *Derhetorizing Paul: A Dynamic Perspective on Pauline Theology and the Law*, Wunt, vol. 124 (Tübingen: Mohr Siebeck, 2000), 96–101.

[6] Karl Barth, *The Epistle to the Romans*, trans. E. C. Hoskyns (Oxford: Oxford University Press, 1968), 33. Cf. James D. Hester, "The Rhetoric of Persona in Romans," in *Celebrating Romans: Template for Pauline Theology* (ed. Sheila E. McGinn, Grand Rapids: Eerdmans, 2004), 99.

[7] Thurén, *Derhetorizing Paul*, 100.

[8] Leonard Victor Rutgers, "Roman Policy towards the Jews: Expulsions from the City of Rome during the First Century C.E.," in *Judaism and Christianity in First-Century Rome* (ed. Karl P. Donfried and Peter Richardson, Grand Rapids: Eerdmans, 1998), 93–116.

Reading Romans as a Roman: The Ideal Audience

It is here that we must offer a broader description of some of those who initially heard the book of Romans. The audience of Romans is a perennially debated issue.[9] This study operates on the assumption that the communities in Rome were predominately, though not exclusively, Gentile. Several internal features of Romans bear out this point. First, in Rom. 1:5-7, Paul indicates that he is the Apostle to the Gentiles, seeking the obedience of the Gentiles. He then specifically indicates in verse 6 that his audience is part of this group. Second, in Rom. 11:13, Paul explicitly states, "Now I am speaking to you Gentiles," again referencing his Gentile congregation. Third, we also mention the cryptic reference in 16:4 to "all the churches of the Gentiles." Again, it bears repeating that although the churches in Rome were predominately Gentile, this does not exclude the presence of Jewish Christians within the communities, as some arguments in Rom. 2:17-29 and the numerous OT quotations from Rom. 9–11 bear out.[10]

Our task in this work is not to deny that there was a Jewish component to the house church(s). There certainly was. Nor is the aim to deny what Paul meant by the phrase ὑπακοή πίστις. This has been adequately dealt with in previous studies.[11] Our task, instead, is to draw attention to the neglected issue of how various Gentiles in Paul's audience may have understood the images and terms related to obedience. Chapters 3–6 have sought to set out the background for such an understanding. Now we turn to a more detailed description of the identity of such persons within the Roman house churches.

We have two ways of understanding the makeup of the house churches in Rome.[12] First, as with all history, we can reconstruct a portrait of Roman society and submit the hypothesis that the Roman house church(s) represented a cross-section of society. To use a Pauline expression, both Roman and Greek, Jew and Gentile, male and female, and slave and free (Gal. 3:28).[13] The house churches in Rome were probably not monolithic and most likely consisted of a broad swath of Roman society.[14] To reiterate

---

[9] Cf. Select articles in Donfried, *The Romans Debate*, 65–84, 85–101; 203–15; 216–30; A. Andrew Das, *Solving the Romans Debate* (Minneapolis: Fortress, 2007), 53–114; Francis Watson, *Paul, Judaism, and the Gentiles: Beyond the New Perspective* (Grand Rapids: Eerdmans, 2007), 167–91; Mark D. Nanos, *The Mystery of Romans: The Jewish Context of Paul's Letter* (Minneapolis: Fortress, 1996), 41–84; Stanley K. Stowers, *A Rereading of Romans: Justice, Jews, and Gentiles* (New Haven: Yale University Press, 1997), 21–33; A. J. M. Wedderburn, *The Reasons for Romans* (Edinburgh: T&T Clark, 1988), 44–65; Paul S. Minear, *The Obedience of Faith: The Purposes of Paul in the Epistle to the Romans* (Naperville: SCM, 1971), 1–45.
[10] See Paul's statement in Rom. 1:7—πᾶσιν τοῖς οὖσιν ἐν Ῥώμῃ ἀγαπητοῖς θεοῦ.
[11] Cf. Garlington, Miller, Davies, and so on. See also the literature review in the previous chapter.
[12] See the helpful articles by Rudolf Brändle and Ekkehard W. Stegemann, "The Formation of the First 'Christian Congregations' in Rome in the Context of Jewish Congregations," in *Judaism and Christianity in First-Century Rome* (ed. Karl P. Donfried and Peter Richardson, Grand Rapids: Eerdmans, 1998), 117–27.
[13] Cf. James S. Jeffers, "Jewish and Christian Families in First-Century Rome," in *Judaism and Christianity in First-Century Rome* (ed. Karl P. Donfried and Peter Richardson, Grand Rapids: Eerdmans, 1998), 128–50. He concludes, "Jews and Christians in first-century Rome were for the most part poor, noncitizen, Greek-speaking foreigners, slaves and former slaves" (149).
[14] Following Edwin A. Judge, "The Social Pattern of the Christian Groups in the First Century," in *Social Distinctives of Christians in the First Century: Pivotal Essays by E. A. Judge* (ed. David M. Scholer, Peabody: Hendrickson, 2008), 1–56. Cf. Lampe, *From Paul to Valentinus*, 173–83.

our question, how would Gentiles within the Roman communities understand obedience from their various sociocultural backgrounds?[15]

Similar work has been undertaken by Peter Oakes.[16] Although relying on a different set of data (and location), Peter Oakes's sociological and archeological description of a "typical" house church is beneficial for this discussion.[17] Based on his detailed analysis of Pompeian evidence, he concludes that the makeup of a household would possibly include a craftsman and his family, craft-working slaves, a domestic slave, and a dependent relative. The house would also include other renters and their spouses who would rent space above the householder, and their slaves and dependents. The house church would also be composed of family members of the owner who do not participate in the house church, slaves whose owners do not participate, freed persons, perhaps some homeless people, and finally those who are renting space in shared rooms (like migrant workers).[18] It is these types of people that this study envisions as some of the first hearers of the book of Romans.

The dissertation by Ben Holdsworth also takes a similar approach to our work and offers helpful considerations for our project.[19] Although his thesis is directed toward issues of ethnicity, the questions concerning the audience are particularly helpful for our work. He raises the primary question, "To what extent can Romans be heard and understood by a readership in Rome within its religio-economic, socio-political, and ethnic context, especially by non-Judeans?"[20] The concerns and questions he poses are similarly shared in this work. He continues, "While the audience situation is discussed by many commentators on Romans, it is often presented from the perspective of Paul and his intended meanings, but not audience reception and their interpretation of Romans. The question is 'What did the audience hear?' versus 'What did Paul say?'"[21] Holdsworth rightly attempts to "hear Romans from this generally neglected perspective, of 'sitting in the audience,' especially with non-Judeans within the context of Roman life."[22] In his attempt to "hear Romans," he focuses on the primary issue of how ethnic identity was understood in the ancient world. He then pays particular attention to the themes of honor, faith, piety, and righteousness. The approach of Holdsworth is beneficial and raises the precise questions and audience issues that this work attempts to address. While the approach may be similar, however, our scope is different. Rather than focusing on ethnicity, this work focuses on obedience language.

Returning to some of our questions, if we were able to "sit in the audience," in light of the evidence from the historians, how would Persis (16:12)—probably a

---

[15] Richard Longenecker emphasizes the importance of the addresses by asking, "What were their civic and social circumstances in the city?" (*Introducing Romans*, 75).
[16] Even more recently this has been expanded upon by Bruce Longenecker, *In Stone and Story: Early Christianity in the Roman World* (Grand Rapids: Baker, 2020).
[17] Peter Oakes, *Reading Romans in Pompeii: Paul's Letter at Ground Level* (Minneapolis: Fortress, 2009), 46–68.
[18] Oakes, *Reading Romans*, 96.
[19] Ben Holdsworth, "Reading Romans in Rome: A Reception of Romans in the Roman Context of Ethnicity and Faith" (PhD dissertation, Durham University, 2009).
[20] Holdsworth, "Reading Romans," 11.
[21] Holdsworth, "Reading Romans," 7.
[22] Holdsworth, "Reading Romans," 11.

slave named for the region from which she was enslaved and taken to Rome—hear discussion of the nations' obedience (Rom. 1:5)? How would she hear that someone can have peace based on entering into faith with God (Rom. 5:1)? Or how would slaves or freed persons understand Paul's discussion of slavery in Rom. 6? We have in mind individuals like these as part of the audience of Romans. They would have been people from diverse backgrounds, various places, and various stations in life who are now part of the Roman congregation(s) and who would bring with them a whole set of assumptions and ideas about obedience.

Reading Romans against Rome?
A Note on Anti-Imperial Readings

Currently, in NT studies and Pauline studies specifically, a revolution is underway regarding the nature of the relationship between the NT and the Roman Empire. The discussion has focused on the ability to detect anti-imperial messages within NT. The rise of this trend is demonstrated by the proliferation of books, monographs, journal articles, and conferences devoted to the topic.[23]

Recent political readings of the NT and Paul found their genesis in two main sources: (1) Krister Stendahl's clarion call to NT studies in his influential article, "The Apostle Paul and the Introspective Conscience of the West,"[24] and (2) the sociopolitical

---

[23] Take, for example, the SBL section "Paul and Politics." Numerous works have been published as a result of their session meetings and related discussions. For a short bibliography see the following works: Christopher Bryan, *Render to Caesar: Jesus, the Early Church, and the Roman Superpower* (Oxford: Oxford University Press, 2005); Richard A. Horsley, ed., *Paul and Politics: Ekklesia, Israel, Imperium, Interpretation* (Harrisburg: Trinity Press International, 2000); Richard A. Horsley, ed., *Paul and the Roman Imperial Order* (Harrisburg: Trinity Press International, 2004); Scot McKnight and Joseph B. Modica, *Jesus Is Lord, Caesar Is Not: Evaluating Empire in New Testament Studies* (Downers Grove: IVP, 2013); Jeffrey Brodd and Jonathan L. Reed, eds., *Rome and Religion: A Cross-Disciplinary Dialogue on the Imperial Cult* (Atlanta: SBL, 2011); Theodore W. Jennings, *Outlaw Justice: The Messianic Politics of Paul* (Stanford: Stanford University Press, 2013); Jacob Taubes, *The Political Theology of Paul*, trans. Dana Hollander (Stanford: Stanford University Press, 2004); Marcus J. Borg and John Dominic Crossan, *The First Paul: Reclaiming the Radical Visionary behind the Church's Conservative Icon* (New York: HarperOne, 2009); Warren Carter, *The Roman Empire and the New Testament: An Essential Guide* (Nashville: Abingdon Press, 2006); Seyoon Kim, *Christ and Caesar: The Gospel and the Roman Empire in the Writings of Paul and Luke* (Grand Rapids: Eerdmans, 2008); Richard A. Horsley, *Paul and Empire: Religion and Power in Roman Imperial Society* (Harrisburg: Trinity Press International, 1997). An early conference was the "New Testament and Roman Empire: Shifting Paradigms for Interpretation" conference, hosted by Union Theological Seminary in New York on October 29–30, 2004, that resulted in a series of articles published in the *Union Theological Review*. Cf. Hal Taussig, "Prologue: A Door Thrown Open," *USQR* 59 (2005): 1–5; John Dominic Crossan, "Paul and Rome: The Challenge of a Just World Order," *USQR* 59 (2005): 6–20; Jean-Pierre Ruiz, "Of Walls and Words: Twenty-First Century Empire and New Testament Studies," *USQR* 59 (2005): 122–30; Elizabeth Schüssler Fiorenza, "Empire and Christian Studies," *USQR* 59 (2005): 131–9; Margaret P. Aymer, "Empire, Alter-Empire, and the Twenty-First Century," *USQR* 59 (2005): 140–6; Susan M. (Elli) Elliott, "Reflections on 'New Testament and Roman Empire'," *USQR* 59 (2005): 172–6; Davina C. Lopez, "Epilogue: Beyond the Threshold," *USQR* 59 (2005): 177–86.

[24] Krister Stendahl, "The Apostle Paul and the Introspective Conscience of the West," *HTR* 56 (1963): 199–215. Richard Horsley points to Stendahl in several of his books on empire and NT studies; see Horsley, ed., *Paul and the Roman Imperial Order*; Horsley, ed., *Paul and Politics*.

situation beginning in the 1960s where former imperial powers divested their control of colonized nations prompting the rise of postcolonialism and postcolonial studies in the fields of sociology, anthropology, and psychology.[25]

Krister Stendahl's work marked a noted shift in Pauline studies, which anticipated much of the later emphases by nearly twenty years.[26] One of the primary components of Stendahl's work is his emphasis on the profound uniqueness of Paul's first-century context. Stendahl argues that the relationship between Jews and Gentiles was *the* issue that shaped Paul's thought more than any other. It is this primary issue of Paul as Apostle *to* the Gentiles in this specific historical situation to which Stendahl draws awareness. By drawing attention to this first-century situation, NT studies were set on a trajectory toward anti-imperial readings. By refocusing Pauline studies on the concrete historical situation of Paul and his first congregations rather than on abstract theological ground, more attention was given to the reality(s) of the first century. Although the first outworking of Stendahl's challenge would primarily still relate to theological terms such as justification, attention would soon turn toward other areas of investigation.

The earliest studies of anti-imperial readings came out of SBL's Paul and Politics group chaired by Richard Horsley who aimed to take up the mantle of Stendahl's concerns.[27] Drawing on the works of rising third-world voices and postcolonial interpreters, these scholars sought to situate Paul and his communities as subjected peoples underneath the sway of imperial power. By focusing on Paul's language of κύριος (lord), εὐαγγέλιον (gospel), ἐκκλησία (assembly), and σωτήρ (savior), terms that were also used by the Roman Empire to describe their rule and rulers, they sought to understand how Paul's message as an individual under an oppressive regime would be understood.[28] To distance my work from empire criticism, this section is an attempt to show my points of agreement and concern with the anti-imperial readings of the Pauline corpus and to clarify my position regarding this

---

[25] Here is a short bibliography on postcolonial studies: Edward W. Said, *Beginnings: Intention and Method* (New York: Columbia University Press, 1985); Edward W. Said, *Orientalism* (New York: Vintage, 1979); Bill Ashcroft, Gareth Griffiths, and Helen Tiffin, *The Empire Writes Back: Theory and Practice in Post-Colonial Literatures*, 2nd ed. (London: Routledge, 2002); Homi K. Bhabha, *The Location of Culture* (London: Routledge, 1994). For a short overview of postcolonial studies and biblical studies see Stephen D. Moore, "Paul after Empire," in *Paul the Colonized Apostle: Paul through Post-Colonial Eyes* (ed. Christopher D. Stanley, Minneapolis: Fortress, 2011), 9–23.

[26] Some of Stendahl's insights had of course been anticipated earlier but had fallen on deaf ears. Stendahl himself admits this in the preface to his work and adds that he was highly influenced by J. Munck, his former teacher. Cf. Johannes Munck, *Paul and the Salvation of Mankind* (Richmond: John Knox, 1959); W. D. Davies, *Paul and Rabbinic Judaism: Some Rabbinic Elements in Pauline Theology* (London: SPCK, 1948).

[27] These resulted in the two works: Horsley, ed., *Paul and the Roman Imperial Order*; Horsley, ed., *Paul and Politics*. Of course these works were preceded by others such as Walter Wink, *Naming the Powers: The Language of Power in the New Testament* (Philadelphia: Fortress, 1984); Dieter Georgi, *Theocracy in Paul's Praxis and Theology*, trans. David E. Green (Minneapolis: Fortress, 1991).

[28] See Brodd and Reed, eds., *Rome and Religion*; McKnight and Modica, *Jesus Is Lord*. Cf. Jeremy Punt, "The New Testament and Empire: On the Importance of Theory," *Studia Historiae Ecclesiasticae* 37 (2011): 91–114; J. Albert Harrill, "Paul and Empire: Studying Roman Identity after the Cultural Turn," *EC* 2 (2011): 281–311. Harrill's article works at deconstructing the vocabulary of empire critics on the level of "culture," "empire," and "propaganda."

matter as some of the findings from my work could be used as evidence of support for anti-imperial readings of Paul.

Empire Criticism: Arguments and Counterarguments

According to empire critics, Paul's gospel confronts the ruling Caesar at various levels. There are open and flagrant criticisms such as in 1 Thess. 5:3 where Paul co-opts an imperial slogan for his purposes, directly flouting the imperial conventions and slogans.[29] There is also Paul's "shared terms" such as his use of εὐαγγέλιον, where it is argued that Paul is contrasting the "gospels" of Christ and Caesar directly. Or as another example, when Paul declares Jesus as *Lord*, it is claimed that he is "de-throning" the reigning Roman emperor. From here, the field splinters with various critics providing their anti-imperial reading of the NT by essentially engaging in a comparative literature project. Indeed, the charge of "parallelomania" is near at hand in many circumstances.[30] Some have rightly wondered, "Are we reading Rome and Caesar *into* the New Testament or are we reading *what is actually there*?"[31]

The Imperial Cult

Many anti-imperial readings of the NT consist of comparing and contrasting the rise of the imperial cult with the rise of Christianity. Subjects for comparison range from persons such as Caesar and Christ, to the imagery used to convey identity and power, to the language employed for descriptions or titles. One of the often-quoted sources on the imperial cult is S. R. F. Price's *Rituals and Power*.[32] His 1984 work is cited ubiquitously in current works on the NT and the imperial cult. For example, Richard Horsley cites Price as a significant contributor to our understanding of the Roman imperial cult. Horsley rightly notes that some NT interpreters undervalued the imperial cult as a "set of empty political gestures" rather than as an expression of "serious religious expression."[33] Horsley emphasizes the contribution of Price in dispelling the often-held notion that the imperial cult was simply a measure of political

---

[29] Harry O. Maier, *Picturing Paul in Empire: Imperial Image, Text, and Persuasion in Colossians, Ephesians, and the Pastoral Epistles* (New York: Bloomsbury, 2013), 38. Paul develops and appropriates that form, including its leading metaphors and vocabulary, to suit his ends.

[30] Samuel Sandmel, "Parallelomania," *JBL* 1962 (1962): 1–13. "We might for our purposes define parallelomania as that extravagance among scholars which first overdoes the supposed similarity in passages and then proceeds to describe source and derivation as if implying literary connection flowing in an inevitable or predetermined direction." As Sandmel goes on to say, the key aspect is "extravagance" (1). One example of this extravagance is Dieter Georgi who suggests that Paul *borrowed* some of his principal imagery and terms from the Roman emperor cult (savior, lord, and faith).

[31] McKnight and Modica, *Jesus Is Lord*, 17; John M. G. Barclay, "Paul, Roman Religion, and the Emperor. Mapping the Point of Conflict," in *Pauline Churches and Diaspora Jews* (Tübingen: Mohr Siebeck, 2011), 345–62.

[32] S. R. F. Price, *Rituals and Power: The Roman Imperial Cult in Asia Minor* (Cambridge: Cambridge University Press, 1984).

[33] Horsley, ed., *Paul and the Roman Imperial Order*, 16.

expediency. There is no area of disagreement on this front with either Horsley or Price's conclusions.

What has been missed by many, and is vitally important to note, is that Price did not conclude his publications with *Rituals and Power* in 1984. Like many others, Price continued to produce more monographs and journal articles. Sadly, many within the NT guild have cited Price's 1984 work authoritatively and have not kept pace with the Price's thoughts on the matter. For example, in the *Cambridge Ancient History* on the Augustan Empire, Price contributes the article, "The Place of Religion: Rome in the Early Empire."[34] Price offers further thoughts on the role of the imperial cult amidst the diversity of the Roman religious environment. His comments deserve a full quotation. Price begins by noting: "In fact, there was no such thing as 'the imperial cult', and in some important contexts imitation of the transformed system of Augustan Rome was of far greater significance than direct worship of the emperor."[35]

Although Price does recognize that the civic space was transformed, he notes that this should not be the entire picture. Even though "the individual elements had earlier parallels, their combination was novel and resulted in a new and remarkably coherent system centered on the emperor. The religion of place was now restructured around a person."[36] However, it is Price's next comments that most scholars have missed:

> But it is misleading to categorize this as "the imperial cult." The term arbitrarily separates honors to the emperor from the full range of his religious activities, and it assumes that there was a single institution of cult throughout the empire. Within Rome, honors to the emperor have to be seen in the light of his holding of religious office, while outside Rome it is wrong to look only for honors to the emperor. In the context of the army and colonies, real clones of Rome, the copying of other Roman religious practices was at least as important. And when, as in Greek towns, religious honors to the emperor were of considerable significance, they were not replications of Roman honors. Indeed the Roman system was not designed to be replicated (except in the army and colonies). Its principal features were specific to the site of Rome, and the growing emphasis on those features served to distinguish Rome from other towns and to express the peculiar position of Rome as the capital of the empire.[37]

Despite the many quotations of Price's *Rituals and Power* by NT scholars, his work seems to have been misappropriated by drawing forth conclusions with which Price would not agree. Many have taken Price's insights on the sincerity of those involved in the imperial cult along with the spreading nature of the imperial cult but have separated this from the wider Roman religious system that incorporated the imperial cult. The balance of Price's observations has been lost on many who use his work unilaterally

---

[34] S. R. F. Price, "The Place of Religion: Rome in the Early Empire," in *The Cambridge Ancient History: The Augustan Empire, 43 B.C.–A.D. 69* (ed. Alan K. Bowman, Edward Champlin, and Andrew Lintott, Cambridge: Cambridge University Press, 1996), 812–47.
[35] Price, "The Place of Religion," 841.
[36] Price, "The Place of Religion," 846.
[37] Price, "The Place of Religion," 847.

without consideration of his wider argument and subsequent work. When the author of the work cited so authoritatively to prove the centrality of the imperial cult expresses disagreement, we may begin to wonder if we have read and used him properly.

S. R. F. Price is not the only classicist to express reservations regarding the use of Empire studies within the NT guild. Karl Galinsky, has expressed considerable reservations regarding Empire-critical studies in the NT. Between 2008 and 2009, SBL and the Society for Ancient Mediterranean Religions organized a cross-disciplinary dialogue that resulted in the 2011 publication of *Rome and Religion: A Cross-Disciplinary Dialogue on the Imperial Cult*.[38] In his plenary address, "The Cult of the Emperor: Uniter or Divider," Galinsky offers his point of view on NT studies as an outsider looking in. He criticizes the unnuanced approach to the imperial cult that presents the imperial cult as "more monolithic and undifferentiated than it was in actuality."[39] He cites in agreement the work of Beard, North, and Price, who argue in a standard reference work on Roman religion that the forms of the imperial cult "are very diverse, because they were located in very different contexts. That is, *there is no such thing as 'the imperial cult'.*"[40] Moreover, Galinsky repudiates any attempt to "superimpose an alien matrix and speak of concepts like 'imperial theology' and 'the gospel of Caesar.'"[41]

Several of Galinsky's conclusions are critically important for anti-imperial investigations of the New Testament. First, the cult of the emperor was often worshipped alongside other gods so that there was not an exclusivity attached to the worship of the emperor. Rather, in the polytheism of the ancient world, the emperor was set alongside the panoply of gods for various Roman devotion and worship.[42] There were, of course, exceptions to this. One thinks of Ephesus, for example, and Galinsky is naturally aware of this site and others where the emperor cult was more prominent.[43] However, Galinsky stresses the embedding nature of the emperor cult where, in cities from Pisidia to Alexandria, both inscriptions and offerings are made to both the emperor and one or more traditional gods (Zeus, Apollo, etc.).[44] He is quick to caution against isolating the emperor cult as an easier target of opposition or polemical partner for early Christianity. Galinsky is certainly firing on all cylinders when he notes that the

---

[38] Brodd and Reed, *Rome and Religion*.
[39] Karl Galinsky, "The Cult of the Roman Emperor: Uniter or Divider?," in *Rome and Religion: A Cross-Disciplinary Dialogue on the Imperial Cult* (ed. Jeffrey Brodd and Jonathan L. Reed, Leiden: Brill, 2011), 2.
[40] Mary Beard, John A. North, and S. R. F. Price, *Religions of Rome*, 2 vols. (New York: Cambridge University Press, 1998), 1:348. Galinsky, "The Cult of the Roman Emperor," 3. Galinsky notes his surprise how little both *Religions of Rome* and the *Cambridge History to the Augustan Age* are cited in these discussions.
[41] Galinsky, *Cambridge History to the Augustan Age*, 3.
[42] For example, see the decree from Cyzicus to Gaius Claudius in 37 CE that honored Claudius as the "new sun God" and in discussing the reign of the emperors note that they "share the rule with such great deities." In M. G. L. Cooley, ed., *Tiberius to Nero*, LACTOR 19 (London: LACTOR, 2011), 270–1. M46.
[43] Noted by Galinsky as well is Steven J. Friesen, *Twice Neokoros: Ephesus, Asia, and the Cult of the Flavian Imperial Family* (New York: Brill, 1993). Galinsky also cites the examples of Aphrodisias, Athens, and Petra.
[44] Galinsky, "The Cult of the Roman Emperor," 4–5.

primary opponents for Paul in Acts 19 are the followers of Artemis and not the cult of the emperor.[45] If ever there was a time for the New Testament to be forthright in its criticism of empire, Ephesus would certainly have been a good place to make the case, but the evidence points in a different direction.

One consequence of embedding the worship of the emperor within the broader religious spectrum is that it brings out important implications for the oft-repeated anthem of resistance. Galinsky argues that this embedded nature of the emperor cult means that "resistance cannot be isolated as resistance to Rome or the imperial cult alone, but to a whole nexus of phenomena."[46] One blurs historical lines by separating the emperor cult from its broader religious matrix, a religious matrix that the imperial cult was indebted to and built upon. Galinsky rightly wonders, "Could you take on just one aspect ... like the imperial cult, without rejecting the remaining network?"[47] From a New Testament perspective, the implications are clear: the resistance to the imperial cult is part and parcel of Jewish monotheism, and Caesar is no worse an idol than Zeus or Mars.[48]

Disagreement may arise with this general assessment that the New Testament's critique of empire is only at the level of a critique of polytheism by noting that Zeus was never a human being. Furthermore, the two of the most prominent human beings who ended up being worshipped in the first century were Jesus and the emperor.

The first century brought many unprecedented changes in religion, and the Caesars are not exempt. However, the complexity of the first century needs to be fully considered. Two issues are worthy of note. One often neglected feature of first-century imperial worship is that Livia, Augustus's life, was declared a goddess under Claudius's reign and had priestesses dedicated to her, as seen in the inscriptions at Neapolis, a port of Philippi.[49] Furthermore, an epigram of Honestus provides a helpful anecdote concerning Livia. It reads, "Twin torches for Peace she lit for every nation ... her genius was the whole wide world's salvation."[50] Such a reality in the first century should caution us against "male-centric" vision of imperial worship.

A second feature should also caution us from limiting divinization to the emperors. The recent work of Cole Spencer has drawn attention to the attempt of Cicero to turn his recently deceased daughter into a god.[51] Such an attempt by Cicero had a precedent in his earlier works where he attempted to divinize the Republican elite of first-century BC Rome.[52] The work of Cohick and Cole shows that the divinization project underway during the first century comprised far more

---

[45] Galinsky, "The Cult of the Roman Emperor," 5.
[46] Galinsky, "The Cult of the Roman Emperor," 6.
[47] Galinsky, "The Cult of the Roman Emperor," 7.
[48] Here the conclusions are not very different from Bryan, *Render to Caesar*.
[49] As noted by Lynn H. Cohick, "Philippians and Empire: Paul's Engagement with Imperialism and the Imperial Cult," in *Jesus Is Lord, Caesar Is Not: Evaluating Empire in New Testament Studies* (ed. Scot McKnight and Joseph B. Modica, Downers Grove: IVP, 2013), 169–70.
[50] As cited in Cooley, *Tiberius to Nero*, 153. She was also declared as "mother of the world" in Anticaria (modern-day Baetica, Spain) in 14 CE.
[51] Spencer Cole, *Cicero and the Rise of Deification at Rome* (New York: Cambridge University Press, 2013).
[52] Cole, *Cicero*, 1–4.

than just the emperor but included his family as well as other notable figures of repute in the first century.

One final aspect of Galinsky's work that bears on our study here is the appropriation of imperial terminology. Galinsky rightly notes that the early Christian movement did have experience with the imperial cult and that it engaged with the Roman Empire. However, Galinsky, by inference, critiques the monolithic approach that equates appropriation with subversion. That is, when the NT writers use terms and symbols that are also used by the Roman Empire, they are assumed to be intentionally subverting those terms. Classic examples include "peace and security" from 1 Thess. 5:3, citizenship language from Philippians, and references to *ekklesia*. He seeks to offer more depth or, in his words, "to enlarge the horizons" as we consider the relationship between the usage of similar terms.

Galinsky's first point is that appropriation is not restricted to the New Testament authors, but that it is a definitive aspect of Greco-Roman authors and texts of the time. A prime example of this appropriation is Augustus's biography, the *Res Gestae*. Galinsky notes that in the very first sentence of one of the most important documents in the Roman period, "every phrase" is appropriated.[53] Augustus has shaped his biography to appropriate images from Alexander the Great to Cicero and Pompey. The key question is rightly pondered and answered: "Is Augustus' appropriation here oppositional? Hardly."[54] More examples of appropriation abound from Greco-Roman literature such as Horace declaring himself *Princeps*, a title Augustus preferred, to poets like Virgil portraying himself as a triumphator.

In each of the three cases—Augustus, Horace, and Virgil—the point is not opposition but "juxtaposition."[55] The conclusion is that these terms were not under the exclusive domain of the empire and that Paul's audience could and would make several associations with these terms depending on their backgrounds.

Galinsky's arguments suggest important conclusions for my work on obedience within the Roman Empire. As will be shown in what follows, Paul uses some of the same terminology and ideas for obedience that Rome expected from the nations under its control. Galinsky's insight helps to show that appropriation of the terminology of the empire does not necessarily entail outright opposition or subversion. Consequently, several possibilities exist for understanding the obedience language. Juxtaposition is certainly a possibility, whereas the obedience Paul seeks carries similarities with Roman obedience but transcends such language with its eschatological flavor. Rom. 1:5 is an example. In this scenario, human obedience only leads so far. The obedience of faith, thinking along the lines of Rom. 5–8 themes, is now obedience to a new degree that can be offered. We could also suggest that obedience was given to various client kings throughout the empire and that this, of course, provoked no degree of opposition to Rome. Further, as we will see, philosophers engaged the question of competing loyalties to divine beings and Rome (cf. Epictetus). Getting ahead of ourselves a bit, a

---

[53] Galinsky, "The Cult of the Roman Emperor," 11.
[54] Galinsky, "The Cult of the Roman Emperor," 11.
[55] Galinsky, "The Cult of the Roman Emperor," 11. If ever there was a politically charged title or role, the princeps and triumphator would be two of the more oppositional roles.

case could be made, reading Rom. 1:5 and Rom. 13:1, that no problem exists for Paul when it comes to giving obedience to Jesus and Rome, but that together these form a web of obedience.

Hidden Transcripts in Rom. 1:5 and 13:1-7?

Another area of anti-imperial readings that deserves comment is the argument for "hidden transcripts." A common refrain among empire critics is that not all subversion of empire is open and flagrant. Rather, subversion can take place through "hidden transcripts." Drawing on the influential work of James C. Scott, several scholars have applied his model to the Pauline letters, and specifically Rom. 13:1-7.[56] The public transcript is a production of the powerful elite that is a "flattering self-portrait" and attempts to show that the ruler governs on behalf of his subjects' interest.[57] In the public transcript, the powerful conceal their exercise of power through the language of benefit, benevolence, and virtue, all the while masking the true notion of exploitation of the powerless.

One immediate problem is that by Scott's argument the hidden transcript of the powerless or subjected groups is "irrevocable for all practical purposes."[58] The only access to their transcript is what Scott says has been "introduce[d] in muted or veiled form into the public transcript."[59] Other problems exist as well, one theoretical and the other historical. First speaking to the theory behind "hidden transcripts," to what degree can Scott's work among the modern poor Malayan peasants equate to the first-century context of ancient peoples? At what point do we engage in an anachronistic endeavor when comparing ancient and modern persons? Certainly, some similarities do exist among subjugated peoples across time, but deciphering these similarities is another issue entirely. The second problem is historical, as complaints are often noted in historical sources where subjugated people are not happy with the rule and reign of Rome, and this is not met with brutality. Sometimes Rome relents and even accommodates the concerns of its subjugated people. It is worth noting the numerous accommodations of the Jewish people by both Julius Caesar and Augustus.

A further historical problem accompanies adopting Scott's "hidden transcripts" approach for an ancient Roman context. To put it bluntly, political elites seem to know how to decipher hidden transcripts whether present or not. One only need to rehearse the sordid history of King Herod of Judea to note the degree of brutality one could encounter when one was merely "suspected" of conspiracy. Further, it appears that the emperors possessed the needed detection skills to perceive "hidden transcripts."[60]

---

[56] James C. Scott, *Domination and the Arts of Resistance: Hidden Transcripts* (New Haven: Yale University Press, 1990). Cf. Neil Elliott, *The Arrogance of Nations: Reading Romans in the Shadow of the Empire* (Minneapolis: Fortress, 2008), 25–58.
[57] Scott, *Domination*, 18.
[58] Scott, *Domination*, 138.
[59] Scott, *Domination*, 138.
[60] Cf. Richard A. Bauman, *Impietas in Principem: A Study of Treason against the Roman Emperor with Special Reference to the First Century A.D.* (München: Beck, 1974).

An example from the Roman historian Cassius Dio about Mamercus Scaurus, a playwright under the reign of Tiberius, is particularly relevant. Dio records:

> Mamercus Aemilius Scaurus, on the other hand, who had never governed a province or accepted bribes, was convicted because of a tragedy he had composed, and fell a victim to a worse fate than that which he had described. "Atreus" was the name of his drama, and in the manner of Euripides it advised one of the subjects of that monarch to endure the folly of the reigning prince. Tiberius, upon hearing of it, declared that this had been written with reference to him, claiming that he himself was "Atreus" because of his bloodthirstiness; and remarking, "I will make him Ajax," he compelled him to commit suicide.[61]

Whether or not Scaurus had intended this to be a hidden transcript is beside the point; although if he had, he had not hidden his elements well enough. What is clear, however, regardless of Scaurus's intention, is that Tiberius is able and capable of detecting what appears to him to be a hidden transcript maligning his rule.[62]

Turning to Paul's letters, bearing in mind the difficulties with appropriating a modern theory of hidden transcripts, I would suggest that the notion of hidden transcripts fails to offer a compelling avenue for understanding Paul's letters. Undue anachronism skews our interpretation of Paul and his challenges. Rather than attempting to decode Paul's letters, more attention should be given to understanding the complexity of the first century than unduly foisting paradigms on the past, which are inappropriate to the context. Empire criticism should not be a totalizing discourse.

---

[61] Cassius Dio, *Histories*, 58.24.3–4.

[62] Criticism on this point has also come from those who are sympathetic to the anti-imperial movement. For example, Maier notes, "Scott bases both notions [public and hidden transcripts] on hundreds of hours of field research of peasant society; with only Paul's letters available as evidence *it is methodologically unsound to posit the apostle's teachings as analogous to such peasant forms of resistance other than in a highly tentative and hypothetical fashion*" (emphasis mine, 36). Cf. Maier, *Picturing Paul*, 36.

3

Obedience in Greek Literature

Terms of the Study

In Rom. 1:5, Paul uniquely combines the terms ὑπακοή and πίστις, leading some, as mentioned in Chapter 1, to say that Paul coins a "unique phrase."[1] This statement is as true as it is misleading. It is certainly true that before the time of Paul we have no evidence of a writer combining the specific term ὑπακοή with πίστις in a genitival relationship. However, this hides the very important fact that we do have passages in ancient Greco-Roman literature where the two terms occur in very close proximity and convey the same concept. In dealing with Paul's phrase, ὑπακοή πίστις, I argue that more attention needs to be given to a broader range of terms for obedience in the Roman Empire. To do this we must, in some sense, go beyond Paul's terms, to build a semantic range for the notion of obedience from his predecessors and contemporaries to provide a broad backdrop with which to compare Paul's terms. The following section attempts to show the process that this project has undertaken to provide a range of terms for obedience. Given the limits and scope of this work, not every term will be able to be pursued. An exhaustive list of Greek and Latin terms is compiled and appears in Appendix 1 at the end of this work.

The support for researching terms other than ὑπακοή is the simple linguistic fact that there is never a singular word used to convey a singular meaning.[2] Language is simply too complex for this to occur. To limit my research specifically to the noun ὑπακοή would result in two important deficiencies. For one, the corpus where ὑπακοή occurs is relatively small. Second, by limiting the notion of obedience to ὑπακοή, we would not have come closer to understanding obedience within the Roman Empire. Greeks and Romans simply used multiple terms to convey the concept of obedience. Therefore, this work, although limited in scope, had to include terms other than ὑπακοή. My work is placed on a better linguistic foundation when we can show that the terms focused on are also used by Paul. The farther we move from Paul's specific terms, the larger degree of uncertainty we entertain, although such investigations are necessary for all linguistic work.

---

[1] Don Garlington, *The Obedience of Faith: A Pauline Phrase in Historical Context* (Tübingen: J. C. B. Mohr (Paul Siebeck), 1991), 3.
[2] James Barr, *The Semantics of Biblical Language* (London: Oxford University Press, 1961).

Given the parameters of this work, my efforts focused on investigating a few specific terms to aid our understanding of obedience in the Greco-Roman world. This work is not an exhaustive attempt to search every term for obedience as such a task would span multiple works. Rather, my goal is to show how certain terms, previously neglected, can aid our understanding of obedience. The following terms provided a large database of citations in TLG and have built the backbone of this research (see Appendix 1 for full list). First, I focused upon the noun ὑπακοή that Paul uses in Rom. 1:5; 5:19; 6:16; 15:18; 16:19, 26. As mentioned above, the places where the noun occurs are relatively small; however, I also investigated the adjective ὑπήκοος that appears quite frequently in the ancient sources. Both ὑπακοή and ὑπήκοος were chosen as they provide the closest parallels to Paul's exact terminology for obedience in Rom. 1:5. Although Paul does not use the adjectival forms of ὑπήκοος, it is in close enough proximity to the noun to warrant further research. Likewise, I also investigated the verbal counterpart in ὑπακούω, which Paul also uses in Rom. 6:12, 16-17; 10:16. I have selected these terms to investigate because they are the terms Paul uses. By surveying the usage of ὑπακοή (obedience), ὑπήκοος (obedient), and ὑπακούω (to obey), in the primary sources, we are in a better position to understand how those in Paul's audience would understand these specific terms. The results from such an investigation of the noun, adjectival, and verbal forms revealed a large number of citations that will help us illuminate obedience from a Greco-Roman perspective.

A further insight occurred when searching the noun and adjectival forms of ὑπακοή within Greco-Roman literature. In contexts where a person or group of people could be described as ὑπακοή, one often finds the verb root πείθ- occurring with a high degree of frequency, even more so than ὑπακούω. In certain contexts, the one who was "obedient" had been "persuaded to obey" (πείθ- root). Therefore, a new line of research was undertaken to discover how the πείθ- root contributed to an understanding of obedience (see Appendix 1 for specific terms used). Support for investigating the πείθ- root is that Paul also uses this verb in Rom. 2:8, 19; 8:38; 14:14; 15:14 in ways similar to how the root is used in the Greco-Roman sources.[3]

This work also focuses on the inverse of obedience language, and I showcase some important examples of disobedience. For that reason, I have also included some terms for disobedience including παρακούω, παρακρόασις, παρακροάομαι, παρακοή, παραβαίνω, ἀπειθέω/ἀπειθόω, and ἀπειθής. One idea that has guided this work is that obedience was, for the most part, the "norm" of the empire. It seems that one

---

[3] Other terms that were initially pursued but showed little promise included ἡμερόω and φυλακτέος that also appeared in some of our Greco-Roman sources. These terms were not investigated with the same degree of depth as the previous terms for two reasons. First, these terms occur primarily in Jewish texts (i.e., Josephus and Philo) and fall outside the scope and aim of this work. Second, neither of these terms is used by Paul in Romans (although Paul does use φυλάσσω in Rom. 2:26). Likewise, given the limits of our work we were unable to include ἀκούω as the database for these term is incredibly large and could constitute a stand-alone project. Further, previous work had been done on this term in the works that investigated the Jewish literature, and many commentaries note the diversity of this term in both Jewish and Greco-Roman sources and cite examples. Therefore, I did not pursue this angle, although as I note in the conclusion, there could be potential future work investigating this field of terms.

possible angle that might better serve the aim(s) of this work was to look at places where the normal procedures of the empire were upended—the thought being that, if groups primarily obeyed Rome, this would probably go without comment by the historical sources. What would register, however, would be those places where the normal practices were violated; these would by nature stand out for comment. By including some terms for disobedience we can construct a more complete picture of how obedience was thought about and documented in the Greco-Roman world, by looking at its inverse.[4]

Other terms such as παρακοή (disobedience), ἀπειθέω (to disobey), and ἀπειθής (disobedient) proved quite beneficial for several reasons. Not only are these terms used throughout Greco-Roman literature, but Paul also uses the same terms in Romans. Paul uses παρακοή in Rom. 5:19, ἀπειθής in Rom. 1:30, and ἀπειθέω in Rom. 2:8; 10:21; 11:30-31; 15:31. As mentioned above, the linguistic foundation is stronger when we can show a direct link between the terms used by Paul in Romans and other Greco-Roman authors.

My aim in this chapter is to establish a spectrum of usage for the language of obedience in Greek literature. The initial question is, how and where does the language of obedience appear in Greek literary sources contemporary with the New Testament, and if possible, is there a connection with the city of Rome? The survey highlighted the instances and places where obedience language occurs and several helpful patterns emerge. By surveying the extant literature from surviving Greco-Roman literature, we are in a better position to listen to Paul's call for obedience with Roman ears and hear the overtone(s) of the echoes of obedience language from throughout the empire.

The survey of obedience language is vast and widespread, so some degree of limitations must be placed for the scope of the work. To this end, we have focused on a select group of Greek authors including Polybius, Dionysius of Halicarnassus, Cassius Dio, Strabo, and Plutarch. Most of the usages of obedience language occur with these authors and provide numerous examples to illustrate just how and where obedience language was used, thus providing a compelling portrait for our understanding of obedience.

Polybius: The Foundations of Obedience in Empire

In 167 BCE, Polybius was met with what had to seem quite unfortunate news: he was being deported. The Macedonians had lost a critical battle to the Romans at Pydna, and as a consequence, the Roman Senate expelled one thousand leading Achaeans to Italy and Polybius was among this number. An already prestigious commander, Polybius had enjoyed a privileged upbringing among elite society in Achaea and reached the

---

[4] Although not every term for disobedience could be fully investigated because of the limits of this work, some terms proved more beneficial than others. For example, although παρακούω and παρακρόασις do appear, their occurrences are primarily in Jewish literature and were not investigated to the same degree as the other terms.

upper echelon of the Achaean league. All of this was seemingly cut short by the loss to the Romans. Polybius's life was marked by both promise, tragedy, and opportunity. However, what initially appeared to be a setback quickly turned into an opportunity when he befriended the Roman general and statesman, Scipio Aemilianus. This friendship turned out to be critical to the trajectory of Polybius's career as his friendship not only brought him into contact with high-standing members of Roman society but also placed him geographically and socially in important places. Geographically, he was able to accompany Scipio to Africa and witnessed the destruction of Carthage in 146 BCE. Socially, this allowed him the vantage point that would be key to his posterity as a historian—from not only witnessing history first hand but also recording it at a critical juncture in Greek history. Polybius was writing not only in the dimming glow of the aftermath of Alexander and certainly far before the bright and illustrious rise of Augustus. He would have a front-row seat to one of the most significant historical transformations with the rise of Rome from a fledgling state in Italy to a worldwide empire.[5]

Our examination of obedience language within the Roman Empire begins with an investigation of obedience in the work of Polybius. Polybius is one of the few Hellenistic historian's writings to survive antiquity. Consequently, he is a key source in documenting the early years of the Roman Empire.[6] The groundwork for Rome's relationships with other nations is set on new trajectories in the early years of Rome's empire.

Polybius sets out his main concern early in the introduction to his *Histories* as, "To know by what means and under what system of polity the Romans in less than fifty-three years have succeeded in subjecting nearly the whole inhabited world to their sole government—a thing unique in history" (1.1.5). Remarking on Rome's dominance, he highlights the role of obedience as, "The Roman conquest, on the other hand, was not partial. Nearly the whole inhabited world was reduced by them to obedience (ὑπήκοος) and they left behind them an Empire not to be paralleled in the past or rivaled in the future" (1.2.3).[7] From his account, the parameters of Roman domination were not merely conquest but to bring the world into obedience. The rest of his work sets out

---

[5] Brian C. McGing, *Polybius' Histories* (New York: Oxford University Press, 2010), 6.

[6] To put this in perspective, for the three-hundred-year span from the death of Alexander the Great to the Battle of Actium (321–31 BCE), there were over six hundred known Greek historians, of which only three have survived, including Polybius. See *OCD*, 1209; *DNP* 11:497-502. Roughly one-third of this source is extant. Polybius maintained a close proximity to the events he reported as his friendship with the Roman general and statesmen Cornelius Scipio allowed him to travel to various locations and events. On reliability see F. W. Walbank, *Polybius* (Berkeley: University of California Press, 1972); Donald Walter Baronowski, *Polybius and Roman Imperialism* (London: Bristol Classical Press, 2011); John Thornton, "Polybius in Context: The Political Dimension of the *Histories*," in *Polybius and His World: Essays in Memory of F. W. Walbank* (ed. Bruce Gibson and Thomas Harrison, New York: Oxford University Press, 2013), 213–30; Nikos Miltsios and Melina Tamiolaki, eds., *Polybius and His Legacy* (Berlin: De Gruyter, 2018).

[7] See also *Hist*. 1.2.7 where he notes, "But the Romans have subjected (ὑπήκοος) to their rule not portions, but nearly the whole of the world and possess an empire which is not only immeasurably greater than any which preceded it, but need not fear rivalry in the future." He also repeats his thesis in 3.3.9, "The one aim and object, then, of all that I have undertaken to write is to show how, when, and why all the known parts of the world fell under the dominion (ὑπήκοος) of Rome."

to describe in detail how this reduction to obedience took place and notes groups that have been "made obedient" by Rome.[8] Obedience and the nations is a standard trope in Polybius's work (cf. Rom. 1:5).[9]

Polybius recalls several episodes to narrate the unfolding process of how the world became subject to Rome. In 3.3.9, he notes that these events "will enable us to perceive how the Romans dealt with each contingency and thus made the whole world obedient (ὑπήκοος) to them." The victories of Rome had succeeded in sending out a compelling message. So much so that Polybius noted, "The growth and advance of Roman power was now complete. Besides which it was now universally accepted as a necessary fact that henceforth all must submit to the Romans and obey (πειθαρχεῖν) their orders" (3.4.2-3). The obedience of the nations is set out as a leitmotif (cf. Rom. 1:5). His reporting of past events is not for historians' curiosity alone but has a present and future function. He wrote, "The present generation will learn from this whether they should shun or seek the rule of Rome and future generations will be taught whether to praise and imitate, or to decry it" (3.4.7). What particular element of imitation does Polybius have in mind? It's worth asking what is to be imitated and what is to be shunned, and his historical work bears out the answer: obedience and submission are worthy of imitation.

The main concern of this work is not necessarily finding specific references to obedience in Polybius's work; such would show only that obedience is of interest to Polybius and the implications for Paul would only be tangential to some degree. What is of greater importance is that the concepts of obedience and faith occur together in Polybius in ways similar to Paul's usage in Rom. 1:5. Several places emerge in the histories that are of interest to this work.

One such place where this occurs is a phrase repeated by Polybius, Ῥωμαῖος πίστις (Roman faith/loyalty), which appears throughout the work and might best be rendered as the faith/loyalty/trust of the Romans. Another important area of focus is the treaties with Carthage that occupy a central role in the *Histories*. These treaties provide an interior look at how Rome subjected their opponents and required obedience from them. How Rome viewed its subjects is of particular importance, but of greater weight is the expectations of Rome on behalf of their conquered subjects. We begin first with a short excursus on surrender or *deditio* within this period, before turning to look at the instances of the *Roman faith*, in Polybius, which will then immediately lead into a discussion of the treaties with Carthage.

---

[8] Some examples are *Hist.* 1.10.5; 2.1.7; 2.18.1; 3.22.12; 7.9.5, 7; 9.34.3; 10.4.7; 15.5.13; 31.1.1.

[9] Obedience language also occurs with people obeying orders from either the Senate or another political group in power; see *Hist.* 2.23.11-14; 4.22.4; 5.2.10; 6.12.2; (to parents) 7.8.9; (satraps to a king) 11.34.14; 15.20.7; 18.53.6, 54.2; 20.4.4-5; 21.22.8; 22.4.10; 23.11.4; 24.9.9; 30.9.18, 32.8; 32.8.6, 9.4; 36.4.6; (Polybius own statement) 36.11.2, 4. Obedience language appears in reference to various laws or aspects of a treaty; see *Hist.* 2.58.7; 3.24.1-6; 6.4.4-5; 7.5.1; 8.35.1; 15.2.2; 22.12.3; 24.8.4, 6, 9.2; 24.12.1-4; 29.27.13; 30.13.9, 23.2-3, 31.8, 31.20. Obedience can occur in contexts where it is refused; see *Hist.* 4.53.4; 5.30.1; 6.57.8; 15.1.2, 4.1-3, 25.13; 22.10.8; 23.3.3; 24.8.4, 9.1; 24.9.14; 25.2.11; 30.8.1, 30.3; 36.9.16-17. A few examples of obedience language fall outside these categories. Two examples refer to the obedience of animals: *Hist.* 3.46.7; 12.4.5. One occurrence of obedience is metaphorical: *Hist.* 33.17.2.

Digression on *deditio*

Since treaties are one of the main reservoirs of obedience language it is essential to grasp how treaties functioned throughout the Roman period. We are greatly assisted in such an endeavor by the recent work of Paul J. Burton, *Friendship and Empire: Roman Diplomacy in the Middle Republic (353–146 BC)*. He explores the four main ways Rome entered into international partnerships during the Middle Republic.[10] The importance of this work is not for the middle Republican period only. As we will show in the work of subsequent historians, the process of *deditio* is important for subsequent Roman periods including the New Testament.[11] Burton's study concludes that Rome entered international partnerships (*amicitia*) through:

- military cooperation,
- diplomatic exchanges,
- unconditional surrender (*deditio*) performed freely with the explicit purpose of receiving Roman protection,
- unconditional surrender (*deditio*) following military defeat by Rome (he calls "surrender under duress" to distinguish it from the voluntary kind").[12]

The first two categories of military cooperation and diplomatic exchange were not as frequent as the two *deditio* categories. The final two categories of surrender (*deditio*) are important as they include the majority of references to obedience language in the work of the historians that comprise this chapter.

Friendships (*amicitia*) with Rome were often initiated through *deditio* or surrender, whether voluntarily as a means of protection or involuntarily as a result of a war. According to Burton, there was a shared cultural assumption whereby "both the Greeks and the Romans appear to have had a shared intersubjective conception of the ritual acts and comportment appropriate to surrenders, which pushed the victor in the direction of exercising leniency and mercy, and pulled the *dediticius* towards ritual displays of humility and gratitude."[13]

Burton draws out the important ramifications of the *deditio* process for international peace. The humble state of the party offering surrender would exert moral pressure

---

[10] Paul J. Burton, *Friendship and Empire: Roman Diplomacy and Imperialism in the Middle Republic (353–146 BC)* (New York: Cambridge University Press, 2011).

[11] Surprisingly Teresa Morgan's work on Roman faith does not add to the discussions of this term. See Teresa Morgan, *Roman Faith and Christian Faith: Pistis and Fides in the Early Roman Empire and Early Churches* (New York: Oxford University Press, 2015), 38.

[12] Burton, *Friendship*, 79. Burton sites the work of both Gruen and Rich in defining the term *deditio*. In the words of Erich Gruen, a *deditio* was the process by which "a state that sought Roman assistance and was accepted into *fides* … would henceforth be judged an *amicus*. Even former enemies, once defeated in war and agreeing to terms … would take on the new status," in *The Hellenistic World and the Coming of Rome*, 2 vols. (Berkeley: University of California Press, 1984), 55. Or as J. Rich has argued, "*deditiones* were made not only by communities under attack, but also by those seeking to avert attack and sometimes by communities voluntarily siding with Rome," in "Treaties, Allies, and the Roman Conquest of Italy," in *War and Peace in Ancient and Medieval History* (ed. Philip De Souza and John France, New York: Cambridge University Press, 2008), 62.

[13] Burton, *Friendship*, 118.

on the victorious general toward "merciful and lenient conditions" and thus "served to mitigate the violent anarchy of the Mediterranean system by imposing a tripwire on aggressive conduct, thereby contributing to the construction of a more collective-security-oriented international system."[14] Friendships were never equal. As Billows notes, "The Romans always viewed themselves, rightly or wrongly, as the superiors in the relationship, the ones to whom gratitude and its accompanying *officium* of deference were owed."[15]

In the case of voluntary surrenders, Barton concludes that this is how most of Rome's international friendships were established.[16] Nations would seek assistance from Rome for protection from either an impending war or to ward off potential threats. Importantly, the issue of *fides*, or the faith of the Romans, is directly tied to these appeals and appears in such contexts. How might we define *pistis/fides* in this context? In many of these contexts, faith in Rome comes closest to the term "trust" or loyalty. Rome was "trusted" to hold up their end of the bargain, whether surrender was voluntary or under duress. Who would enter into the "faith of Rome" if this faith was known to be hollow? If Rome couldn't be trusted then the faith in their treaty would be empty. Barton highlights the role that *fides* played in these international relationships:

> There can be no question that the Romans were gradually earning themselves a reputation in the region as preservers of *fides*: a *stater* issued by Epizephyrian Locri, probably in 282 BC, depicts the goddess *pistis* (= *fides*) crowning the goddess Roma. At some point in the 250s/240s, the Romans monumentalized the worship of the goddess Fides, a cult of perhaps great antiquity, with the establishment of a permanent stone temple to her on the Capitoline. The timing is probably no great coincidence: the temple was a public-relations ploy designed to advertise Rome's *fides* to the world, and perhaps, by implication, to denigrate the perfidy of her Carthaginian foe ... the Romans took their *fides* quite seriously, especially towards surrendering states, and could be expected to respond in some positive fashion to the moral pressure being exerted.[17]

Interestingly, the breaking of such treaties described as "entering into the Roman faith" was not termed as a violation of a treaty but contained moral overtones that resulted in the language such as "breaking *fides* and violating the bonds of *amicitia*."[18] Breaking faith or in many contexts faithfulness toward Rome fractured the treaty.

---

[14] Burton, *Friendship*, 119, 121.
[15] Richard Billows, "International Relations," in *The Cambridge History of Greek and Roman Warfare: Greece, the Hellenistic World, and the Rise of Rome* (ed. Philip A. G. Sabin, Hans van Wees, and Michael Whitby, New York: Cambridge University Press, 2007), 1:320.
[16] An actual historical *deditio* was found on an inscription from Alćantra, Spain, and dated to 104 BCE. See Burton, *Friendship*, 119.
[17] Burton, *Friendship*, 132-3.
[18] Burton, *Friendship*, 139. Dionysius of Halicarnassus uses the precise language of "breaking faith" (see section below). Cf. David Potter, "Old and New in Roman Foreign Affairs: The Case of 197," in *Imperialism, Cultural Politics, and Polybius* (ed. Christopher John Smith and Liv Mariah Yarrow, New York: Oxford University Press, 2012), 135.

Such relationships between Rome and their subjects is important as it begins to provide a working definition for the type of obedience Rome required of its conquered subjects. The implications for such a group bear directly on Paul's letter to the Romans and the audience members who may have come to Rome as subdued persons. Treaties would have provided the framework and language of obedience and serve as a point of contact for some persons in Paul's audience as they reflect on Paul's call for the obedience of faith. The connection between obedience and faith leads us to the next area of importance in Polybius, his usage of the phrase Ῥωμαῖος πίστις.

The Faith of the Romans

The phrase Ῥωμαῖος πίστις first appears in *Histories* 2.11, where Polybius notes that the Corcyreans "committed themselves also unconditionally to the Roman faith; believing that this was their only security in the future against the piratical incursions of the Illyrians" (2.11.5).[19] Several things ought to be noted in this first occurrence of the phrase Ῥωμαῖος πίστις. First, the motivating factor for this decision is fear; the general Demetrius seeks correspondence with Rome for assistance—a "voluntary surrender" in Roman terms. He offers to provide all that lies within his control to the disposal of the Romans. When the Romans appear, the Corcyreans not only give up their garrison but also give themselves "unconditionally" to the Romans. The aftermath of surrender requires obedience over the long term to Rome's demands. Whether defeated through war or acquiesced through treaties, as subjects, they now serve on behalf of Rome's commands when their services are required (3.12.5-6). A frequent theme emerges within Polybius's work—Roman dominance issuing forth the unconditional obedience of the defeated party.

One of the most important references to obedience occurs in Book 16 where Polybius rehearses the relationship between Rome and Philip of Macedon. Polybius notes that Roman legates were in Athens and requested that Philip refrain from attacking any Greek state. Rome laid out the terms of their request as follows: "If he [Philip] acted so, they added, he might consider himself at peace with Rome, but if he refused to obey (πείθω) the consequences would be the reverse" (16.27.3). Polybius repeats the same phrase three times, noting, "If he acted so he would be allowed to remain at peace, but if he did not at once obey these terms he would find himself at war with Rome" (16.34.4), thus stressing the importance of the decision to obey.[20] The terms of the agreement are clear: obedience results in peace, and disobedience to Rome's commands results in war. The theme of disobedience leading to destruction is also found in Rom. 6:20-23.

We still have yet to discuss just what those conquered by Rome were surrendering to? As one might guess, the common expression *Pax Romana* looms in the discussion. Certainly, surrender warded off death on the one hand, but on the other, it also was the offer of peace that may have been extended. One of the results of entering into a

---

[19] On Ῥωμαῖος πίστις see *Hist.* 3.18.6-7 (of the Ilyrians); 3.30.1 (of the Carthaginians); 10.34.6 (of the Edetani); 10.40.2 (of the Iberians); 18.38.5 (of the Thebes).
[20] Other occurrences, *Hist.* 16.27.3, 34.7.

treaty with Rome through a *deditio* was peace. The notion of Roman *Pax*, or "peace," requires further definition. Carlos Noreña offers a helpful definition of Roman peace in relationship to conquered nations. Peace has a twofold meaning. Within the city of Rome, peace often meant the absence of civil war and is closer to our modern concept of peace. What Noreña calls "civic peace" is often linked with issues of concord and justice. Noreña warns that we should not confuse civic peace with the peace that Rome had with subject peoples. He notes, "This 'militaristic *pax*' originally referred to 'a pact' concluding a war ... but which came to take on the more general meaning of capitulation to Rome, was the product of foreign conquest and depended on the military *virtus* of the Roman soldiers and generals who had brought it about."[21] Peace in Rome did mean the absence of hostilities, but peace in a region that voluntarily surrendered or conquered meant something closer to "pacification." In the following examples, peace with Rome must be understood within this militaristic context. Continued obedience was paramount to securing this lasting accord with Rome. We might contrast such a paradigm with Paul's statements in Rom. 5:1 that bear out the inverse relationship.

Not all treaties with Rome went smoothly; submission to the faith of Rome often entailed misunderstanding. Just what did the Romans expect from those "entering into faith with them?"[22] It is confusion among the defeated that drives more precise definitions. Polybius highlights this in recounting the Aetolian episode in Book 20. After losing several battles, the Aetolians seek a peace treaty with Rome. They send an embassy to Manius Acilius Glabrio to beg for a peace treaty. Glabrio is charged with representing Rome and working out the treaty with the Aetolians. The Aetolians had discussed among themselves what they thought Rome would require of them, perhaps even working up an initial list of offerings to appease the Romans. However, Polybius recounts that they had "no comprehension" of what they were agreeing to in this relationship. It is here that Polybius seeks to define the term for his readers. Polybius describes that the Aetolians were misled by the word "faith" into supposing that the Romans would thereby be more inclined to grant them terms. But with the Romans for a man "to commit himself to their good faith" is held to be equivalent to "surrendering unconditionally" (20.9.10-12).

The account offers Polybius a chance to provide a working definition for Ῥωμαῖος πίστις. What exactly is πίστις in this context of the treaties? What does it mean to enter into the "πίστις of the Romans." The faith of the Romans results in unconditional surrender or obedience. Polybius shows that what the Romans meant by faith was total obedience to their requests. The Anatolians thought that they might be looked upon favorably by the Romans and this was not the case. No favored position was granted and it indeed was a mischaracterization of the Romans' position. Paul makes similar claims in terms of God's outlook that he

---

[21] Carols F. Noreña, *Imperial Ideals in the Roman West: Representation, Circulation, Power* (New York: Cambridge University Press, 2011), 127.
[22] A. M. Eckstein, "Glabrio and the Aetolians: A Note on Deditio," *TAPA* 125 (1995): 271–89; Álvaro M. Moreno Leoni, "The Failure of the Aetolian Deditio as a Didactic Cultural Clash in the Histories of Polybius," *Histos* 8 (2014): 146–79.

does not show favoritism and requires obedience from all, Jew and Gentile alike (Rom. 2:11).

Further, if we set this story alongside Paul's argument in Rom. 6:1-21 it illumines the passage in a new way. In Rom. 6:1-21, Paul offers some avenues for how Gentiles may have thought about obedience. Gentiles in Paul's audience could be tempted to think that this new freedom in Christ meant no longer having to obey (see Rom. 6:1). Paul has to correct this misunderstandings of obedience to this new Lord in analogous ways to the situation described by Polybius. Further illuminating is that Paul's discussion in Rom. 6:1-21 involves military language of weapons, peace, and wrath as well.

Glabrio is charged with taking back the message that to enter into faith with them is to accept the treaty as one of unconditional obedience to their demands. The outcome of submitting to the faith of Rome results in directives to be obeyed. The directives relayed by Glabrio were that the Aetolians can no longer cross into Asia, they must turn over an enemy to Rome, and tone rather startling demand. In an absurd show of power, Glabrio charges, "Why, I might if I chose put you all in chains and commit you to prison!" With these words he ordered his men to bring a chain and an iron collar and put it on the neck of each of them (20.10.1-5). The last requirement seems to show the depths to which obedience must be rendered, even to the most shameful of actions.[23] The definition and application of obedience shock the Aetolians (20.10.8-9).[24]

With different groups, the results of entering into the Ῥωμαῖος πίστις carried various requirements for maintaining peace. Violating or disobeying such stipulations meant running the risk of incurring the wrath of Rome. Certainly, some of the demands of Rome were sure to raise objections, such as in the case of Aetolians being put in iron collars. Polybius raises such objections and then answers the problems in offering obedience to Rome toward the end of his work in a discussion of the Roman treaty with the Carthaginians.

In Book 36, Polybius covers the events of the Third Punic War between Rome and Carthage.[25] Although Rome and Carthage had a formal treaty, Rome was looking for a pretext for war with Carthage. One such justification was found in the rumor that Carthage was raising an army in violation of their treaty with Rome. Rather than risk war with Rome, it appears Carthage chose the "lesser of two evils," to use Polybius's own words. They chose to surrender to Rome unconditionally (36.3).[26] At this point in

---

[23] So also Billows, *Cambridge History of Greek and Roman Warfare*, 324. He notes that after such an experience the Aetolians had no trust any longer in the Roman faith.

[24] The details of such acceptance of Roman faith are reiterated again in Polybius's discussion of the campaign in Italy against the Decietae around 154 BCE (*Hist.* 33.10.11).

[25] There are notorious issues with the various translations of the thirty-sixth book of Polybius's *Histories*. Most notably, and bearing importantly on this section, the insertion of the word "faith" at various places where the existing manuscripts lack such word. The Loeb edition has recently had a revision in 2012 by renowned Polybius scholar F. W. Walbank to remedy some of the deficiencies of the original volume. Weaknesses still remain including Walbank's retention of the original translator's (W. R. Paton) mistakes including four references to "faith" in Book 36 when no form of *pistis* is in the Greek manuscripts. See the helpful review by Liv Mariah Yarrow, "Book Review (Review of Polybius: The Histories Books 28–39. Translated by W. R. Paton. Revised by F. W. Walbank and Christian Habicht)," *Histos* 7 (2013): 1–5.

[26] On the long and complex relationship with Rome see John E. Lazenby's article, "Rome and Carthage," in Harriet I. Flower, *The Cambridge Companion to the Roman Republic* (New York: Cambridge University Press, 2006), 225–41.

Polybius's narrative, he reiterates one aspect that he has repeated throughout his work, the meaning of surrender:

> I have spoken before about what this implies, but I must in this place also briefly remind my readers of its import. Those who thus surrender themselves to the Roman authority, surrender all territory and the cities in it, together with all men and women in all such territory or cities, likewise rivers, harbors, temples, and tombs, so that the Romans should become actual lords of all these, and those who surrender should remain lords of nothing whatever (36.4.1-3).

Although the phrase Ῥωμαῖος πίστις does not appear in this section, all the formal features mentioned above in entering the Roman faith, primarily the aspect of ultimate surrender, are in play here.[27] Surrender to Rome is couched in terms of obedience to Rome's demands, however drastic they might be. The aftermath of disobedience is portrayed. To disobey is to provoke a war with Rome.[28]

The relationship between Carthage and Rome impacted Roman identity. Even though the defeat of Carthage was in the distant past, it still had profound ramifications for Polybius's Rome. Even for subsequent writers in the Augustan period, the rise of Rome was inextricably linked with Punic Carthage. Polybius's influence on subsequent historians and his descriptions of Carthage are important for the subsequent building of Roman identity. As Richard Miles has noted about the educated elite, "To be Roman was to know the city itself. To know the city of Rome required knowledge of Punic Carthage. This was a discourse which was still strikingly relevant to Roman authors writing many generations after the re-foundation of Carthage as a Roman city."[29] The story highlights the importance of obedience and disobedience to Rome by the nations (cf. Rom. 1:5).

---

[27] Polybius notes that Carthage agreed to these terms, but that the Praetor added one further condition: that they must send three hundred hostages from the Carthage Senate "to obey (πειθαρχήσωσιν) whatever commands the consuls of Lilybaeum might request" (*Hist.* 36.4.6, cf. 36.5.3-6).

[28] Cf. *Hist.* 36.9.7-8; 36.19.17. At the end of Book 36, Polybius notes that even within his own day, controversy surrounded Rome's attack and defeat of Carthage, given their treaty and Carthage's obedience to all of Rome's demands (36.9.1-17). At this point we enter into the causation of the Third Punic War, a topic of no considerable controversy within scholarship on Polybius. We face several problems, one being the reality that only fragments of Books 36–38 exist and are at a considerable loss of valuable information. Donald Baronowski has argued that there were two stages of the war. He argues, "The inception of hostilities, culminating in the surrender of Carthage, marks the first stage, and the subsequent decision of the Carthaginians to resist, which ultimately led to the destruction of their city and the annexation of their country by Rome, constitutes the second stage." The paragraphs immediately above discussing Polybius's definition of surrender and the speech of Mago Brettius would correspond to Baronowski's first stage. See Donald Walter Baronowski, "Polybius on the Causes of the Third Punic War," *CP* 90 (1995): 16–31. Given the fragmentary nature of Books 36 and 38, and because Book 37 is entirely missing, it is hard to judge exactly which position Polybius would have chosen in the debate over Rome's actions with Carthage. In our view, however, Polybius goes out of his way to clearly define the concepts of obedience and surrender several times in his work. It would seem that the second view proposed by Polybius, where Carthage at some point resisted and disobeyed Roman orders, would align closer with Polybius's own views on the matter for the cause of the Third Punic War.

[29] Richard Miles, "Rivaling Rome: Carthage," in *Rome the Cosmopolis* (ed. Catharine Edwards and Greg Woolf, New York: Cambridge University Press, 2006), 129.

Polybius on Obedience

Obedience in Polybius occurs primarily in the relationships between Rome and foreign nations. Whether this refers to a king or a nation, obedience is expected to fulfill the expectations in a treaty with Rome. Obedience is the mechanism by which peace with Rome is *obtained and maintained*, while disobedience violates treaties / alliances and can provoke a war with Rome.

Most intriguing and illuminating was the relationship between Roman faith or loyalty and obedience, where obedience is the outworking of entering into the faith of Rome. Key to Rome's history and rise to power was the role that "subject" peoples played in Rome's dominance of its ever-expanding empire. Obedience was essential to Rome's empire and expected on behalf of those it had subjected to retain peace and avoid war. This was in keeping with the "good faith" of the Romans. To repeat a central claim, to enter into "faith with Rome" was to commit oneself or one's nation to complete obedience to Rome.

Reflecting on Paul's letter to the Romans, this work is not suggesting that Paul has drawn on these accounts or even the language. The previous section is part of my major argument in constructing a background for "how" obedience language appears in Greek and Roman literature. Certainly, there are parallel ideas with Paul's language in Romans, such as the language about obedient nations and the discussion of enemies, but the primary emphasis is on understanding how those in Rome might have recognized obedience language within their social context(s).

Dionysius of Halicarnassus and the Rhetoric of Obedience

With the dust of the civil war of Rome barely settled, a Greek rhetorician arrived in Rome in 30/29 BCE as the young Octavian was asserting his new role. It was a time of peace and celebration. Octavian would celebrate the year 29 BCE with three consecutive triumphs in Rome for his victories in Illyricum, Actium, and Egypt. The doors to the temple Janus would also be closed, for only the third time in Roman history, signaling peace. This era provided the context for a Greek rhetorician to spend the next two decades researching and compiling his historical work with the first volume appearing in 7 BCE. His work was one of reconciliation and a literary rapprochement showing how Greek ideals were the basis for the Roman Empire in hopes to persuade Greeks of Roman rule.[30] Such language can obscure important details, such as, why should the Greeks submit or obey the Roman rule?

---

[30] This is a complex literary, historical, and social point; see Richard Hunter and Casper C. de Jonge, eds., *Dionysius of Halicarnassus and Augustan Rome: Rhetoric, Criticism and Historiography* (New York: Cambridge University Press, 2018), 201–66. Also Nicolas Wiater, *The Ideology of Classicism: Language, History, and Identity in Dionysius of Hallicarnassus* (Berlin: De Gruyter, 2011), 60–119.

The survey of obedience language within the Roman Empire now moves to an investigation of obedience in the work of Dionysius of Halicarnassus, the Greek historian of Rome's early Republican period.[31] The *Roman Antiquities* (*RA* hereafter) comprised twenty volumes that traced Rome from its mythical beginnings to the start of the First Punic War (264 BCE).[32] The *RA* begins with Dionysius's preface stating the intention of his work. His aim in comparing Rome to previous empires is to

"determine which of them obtained the widest dominion and both in peace and war performed the most brilliant achievements" and concludes unsurprisingly that "the supremacy of the Romans has far surpassed all those that are recorded from earlier times, not only in the extent of its dominion and in the splendor of its achievements … but also in the length of time during which it has endured down to our day." (1.2.1)

Of particular note are the Persians whom Dionysius singles out for not reducing various nations to "submission" (ὑπάγω) (1.2.2). Likewise, the Macedonians are castigated for they did not "subjugate (ὑπήκοος) every country and every sea" (1.2.4).

Naturally, the failures of previous empires are avoided by Rome itself, with the logical conclusion that, in light of the failures of Persia and Macedonia to subjugate or make obedient their neighboring countries, Rome has done so. As Dionysius notes, Rome now "rules every country" and the boundaries of Rome's dominion are the rising and setting of the sun (1.3.3). The entire passage indicates the parallel between Rome's dominion and the obedience of other nations in contrast to the previous empires.[33] Dionysius states this explicitly in 1.3.4, noting, "For from the very beginning, immediately after her founding, she [Rome] began to draw to herself the neighboring nations, which were both numerous and warlike, and continually

---

[31] As a resident of Rome, he published his historical work twenty two years after the end of Rome's civil wars. Cf. *OCD*, 478. Of the twenty books only eleven have survived antiquity, the first ten in their entirety, Book 11 is incomplete, and Books 11–20 exist in fragments.

[32] *DNP* 4:482; John Marincola, ed., *A Companion to Greek and Roman Historiography* (Malden: Wiley-Blackwell, 2011), 1.

[33] One of the unique traits of Dionysius's work is the religious tinge that accompanies such obedience language. For example, see Decius's speech in *Ant. Rom.* 7.43.1. Though unique to Dionysius's work, the religious character of battle and treaties was integral to the Roman system through the administration of the *fetiales* who were priests that oversaw the treaty-making process. Cf. Richard Billow's article "International Relations," in *Cambridge History of Greek and Roman Warfare*, 315. He notes,

> The *fetiales*, as overseers of Rome's international relations also oversaw the making of treaties. The decision to make a treaty, and as to the precise terms, was taken by the Roman authorities, but it fell to the *fetiales* to formalize the treaty by giving it religious sanction. Again, one of the *fetiales* was nominated *pater patratus*, and he then swore an oath on behalf of the Roman people, recited the terms of the treaty, and, striking a sacrificial pig with a special flint, called on Jupiter to smite the Roman people as he was smiting the pig, if the Romans failed to fulfill and abide by the terms just recited by the priest. The representative of the other community was present for this oath and sacrifice, and committed his people to the treaty in his own way at the same time. (315)

advanced, subjugating every rival." Rome made rival nations into its slaves. The notion of slavery carries the corollary of obedience.

In light of this, sections such as Rom. 5–6 seem to indicate that slavery language was an apt metaphor for Paul's audience. This is all the more important if some of his readers were from ethnic groups conquered by Rome and may indicate that this is one of the primary ways persons in Rome understood the concept of obedience.

In the *RA*, obedience language appears in similar settings as those we found in Polybius. Obedience language is predominately featured in discussions of Rome's wars and treaties.[34] In 3.6.1, Dionysius focuses on two groups, the Veientes and Fidenates, who had gone to war with Romulus but lost and were "forced to become subjects of the conquerors." His description of this subjugation bears similarity to the *deditio* under duress discussed in the section above. However, as time passed, these groups grew in population, wealth, and prosperity, so much so that "they again aspired to freedom, assumed a bolder spirit, and prepared to yield obedience to the Romans no longer." These actions led to grounds for war as Dionysius alleges, "The grounds he alleged for the war were that this people, being called upon to justify themselves in the matter of the plot that they had formed against the Romans" and that by "taking up arms, shutting their gates, and bringing in the allied forces of the Veientes, had openly revolted" (3.23.1).[35]

An apt comparative point with Romans emerges with Paul's discussion of wrath and disobedience in Rom. 1:18-32 where we see connections between these concepts. For Paul, disobedience produces wrath for those who fail to obey. In Rom. 2:8-9, Paul will state that those in opposition to God will experience a litany of negative outcomes, including wrath (ὀργή), fury (θυμός), anguish (θλῖψις), and distress (στενοχωρία). Similar rhetorical features are at work in both works—an attempt to dissuade disobedience and encourage obedience. The disobedience and subsequent wrath are also dissimilar in Paul's argument given the nature of rescue Paul will go on to describe (see Chapter 8). Regardless, such an initial link between disobedience and wrath for a gentile audience would not be lost.

Similar themes with Polybius emerge in the *RA*: loss in war results in a nation becoming obedient to Rome and over time that obedience must be maintained. Likewise, the notion of obedience—or lack thereof, in this case—closely resembles Polybius's definition of obedience as unconditional surrender (*deditio*) evidenced by the giving up of arms and cities. Particularly important is that Tullus considers the actions of the Fidenates as "breaking faith" (3.28.2).[36] A similar approach appears in

---

[34] Obedience and disobedience language frequently appears in the language of oaths, laws, and treaties and if these are upheld or violated. Cf. *Ant. Rom.* 1.20.2; 2.26.3 (of children), 40.1; 3.23.3 (refers to a command itself); 3.34.1 (of cities); 4.5.3, 45.2, 70.5; 5.54.2; 7.14.5, 23.1, 56.4; 8.16.2, 35.2, 81.3; 9.37.2, 41.1, 60.1; 10.5.3, 18.3; 11.4.2 (of senators), 32.1, 43.2 (of soldiers); 15.7.2; 16.4.1; 20.13.3. See also 1.23.4; 2.3.6, 8 (of Romulus); 3.3.4, 34.3 (not obeying the rule of the Romans); 3.51.1-3; 5.63.1, 71.1-3; 6.89.4; 8.36.4, 68.2; 11.56.1-2; 12.13.2.

[35] On the disarmament of Rome's subjects see P. A. Brunt, "Did Imperial Rome Disarm Her Subjects?," in *Roman Imperial Themes* (New York: Oxford University Press, 1990), 255–66. Contra Ramsay Macmullen argues that there was a universal disarmament by the Romans of their subjects in *Roman Social Relations: 50 B.C. to A.D. 284* (New Haven: Yale University Press, 1974), 35–6.

[36] On violations of *fides* see Burton, *Friendship*, 250–99.

Paul's language in Rom. 2:25-27 that operate on similar conceptions of obedience and disobedience. In 2:25 Paul even utilizes the breaking language (παραβάτης) to discuss disobedience. We could compare Paul's statements in Rom. 2:27, when he states that the Gentiles will "condemn you that have the written code and circumcision but break the law" (σὲ τὸν διὰ γράμματος καὶ περιτομῆς παραβῆτην νόμου) as comparable to those who have a Roman treaty of peace, yet disobey and doing actions inconsistent with the requirements of Rome.

The idea that other nations were destined for obedience and that the Romans were destined for freedom is explicitly raised in the latter part of Book 3 in a speech by the Roman king Tullus Hostilius.[37] Embarking on the war with the Fidenates, Tullus charges his soldiers to "promptly obey orders … remembering that we are not contending for liberty upon the same terms as other people, who have been accustomed to obey others and who have received that form of government from their ancestors" (3.23.18). Rather, Tullus champions, "For we are freemen descended from freemen, and to us our ancestors have handed down the tradition of holding sway over our neighbors as a mode of life" (3.23.19). From the preceding section, Roman soldiers obey orders so that nations that are destined to be ruled may be conquered. Roman obedience leads to their right to rule (cf. Rom. 1:5).

Not all of Rome's problems were external; quelling internal disputes and ending foreign wars were a perennial problem in Rome. The political move required to quiet the dissension would be advanced by the consuls who attempted to divert the dissatisfaction of the people to a foreign war with the Volscians (6.23.1). The raising of an army would be required for such a task. At the consuls' demand that all military-aged men take the military oath, the plebeians, "though repeatedly summoned to take the military oath, would not obey (ὑπακούω) the consuls" (6.23.2).[38] The immediate task of the Senate was how to respond to the disobedience of the plebeians. One side sought to be lenient toward the disobedient and to encourage rather than compel the plebeians (6.23.3). Others sought a different course of action, noting that the plebeians had not yielded "prompt obedience" to their commands before (6.24.2). At the same time, the Senate noted that there was an obedient group of the patrician youth and that this, combined with the Roman Senate, the "great weapon," would "subdue the plebeians" (6.24.3). For the first time in the *RA*, obedience is regarded metaphorically as a weapon. A similar concept occurs in Paul's language in Rom. 6:12-13; 13:12 concerning "weapons" of obedience. Likewise, this section shows the concern the Roman elite had with the obedience of the city's inhabitants that provides context for Paul's remarks in Rom. 13:1-7.

The disobedience of the plebeians only added to the problems facing the Romans. The adverse circumstances were mounting, as Dionysius notes "in a short time the city was full of disorder and tumult. And as the sedition increased in the city, the

---

[37] Many references to obedience simply refer to countries that are obedient to Rome or another nation. Cf. *Ant. Rom.* 1.9.2, 35.1; 3.4.1, 23.9; 4.9.2; 6.18.2, 19.4, 75.3, 76.1, 91.4; 8.68.3, 70.2, 77.2, 3; 9.5.2, 59.5, 6, 69.3; 10.21.8; 15.5.1, 2, 7.5, 8.4; 19.10.2; 20.1.5. See the one important example where nations are explicitly referred to as αἱ τῶν ὑπηκόων (8.83.3).

[38] On the military oath see J. B. Campbell, *The Emperor and the Roman Army, 31 BC–AD 235* (New York: Oxford University Press, 1984), 19–32.

preparations of the enemy for overrunning their territory increased." Adding to these pressures, "ambassadors came from all the peoples who were obedient (ὑπήκους) to the Romans, asking them to send aid, since their territories lay in the path of the war" (6.34.3). The phrase "subject to Rome" can be translated as "all those who were obedient to the Romans." The request for help by Rome's obedient territories only exacerbated Rome's problems when combined with the internal dissension and external threats by their enemies. Such monumental dilemmas were not lost on Titus Larcius. In his speech, he notes,

> If we do not soon put a stop to them, they will prove to be the causes of the utter overthrow and ruin of the commonwealth. I refer to the disobedience (ἀπείθω) of the plebeians, who refuse to carry out the orders of the consuls, as well as to our own severity against this disobedient and independent spirit of theirs. It is my opinion, therefore, that we ought to consider nothing else at present than by what means these evils are to be removed from the state and how all of us Romans with one mind are to prefer public to private considerations in the measures we pursue. For the power of the commonwealth when harmonious will be sufficient both to give security to our allies and to inspire fear in our enemies, but when discordant, as at present, it can effect neither. (6.35.1-2)

A clear point is made by Dionysius with his rehearsal of Rome's early history. Roman disobedience is as grave a threat to the Roman way of life as are the external threats by Rome's enemies. A similar point will be made by the philosopher Seneca the Younger. Both the disobedience of Rome's citizens and Rome's enemies have the capability of bringing Rome to ruin. Such examples intersect well with some of the themes we identify in Romans (see Chapters 7–8). Namely, the seriousness of quelling internal disputes in Rome adds context to the importance of Paul's admonition in Rom. 13:1.

Unrest within Rome continued to be a problem in the Early Republican period.[39] The unrest between the patricians and plebeians came to a head when an army again needed to be enrolled for war against the Tyrrhenians who no longer offered their obedience (11.54.2). Dissension at home could not be tolerated amid the pressing need to quell revolts and defend cities loyal to Rome that lay in the path of conflict. The unrest at Rome began with the consuls being instructed "to inflict any punishment on the disobedient (ἀπειθω)" who failed to take the military oath (11.54.3). Given these problems, Gaius Claudius lays out an ominous threat: "All who attempted to disturb the established customs and to corrupt their ancient form of government, he said, were aliens and enemies of the commonwealth" (11.55.2). In an alarming move, Claudius proposes that even the residents of Rome who stir up unrest or disobey should be declared enemies of Rome.[40]

We have noted so far in this work this demands that Rome placed on conquered subjects and the extent to which they expected obedience. We have not, as of yet, shown

---

[39] On unrest in Rome see *Ant. Rom.* 5.59.1-75.3; 6.23.2-3, 35.1, 56.5, 91.4; 7.19.2, 27.1, 46.4; 8.87.3; 9.3.2; 10.4.4, 33.3, 43.2; 11.45.2.
[40] These residents are termed παραβαινωσι or disobedient.

if those demands over the longevity of the treaty proved to be too much to sustain. Another episode indicates that the Romans' conditions for obedience could be too much to bear for certain nations. In similar ways, misunderstandings—almost always on the part of the conquered—could result in the termination of a treaty with Rome. The Samnite Wars provides an example. The confusion begins almost immediately as "the Samnites, having listened to the ambassadors, were indignant and declared in their own defense, first of all, that they had not made the peace on the understanding that they were to count no one as their friend or enemy unless the Romans should bid them to do so" (17.18.2.1).[41]

The Roman response was to insist that the treaty with them was contingent on their obedience to whatever orders they might issue. The Roman response was "that subjects (ὑπηκόους) who had agreed to follow them and had obtained a termination of the war on that condition must obey (πείθεσθαι) all orders of those who had assumed the rule over them, and threatened to make war upon them if they did not voluntarily do as they were ordered" (17.18.2.2). Such conditions proved too difficult to entertain any longer for the Samnites, and they regarded the "the arrogance of Rome as intolerable." The difficulties of the demands of Rome led the Samnites to suspend their obedience and begin to make preparations for war. Important for this discussion is that the Samnites themselves know that when their obedience formally ends, war is on the way. Here we see the Samnites taking the initiative to prepare for the impending war with Rome (17.18.2.3).

This Samnite example from the *RA* is important for several reasons. First, it shows the dual understanding that disobedience was a cause for war with Rome. Something the Samnites readily understand. Second, it evidences that there was little to no room for negotiation with Rome on the terms of obedience, regardless of how requirements were perceived by the opposing party, whether justly or unjustly. Third, such a text is important for it shows the linguistic relationship between the adjective ὑπήκοος (obedience) and the πείθω (to persuade) root. The group that is "persuaded to obey" is described by their actions as "obedient." Such a connection between persuasion and obedience is also seen in Rom. 2:8-9.

Dionysius of Halicarnassus's Perspective on Obedience

Obedience in Dionysius of Halicarnassus occurs primarily with foreign affairs with Rome, as was the case with Polybius. "Obedience" is a term that is applied to persons or nations that Rome controls or exercises power over. Unique to Dionysius's portrayal of obedience in the early Roman period is the internal unrest in Rome that is described as disobedience and the threat that this provides to the empire's security and future. In contrast to the previous section with Polybius, Dionysius includes an episode where obedience to Rome does not forestall the impending destruction of a city (12.13). Likewise, we find obedience in the social relationships between

---

[41] See parallel account in Livy 7.30.1.

generals and soldiers, especially obedience to the military oath, as paramount examples of obedience. The now familiar trope reemerges in Dionysius's accounts of Rome. Obedience to Rome and its demands lead to peace, while disobedience invites Rome's wrath.

Cassius Dio on Obedience

Between the years of 193 and 211, Rome underwent a physical transformation not seen since the years of Augustus.[42] Amidst the reconstructions, building projects, and rubble stood the Roman senator Cassius Dio who happened to be residing in Rome during these years. Living through the construction and renovation of the city left an indelible mark on the senator. Perhaps it was this reconstruction that spurred Cassius Dio to refer to the city's foundations both literally and metaphorically. Literally, Dio comments more often on the monuments and buildings of Rome than other authors.[43] Metaphorically, Dio is interested in understanding Roman history and in particular its underlying structure or foundation of society and the interaction of both Roman institutions and individuals such as emperors, statements, citizens, soldiers, and foreigners.[44]

As a historian, Cassius Dio authored an eighty-volume work on the history of Rome.[45] His work traces the rise of Rome from its foundation to 229 CE. Dio is the only historian who tracks the history of Rome over more than a thousand-year period.[46] Of the original eighty books that comprised his history, only Books 36–60 and 78–79 survive. They describe the periods of 68 BCE–47 CE and 216–218 CE, respectively.[47] As one of the few remaining Greek works on this period, Books 36–60 are an invaluable source of insight into the Imperial period.

Dio's thirty-seventh book spans the career of Pompey the Great through the establishment of the First Triumvirate of Crassus, Caesar, and Pompey.[48] In chapters 10–14, Cassius rehearses the demise of one of Rome's most formidable opponents, the King of Pontus, Mithridates.[49] During the last throes of his empire, Mithridates set out to invade Italy while Pompey was warring in Syria (37.11.1). This was a historically unwise move given the dwindling prospects of Mithridates's success, as his soldiers began to mutiny, and faith in his leadership was crumbling. Dio offers

---

[42] Alain M. Gowing, "Cassius Dio and the City of Rome," in *Cassius Dio: Greek Intellectual and Roman Politician* (ed. Jesper Majbom Madsen and Carsten Hjort Lange, Leiden: Brill, 2016), 117–18.
[43] Gowing, "Cassius Dio and the City of Rome," 118.
[44] Madsen and Lange, eds., *Cassius Dio: Greek Intellectual and Roman Politician*, 3.
[45] *OCD*, 299.
[46] Madsen and Lange, eds., *Cassius Dio: Greek Intellectual and Roman Politician*, 2.
[47] *DNP*, 1171; Martin Hose, "Cassius Dio: A Senator and Historian in the Age of Anxiety," in *A Companion to Greek and Roman Historiography*, 463.
[48] Pompey is mentioned twice with reference to obedience. He subdues the sea (36.37.3) and also perishes on the sea he subdued (42.5.3).
[49] On the notorious problems with Mithridates see Catherine Steel, *The End of the Roman Republic, 146 to 444 BC: Conquest and Crisis* (Edinburgh: Edinburgh University Press, 2013), 140–7.

this penetrating critique: "Mithridates ... did not recognize the fact that neither arms nor a multitude of subjects (ὑπήκους) is of any real strength to anyone without their friendship; on the contrary, the more subjects a ruler has, the greater burden they are to him, unless he holds them faithful?" (37.12.2).

The importance of this text is that it is one of the few texts within Greco-Roman literature to combine both obedience (ὑπακοή) and faith (πίστις) that exemplifies the relationship between obedience and faith.[50] Subjects of a king are described as obedient, and every empire or kingdom aims to hold those obedient subjects loyal or faithful. Faithfulness or continued obedience is the ongoing position that is expected from the subjects of a ruler. The inherent problem with a large kingdom, whether Rome or Pontus, is that the more populous the empire, the increased chance for disobedience or rebellion. The art of ruling is to keep subjects obedient.[51]

As Dio's narrative rehearses the rise of the first triumvirate, many occurrences of obedience language appear within the military campaigns of Julius Caesar, Pompey, Antony, and their soldiers.[52] Such examples focus on the ability of Rome to "rightly manage" their obedient subjects. The task of ruling the obedient is rooted in Roman identity as Caesar states, "When, accordingly, in the face of these facts, anybody declares that we ought not to make war, he simply says that we ought not to be rich, ought not to rule others, ought not to be free, ought not to be Romans" (38.40.8-9). Caesar's point is clear: being Roman means ruling over obedient subjects.

Dissension and disobedience within the army were a constant refrain and always a cause for concern on behalf of Roman generals.[53] In Book 41, Caesar's army begins to splinter into mutinous factions and Caesar must once again inspire the obedience of his soldiers. He praises the obedience of most of his soldiers but singles out the disobedient among the group for concern: "Most of you obey (πείθω) my orders very scrupulously and satisfactorily and abide by your ancestral customs, and in that way have acquired so much land as well as wealth and glory; but some few are bringing much disgrace and dishonor upon us" (41.28.2).[54] The few who are attempting to mutiny receive the main focus of Caesar's speech:

---

[50] Such a linguistic connection is one of the lacunas of the work of Garlington mentioned in the literature review in the earlier chapter.

[51] On obedient nations see *R.H.* 36.36.4, 47.2; 37.25.4; 38.10.1, 41.5; 40.30.2; 41.55.2, 57.3, 59.4; 42.3.4, 20.4, 44.1; 43.9.2; 44.44.2, 45.2; 45.9.2; 47.22.3, 24.2, 39.3; 48.49.1; 50.16.1; 50.33.2; 51.18.1; 52.5.4, 19.2-3,5 21.8, 27.1; 53.5.4, 10.5, 19.5, 26.3, 32.5; 54.9.1, 32.1; 55.34.5; 56.25.6, 33.4, 41.4; 58.25.1; 59.21.3; 60.9.5; 68.14.3, 5, 23.1; 69.5.3; 70.30.1.

[52] One such occurrence is noted by Dio when Caesar "feared his soldiers might perchance refuse obedience (ἀπειθήσαντες)" (*R. H.* 38.35.3). Caesar's speech shows that the soldiers' obedience to him was paramount in keeping Rome safe, as "not that we may take our ease or neglect our duties, but for the purpose of managing rightly the affairs of our subjects (ὑπηκόων), preserving in safety the property of those bound to us by treaty, repelling any who undertake to do them wrong, and increasing our own possessions" (38.36.5) (cf. Dionysius of Halicarnassus 6.35; 11.54; Rom. 13:1).

[53] Even into the later empire with Trajan and obedience of his soldiers (*R.H.* 69.5.2). Dio seems to take a generally negative view of soldiers; see Verena Schulz, *Deconstructing Imperial Representation: Tacitus, Cassius Dio, Suetonius on Nero and Domitian* (Leiden: Brill, 2019), 173-4.

[54] Obedience in Dio's work is often directed toward various persons: *R.H.* 36.46.2 (to Lucullus); 38.47.1; 40.5.3 (to Caesar); 40.62.4 (Pompey disobedience); 46.50.6 (to Senate); 47.39.2; 52:42.1-3; 56.19.1 (to Augustus); 57.15.8 (to Tiberius); 60.22.4 (to Messalina); 69.22.2 (to Hadrian).

> Now I do not believe it a good thing in any case for a ruler to be overridden by his subjects, nor do I believe there could ever be any safety (σωτήριος) if those appointed to obey (ὑπηρετέω) a person attempted to get the better of him. Consider what sort of order would exist in a household if the young should despise their elders, or what order in schools if the scholars should pay no heed to their instructors! What health would there be for the sick if the afflicted should not obey (πείθω) their physicians in all points, or what safety for voyagers if the sailors should turn a deaf ear to their captains? Indeed, it is in accordance with a natural law, both necessary and salutary, that the principle of ruling and of being ruled have been placed among men, and without them it is impossible for anything at all to continue to exist for even the shortest time. Now it is the duty of the one stationed over another both to discover and to command what is requisite, and it is the duty of the one subject to authority to obey (ὑποτάσσω) without questioning and to carry out his orders. (41.33.3-4)

Several aspects of Caesar's speech are important for our study of obedience. The first aspect to note is linguistic. "To obey" is conveyed by the two verbs ὑποτάσσω and πειθαρχέω that indicate their proximity within a semantic domain of the terms. Such varied usage of terms within one context points to the multifaceted linguistic nature of obedience where one term is not sufficient to convey the complete concept of obedience. Second, and more importantly, the person who is subjected to the rule of another, conveyed by the verb ὑποτάσσω or the noun ὑπακοή, must obey without questioning. Those who are subject are expected, even demanded, to obey. We can compare and contrast such language with Paul's own in Rom. 2:6-9 where the same values of honor and glory also appear.

The three social metaphors that Caesar uses are also critical in conveying the importance of obedience. The examples of household, education, and health outline the "natural order" of things. The use of these examples argues that without obedience, society as a whole is opened to disastrous consequences. In each of the metaphors, the person in the dominant social position is given obedience by the social inferior. By use of the social metaphors, Caesar weaves obedience into the social fabric of the *polis* and communicates the naturalness of obedience to social superiors. The use of such metaphors in moral discourse is seen in Cicero and Seneca the Younger as well as in Rom. 6.

One might object that this context speaks only of soldiers, friends, or allies, and not everyday Romans. However, Caesar makes clear in his speech that the requirement of obedience is not for soldiers alone: "Do not think, now, that, because you are soldiers, that makes you better than the citizens at home; for you and they alike are Romans, and they, as well as you, both have been and will be soldiers" (41.31.1). Obedience is expected by all within the reach of Rome—soldiers and citizens alike. Such an account gives us another example, at ground level, of how obedience language functioned within the empire.

The result of Caesar's speech is important as well. The punishment for the disobedient and rebellious was death by execution through the casting of lots. The most flagrant of the disobedient were executed, whereas the rest of the disobedient were dismissed and, after repenting (μετανοέω), rejoined the campaign (41.35.5). We should not miss the link of terms and outcomes in this section. The disobedience sets up the two outcomes. If there is repentance, restoration was offered, but if disobedience was not responded to with repentance, death is the outcome. We see the train of thought clearly: disobedience—repentance—restoration.

After Caesar's death, Dio includes the summary of a funeral speech given by Antony extolling and praising the qualities and character of the deceased ruler. After discussing his lineage (44.37.1-6) and private affairs (44.39.1-5), Antony turns to discuss his public activities. Antony praises Caesar's leadership by noting that it is far more difficult to keep people obedient (ὑπηκόους) than to merely conquer them: "Keeping a thing is more difficult than acquiring it, and reducing men to a condition where they can never again become rebellious is more profitable than making them subject (44.41.1-2). The harder political task is not the military campaign but the governmental affairs of keeping day-to-day operations running. The easier task of a ruler who sets out to conquer a nation is reducing that nation to obey the terms of a treaty. Long-lasting obedience, where the people do not desire rebellion, is far more worthwhile for a leader (44.41.2). Antony praises Caesar for holding Spain accountable for hiding their disloyalty and eliminating their rebellious desire by force. Although the rhetoric may be a bit hyperbolic, and history certainly showed Spain would continue to be a problem for Rome, the point of the value of long-term obedience is clear.[55]

Several notable features stand out in Antony's speech. First, we get an indirect witness to the inner working of conquered groups who, although they externally conform to Rome's terms, were not loyal to Rome and its interests.[56] Second, Caesar is directly praised for his ability to root out disloyalty. We see here that it was in the interest of the Romans themselves to examine the "faith" of various subjected nations. For if they neglected this task, one might not be able to root out disloyalty. Third, force is shown as one means that Rome used for obtaining obedience. Antony's speech makes this explicitly clear when he says that Caesar "brought them to their senses against their will" (44.41.1). The speech indicates that those in Spain would not willingly change their course. Given the choice to be loyal to Rome, Spain refused. The term μετεμέλοντο from the root μεταμέλομαι refers to repentance or a change of conduct or purpose (cf. Rom. 2:4-5). Since they would not willingly relent

---

[55] Martin Goodman states, "The continued stationing in Tarraconensis of three legions (one after AD 63) for the next 150 years may suggest something less than total pacification, let alone Romanization." See "The Iberian Peninsula," in *The Roman World: 44BC-AD180* (New York: Routledge, 1997), 197-202.

[56] Dio relates another story of the Atrebatians who likewise feigns peacemaking,

> Before any terms were made, however, he was wounded by one of the Romans, who surmised that it was not his real intention to make peace; but he escaped and again proved troublesome to them. At last, despairing of his project, he secured his associates unconditional amnesty for all their acts, and pardon for himself, as some say, on the condition of his never appearing again within sight of any Roman. So these foes became reconciled on these terms, and later the rest were subdued, some voluntarily and some when conquered in war; and Caesar by means of garrisons and punts and levies of money and assessments of tribute humbled some of them and tamed (ἡμέρωσε) others. (*R. H.* 40.43.1-3)

or repent, Caesar was compelled to force them back to their "senses." Disloyalty to Rome in this context is characterized as aberrant or abnormal behavior. The inverse is likewise then true; obedience is the most natural of behavioral reactions to Rome's rule.

Shifting to the reign of Augustus, on January 13, 27 BCE, Augustus entered the Roman Senate to give a speech and returned the entire Roman state to the Senate and the people.[57] Midway through his speech, Augustus recites some of his achievements that bear a striking similarity to his *Res Gestae*. Augustus enumerates the various military campaigns of Galatia, Pannonia, Moesia, Egypt, Juba, and the Britons—among others—noting that these "deeds were more important than any previous Roman had accomplished" (53.7.1). The various nations are all aligned under the single theme of victory, although each nation is given a different term to describe this victory. Augustus states that Galatia was "conquered" (ἅλωσις), Pannonia was "enslaved" or "made a slave" (δουλόω), Moesia was "subjugated" (χειρόω), and Egypt was "overthrown" (καταστροφή). Although different terms are used, they all bear testimony to the fact that these regions were under Roman control.[58] This also shows the semantic domain of terms Rome used to describe its territories.

In describing the power of Rome itself, the language of quiescence and resistance is critical. Augustus notes that Rome overpowered "as enemies all who *resisted*, but sparing as friends all who *yielded*; therein setting an example, so that if it should be fated that our city should ever again be afflicted, one might pray that it should conduct its quarrel in the same way" (53.7.2). Augustus terms two groups as either

---

[57] Cf. Erich S. Gruen, "Augustus and the Making of the Principate," in *The Cambridge Companion to the Age of Augustus* (ed. Karl Galinsky, New York: Cambridge University Press, 2005), 33–54. Also of note is the speech by Augustus's advisor, Agrippa who counsels him on various aspects of his rule. Agrippa notes,

> It is most important to restrain the rash enterprises of communities, and if they are attempting to coerce others or to go beyond their capacity or means in any undertaking or expenditure, to forbid it, even though in their petitions they invoke blessings upon the empire and pray for your welfare and good fortune. It is important also to eradicate their mutual enmities and rivalries, and not permit them to assume empty titles or to do anything else that will bring them into strife with others. And all will readily yield obedience (πειθαρχήσουσιν) to you, both individuals and communities, in this and in every other matter, provided that you make no exceptions whatever to this rule as a concession to anybody; for the uneven application of laws nullifies even those which are well established. (52.37.9-10)

Agrippa advises the dissolution of these groups despite the fact that they offered signs of support such as blessings or praying for the good of the state and future of the empire. He singles out groups that seek to upset the social order by coercing others or are factious and run the risk of strife with others (cf. Rom. 12–15). The similarity here to early Christianity should not be missed (Rom. 13:1-7; 1 Pet. 2:13-17). The eradication of strife, even potential strife, is of grave concern for the running of the empire. What is at stake is the upholding of justice by enacting the laws equally to all. If this is done as Agrippa admonishes, obedience is the reward for the fairness of the legal and political system (cf. Rom. 13:1).

[58] Myles Lavan has drawn attention to the use of slavery language to depict Roman rule and notes the unique contribution of Cassius Dio who repeatedly describes "Roman conquest as enslavement" and "constitutes a break with the representation of Roman rule in earlier Greek historiography." See Myles Lavan, *Slaves to Rome: Paradigms of Empire in Roman Culture* (New York: Cambridge University Press, 2013), 108.

friends or enemies based on whether they resisted or yielded to Rome (cf. Rom. 5:3-11). Given our previous examples of obedience and treaties, along with Rome's process of navigating international contexts, this indicates that although obedience is not explicitly mentioned it forms the background to Augustus's statement.

Confirmation of such a theory comes to us a few lines later in Augustus's speech when he notes that both "Rome and allies" are devoted to him (52.8.1) and when "at a time when there is no longer any foreign enemy making war upon me and no one at home is engaged in sedition, but when you are all at peace, are harmonious and strong, and, greatest of all, are content to yield obedience (πειθαρχέω)" (53.8.2). Obedience, whether from foreign nations or Roman citizens, is part of the themes of victory, harmony, and strength that Augustus lists as facets of his accomplishments.

In a move that surprised many senators, Augustus did not assume the position of sole ruler of the empire (53.11.1). In a politically advantageous move, he divided control of the empire between himself and the Senate and gave them the provinces that were weaker on the basis that they were "peaceful and free from war." Augustus took the more powerful provinces on the basis that they were "insecure and precarious and either had enemies on the borders or were able on their own account to begin a serious revolt" (53.12.2). Such a move also provided the rationale for Augustus to retain control over large parts of the Roman army. A move no doubt that cemented his power more fully. Dio argues that there were more subversive intentions on the part of Augustus as now the Senate had provinces that were unprepared for battle, while he maintained the provinces that were ready for war (53.12.3).

Another way of viewing Augustus's division of the provinces is through a lens of obedience and disobedience. Given the nature of the treaties Rome made with foreign nations, Augustus's proposal was, in essence, a division of the provinces *based on obedience*. Nations that were already obedient or subject to Rome are given to the Senate; Augustus retained those nations that were under suspicion of disobeying (cf. *Res Gestae* 26.1). Obedience and disobedience played a part in the division of the empire between the control of the Senate and that of Augustus. Dio's work makes this clear. Augustus "promised to reduce them to order within this period, and boastfully added that, if they should be pacified (ἡμερόω) sooner, he would the sooner restore them, to the Senate" (53.13.1). Pacification of the provinces means nothing less than reducing them to obedience as stated in Augustus's recounting of his deeds in the *Res Gestae* 26.1.

Augustus also sought obedience in the social realm. The Augustan period was well known for the various laws enacted for the upholding of morality and marriage.[59] Karl Galinsky has noted that "Augustus was the prime mover behind this unmistakable legislative program. It was central to his reign."[60] The Augustan laws on marriage were part of the larger legislation on morality passed in 17 BCE

---

[59] Obedience or disobedience of laws or treaties is also frequent *R. H.* 39.60.1; 40.65.4; 41.11.2; 47.13.2; 48.2.4; 50.17.5 (Antony); 53.1.13 (Augustus); 54.19.2; 60.6.7 (Claudius and Jews).
[60] Karl Galinsky, *Augustan Culture: An Interpretive Introduction* (Princeton: Princeton University Press, 1996), 128.

and were designed as a remedy to the perceived problem of men's reluctance to marry. One particular law, the *Lex Iulia de maritandis ordinibus*, required marriage and remarriage for men and women between certain ages and included penalties for failing to do so.[61] Tax relief was also available for those who obeyed the law. Although gauged in moral terms, clearly such legislation aimed to fulfill a practical necessity of the growing empire—the ability to have a supply of soldiers for the army as well as future administrators (consequently, many of the laws were aimed at the wealthier classes and freedmen).[62]

Such significant legislation provoked numerous protests and hostility in Rome. Augustus addressed resistance to the laws in a speech in 9 CE with the equestrians. In the speech, he raises the specific issue of obedience and disobedience to the laws on marriage. "I, now, have increased the penalties for the disobedient (ἀπειθέω), in order that through fear of becoming liable to them you might be brought to your senses; and to the obedient (πειθαρχέω) I have offered a more numerous and greater prizes than are given for any other display of excellence" (56.6.5). Such concern for penalties and rewards related to the laws points to the degree of dissatisfaction many in Rome felt toward the legislation.[63] The anger toward the new laws was such that Dio remarks that their introduction was the beginning of conspiratorial plots against Augustus (54.15.1).[64]

Since the Roman ruling class was the target of such legislation, the ramifications for obedience and disobedience to the "new laws" of Augustus had profound implications. Establishing peace and tranquility at home was integral to establishing peace abroad, both literally in the necessity of producing males to become soldiers—hence the laws on childbearing—and more figuratively in preserving the status of the ruling class—hence the laws on marriage and adultery. The new laws aimed at the running of the state were focused on stability and would require obedience. The importance of a text like this one is that it shows how obedience was expected and how it functioned at "ground level" in Rome itself and among its inhabitants' daily lives.

Turning to other events, one wonders what episodes of national memory stood out to the Roman people? What were the hallmark pictures of obedience or disobedience? One of the most catastrophic episodes in Roman history was Varus's defeat by the Germanic tribes and the loss of the Roman standards in 9 CE. Such a significant event also provides an opportunity for an important discussion of obedience. Beginning in Book 56, the Romans held small portions of the area. These

---

[61] Galinsky, *Augustan Culture*, 130; *CAH* 10:888. See also Beryl Rawson, "Marriages, Families, Households," in *The Cambridge Companion to Ancient Rome* (ed. Paul Erdkamp, New York: Cambridge University Press, 2013), 93–109.

[62] *CAH* 10:889.

[63] Dio also relates the advice of Livia to Augustus to rule mercifully,

> Gentle words, for example, cause all one's inflamed passion to subside, just as harsh words in another case will stir to wrath even the spirit which has been calmed; and forgiveness granted will melt even the utterly arrogant man, just as punishment will incense even him who is utterly mild. For acts of violence will always in every instance, no matter how just they may be, exasperate, while considerate treatment subdues / tames (ἡμεροῦσι). (*R. H.* 55.17.3)

[64] *CAH* 10:94.

districts had been subdued by the Romans (56.18-19). Under Augustus, Rome had been campaigning in the Rhineland from 17 BCE to 9 CE in an attempt to extend control as far east as the River Elbe.[65] These areas had been stationed with soldiers and Roman cities began to be built.

Commenting on the local inhabitants, Dio remarks, "The barbarians were adapting themselves to Roman ways, were becoming accustomed to hold markets, and were meeting in peaceful assemblages. They had not, however, forgotten their ancestral habits, their native manners, their old life of independence, or the power derived from arms" (56.18.2). Slowly, the barbarians were adapting themselves to the Roman way of life; however, with the hindsight of history that Dio possesses, he notes the underlying suspicion that they had not truly given up their "old life of independence." He continues, "So long as they were unlearning these customs gradually and by the way, as one may say, under careful watching, they were not disturbed by the change in their manner of life, and were becoming different without knowing it" (56.18.3). The process of Romanization seemed to be underway.[66]

Such a gradual process may have continued apace if it weren't for the actions of Quintilius Varus who, despite his success in Syria and Africa, failed rather quickly in Germania. According to Dio, when Varus became governor, he sought to change the barbarians "more rapidly" by not only "issuing orders to them as if they were actually slaves of the Romans, he exacted money as he would from subject nations" (56.18.3-4). Varus's treatment of the barbarians like a conquered nation was not amenable to the leaders of these regions, who, as Dio notes, "were in no mood to submit, for the leaders longed for their former ascendancy and the masses preferred their accustomed condition to foreign domination" (56.18.4).

Given the current state of Roman troops in the region, rather than outright revolt that would surely result in a loss, the barbarians employed a different tactic. They embarked on an ambitious program of covert deception whereby "they received Varus, pretending that they would do all he demanded of them, and thus they drew him far away from the Rhine into the land of the Cherusci, toward the Visurgis, and thereby behaving in a most peaceful and friendly manner led him to believe that they would live submissively without the presence of soldiers" (56.18.5). Varus is led out into the densely wooded forest on the pretense of obedience to his commands and the commitment to live submissively as obedient subjects. At the opportune moment, "they came upon Varus in the midst of forests by this time almost impenetrable. And there, at the very moment of revealing themselves as enemies instead of subjects (ὑπήκοος), they wrought great and dire havoc" (56.19.5).

The failure of Varus to understand the deteriorating situation is offset by an important consideration relating to obedience and loyalty. Given the history of the Germanic tribes' accommodation to Roman ways and the current offer of obedience by those who

---

[65] Goodman, *The Roman World*, 217.
[66] On Romanization see Ramsay MacMullen, *Romanization in the Time of Augustus* (New Haven: Yale University Press, 2000), 85–123.

led Varus into the forest, there was no reason to suspect any sedition on behalf of the tribes. Their previous stability and their past obedience seemed to indicate no concern for their future obedience.[67] Dio's account of this infamous disaster is punctuated with the language of enemies and obedience. Rather than continuing to be obedient subjects, the barbarians revealed themselves to be enemies of Rome (cf. Rom. 5:1-11).

In this case, the important point made in this account is that the opposite of obedience is not disobedience but being declared an enemy of Rome. Disobedience equates with being an enemy of the state. In light of this discussion, Paul's phrase "while we were yet enemies" in Rom. 5:8 is of clear relevance. Paul shares a similar idea of disobedience equating to enmity, yet Paul transforms this paradigm with the flow of his argument that it is God's love that compels (in this instance) Christ's death for his enemies.

Another area for comparison is Paul's description of God's mercy to Israel despite Israel's killing of God's messengers (Rom. 11:3-5). Many Gentiles may have tacitly assumed that God would outright reject Israel for its disobedience. The surprise for many is that God extends further mercy to a disobedient people. Such far-ranging mercy would have upended many Gentiles conceptions; if merely not following Rome's commands could provoke a war with Rome, killing Rome's messengers would certainly have been a death knell to any potential hope for that people. Gentiles familiar with these recent events would be quite astounded at a God who responded in grace and mercy even at the death of his messengers. Further, such a context brings added understanding to Paul's admonitions in the direction of submission in Rom. 13:1 because disobedience could identify the house churches as enemies of Rome.

Moving from the reign of Augustus to the reign of Tiberius, we find another helpful example of obedience. The transition from Augustus to Tiberius, although easier than some subsequent transitions, was not without complications.[68] Tiberius's acceptance entailed both the loyalty and favor of every Roman who had been devoted to Augustus. An interesting feature takes place with Tiberius. Dio notes that it was custom every New Year's day for the public to renew the oath to the emperor; however, Tiberius refused to receive this for himself and directed it, instead, to the deceased Augustus. This was an oath Tiberius took himself as well (57.8.4-5). T. E. J. Wiedemann has noted the importance of the oath:

> The oath to protect him and the rest of the *domus* whose *paterfamilias* he had now become, [was] taken as soon as they heard the news by the consuls, and the prefects of the praetorian guard and of the corn supply, and then administered to the Senate, the equestrian *ordo* and the Roman people. Similar oaths were subsequently sworn by communities elsewhere in the empire; a copy of an oath to Tiberius and his whole

---

[67] J. S. Richardson, *Augustan Rome 44 BC to AD 14: The Restoration of the Republic and the Establishment of the Empire* (Edinburgh: Edinburgh University Press, 2012), 183–4.

[68] See *CAH* 10:198–209. According to Dio, it was Germanicus who had the "good will of absolutely all the Romans as well as of their subjects (ὑπηκόων)," but who refused the role (57.6.2). It was at this point when "no further news of any rebellious moves came and the whole Roman world had acquiesced securely in his leadership, Tiberius accepted the rule" (57.7.1).

household taken by the cities of Cyprus survives. This oath illustrates the dependence of groups as well as individual magistrates on the head of the imperial family as the source of patronage, honour and decision-making. But—unlike the *sacramentum*, the military oath taken by a soldier to the emperor as his commander-in-chief—its force was private and personal, not public or constitutional.[69]

Several copies of these oaths survive and provide a unique glimpse into the obedience expected at ground level to the emperor and his family throughout the empire. Tiberius's attempt to direct such loyalty to his successor was no doubt political nuance at such a critical juncture of transition between leaders.[70] The point bears considerable importance for our reading of obedience in Romans, particularly our attempt to understand how a Gentile audience in Rome would understand a call to obedience, as the oath to an emperor was a primary way the residents of Rome would have understood a call to obedience.

Following the death of Germanicus, Dio notes a marked shift both in the personality and practice of Tiberius, whereby he drifted into vices (57.13.16).[71] As the despotism of Tiberius grew, he was more inclined to hear charges of any crime and became crueler in his punishments. Such despotic rule is captured in Tiberius's remark, "Nobody willingly submits to being ruled, but a man is driven to it against his will; for not only do subjects delight in refusing obedience, but they also enjoy plotting against their rulers" (57.19.1b). Tiberius's view seems to be that the default position of his subjects is disobedience. The subjects must be compelled or forced against their will to be ruled.

Two final examples of obedience from Dio's history will conclude our survey. Both come from the reign of Claudius. It is well known that Claudius was not well-liked. Most ancient sources depict him as foolish. For example, Seneca's *Apocolocyntosis*, written only months after Claudius's death, depicts him as full of fear, rife with stupidity, and cruel.[72] Claudius became emperor in 41 CE after the brutal murder of Caligula by the

---

[69] *CAH* 10:203. On his ascension to emperor, in 41–42 CE, a coin was minted intending to show the loyalty of the Praetorian Guard to Tiberius Claudius. The reverse of the coin shows Tiberius Claudius holding hands with a long-haired soldier holding a shield and legionary eagle bearing the inscription, "PRAETOR RECEPT" (the praetorians received). The coin was meant to show Tiberius Claudius accepting the loyalty of the Praetorian Guard. See M. G. L. Cooley, ed., *Tiberius to Nero*, LACTOR 19 (London: London School of Classical Teachers, 2011), 179.J12b. Another very similar *aureus* minted at the same time shows the "battlements of the praetorian camp at Rome in which a solider stands holding a spear and next to a legionary eagle (*aquila*)" bearing the inscription IMPER RECEPT (the victorious commander welcomed) on the reverse. See *RIC* Claudius 7.

[70] Velleius Paterculus notes the potential for disorder at this time and that the posting of a large number of troops at Augustus's funeral seems to confirm (11.124).

[71] The *Tabula Siarensis*, fragment b, column II lines 1–19 note the "loyalty of Drusus Caesar." Lines 20–31 note "the loyalty of all orders towards the Augustan household and the consensus of all citizens in honoring the memory of Germanicus Caesar." Cited in Cooley, *Tiberius to Nero*, 170. J8G-H. These eulogies were to be inscribed in public places around the empire. Cf. David S. Potter, "The 'Tabula Siarensis,' Tiberius, the Senate, and the Eastern Boundary of the Roman Empire," *ZPE* 69 (1987): 269–76.

[72] *CAH* 10:229. Modern accounts of Claudius have not been kind either; Edward Gibbon declared that Claudius was "the stupidest of emperors." See Edward Gibbon, *The History of the Decline and Fall of the Roman Empire*, vols. 1–6 (New York: Penguin, 1996), 1.33.

Praetorian Guard. As the recent work of Josiah Osgood suggests, Claudius inherited a unique problem from his predecessors. Osgood writes, "The principate was supposed to draw inspiration from the institutions of the Republican past, and Claudius, as a historian, was attuned to that. Yet at the same time, Rome was now a world Empire, and must try to dispense justice based on humanity to all of its subjects, not just citizens."[73] Such a dilemma leads Osgood to explain the hostility toward Claudius from the ancient (senatorial) sources like Cassius Dio. Dio includes hostile remarks such as, "Hence he [Claudius] had acquired none of the qualities befitting a freeman, but, though ruler of all the Romans and their subjects (ὑπήκοος), had become himself a slave" (60.2.5).

Dio signals that although Claudius was ruler over all of Rome, the combination of his upbringing by his grandmother out of the political light and his vices of "drink and sexual intercourse" render him a slave, obedient to those vices; therefore, he was "incredibly easy to master" (60.2.6). Obedience to the passions (sometimes deemed vices) was a frequent refrain of the philosophers (see Chapter 5) and Paul (cf. Rom. 6:12). This example shows the moral qualities of obedience that play out in the practical realm. In a rather unbefitting move, Claudius is "worse than these" for failing to live up to the stature of his position, since he ought to have commanded obedience from all Roman citizens and conquered subjects.

In 43 CE, during Claudius's third consulship, one of the most remembered aspects of his reign occurred, the annexing of Britannia. Dio records that the cause of the war between Rome and Britannia was the slaying of eighty thousand Romans. Adding insult to injury, the loss came at the hands of the female general Boudica (62b.1.1). At the start of the war, Dio records a speech given by Boudica to her army of 120,000, declaring the Roman rule injurious to the British way of life. Her entire speech revolves around the issues of freedom and slavery and decries the "alluring promises of the Romans" (62b.3.1), which may allude to a *deditio*. After rallying her army, she sacked two Roman cities and wreaked havoc on those Roman inhabitants (62b.7.1-3).

The Roman general Paulinus, absent from Britannia at the time of its sacking, returned to do battle with Boudica. Paulinus sought to rally his troop. In a speech to the third division, he argues that this battle will simultaneously show Roman clemency and wrath. He remarked,

> Choose, then, whether you wish to suffer the same treatment yourselves as our comrades have suffered and to be driven out of Britain entirely ... or else by conquering to avenge those that have perished and at the same time furnish to the rest of mankind an example, not only of benevolent clemency toward the obedient (πειθαρχέω) but also of inevitable severity toward the rebellious. (62b.11.2)

Paulinus's charge to his soldiers contains several important points. First, the battle has global ramifications as it serves as an example to the rest of the world of how

---

[73] Josiah Osgood, *Claudius Caesar: Image and Power in the Early Roman Empire* (New York: Cambridge University Press, 2011), 18.

Rome deals with disobedience. Rebellion is equated with disobedience and incurs the violent backlash of Rome, whereas obedience results in "benevolent clemency" to those who are or remain obedient. The speech by Paulinus reaffirms what has been seen throughout this study: disobedience to Rome invokes Rome's wrath, whereas obedience results in clemency and benefits. The importance of these events and examples is that they occur roughly a decade before the writing of the book of Romans.

A familiar Roman pattern occurs with the disobedience provoking wrath structure (this was identified earlier in how common a refrain it was and statements like Rom. 1:18-32 fit within such a paradigm). Of course Romans is much longer than the first chapter. What remains rather surprising in light of the entirety of Paul's letter is the extent to which God's mercy is extended toward those who are disobedient. This is nowhere more apparent than Paul's statements about "Israel" and God's mercy in Rom. 11:30-32; 12:1. Indeed, the shocking nature of Paul's statement in Rom. 11:32, "For God has imprisoned all in disobedience so that he may be merciful to all," would go beyond the categories most Gentiles in Paul's audience would have been familiar with in light of their experiences of Roman power.

Paulinus would, of course, conquer Britannia, and this would serve as one of the highlights of Claudius's lackluster reign as emperor. Such an accomplishment should not be underestimated for the Roman program, as the island of Britannia held "symbolic importance for Romans: its conquest would indicate that not just the whole world, but even lands beyond the edge of the world, were subject to the dominion of the Roman people."[74] The subjugation of Britain had eluded the Romans since the time of Julius Caesar; but now, through Claudius's efforts, Roman expansion had finally seized this elusive island. The crowning jewel of Claudius's reign would be known throughout the empire, whether through celebrating the triumph in Rome itself or stamped on coins, and finally epitomized in the Arch of Claudius in 51 CE.

Dio and the Theme of Obedience

Obedience in Dio is a term used to describe a people or nation under the control of Rome (cf. Rom. 1:5). Likewise, obedience language often occurs within military contexts, like speeches to soldiers. However, even in speeches to soldiers, the citizens of Rome are not far off, as Caesar explicitly makes clear. The clear function of such examples is emulation. Obedience was also key to Augustus's reign, as epitomized in the introduction of his marriage laws, showing how obedience language functioned outside a military context and intersected with the life of Rome's citizens. Obedience was also seen in the oaths the Roman people took to the emperor. Certainly, obedience also formed part of the collective memory of Rome in one of the darkest chapters of Roman history, the Varian disaster.

---

[74] *CAH* 10:235.

Obedience also appears in a speech by Tiberius that shows how the emperor viewed obedience and his subjects—a condition that, according to him, did not come naturally. Finally, despite all of Claudius's perceived or real faults, none could debate the importance of securing Britannia under Rome's rule. The pinnacle of Claudius's reign involved important battles where obedience and disobedience were central. Such a momentous event would not go unseen; many throughout the empire would see the victorious campaign commemorated on coins or through the triumphal arches that documented the victory in Rome and abroad. Despite the changing nature of this growing empire, obedience still formed part of the Roman identity, both for its citizens and for those under Roman control.

Select Examples from Other Greek Authors

Although we have primarily focused on the Greek historians in this chapter, obedience language appears outside the three major Greek historians of Rome's rise to power, most notably in Strabo and Plutarch.[75] This, of course, does not include much of the early sources of the Greek period.[76] The following section will briefly survey the important examples of obedience in both Strabo and Plutarch, as these examples bear out further similarities to examples shown in the historians above.

Strabo and the Geography of Obedience

Strabo's *Geography* is immensely valuable for understanding the geography of the Augustan period. Comprising some seventeen volumes, his work provides critical data for the expansion of the Roman program.[77] Frequently throughout the *Geography*, the standard usage of obedience language refers to conquered nations and regions under Roman control, as we have seen in the historians.[78]

---

[75] Other important examples include Appian *Libya* 240.4; *Bell. civ.* 1.5.42, 11.101; 2.4.33; 3.8.63, 11.82; 5.3.21, 6.57; Dio Chrysostom *Orat.* 1.13.5; 2.75-76; 2.77.1; 3.5.6, 40.5; 6.51.3;14.8.4; 23.12; 35.14.6; 56.6.1, 10.2; 57.1-3; 62.4.4, 5.3; 76.5.4; 80.3.2.

[76] Some examples of obedience language in these sources would include Demosthenes *Meg.* 23.6; *On the Accession of Alexander* 14.2; 17.1; *Cor.* 167.7; *1–2 Aristog.* 1.20.8; 21.2; 26.1, 27.1; 2.25.2; *1 [2] Boeot.* 13.9; [*Macart.*] 6.5; 72.10; [*Olymp.*] 27.4; [*Poly.*] 65.9; [*Theocr.*] 49.5; Diodorus Siculus *The Library of History* 1.27.2; 2.21.5; 3.6.3, 49.3; 4.11.1.4, 16.2, 31.5; 5.8.2; 7.12.2; 11.65.2; 12.16.3, 26.3, 29.2; 39.5; 14.6.2; 16.8.1; 17.5.4, 65.4,104.4; 18.59.3, 63.3; 19.61.3, 84.6; 20.57.2, 5, 111.1-2, 4; 21.21.11; 29.22.1; Herodotus *Hist.* 1.24.11, 126.4-5; 1.141.1; 3.73.10; 4.15.15-16, 137.4; 5.29.2 –5.30.1, 33.4, 91.3, 98.10; 6.12.4, 20, 35.13, 41.15; 7.16.6; 8.69.10, 110.4; 9.53.6; Homer *Il.* 1.274, 295; 12.238; *Od.* 2.27; Thucydides *History of the Peloponnesian War* 5.9.9; 7.73.2; *Hist.* 1.35.3; 6.22.1; 7.20.2, 57.4; 8.64.1, 5; Xenophon *Hell.* 1.6.6, 8; 2.2.22, 3.34; 2.4.23; 3.1.13; 6.1.1; 7.1.8, 5.19; *Oec.* 5.15; 13.5-10; 21.4-5; *Mem.* 1.2.34; 2.2.11; 3.3.8-10; 3.9.11; 4.4.13-17; *Apol.* 20.2; *Anab.* 1.3.6, 9.5; 6.6.20; *Cyr.* 1.1.2-3, 8, 6.13-14, 20-22, 26, 42; 2.2.8, 3.8, 4.22; 3.1.18, 20, 3.9, 70; 4.1.3, 4.8; 5.1.11, 3.6; 7.5.69, 70; 8.1.3-4, 29, 3.6, 6.2; *Ages.* 6.4.6.

[77] For introductory issues see Strabo and Duane W. Roller, *The Geography of Strabo* (New York: Cambridge University Press, 2014), 1–34. Cf. *OCD*, 1447.

[78] See Strabo *Geogr.* 5.3.2 (2x), 4.1.12; 5.3.4; 6.1.13, 2.10, 4.2; 5.3.4; 7.1.4, 4.3 (2x), 4.4; 8.4.1; 9.1.20, 5.5; 10.2.13, 4.11, 5.19; 11.2.3, 10-11 (2x); 12.3.28; 12.3.34, 6.2, 7.3; 8.9; 15.2.7, 3.12; 16.1.18, 24,

One important example of obedience language from Strabo's account is Pompey's installation of Archelaus as a ruler in the region of Comana in Asia Minor. Strabo relates Rome's policy of indirect rule as "Pompey took over the authority, he appointed Archelaus priest ... and ordered the inhabitants to obey (πειθαρχέω) his rule" (12.3.34). The importance of this account for our study of obedience is that the authority of client kings was the way most outside Rome and the Italian provinces would have experienced Roman rule. Often, inhabitants of the empire would exchange one form of rule for another in the ever-changing political landscape.[79] Strabo relates such an incident earlier in his work while discussing the Athenians who are ruled by a client king named Cassander, and Strabo comments that although the Athenians had experienced oppression before, through "forced obedience" (ὑπακούω), they still kept their form of government. Even when Cassander took overrule for Rome, he had "reduced the city to subjection ... be that as it may, the Romans, seeing that the Athenians had a democratic government when they took them over, preserved their autonomy and liberty" (9.1.20).

The Athenians are first subjected to and made obedient by the Macedonian kings. In turn, they are conquered by the Romans and come under Roman rule. Rome preserves their form of government, but they are dependent and obedient to Rome. At ground level, obedience is not the exclusive prerogative of Rome. Rather, citizens of a vast number of cities, at least from the time of Alexander the Great, had seen a change in their way of life. They were now subordinate to a foreign ruler and obedience to the new regime was expected. Such a scenario may be compared closely with Paul's call for obedience to Christ as Lord (1:5) and his admonitions in Rom. 13:1.

One example from Plutarch will finish our survey of obedience in the Greek sources. Although obedience language appears frequently in Plutarch, these examples are worth citing in full.[80] Plutarch discusses the art of instilling obedience in his biography of Lycurgus and his description of the Lacedaemonians. Previous examples have simply stated that a nation was obedient or disobedient; however,

---

2.14, 4.21. Strabo can describe the process of making other nations obedient as "subduing" or "civilizing." A good example of this is early on in Strabo's work, "yet even the regions of poverty and piracy become civilized as soon as they get good administrators ... The Romans, too, took over many nations that were naturally savage ... also taught the more savage how to live under forms of government" (2.4.26). Other examples include Strabo *Geogr.* 3.4.13; 4.6.6; 6.3.9; 9.3.12. Obedience of animals in *Geogr.* 5.1.9.

[79] See *Geogr.* 4.1.5; 6.4.2; 15.3.23-24. See P. A. Brunt's "Romanization of the Local Ruling Classes," in *Roman Imperial Themes*, 267–77. One should also note the statement of Claudius to athletes in 46 CE, where he notes that on sending their victory crowns to him, he received them as a "perpetual symbol of your loyalty to me" (*Papyrus of London* 3.215, as cited in Cooley, *Tiberius to Nero*, 298. N21).

[80] See Plutarch *Aem.* 3.7.3; *Ages.* 1.2.3, 28.3; *Ant.* 40.5, 61.2; *Arat.* 9.5-6; *Arist.* 5.2.5; *Caes.* 15.2; *Cato. Maj.* 12.1-2; *Cat. Min.* 1.4-5; *Cic.* 21.5.5; 36.2.1; *Comp. Lys. Num.* 2.3.11; *Cor.* 16.4-5; 18.1; *Demetr.* 15.1; 38.8; *Fab.* 4.3.3; *Flam.* 12.11.1; *Luc.* 29.6; *Lyc.* 15.2; *Mar.* 14.2; *Num.* 6.2, 20.1, 3, 8; *Per.* 29.6.2; *Phoc.* 24.3; *Pomp.* 6.2.2; 12.4.1; 13.2; 31.1; 41.1; 54.4; 59.2.1; 65.1.4; 70.1-3; 75.2; *Publ.* 11.4; *Sert.* 3.2; *Sol.* 8.3.4; *Sull.* 16.4; *Ti. C. Graech.* 3.1; 10.8; *Tim.* 10.1. For philosophical works see *Amat.* 753E; *[Apoph. lac.]* 219A; 236E; *Cohib. ira* 455B; *Comm. not.* 1060D; *Fort. Rom.* 322F; 325D-E; *Gen. Socr.* 581F; 592C; *[Reg. imp. apophth.]* 192D-F; *Her. mal.* 863D; *Princ. iner.* 779A; 780B-C, F; *Quaest conv.* 618C; 620B; 708A; *Sera* 550B; *Vit. pud.* 529E.

this passage investigates the process whereby obedience is instilled at ground level. Plutarch ponders,

> Wherefore, I for one am amazed at those who declare that the Lacedaemonians knew how to be ruled, but did not understand how to command, and quote with approval the story of King Theopompus, who, when someone said that Sparta was safe and secure because her kings knew how to command, replied: "Nay, rather because her citizens know how to obey (πειθαρχικός)." For men will not consent to obey (ὑπομένω) those who have not the ability to rule, but obedience (πειθαρχία) is a lesson to be learned from a commander. For a good leader makes good followers, and just as the final attainment of the art of horsemanship is to make a horse gentle and tractable, so it is the task of the science of government to implant obedience (εὐπείθεια) in men. And the Lacedaemonians implanted in the rest of the Greeks not only a willingness to obey (εὐπείθεια), but a desire to be their followers and to be obedient (ὑπακούω). (*Lyc.* 30.3-4)

This example from Plutarch highlights several important features of obedience language. First, we see the semantic range of obedience language represented in this text by the usage of πείθω verb and the ἀκούω being used synonymously. Furthermore, obedience is predicated on the ability of the ruler to rule well, something that the Romans took seriously (see Chapter 5).

In Plutarch's estimation, obedience is something that is not naturally inherent in humanity, but it is a quality that is developed. Plutarch issues two metaphors to illustrate his point: the military metaphor of a soldier learning from a general and that of a horse obeying its master. The imagery is appropriate as obedience language often occurs within a military context. Apparently, from Plutarch's employment of the metaphors, he can take for granted that his readership would understand the parallel and grasp the metaphors. Plutarch argues that it is the task of government to instill this quality into its people, a requirement of the ability to rule. He holds up the Lacedaemonians as being exceptionally adept at such a task because of their effectiveness in training the Greeks to willingly obey them and become their followers.

Two issues are of note for our reading of Romans. First, both Plutarch and Paul assume the ability of a ruler to govern well (cf. Rom. 13:1), and this is tied to the obedience of subjects. Second, we see again the metaphors from a martial context are applied in moral discourses and provide apt metaphors that are sure to be understood by the audience.

Perspectives on Obedience in Greek Literature

We are now in a position to offer some initial conclusions on obedience language in the Greek sources. First, it is clear from Polybius to Plutarch that the adjective ὑπήκοος is the preferred term for describing those territories and peoples that are subordinate to Rome. Such use of a term highlights the central role of obedience in Rome's process of describing and identifying those within its empire. Paul's usage aligns with such a characterization (Rom. 1:5) that nations obey.

Second, from the survey of the available literature, the obedience of subject territories or nations to all that Rome demands is central to a relationship with Rome. The consequence of disobedience is a cessation of peace and can provoke a war with Rome. Continued obedience to Rome was the prerequisite for maintaining peace and avoiding destruction. Polybius would describe this as entering into the "faith of the Romans." One enters the faith of the Romans and then obedience is expected.

Third, perhaps not surprisingly, obedience language appeared in military contexts in the speeches of generals to their soldiers. Whether referring to Sulla or Julius Caesar, the ability of a commander to obtain the loyalty of his soldiers was indispensable for the success of any campaign. The relationship between soldiers and commanders and the larger citizen body of Rome is seen in that citizens often became soldiers and vice versa. Likewise, such contexts provided metaphors for obedience in moral discourses.

Fourth, obedience was the key to stability. From the peasant to the solider to the upper classes, obedience was required for the continuation of the empire. The periods of unrest within the city of Rome exposed it to more significant dangers from the outside. The ability to guarantee the loyalty or faithfulness of one's subjects is seen as the primary task of any emperor's relationship with his people. Further, such disobedient groups are labeled as enemies. As previously mentioned, such accounts bear important consideration for Paul's exhortation to submit to the governing authorities.

Fifth, and finally, we ought not to disregard the way Rome's history would have impacted its citizens. Rome was a cosmopolitan city that saw massive waves of immigration into its urban landscape. Those who immigrated to Rome would have experienced Rome in one way or another even before coming to the city. The relationships Rome had maintained or eliminated were sure to have had an impact on the cultural memory of its new residents. Since Rome characterized its history in terms of obedience and disobedience, many coming into the city would have experienced Roman benefits or punishments firsthand and would have been acutely aware of the importance of obedience in Rome's success. Such a survey offers a fuller understanding of how the Roman communities would have experienced and received calls to obedience, such as Paul's exhortation in Rom. 1:5.

4

Obedience in Latin Literature

In the previous chapter, we saw several important patterns emerge on the nature of faith and obedience in relationship with Rome among Greek authors. Through a variety of works, authors, and periods the nature of obedience was a condition of peace with Rome and the treaties with other nations. This chapter finds its focus on obedience language in the Roman Empire by investigating key evidence from Latin literature.

Livy and the Foundations of Obedience

The allure of Rome and its fame was not for political insiders alone. One might expect such darling portraits of a city and its leadership from those acutely invested in it, such as generals, statesmen, and elite society. They have a vested interest and the enchantment that results from proximity to the center of power in the ancient world. Exceptions existed. The allure and fascination captive others outside the orbit of Rome's centrifugal power, which makes them all the more interesting for study. The person of Livy is one of those anomalies. We know very little about the person of Livy. Unlike the other figures in this study, Livy never held public office nor was he involved in military affairs. Complicating this further is that he gives sparse detail about his own life in his work. But perhaps this is the unique contribution of Livy who writes from a nontraditional vantage point. He seems to be motivated by the love of Rome, so much so that he begins writing about the city before ever stepping foot there.[1] He arrived at Rome right after the civil war to witness the triumph of Augustus in 29 BCE. As a dedicated historian, he provides unique insight and scope of his work that makes it valuable for our interests here.

We begin with the work of Livy, *Books from the Foundation of the City*. This work is characterized by a "phenomenal expansiveness" covering Roman history from the period of Rome's origin to 9 BCE.[2] Livy's work, like that of many Roman historians, relies on literary sources rather than eyewitness accounts.[3] At points, it is clear that

---

[1] Ronald Mellor, *The Roman Historians* (New York: Routledge, 1998), 49.
[2] *OCD*, 877–8; John Marincola, ed., *A Companion to Greek and Roman Historiography*, vol. 1 (Malden: Blackwell, 2007), 283. Cf. Jane D. Chaplin and Christina Shuttleworth Kraus, eds., *Oxford Readings in Classical Studies: Livy* (New York: Oxford University Press, 2009).
[3] Charles W. Fornara, *The Nature of History in Ancient Greece and Rome* (Berkeley: University of California Press, 1983), 47–90.

Livy has followed Polybius in his narration of events, but that he adapted his narration for a Roman audience with various additions.[4] Livy writes from a Roman viewpoint, chronicling Rome's rise to power, beginning in Italy and—finally, by his time—conquering most of the Mediterranean. Livy does not interrogate issues of Rome's right to rule; but, like Polybius, he is more interested in the process of acquisition. Furthermore and germane to the work here, Livy is interested in the behavior and character of Roman citizens and ultimately toward the end of the unity or concord, which he views as a central feature to the rise of Rome.[5] Therefore, the discussion of obedience and disobedience takes on a particular importance for our study.

The preface to Livy's work notes that the foundational stories of any city are always fraught—or to use his term, "mingled"—with both "poetic legends" and "historical proofs" (1.7).[6] Even so, Livy permits that

> if any people ought to be allowed to consecrate their origins and refer them to a divine source, so great is the military glory of the Roman People that when they profess that their Father and the Father of their Founder was none other than Mars, the nations of the earth may well submit (*gens humanus patior*) to this also with as good a grace as they submit to Rome's dominion (*imperium*). (1.8)

Livy attaches little importance to these stories (1.9) but provides a moral tone, stressing the importance of "what life and morals were like; through what men and by what policies, in peace and in war, empire was established and enlarged" (1.9). Worth noting is the language of submission of the nations that characterizes the mythic past of Rome and provides current for his day. The examination of the past functions as a mirror for current reflection for Livy's audience (1.10-12).[7]

Livy's description of the Samnite Wars provides another insightful glimpse into obedience within the Greco-Roman world. He provides an important parallel account to the descriptions of obedience, surrender, and friendship that we saw in Polybius in the last chapter. Rome's ever-growing friendships with new nations could lead to problematic relations with their older allies. Such is the case with the Samnites, whom Livy notes were "united in friendship and alliance" with the Romans at the time when the Samnites attacked the Campanians (7.29.6). With their options dwindling, the losing Campanians reach out to Rome for assistance, albeit against one of Rome's allies (7.29.7). Events like this indicate a *deditio* under duress, to use our categories from the last chapter. The Campanian ambassadors seek a perpetual friendship with Rome (7.30.1) and acknowledge the embarrassing fact that they had not sought friendship

---

[4] *OCD*, 878. On some of the problems with Livy vis-à-vis other historians see Ronald T. Ridley, "The Historian's Silences: What Livy Did Not Know—or Chose Not to Tell," *JAH* 1 (2013): 27–52; H. Tränkle, "Livy and Polybius," in Chaplin and Kraus, eds., *Oxford Readings in Classical Studies: Livy*, 476–95.

[5] Daniel J. Kapust, *Republicanism, Rhetoric, and Roman Political Thought: Sallust, Livy, and Tacitus* (New York, Cambridge University Press, 2011), 83.

[6] On the importance of Livy's preface see J. L. Moles, "Livy's Preface," in Chaplin and Kraus, eds., *Oxford Readings in Classical Studies: Livy*, 49–90.

[7] Such of course is standard ancient historiography practice; see Polybius, *Hist.* 2.61.3; Tacitus, *Ann.* 3.65.

before the unfortunate turn of events that now place them in a dire position. In a rhetorical move of immense proportions, the envoys argue that if they had sought friendship when "equals," they would not have been as accepting of the terms as they are now (7.30.2).

One advantage that the Campanians offer the Romans is their geographical position as a defense against Rome's enemies—the Volscians and the Aequinians (7.30.7) and furthering Roman territory. The ambassadors remark, "When once you have subdued (*subactis*) these nations that lie between our boundaries and your own—a thing which your valor and good fortune guarantee will speedily come to pass—your rule will extend unbroken all the way to our frontier" (7.30.8). One final offering of the Campanians is a pragmatic one. Campania will end up being one of Rome's friends or enemies, and the envoys exploit this feature before the Senate, noting, "Defend us, and we are yours; desert us, and the Samnites will possess us. Consider therefore whether it be your preference that Capua and all Campania augment Rome's power, or that of Samnium" (7.30.9-10). The Campanians offer their territory as an "augment" to Rome's power and a decision that they ought to make in their self-interest. The increase of power of the Samnites, by acquiring Capua, also functions as a threat against Roman interests and, thus, an impetus for siding with the Campanians. The final offering of the Campanians is the obedience of their colony:

> The shadow of your help therefore is enough to protect us, and we shall regard whatever we have, whatever we are, as wholly yours. For you the Campanian soil shall be tilled, for you the city of Capua shall be thronged; you we shall regard as our founders, our parents, yes, even as gods; there is not a single one amongst your colonies that will surpass us in obedience (*obsequium*) and loyalty (*fides*). (7.30.18-19)

The Campanians end their appeal to Rome in terms of competing obedience and argue that their obedience will surpass that of all the other Roman colonies as a testament to their loyalty (*fides*). The ambassadors frame their appeals to Rome in terms of military assistance against Roman enemies, extending the geographical reach of the empire, their self-interest, and, finally, in terms of surpassing obedience. Again we see a linkage between obedience and faith language whereby one's obedience spells out and witnesses one's *fides* to Rome.

The Roman Senate initially responded negatively. They cite their previous friendship with the Samnites as preventing them from entering into a friendship with the Campanians. The Senate remains firmly committed to their treaty with the Samnites and requests that the Samnites not attack Capua. Next, the politicking of the Campanian envoy kicks into high gear.

In a brilliant move, knowing that Rome will defend what is theirs, the Campanians willingly surrender themselves to Rome (*deditio*), saying, "Wherefore we now place under your sway and jurisdiction, Senators, and that of the Roman people, the people of Campania and the city of Capua, its fields, its sacred temples, all things human and divine" (7.31.3). The Senate is "deeply moved" by the actions of the envoy, and Livy notes, "It at once became a matter of honor that men who had formally surrendered themselves should not be left to their fate, and it was resolved that the Samnite nation would commit a wrongful act if they attacked a city and territory which had by surrender become the possession of Rome" (7.31.7). The system of obedience seems to work both ways, as obedience can provoke the hand of the Romans and be used in ways that secure one's interests.

The Romans then dispatched envoys to the Samnites requesting that they not attack the territory of Campania. The Samnites' friendship with Rome would legally entail that they follow Rome's request and not attack a territory, however new, under Rome's control. Such a request outrages the Samnites who immediately send their army to ravage the Campanian territory (7.31.11). The Samnite disobedience to Rome's request results in Rome declaring war against the Samnites (7.32.1-3).

The cause of the Samnite War shows the importance of obedience to Rome's requests, even when those directives go against a nation's self-interest.[8] Rome's interests appear paramount regardless of the complexities of international conflicts. Certainly, the Campanian envoys masterminded a politically savvy move to defend themselves. Despite the problems this created for the Samnites and their interests, Rome expects the Samnites to obey their request. Such an account indicates the seriousness with which the Romans took the obedience that was due to them from various nations (cf. Rom. 1:5).

The Roman relationship with the Volscians provides another important example of obedience language that parallels our findings in the Greek sources. In Livy's description of the consulships of Crassus and Veno, he notes that ambassadors from the Volscian people came to Rome seeking an alliance or to solicit faith from the Romans. Livy describes the terms that the Volscians seek, namely for the Romans to defend them against Samnite aggressions. In doing so, the Volscians continue to offer their faith (*fides*) and obedience (*oboedio*) to the Roman people (8.19.2). The Senate sent their ambassadors to direct the Samnites to refrain from attacking these territories, and they agreed, "not so much because the Samnites were desirous of peace, as because they were not prepared for war" (8.19.3).

As we saw in the Greek sources with Polybius, Livy's description of these events utilizes the equivalent Latin terms: *fides* and *oboedio*. Roman faith is entered into by friends of Rome on the condition of their continued obedience.[9] Those already indebted to Rome, in this case, the Samnites, are expected to obey Rome's demands. Livy provides an internal view of the relationships between Rome and her allies and shows that not all obedience was enthusiastic. Pragmatism often won the day rather than one's interests. In this case, the Samnites' ability to resist Rome is outweighed by their inability to prepare for the war that their disobedience would provoke. The relationship between faith and obedience is important for our study of Romans and Paul's usage of similar Greek terms (cf. Rom. 1:5).

Rome's relationship with Hannibal also provides several important examples of obedience in Livy's *History*. The campaigns of Hannibal certainly produced anxiety for

---

[8] On obedience of nations or enemies see Livy 6.4.-5; 8.13.16-18; 9.36.7; 28.16.11; 29.15.2-3; 38.16.10; 38.43.1-6; 39.42.16; 38.31.5-6, 34.1-4; 39.53.11; 45.31.9-10.
[9] Cf. Livy, 27.10.10; 32.8.8-10.

the Roman allies in these regions. Hannibal used his allies to attack various territories, and Livy recounts how the Numidians "wrought great havoc and spread dismay and terror" (23.13.10). However, Livy mentions that

> this terror, even though all the country blazed with war, did not cause the allies to waver in their loyalty (*fides*), assuredly because the rule under which they were governed was just and temperate, nor did they refuse—and that is the only guarantee of loyalty (*fides*)—to yield obedience (*pareo*) to their betters. (23.13.11)

One of the best examples of obedience in Livy's work comes in Book 30 with the end of the Second Punic War. Scipio's defeat of the Carthaginians provides an excellent example of obedience, and Livy's narration of events mirrors Polybius's description of the same event. This example is important as it shows the crossover between Greek and Latin terms for obedience.

In Book 30, Livy narrates the events that led to the surrender of the Carthaginians. Following their defeat, the Carthaginians

> now listening no longer to any who advocated war, they sent thirty of their principal elders as deputies to solicit peace ... They implored pardon for their state, which had been now twice brought to the brink of ruin by the temerity of its citizens, and would again owe its safety to the indulgence of its enemies. They said, the object the Roman people aimed at in the subjugation of their enemies was dominion, and not their destruction; that he might enjoin what he pleased upon them, as being prepared submissively (*servio*) to obey (*oboedio*). (30.16.2-7)

Given the Carthaginian request for peace, they take the steps necessary to show that they are serious in their pleas by prostrating themselves (30.16.3) and seeking pardon, but most importantly by noting that they were prepared to obey (30.16.7). Scipio's response bears out the same features we saw in Polybius for a *deditio* under duress:

> Still, though he had victory in a manner within his grasp, he would not refuse all accommodation, that all the nations of the world (*omnis gens*) may know that the Roman people both undertake and conclude wars with justice. (30.16.9-10)

As we saw in Polybius, Rome issues the demands to be obeyed and peace is dependent on the subjected nation accepting these terms. One interesting feature, unique to Livy's account, is Scipio's statement reveals that the global image of Rome is at stake in making this treaty, and Rome must appear to be just before all the nations. We see the emergence of a triad of concepts: obedience, justice, and the nations (cf. Rom. 1:5; 16–17).

The ability of Rome to defend friends and allies was paramount to securing their reputation around the known world (cf. 30.16.19). As seen in Polybius, with the stater from Ephizephyrian Locri (282 BCE), the Romans were establishing their reputation in the region as "preservers of *fides*." The ability to uphold treaties and offer protection for those that relied on Rome is raised in Book 42 with Marcus Popilius's attack on the Ligurians. Such an attack by a Roman praetor in 173 BCE was grounds for another praetor, Aulus Atilius, to offer an invective against him. According to Livy's accounts, Marcus Popilius had attacked the Ligurians and brought them to the point of surrender (42.7.1–42.8.1). The Ligurians, having been defeated, surrendered without stipulating any terms (42.8.1). However, Popilius "immediately took their arms from them, razed their town, and sold themselves and their effects" (42.8.2). The Senate deemed Popilius's actions "outrageous," stating

> that the Statellates, who alone of the Ligurians had not made war on the Romans, who even on this occasion had been attacked although they had not begun a war, who had entrusted themselves to the good faith (*fides*) of the Roman people should have been harassed and destroyed with every form of extreme cruelty, that so many thousands of innocent persons, calling upon the Roman people for protection, should have been sold—a fate which established the worst possible precedent and issued a warning that no one should ever dare in the future to surrender—and, scattered in every direction, should, though at peace, be slaves to those who had once been downright enemies of the Roman people. (42.8.4-6)

The Senate is outraged with Popilius's actions as they called into question the purpose of surrendering to Rome in the first place. Not only had the Ligurians been defeated and sought a *deditio* but they had not made war on Rome. Rather than harassing and mistreating them, actions the Senate deems "extreme cruelty," they should have been accepted into the faith of the Romans and guaranteed protection rather than annihilation. Aulus Atilius draws out the illogic of Popilius's actions, whereby if Rome always acted this way, who would want to surrender in the future?

The obedience of a surrendering nation has ramifications for Rome, where it is in Rome's best interest to honor the obedience of a subordinate group (cf. Rom. 13:1). Failure to honor the obedience of a conquered territory or people runs the risk of deterring future surrender from their enemies.[10] Obedience, therefore, forms a channel of international diplomacy on behalf of the weaker group.

Further we might remark on how Livy is using the story of Populius in his narrative as an example of disobedience and as a character not worthy of emulation. Paul will offer a similar comparison of disobedient characters unworthy of imitation in Rom. 9:13-18 and the characters of Jacob, Esau, and Pharaoh. The rhetorical aims are similar whereby their actions are meant to dissuade the listener from pursuing similar actions.

A final example of obedience occurs in Book 44 during Rome's campaigns against King Philip of Macedonia and his heir-apparent son, Perseus (Books 41–45).[11] This

---

[10] Popilius refused to follow the Senate's orders. Rather, "the same ungovernable temper which the consul had displayed towards the Ligurians he now showed in refusing to obey the Senate" (42.9.1). Such disobedience toward the Senate was not received well and he was censured (42.9.6). Livy's account of this event shows that a disobedient praetor acts disobediently toward other nations. Or, to put it in other words, it appears that the events of Popilius are narrated first, and Livy's description of his disobedience to the Senate serves to mitigate his poor choices with the Ligurians. On obedience to governmental officials (tribunes, consul, Senate) see Livy, 3.38.13–3.39.1; 4.5.5; 5.12.13; 6.6.8, 18; 8.32.3; 9.4.15-16; 9.34.24 (to laws); 26.36.3; 41.10.7-8.

[11] On obedience to/from kings see Livy, 1.35.5; 36.16.9; 39.25.12-15; 40.21.8; 44.10.1.

instance is unique as it shows how Rome responded to calls for their obedience from other nations. So far, every example has shown Rome in the superior position, requesting obedience from nations that seek Roman friendship. In 44.14, we find a situation where Rome is not in a superior position. Instead, they are part of a larger coalition of forces working to end a war. Livy notes that the war with Macedonia was a cause for concern (41.19.6).[12]

In this buildup to war with Rome, the loyalties of several nations were called into question, especially the Rhodians. By 172 BCE, preparations for war had already begun. To avoid war with Rome, Perseus sent an envoy to the Roman Senate. This effort would prove to be unsuccessful. The Roman general Crassus lost the battle with Macedonia, and Perseus attempted to offer peace to Rome. Rome's loss was, of course, heralded around the known world and set off a chain of problems for territories under their control. Perseus sent the Rhodians, despite their concerns, to be arbiters of a peace treaty between Rome and Macedonia (44.14.6). Unique to this situation is that Rome is no longer the victor but the defeated party.[13] Such a request or demand to Rome was not lost on many, as Livy notes some of the responses:

> And now the Rhodians pass judgment throughout the world as to peace and war! At the beck and call of the Rhodians will the Romans take up and lay down their arms! Now we are no longer to call upon the gods to witness treaties, but rather the Rhodians! Unless obedience (*pareo*) is rendered to them, and our armies are removed from Macedonia, the Rhodians will see, will they, what they must do? What the Rhodians will see, they themselves know. But surely the Roman people, after their conquest of Perseus, which they hope will take place any day, will see that they repay a suitable reward for the actions of each state during the war. (44.15.3-8)

Roman anger toward their subservient position is quite understandable. Although this is in an early period of Rome's Republic, history would show that they would not be in this position for long. Such an episode offers the revealing look into Rome's understanding of their position and power. The Romans regard obedience to any other nation as beneath the dignity of being Roman. In an interesting charge against the Rhodians, the Romans balk at their attempt to adjudicate issues of peace and war (44.15.4) as it shows the Rhodians usurping a Roman prerogative and expropriating Rome's place in the wider region. Eventually, Macedonia would fall to Rome, so their obedience to other nations would be short-lived.

---

[12] *CAH* 8:303.

[13] Claudius would eventually annex Lycia in 43 CE after disturbances in the region. A milestone from 45/46 CE was found in Lycia bearing the inscription in honor of Claudius, "the savior of the their nation: the Lycians, Rome-loving and Caesar-loving, faithful allies, set free from faction, lawlessness and brigandage through his divine foresight" (G. L. Cooley, ed., *Tiberius to Nero*, LACTOR 19 (London: London School of Classical Teachers, 2011), 304n.40).

Livy on the Importance of Obedience

Given the similarities between Livy and Polybius's histories, several degrees of overlap can be found with the obedience language. Unrest at Rome, treaties, and war comprise the contexts for obedience that Livy shares with Polybius. Continued obedience forms a common refrain in Latin literature. Unique to Livy is the Roman loss to Perseus and outrage at demands for Roman obedience to the Rhodians.[14] As seen in other contexts, obedience primarily occurs within military and diplomatic domains within Livy's work. Finally, we also highlight that several examples in Livy include references to faith and obedience, particularly nations that show themselves faithful by their obedience. Such examples have consideration for our understanding of Paul's genitive construction in Rom. 1:5.

Tacitus: Obedience in the Aftermath of Chaos

In 96 CE, after the murder of Domitian, Tacitus who had adeptly navigated the maddening and paranoid years of Domitian would take the prestigious role of consul. He was young, gifted, and uniquely poised to write some of the history that he had lived through. Political experience of course being a major prerequisite of history writing. A native of southern Gaul and born into the equestrian class, Tacitus had been educated and brought up among the elite; he would utilize those skills to be one of the best remembered Roman authors. His introduction into the Senate was in the aftermath of the civil wars of 69 CE and Vespasian recruiting numerous Spaniards and Gauls into the Senate.[15] His ambition was only matched by his success. Arriving in Rome by 75 CE, his career spanned the reigns of Vespasian, Titus, and Domitian.[16] The civil unrest that preceded his career certainly shapes some of the context of the importance of obedience in his work.

By the early second century, Tacitus was at work on his *Histories* that would cover the years 69–96 CE and consist of some twelve to fourteen books. The only portions to survive antiquity are the first four books that bring the narrative up to 70 CE and cover the tumultuous year of 69 CE with the reigns of Galba, Otho, Vitellius, and Vespasian.[17] Tacitus's second historical work, *The Annals*, or more accurately *Ab excessu divi Augusti*, covers the Julio-Claudian dynasty beginning with the ascension of Tiberius. The original sixteen to eighteen books were to cover the reigns of Tiberius, Gaius, Claudius, and Nero.[18] His value is inestimable as nearly all of the Roman historians from the Republican period have been lost. Of the three great Roman historians,

---

[14] Also unique is his description of obedience and religious cults as seen with the Bacchus cult (39.16.213).
[15] Ronald Mellor, *Tacitus' Annals* (New York: Oxford University Press, 2010), 11.
[16] For introductory matters see Andreas Mehl, *Roman Historiography: An Introduction to Its Basic Aspects and Development*, trans. Hans-Friedrich Mueller (Malden: Wiley-Blackwell, 2011), 136–51.
[17] *OCD*, 1469.
[18] Although much is lost of Book 5, all of Books 7–10, the first half of Book 11, and everything from the second half of Book 16. *OCD*, 1469.

only Livy and Tacitus remain, while the works of Sallust are entirely lost. Even for the historians who remain, we lack over one hundred books from Livy and over two-thirds of Tacitus's historical works.[19] Therefore, although Tacitus is a second-century work, his purview is the first century. Given the paucity of historical sources for this period, Tacitus must be used to construct an understanding of obedience for the first century. We will begin with *The Annals* since the time frame is closest to Paul and Romans before moving onto *The Histories*.

Obedience in *The Annals*

Book 1 of Tacitus's *The Annals* is a short preface detailing Rome's rulers, rapidly moving from Rome's early kings, through dictatorships, and quickly arriving at the preceding generation of rulers from Augustus onward. Tacitus's description of his work states that he has chosen to focus on the end of Augustus's reign and then on the Emperors Tiberius, Gaius, Claudius, and Nero (1.1). In describing Augustus, Tacitus notes it was Augustus "who, when the world was wearied by civil strife, subjected it to Empire under the title of 'Prince'" (1.1). Although Augustus is only briefly covered in *The Annals*, his subjection of the world tops the list of remembered deeds (cf. *Res Gestae*).

As with any succession, Tiberius's ascension to the role of emperor had the potential for strife. Although he was adopted by Augustus in 4 CE and granted important titles thereafter, his initial balking at the title did little to strengthen public support for his new role. In addition to this precarious context was his brother Germanicus control of the army and vast auxiliary forces at his disposal, which also did little to strengthen Tiberius's attitude toward his role or the perception of the Roman people. Nevertheless, Tiberius took the necessary steps to secure his position.

Tacitus quickly recounts the first responders to Tiberius's ascension, including two Consuls, the commander of the Praetorian Guard, and the holder of the corn supply.[20] Each of these three positions would be essential to Tiberius's smooth transition to power. Tacitus notes that all four of these men took the "oath of allegiance" (*iuravere*) and that the Senate, the soldiers, and the people did the same (1.7).[21] Valerius Messalla went further suggesting that "the oath of allegiance to Tiberius should be renewed annually" (1.8). The role of obedience and the nations is certainly implicit in the oath of allegiance (see Chapter 5).[22]

In a politically opportune move, one of Tiberius's first acts was to write to every provincial army. The death of any ruler provided the opportunity for mutiny and revolt on behalf of the armed forces (as would be well documented with other successions). Therefore, the key to Tiberius's ascension was securing the army. Augustus's death had

---

[19] Marincola, *Companion to Greek and Roman Historiography*, 1.
[20] On the importance of the Praetorian Guard see Sandra Bingham, *The Praetorian Guard: A History of Rome's Elite Special Forces* (Waco: Baylor University Press, 2013).
[21] On obedience of citizens, plebes see *Ann*. 3.65; 4.20; 6.10-11. Tacitus includes a disparaging comment on Tiberius relationship to his mother, "For with Tiberius obedience (*obsequium*) to his mother was the habit of a life" (*Ann*. 5.3).
[22] On the obedience of other nations see Tacitus, *Ann*. 4.46, 72; 12.11; 12.54 (Jews); 13.54; 14.24.

reinvigorated some of the poorer sensibilities among those in the army on the Danube and Rhine rivers. T. E. J. Weidemann rightly notes:

> Augustus' death gave the Roman conscripts serving in Pannonia and Germany an opportunity to express their long repressed resentment at their terms of service. The Roman soldier's oath of loyalty was not only to the *res publica*, but to the individual *imperator* who had called him up for that particular campaign. This was the first time in almost half a century that an *imperator* had died and needed to be replaced by a new one—albeit one who had seen many years' service both in Pannonia and Germany ... Tacitus describes these events as a complete collapse of discipline, and maximizes both the moral disgrace and the potential danger to Tiberius.[23]

Within this context, Tacitus records a speech attributed to Percennius delivered to the army at Pannonia that contains the first explicit reference to obedience in *The Annals*.[24] Tacitus blames the mutiny of the Pannonian legions on the change of emperors. According to Tacitus, it was those under the command of Junius Blaesus who, having heard of Augustus's death, gave his troops a reprieve from their duties. Such a lull provided fuel for the embers of dissension that, according to Tacitus, Percennius flamed to his advantage (1.16). In this recorded speech, Percennius asks, "In the tone of a demagogue, why, like slaves, they were obedient (*oboedio*) to a few centurions and still fewer tribunes" (1.17). Not entirely surprisingly, this account links slavery with obedience, and Percennius exploits this point with his Roman audience. Again, the linkage between obedience and slavery is well established (cf. Chapter 5 and Rom. 5–6).

In his response, Junius Blaesus reprimands Percennius's attempt to stir up dissension among the troops. Blaesus remarks, "Better imbrue your hands in my blood: it will be less guilt to slay your commander than it is to be in revolt from the Emperor. Either living I will uphold the loyalty of the legions (*incolumis fides*), or pierced to the heart I will hasten on your repentance" (1.18). Blaesus contrasts Percennius's disobedience with his charge to upload the loyalty of the legions for the emperor. In this example, disobedience is equivalent to "revolt from the Emperor" (1.18).[25]

Similar factions plagued the legions on the Lower Rhine, and Tacitus's account focuses on Germanicus's response to this situation. This is important for several reasons. First, he certainly could have been a formidable rival to Tiberius had he wanted to be. Second, in his response, Germanicus connects the oath of allegiance to the emperor and our topic of obedience. Third, Germanicus's dramatic act highlights

---

[23] *CAH* 10:207. Note the Claudian *aureus* that celebrates Drusus's victories over the Germans between 12 and 9 BCE. The coin bears the image of Nero Claudius Drusus wearing a laurel wreath on the obverse and on the reverse has the image of two shields with two crossed spears and trumpets before a standard, bearing the description, "*DE GERMANIS*" (over Germany). Cf. Cooley, *Tiberius to Nero*, 159.

[24] On the obedience of soldiers see Tacitus, *Ann.* 1.19, 21, 28, 35, 40, 65; 2.55; 3.12; 4.18; 6.44; 15.6.

[25] On obedience to generals in Tacitus, see *Ann.* 1.84; 2.43; 3.50; 15.25. Cf. Drusus's wife Antonia was signaled out for her "loyalty" (*fides*) to her husband's love by Valerius Maximus (*Mem. Deeds.* 4.3.3).

the importance attached to obedience. We will take each of these important issues in reverse order.

On hearing of the dissensions and disloyalty of legions on the Lower Rhine, Germanicus declares that "he would rather die than cast off his loyalty (*fides*)" (1.35). Then in a daring display, he "plucked his sword from his side, raised it aloft and was plunging it into his breast, when those nearest him seized his hand and held it by force" (1.35). Germanicus's vivid display drives home the importance of obedience and loyalty. Second, after having his self-flagellation stayed, Germanicus's speech invokes the memory of Julius Caesar's and Augustus's ability to lead:

> The Divine Julius once quelled an army's mutiny with a single word by calling those who were disobeying their military (*detrecto*) oath "citizens." The Divine Augustus cowed the legions who had fought at Actium with one look of his face. … You too, in whose faces and in whose hearts I perceive a change, if only you restore to the Senate their envoys, to the Emperor his due obedience (*obsequium*) … This will be a pledge of your repentance, a guarantee of your loyalty (*fides*). (1.42-43)

Germanicus's speech to the mutinous legions hinges on invoking the memory of important figures like Julius Caesar and Augustus to inspire the renewed obedience of the troops. He emphasizes obedience to the military oath and the obedience due to the emperor from his armies.[26] Extremely important is Germanicus's charge that by returning their obedience to the emperor they show that they have repented and guaranteed their faith/loyalty. Obedience is a sign of repentance and faith. The army's loyalty or faith is evidenced by their obedience. What remains for the soldiers who by their obedience show they have repented? Later on a Roman knight, Marcus Terentius will remark that all that is left "for us is left the glory of obedience" (*obsequii gloria*) (6.8). The benefit gained is glory, an exceedingly important Roman value. Paul likewise links obedience, repentance, and glory in Rom. 2:7, for those Gentiles who by their obedience show their repentance and also received glory and immortality. We have another example of faith and obedience language occurring in relationship to one another. In this account, faith is evidenced by one's obedience (cf. Rom. 1:5, 3:1; 9–11).

In 17 CE, Tiberius would nominate his longtime friend Cnaeus Calpurnius Piso as his legate to Syria. By 20 CE, after his death, Piso's trial would be well underway. The importance of this trial for Tacitus is seen in the ten chapters he devotes to it, more than any other trial in *The Annals*.[27] The trial of Piso is told indirectly through the

---

[26] Weidemann notes,

> It would be wrong to accept the implication that Germanicus was a rival or a threat to Tiberius during his lifetime. On the contrary, there is epigraphical and other evidence that Germanicus was recognized as Tiberius' successor by men who had no wish to show disloyalty to Tiberius himself. When Ovid, in exile at Tomi on the Black Sea, addressed Germanicus as a *princeps*, he will hardly have assumed that he would be understood to want Germanicus to be Emperor in Tiberius' place. (*CAH* 10:208)

[27] No trial occupies more than three chapters and some far less than that; see Cynthia Damon, "The Trial of Cn. Piso in Tacitus' Annals and the 'Senatus Consultum De Cn. Pisone Patre': New Light on Narrative Technique," *AJP* 120 (1999): 146.

speeches of Tiberius, the prosecution and defense, as well as the reading of Piso's letter of self-defense to Tiberius (3.16).[28] Although a full survey of the events and trial falls outside the scope of this project, we will focus on key examples of Piso's story where obedience forms a central feature of the narrative.

Beginning in 3.16, Tiberius reads a note from Piso before the Senate. Piso's letter is important as it not only represents an occurrence of faith and obedience together but also fleshes out the relationship. Tacitus's recounts:

> Crushed by a conspiracy of my foes and the odium excited by a lying charge, since my truth and innocence find no place here, I call the immortal gods to witness that towards you Caesar, I have lived loyally (*fides*), and with like dutiful respect towards your mother. ... And therefore I pray the more earnestly that the innocent may not pay the penalty of my wickedness. By forty-five years of obedience (*obsequium*), by my association with you in the consulate, as one who formerly won the esteem of the Divine Augustus, your father, as one who is your friend and will never hereafter ask a favor, I implore you to save my unhappy son. (3.16)

Piso's forensic defense of himself stresses that he had lived "loyally" or "faithfully." Calling on the gods as his witnesses, he seeks divine assistance in effecting his plea. After petitioning protection for his children, he notes his forty-five years of obedience. The important point is that Piso cites the evidence of his faithful life toward Tiberius by his forty-five years of continued obedience.[29] Obedience is the outworking of a faithful life in this judicial context. Although all of this forensic oratory is aimed at saving his son, we should not miss the way that obedience and faith work together in this forensic context (cf. Rom. 1:5).

Moving forward to the reign of Claudius, the fall of Sejanus in 31 CE, allowed several figures to rise in the political vacuum. One of them was Lucius Vitellius who became an advisor to Claudius.[30] In 35 CE, he would be sent to Syria to nominate Tiridates to the throne of Armenia. Tacitus records:

> Vitellius thought it enough to have displayed the arms of Rome, and he then bade Tiridates remember his grandfather Phraates, and his foster-father Caesar, and all that was glorious in both of them, while the nobles were to show obedience (*obsequium*) to their king, and respect for us, each maintaining his honor and his loyalty (*fides*). (6.37)

---

[28] Damon, "Trial of Cn. Piso in Tacitus' Annals."
[29] Tiberius accepted other families into formal friendships. See the inscriptions from Lusitania from 31 CE where Tiberius accepts the Quintus family into the "good faith" of himself. Cooley, *Tiberius to Nero*, 280.M65.
[30] Also from Claudius's reign is the account in *Ann.* 11.24, where Tacitus comments on the loyalty of the Gauls. He points to Romulus as an example of how to accept foreigners, as Romulus "regard[s] several people as enemies one day and Roman citizens the next." In using this as an illustration for accepting the Gauls, he comments that since their war, "peace and loyalty has been unbroken. Now that they have been assimilated into our customs, culture, and even our families."

The significance of this example is twofold. First, the nobles of the region maintained faith and were still able to show subsequent obedience to their king (cf. Rom. 13:1). Second, and more importantly, obedience to their kings was not in competition or a threat to the Romans to whom they still showed respect (*reverentia*).[31] This shows perhaps most clearly that obedience could be given to another political figure without questioning one's loyalty or faith. Perhaps the Roman situation and Paul's call to obedience might be best viewed in this light. Christians would be allowed to show obedience to Christ and still retain a respect for Rome without incurring the charge of sedition or subversion (Rom. 13:1). Finally, we again see the linkage between the intertwined concepts of obedience and faith.

The highlight of Claudius's reign was the conquering of Britannia. He celebrated his victory by constructing a triumphal arch in Rome in 51–52 CE with an inscription bearing the words "the senate and people of Rome (set this up) because he received submission (*deditio*) of eleven kings of the Britons, [conquered without] any loss because he was the first to bring barbarian tribes [beyond Ocean] into the dominion [of the Roman people]."[32] Again, the importance of such an account is its proximity, some three to five years before Paul's writing of the letter to the Romans. This example of obedience comes in "recent memory" for those in Rome.

Several other examples of obedience in *The Annals* are important as they occur during the reign of Nero and are close to the writing of Romans. In 58 CE, Nero's general Corbulo attacked Tiridates and captured Artaxata. The army of Rome was relentless in their attack. Tacitus recounts, "Finding that there was no breaking of our ranks from rashness, and that only one cavalry officer advanced too boldly, and that he falling pierced with arrows, confirmed the rest in obedience (*obsequium*) by the warning" (13.40). The failure of one officer and his death suffices as a negative example and results in inspiring the obedience of others. Such imagery provides a helpful comparison between the actions of Christ and Adam (cf. Rom. 5:17).

Tacitus highlights the person of Boiocalus as a paragon of obedience. After describing him as "famous among the nations and loyal to Rome," Boiocalus reminds the Romans that "he had served under the leadership of Tiberius and of Germanicus, and that to a fifty years' obedience (*obsequium*) he was adding the merit of subjecting (*subicio*) his tribe to our dominion" (13.55). As seen in numerous examples (cf. 3.16), one's loyalty or faith to Rome is expressed through obedience. Not only is Boiocalus's obedience highlighted but it is also connected with his subjection of his tribe to the rule of Rome. The significance of this example is the inclusion of references to nations, faith, and obedience (cf. Rom. 1:5).

During Nero's reign, there were several trials of various Romans for extortion. One such example was the prosecution of Claudius Timarchus by Thrasea Paetus who thought that Timarchus's power had grown too large. According to Tacitus's record, Thrasea was angered that Timarchus had "repeatedly declared that it was in his power to decide whether the proconsuls who had governed Crete should receive the thanks

---

[31] Although see the instance of 14.31 where a token of obedience does not result in a good outcome.
[32] Smallwood 43b; Cooley, *Tiberius to Nero*, 19, N25, 299. Cooley also notes that the arch displayed battle scenes between Romans and the Celtic barbarians.

of the province" (15.20). Tacitus's record of Thrasea's remarks in the speech is revealing for our study of obedience: "Formerly, it was not only a praetor or a consul, but private persons also, who were sent to inspect the provinces, and to report what they thought about each man's obedience (*obsequio*)" (15.21). According to Thrasea's account, during Nero's reign, it was the custom for certain persons, including private citizens, to test the obedience of various officials, most likely to see if there was any cause for concern for sedition or revolt. What this text makes clear is that obedience is something that must remain in check, and continued obedience on behalf of the provincial officials was an important matter (cf. Rom. 1:5; 13:1).

One final account of obedience will conclude our survey of obedience in *The Annals*. The first five years of Nero's reign, known as the *quinquennium*, refer to the time when Nero was advised by both Seneca and Burrus. Weidemann, remarking on the *quinquennium*, notes that it was "an attempt to explain why so many Senators who later reviled Nero as a monster were prepared to support him for so many years."[33] Such a degree of optimism is also seen in the famous poet Calpurnius Siculus's *Eclogue* where one of his characters, Cordyon, praises Caesar (Nero). "I beg you, rule this world, govern the nations as our king forever ... never desert this peace you have begun" (4.145-6). The peace would quickly desert Nero's reign as the golden years would come to an abrupt end when Nero killed his mother and Senator Thrasea Paetus. The death of the latter was the result of his failure to believe the reason for Agrippina's death. The "official" explanation for Agrippina's death was a conspiracy to replace Nero (which, ironically, could have been true). On hearing this, Thrasea Paetus walked out of the Senate in disbelief and disgust.

In 66 CE, as a result of his building anxieties, Nero began to execute those whom he feared, including a governor of Britannia who had consulted astrologers to see how long Nero would live. Included in this culture of fear was the Stoic-influenced Senator Thrasea Paetus. Of primary concern for the Stoic senator was the idea of *libertas*. He became more outspoken at the frivolity of the court and the multiplication of honorific titles and statues as such things distracted from the single-minded pursuit of governance. From the late 50's to the early 60's, Paetus had frequently voiced his disdain of current practice and hearkened for a return to the old Roman values.[34]

Nero could not take up such a charge against a senator, so this task was left to Capito Cossutianus, a Roman politician, who had his own ax to grind against Paetus. In a speech, Capito brought more devastating charges. "Thrasea, he said, at the beginning of the year always avoided the usual oath of allegiance (*juro*); he was not present at the recital of the public prayers, though he had been promoted to the priesthood of the Fifteen; he had never offered a sacrifice for the safety of the prince or for his heavenly voice" (16.22). To this, Capito added:

> The country in its eagerness for discord is now talking of you, Nero, and of Thrasea, as it talked once of Caius Caesar and Marcus Cato ... He [Thrasea] is the only man who cares not for your safety, honors not your accomplishments. The

---

[33] *CAH* 10:244.
[34] On the obedience of senators or consuls see Tacitus, *Ann.* 3.55, 75; 12.47; 14.13.

prince's prosperity he despises. Can it be that he is not satisfied with your sorrows and grief? It shows the same spirit not to believe in Poppaea's divinity as to refuse to swear obedience (*non juro*) to the acts of the Divine Augustus and the Divine Julius. (16.22)

The reader of the account ought to know that this long list of injurious offenses contains false charges against Thrasea.[35] Tacitus's disparaging accounts of both Nero and Capito's character lend a degree of incredulity toward the charges against Thrasea. Further, Tacitus's defense of Thrasea includes him writing a note to Nero to seek out the charges and defend himself (16.24). Ultimately, Nero called up the Senate, which proceeded to condemn Thrasea. He was given the penalty of death.

This final story from Tacitus's *The Annals* includes the disastrous destruction of Nero's *quinquennium*, revolving around the suicide of Thrasea Paetus who has been charged with disobedience to Nero. The remaining two years of Nero's reign are lost, but if this last story is any indication, what followed was the eventual decline of Nero's rule into a rule of terror. Such recent accounts have considerable importance for Romans and especially for Rom. 13:1. It is of note that news of this story could have circulated through the streets of Rome, streets that contained the very house churches that Paul wrote Romans. Disobedience, real or invented, was cause for death.

The Histories and Obedience

The Histories begin by covering the difficult year of 69 CE, which saw four emperors perish by assassination (1.2).[36] Three civil wars would plague Rome until ultimately Vespasian would rise and retain power. Not only were there difficulties in Rome but also sedition raged across the Roman Empire. Tacitus sets out his goal to "review the condition of the capital, the temper of the armies, the attitude of the provinces, and the elements of weakness and strength which existed throughout the whole Empire" (1.4). Nero looms large in Tacitus's work. As Holly Hanes has argued, "Nero's influence is written all over this story … [his death] opens the floodgate for all the problems of Empire that the shadow of Augustus previously kept in check."[37] The death of Nero set off a chain reaction of events among numerous groups, including senators, the people, the generals, and the armies.

After detailing the state of the provinces and legions and the rise and fall of various important figures, Tacitus turns to reflect on Galba, the first of three short-lived

---

[35] In the closing chapters of the final book that survives of *The Annals*, Tacitus includes a damning account of Nero's treatment of those he disliked. Tacitus excoriates Nero, noting, "After having butchered so many illustrious men, at last aspired to extirpate virtue itself by murdering Thrasea Paetus and Barea Soranus" (*Ann.* 16.21). Nero's disdain for Thrasea was well known to Tacitus who remarks, "He [Nero] had hated of old, Thrasea on additional grounds, because he had walked out of the Senate when Agrippina's case was under discussion" (*Ann.* 16.21). Other causes for the hatred were singing in a tragedian's dress at Patavium, proposing a more merciful sentence than Nero, purposefully not giving divine honors to Poppaea, and missing her funeral.
[36] Martin Goodman, *The Roman World: 44BC–AD180* (New York: Routledge, 1997), 58–66.
[37] Holly Haynes, *The History of Make-Believe: Tacitus on Imperial Rome* (Berkeley: University of California Press, 2003), 34.

emperors. The first occurrence of obedience in *The Histories* finds Galba warning Piso that obedience can be used to soften one's resolve. Tacitus recounts:

> You indeed will cling with the same constancy to honor, freedom, friendship, the best possessions of the human spirit, but others will seek to weaken them with their obedience (*obsequium*). You will be fiercely assailed by adulation, by flattery, that worst poison of the true heart and by the selfish interests of individuals. (1.15)

Galba's warning is that obedience can be used to exert control and that one must be cautious regarding obedience. Such an account has important ramifications for the notion of hidden transcripts (cf. Rom. 13:1). Piso was a very unremarkable successor with little political aspirations. The more obvious successor to Galba was Otho.

Otho had many marks in his favor as a successor. He had been associated with Nero's *quinquennium*, he had the favor of the Praetorians, and he enjoyed support from the "house of Caesar."[38] After executing a successful coup, Galba and Piso were both assassinated on January 15, 69 CE. The removal of Galba and Piso did not affect Otho's other competitors for the throne. However, one legion after another would give their loyalty to Otho.

Throughout our study of the Roman historians, we have seen references to the oaths of loyalty or allegiance to various emperors. However, the notion of obedience has remained implicit. Tacitus, likewise, includes such oaths but helpfully elaborates on the ramifications, particularly the relationship between the oaths and obedience. One early example of this is at the beginning of Otho's reign. Tacitus records the loyalty of various legions to the persons vying for the throne, noting, "The first encouraging tidings came to Otho from Illyricum. He heard that the legions of Dalmatia, Pannonia, and Moesia had sworn allegiance to him" and that "the army of Judea under Vespasian, and the legions of Syria under Mucianus, swore allegiance to Otho" (1.76). Tacitus notes, "Nowhere was there any loyalty or affection; men changed from one side to the other under the pressure of fear or necessity" (1.76).

After describing such oaths of loyalty to Otho, Tacitus remarks that Africa, following the lead of Carthage, "displayed the same obedience (*obsequium*)" (1.76).[39] Tacitus makes it clear that the oath of allegiance or loyalty is also an oath of obedience by use of the demonstrative pronoun *idem*. This is one of the first texts that explicitly connects obedience to the oaths of allegiance; although previously this could be inferred, such an explicit connection is revealing. The example is important as it contains an explicit reference to the nations swearing obedience (cf. Rom. 1:5).

Given the tumultuous nature of the year 69 CE and the various persons vying for the allegiance of the legions, it is no surprise that the obedience language occurs almost exclusively within militaristic contexts. Obedience on the part of the soldiers

---

[38] *CAH* 10:265.

[39] One should also note the three bronze tablets found in Northern Italy from 28 CE that feature a patronal agreement between Silius Aviola and Siagu. Aviola was a patron of communities in North Africa; he was chief magistrate of towns with a Punic background. The inscription reads, "Aviola … received them and their descendants into allegiance (*fidem*) and client-relationship." Cf. *ILS* 6099; Cooley, *Tiberius to Nero*, 280.M64.

is as important as other aspects of battle such as weapons, towers, and walls.[40] In recounting the success of General Vestricius Spurinna, Tacitus writes, "The walls were strengthened, battlements were added, and the towers were raised in height. It was not only of the implements of war that provision and preparation were made, but of the spirit of subordination (*pareo*) and the love of obedience (*obsequium*)" (2.19). This text is important for a few reasons. First, linguistically it connects the verb to submit (*pareo*) to the noun obedience (*obsequium*), showing the conceptual relationship between the verb and noun in ways similar to the Greek sources with the πείθω (to persuade) root and the adjective ὑπήκοος (obedient). Second, the importance of the physical preparations for the battle is equated with the obedience of soldiers. In war, love of obedience is as important as walls and towers.

Faith and obedience appear in several other places in *The Histories*. Rome's relationship to the Suebi nation provides one example, where Vespasian draws their kings over to his side. Regarding these people, Tacitus remarks, "Their obedience to the Roman people was of long standing and whose people were more inclined to remain faithful to Rome than to take orders from others" (3.5).[41] The Seubians' faith is evidenced by their long-standing obedience to the Romans' directives that are showcased in supplying Vespasian with auxiliary troops (cf. Rom. 1:5).

Another example of faith and obedience occurs in Tacitus's discussion of the armies following the death of Vitellius in Book 4. Following a defeat by the German army, the Romans attacked their commander Gallus and charged him and Hordeonius with treachery. They beat them and placed them in chains, until Gallus wisely charged Hordeonius with the crime, barely saving himself. Such sedition among the troops was, of course, a problem, especially at this moment of political upheaval. When the pro-Vitellius legate Vocula arrived, he suppressed the dissension by killing the leaders of the mutiny. Tacitus comments on the situation:

> Such wide extremes of license (*licentia*) and obedient submission (*patientia*) were to be found in that army. The common soldiers were undoubtedly loyal (*fides*) to Vitellius, but all the most distinguished men were in favor of Vespasian. The result was an alternation of outbreaks and executions, and a strange mixture of obedience (*obsequium*) and frenzy, which made it impossible to restrain the men whom it was yet possible to punish. (4.27)

This text is important as it shows the difficulty with transferring loyalty from one leader to another, especially during times when loyalties were quickly changing. Tacitus records the soldiers' disposition, which diverged radically between the options of obedience and disobedience.

One final example concludes our survey of obedience in *The Histories*. A reference to obedience occurs in a speech of the general Cerialis to an assembly of the Teveri and Lingones at Trier around 70 CE after the Batavian revolt had been quelled. After noting

---

[40] On obedience of soldiers see Tacitus, *Hist.* 1.80, 82, 83-4; 2.27, 97; 3.15, 50; 4.19, 56, 72.
[41] The relationship between Rome and the Suebi was established in 19 CE by the younger Drusus.

that it was their ancestors who had sought out Rome during a time of duress and that Rome had intervened to help both friend and foe (4.73), Cerilias remarks,

> We, though so often provoked, have used the right of conquest to burden you only with the cost of maintaining peace. For the tranquillity of nations cannot be preserved without armies; armies cannot exist without pay; pay cannot be furnished without tribute; all else is common between us ... Should the Romans be driven out (which God forbid) what can result but wars between all these nations? ... Give therefore your love and respect to the cause of peace, and to that capital in which we, conquerors and conquered, claim an equal right. Let the lessons of fortune in both its forms teach you not to prefer rebellion and ruin to obedience (*obsequium*) and safety. (4.74)[42]

Several features of Cerialis's speech are worth noting. First, as we have seen in other historians, Cerilias seems to highlight that the two groups had come to Rome seeking a friendship under duress from their more powerful neighbors. Rome accepted their surrender and came to their aid. Second, his speech raises the interesting notion of "maintaining peace," which, in this context, appears to be paying the armies. Third, Cerilias also warns the tribes that if they fail to uphold their obedience to Rome, then the removal of Rome would result in the cessation of peace. Fourth, Cerilias charges them to love and respect the cause of peace, the city of Rome, and the conquerors themselves. Calling on fortune, a key Roman theme—obedience and safety—should be preferred to destruction.

Obedience is crucial to maintaining their peace and safety. In this context, it refers to keeping their treaty with Rome by agreeing to continue to pay tribute. The lack of obedience would result in the removal of peace that Rome has secured among the various nations and, thus, to the defeat of the Teveri and Lingones tribes. Rebellion in this example is seen as equivalent to disobedience (Rom. 1:18-32). Disobedience brings ruin while obedience maintains peace.

Reflections on Obedience in Tacitus

Tacitus conforms to the thematic aspects of obedience. Obedience is a term that describes the relationship nations have with Rome and obedience is expected for peace to be maintained. Obedience, especially in *The Histories*, often occurs within military contexts where it describes the obedience demanded from soldiers and armies. Two unique features stand out from Tacitus's work. The connection between the oath of

---

[42] On the obedience of Gaul see Tacitus, *Hist.* 4.71. Likewise see Claudius's speech on admitting the Gauls into the Senate in 48 CE. Claudius notes that even though Gaul was a nuisance to Julius Caesar, he contrasts this with "one hundred years of resolute loyalty (*fidem*), an allegiance (*obsequiumque*) which has more stood the test of many difficult crises in the Empire." See *ILS* 212. Although Claudius neglects the revolt of Florus and Sacrovir under Tiberius, which is reported in Tacitus, *Annals*, 3.40. Noted by Cooley, *Tiberius to Nero*, 252.M11D. See Tacitus's account in *Ann.* 11.24, which also includes a reference to "peace and loyalty."

allegiance to the emperor and obedience is highlighted by Tacitus. Linguistically, the connection between the verb *pareo* (to obey, to submit) and the noun *obsequium* (obedience) is established in several occurrences. Most importantly, faith and obedience appear in close context, where nations are deemed faithful by showing their obedience.

Perspectives on Obedience in Latin Literature

The primary examples of obedience in the Latin sources have similar features to those at work in the Greek sources, particularly with the relationship between obedience and faith. As seen in both Livy and Tacitus, obedience is the demonstration of faith or loyalty. When one wants to prove one's faith, one can point to obedience. The Latin sources also bear out that obedience language occurs primarily in the martial contexts of war and treaties (similar to the Greek sources). Several examples of obedience in the social contexts of slavery were noted. Unique occurrences of obedience are found particularly with Tacitus, who provides illuminating help in his discussion of the oath to the emperor and the necessity of obedience. Finally, several examples before the writing of Romans show how obedience language functioned around the time of Paul's call for obedience to those in Rom. 1:5.

As stated previously, our aim is not to create parallelomania between Romans and the Latin sources. Rather, the intention is to construct a broad portrait to show how obedience functioned as a possible avenue for how those in Rome, or brought to Rome from the provinces, may have understood the concept of obedience. In summary, throughout the Latin sources, obedience is connected with the nations and is the evidence of faith and is the key to securing peace. Likewise, disobedience or rebellion brings about punishment and destruction.

5

Philosophizing on Obedience

The previous chapters looked at the role of obedience in Roman statecraft and its relationships with other nations in their treaties. This survey, important as it is, is still incomplete. The aspects of the empire that touched on obedience were not military and empire building alone. Rather they were supported by, and ultimately furthered, the philosophical discussion on the nature of obedience in relationship to Rome.[1] To limit our understanding to the occurrences of obedience language in the histories of Rome or its military contexts would produce an imbalanced portrait of obedience in the Roman Empire. We must add to this emerging paradigm of faith-obedience by looking more broadly into the avenue of ancient moral philosophy. We begin with an example from one of our authors: Epictetus.

Perhaps no one represents the interlocking nature of philosophy, power, and empire better than the Stoic philosopher, Epictetus. He was likely born a slave to the powerful freedman, Epaphroditus, who himself was a secretary to both Nero and Domitian. Epictetus represents the intense complexity of the ancient world, a powerless slave connected to power brokers. This precarious position granted him access not only to the interworkings of the imperial house but also to education as he was allowed to sit under the teaching of the Stoic philosopher Musonius Rufus and began his new pathway out of slavery.[2] He even taught in Rome, but this was to be short-lived. In 95 CE, Domitian banned all philosophers from Rome, thus forcing Epictetus to take up residence in Nicopolis where he gathered students—often from elite backgrounds at that—who themselves were on their way up the social ladder. Epictetus's philosophy was impacted by his servile background under the shadow of the empire. His teaching and person transgressed the boundaries, of philosophy, empire, allegiance, and obedience. The complexity that marked Epictetus would also in similar ways mark Paul and his audience. These understandings of obedience would be woven with nuance, subtlety, and show forth the tension(s) that existed in the realm of obedience and empire.

---

[1] Livy would be another excellent example of the intersection between philosophy and history, but it is harder to trace the Stoic influence. See Ronald Mellor, *The Roman Historians* (New York: Routledge, 1998), 50.
[2] A. A. Long, *Epictetus: A Stoic and Socratic Guide to Life* (New York: Oxford University Press, 2002), 10; C. Kavin Rowe, *One True Life: The Stoics and Early Christians as Rival Traditions* (Grand Rapids: Eerdmans, 2016), 43–4.

In this chapter, the philosophers' discourses on obedience form a natural parallel with Paul's aims to persuade and motivate communities across the Mediterranean to pursue a way of life that bears a striking resemblance to the goals of philosophers in the ancient world.[3] Our focus will be limited, given the parameters of this study, and focus on Aristotle, Cicero, Seneca the Younger, Epictetus, and Plutarch. These authors are chosen for a variety of factors including: (1) their influence on subsequent tradition; (2) quality of illustrative examples; and (3) their proximity to Paul and the writing of Romans.[4] This survey aims to show the multiplicity of ways that obedience language was used within the philosophical frameworks of the ancient world. The primary purpose is to see how obedience shaped the thought and ethics of persons in Paul's world.

Obedience in Aristotle

We begin with Aristotle whose influence on subsequent philosophy, politics, and ethics is unsurpassed. The main focus in this chapter will surround his *Politics* and *Nicomachean Ethics* (*EN* hereafter), although we will draw on more works than these to show how Aristotle sets out the parameters of the philosophical and ethical discussion of obedience. It is his discussions of justice and obedience that will prove important for all those who follow.

Aristotle's twin topics of cities and ethics are intertwined. Malcolm Schofield draws our attention to the relationship between *polis* and *ethos* as "ethics—as its name indicates—is the subdivision of politics concerned with understanding the *habits* (italics original) of character which constitute the moral virtues necessary for human fulfillment."[5] To restate this, Aristotle's *Politics* and *EN* deal with the same subjects but from different angles. To use Aristotle's own words, "The true statesman seems to be one who has made a special study of goodness, since his aim is to make the

---

[3] Abraham J. Malherbe, *Paul and the Philosophers* (Minneapolis: Fortress, 1989); Wayne A. Meeks, *The Moral World of the First Christians* (Philadelphia: Westminster, 1986); John E. Stambaugh and David L. Balch, *The New Testament in Its Social Environment*, ed. Wayne A. Meeks (Philadelphia: Westminster, 1986); Troels Engberg-Pedersen, ed., *Paul in His Hellenistic Context* (Edinburgh: T&T Clark, 1994); Troels Engberg-Pedersen, *Paul and the Stoics* (Louisville: Westminster John Knox, 2000); James W. Thompson, *Moral Formation According to Paul: The Context and Coherence of Pauline Ethics* (Grand Rapids: Baker, 2011); Runar M. Thorsteinsson, *Roman Christianity and Roman Stoicism* (New York: Oxford University Press, 2010); Tuomas Rasimus, Troels Engberg-Pedersen, and Ismo Dunderberg, eds., *Stoicism in Early Christianity* (Grand Rapids: Baker, 2010); Edwin A. Judge, *Social Distinctives of Christians in the First Century: Pivotal Essays by E. A. Judge*, ed. David M. Scholer (Peabody: Hendrickson, 2008). One must be aware that such comparisons are never one for one and fraught with potential for misunderstanding. Such issues have been raised by Rowe, *One True Life*, 1–12. Rowe raises critical methodological reflections on the nature of comparative work that must be considered. Although when stressed too much the traditions become unrecognizable to one another, or in Rowe's terms "incommensurable difference" fundamentally breaks down. Although his point about the traditions being rivals for a way of life is exactly correct.
[4] By proximity I mean both chronologically and also in aims and intentions, like Epictetus.
[5] Malcolm Schofield, "Aristotle: An Introduction," in *The Cambridge History of Greek and Roman Political Thought* (ed. Christopher Rowe and Malcolm Schofield, New York: Cambridge University Press, 2006), 310.

citizens good and obedient (ὑπηκόους) to the laws" (*EN* 1.13). At the outset, therefore, Aristotle's ethics and politics are intertwined, and obedience forms an important part of his political and ethical framework.

In several places in the *Politics*, Aristotle discusses obedience and its relationship to the dialectical aspect of politics—those who rule and those who are ruled. In 3.2.7, he notes, "We praise the ability to rule and to be ruled (ἄρχω), and it is doubtless held that the goodness of a citizen consists in ability both to rule and to be ruled well." Key to both aspects of ruling and being ruled are obedience and justice. Aristotle makes this clear in 1.5.5: "For if the ruler is not temperate and just (δίκαιος), how will he rule well? And if the ruled, how will he obey (ἄρχω) well?"

The success of any political program is contingent, for Aristotle, on both ruler and subjects possessing virtue. The virtue of the ruler is highlighted in 8.3.4-5: "Hence in case there is another person who is our superior in virtue and in practical capacity for the highest functions, him it is noble to follow and him it is just to obey (πείθω); though he must possess not only virtue but also capacity that will render him capable of action." How ought a community respond to such an individual? Aristotle argues that "it only remains for the community to obey (πείθω) such a man, and for him to be sovereign not in turn but absolutely" (3.12.13). A just and virtuous leader commands the obedience of the community. It is persons like these that Aristotle suggests "all" are required to obey and to make kings "for all times" (3.2.7). We see the intertwining discourse of obedience, lordship, and community that makes for a thriving polis.

Alongside the virtue of the king and an obedience community, Aristotle acknowledges the insufficient nature of these elements for a well-run *polis* by themselves. In addition to these, laws are essential to the *polis*, as is the development of virtue among its citizens, as "one form of good government must be understood to consist in the laws enacted being obeyed (πείθω), and another form in the laws which the citizens keep being well enacted (for it is possible to obey (πείθω) badly enacted laws)" (4.6.3-4).

Obedience is central to a well-run political program; laws are, of course, a necessary component, although even Aristotle remarks that "the law has no power to compel obedience (ὑπάρχω)" (2.5.14). Where Aristotle applies reason, Paul applies the Spirit. For Aristotle, this opens up the possibility that, even if one enjoyed a virtuous king and impeccable laws, there remains a weakness in the framework. Some would be unwilling to obey and thus a king needs the power to enforce obedience (3.10.10).

In addition to the virtuous king, the "best laws" (4.6.3), and the power to enforce them, one more item is needed for a thriving community. The citizens must be virtuous for the political program to function properly. The development of virtue within those ruled forms the focus of Aristotle's *EN* to which we now turn.

At the end of *EN*, Aristotle focuses on the life of those living within the *polis*:

Accordingly we shall need laws to regulate the discipline of adults as well, and in fact the whole life of the people generally; for the many are more amenable to compulsion and punishment than obedient (πειθῶ) to reason and to moral ideals. Hence some persons hold, that while it is proper for the lawgiver to encourage and exhort men to virtue on moral grounds, in the expectation that those who have had a virtuous moral upbringing will obey (ὑπακούω), yet he is bound to impose chastisement and penalties on the disobedient (ἀπειθέω) and ill-conditioned, and to banish the incorrigible out of the state altogether. For (they argue) although the virtuous man, who guides his life by moral ideals, will be obedient (πειθαρχέω) to reason, the base, whose desires are fixed on pleasure, must be chastised by pain, like a beast of burden. (10.9.9-10)

For Aristotle, the two types of citizens are the virtuous person and the base person. What separates these two is obedience to reason that marks the "virtuous man."[6] Virtue and obedience are related to one another as virtue is obedient to reason or the "rational principle."[7] The virtuous person can discern between good and evil and have the self-control to choose the virtuous. Elsewhere Aristotle will note, "He who disobeys this right Principle is self-indulgent, while he who obeys it and is not led by his desires is self-controlled" ([*Mag. mor.*] 2.6.18). Obedience is tied to the pursuit of virtue and self-control (cf. Rom. 6:12).[8] Obedience, therefore, takes on a particular moral connotation that is important in the pursuit of virtue. But in what domain might one learn such principles? Unsurprisingly, Aristotle turns to the smallest microcosm of community in the ancient world—the home.

Not only is the lawgiver or philosopher essential to advancing in virtue, but the social domain of parenthood is also a primary location of obedience language in Aristotle. Several times throughout the *NE*, the upbringing of children is key, not only to metaphors for obedience (3.8-9) but also in the effort to provide practical examples of obedience and justice in microcosm.[9] A primary example of this is *EN* 10.14-15:

Paternal exhortations and family habits have authority in the household, just as legal enactments and national customs have authority in the state, and the more so on account of the ties of relationship and of benefits conferred that unite the head of the household to its other members: he can count on their natural affection and obedience (εὐπειθέω) at the outset.

The role of the home and the relationship between father and child serves at the most basic level as a representation of the type of obedience expected at the political level. Just as the natural world is obedient to the "laws of God," obedience in the home teaches one to obey the laws of the state.[10] Hence, some light is shed on Paul's citation of rebellion to parents in Rom. 1:30.

The keeping of laws is also tied to justice. As Aristotle states in *Metaphysics* 11.3.6, "The just (δίκαιος) man is 'one who is obedient to the laws' ... the unjust man (ἄδικος)

---

[6] Cf. *Eth. nic.* 1.7.13-14, *Pol.* 4.9.4.
[7] "And virtue cannot be in opposition to Virtue; since its very nature is to obey rational Principle" ([*Mag. mor.*] 2.3.13).
[8] See Luke Timothy Johnson, "Transformation of the Mind and Moral Discernment in Paul," in *Contested Issues in Christian Origins and the New Testament: Collected Essays* (Boston: Brill, 2013), 255–76.
[9] See *Rhet.* 2.12.3; *Eth. nic.* 1.13.18-9, 3.12.16-7, 9.2, 10.12; *Soph. elench.* 12.2, 15.40; *Top.* 1.14.20.
[10] *Cael.* 400B; 401A.

will not be entirely deprived of the whole definition, but will be 'one who is in some respect deficient in obedience to the laws.'" Or, as in Aristotle's *Rhetoric to Alexander*, "Doing justice means following the common customs of the city, obeying the laws, and abiding by one's agreements" (2.2.24).[11] For Aristotle, obedience and justice are linked to the laws and customs of the city. To break the law, therefore, is to practice a form of injustice and not pursue virtue or wisdom.[12] Here, as in Paul, there is a connection between δίκαιος and obedience, and both bear on behavior. Indeed, Aristotle regards disobeying the laws as injustice:

> And it belongs to unrighteousness to transgress ancestral customs and regulations, to disobey the laws and the rulers, to lie, to perjure, to transgress covenants and pledges. Unrighteousness is accompanied by slander, imposture, pretense of kindness, malignity, unscrupulousness. ([*Virt. vit.*] 7.1-5)

Aristotle uses a vice list to detail his definition of unrighteousness (cf. Rom. 1:18-32). Disobedience and unrighteousness are linked and are made manifest in particular vices. Further, these are connected to the ability of a community to flourish.

Although not every aspect of Aristotle's understanding of obedience is paralleled in Paul—nor should that be expected—the importance of Aristotle is that he provides the foundation and framework for subsequent philosophical and political systems into the time of Paul. The ideas of justice along with obedience and disobedience within the political and moral spheres of ancient life would continue to exercise influence on subsequent philosophers. Aristotle's account is particularly important for Paul's discussion in Rom. 13:1-7, where Paul likewise assumes that the ruler is just and that he is administering actual justice and should thus be rendered submission.

Obedience in Epictetus

Obedience appears most frequently in the *Discourses*, which will form the focus of our efforts in this section.[13] Early on in the *Discourses*, Epictetus compares oaths to political leaders and a deity. In 1.14.16-18, within a discussion of an omnipresent god, Epictetus remarks that "to this god you also ought to swear allegiance, as the soldiers do to Caesar" (1.14.15). Epictetus draws a comparison between the allegiance due to a god and that due to Caesar. However, he is quick to point out the differences between such oaths. Epictetus contrasts the dedication of the soldiers to Caesar with the person who has "been counted worthy of blessings so numerous and so great" (1.14.15) from a deity. The blessings from the deity are so great that to reject the oath would be absurd. For those who take the oath, Epictetus emphasizes the importance of

---

[11] Aristotle also discusses obedience and disobedience to contracts and covenants in *Rhet.* 1.25.21-3.
[12] Cf. *Metaph.* 1.2.3.
[13] *OCD*, 532. See A. A. Long, *Epictetus: A Stoic and Socratic Guide to Life* (New York: Oxford University Press, 2002).

abiding by it (1.14.16). The oath to the deity, although similar to the oath to Caesar, is of a surpassing quality given the nature of the benefits received.

Epictetus details the parameters of the oath to god as "never to disobey under any circumstances, never to prefer charges, never to find fault with anything that God has given, never to let your will rebel when you have either to do or to suffer something that is inevitable" (1.14.16). The oath to the deity is an oath of obedience. Epictetus concludes this discourse by once again comparing the oaths to the deity and those offered to Caesar. He comments, "Can the oath of the soldiers in any way be compared with this of ours? Out there men swear never to prefer another in honor above Caesar; but here we swear to prefer ourselves in honor above everything else" (1.14.17-18). The oath to the deity far surpasses the oath made to a human ruler, even—or one may even say, despite—an oath offered to Caesar.

Epictetus's discourse is important for our study of Romans as it provides a near-contemporary explanation of how a person living in the Roman world might manage loyalty to both God and Caesar. A fruitful comparison arises as we bring together Epictetus's notion of an oath to Caesar and the loyalties at stake in Paul's conception of the covenant (cf. Rom. 9:1-3).[14]

For Epictetus, these loyalties are not antithetical, even though the oath to God is superior and appears to be the oath of higher importance. Paul would certainly agree with this conclusion. We might imagine a scenario in the Roman house churches where a member might wonder how their loyalty to Jesus is related to other relationships in the political world of their day. We see Paul discussing similar realities in Rom. 13:1-7, and Epictetus's account shows at least one approach to managing those loyalties. Given the current political realities of Paul's audience, it appears, at least from Epictetus, that an individual could prioritize his oath to a deity over that of an emperor. Although not as important as the writing of Romans during the *Quinquennium* of Nero, it would certainly become relevant for the Early Christians soon as they navigated the ever-changing landscape of Rome's political leadership.

Another important example of obedience language occurs in 4.12 in a similar context as the example above, this time with the language of submission. In a discourse "on attention," he discusses external disturbances that may distract one's focus. His first example is that of the tyrant. "What kind of tyrant inspires fear?" (4.12.9).[15] Similar language appears in Rom. 13:3 in the opposite sense, namely "For rulers are not a terror to good conduct." The tyrant is not an acceptable distraction. As Epictetus notes, "He is not my judgment, is he?—No.—Why, then, do I care any longer?—But he has the reputation of being somebody … but I have one whom I must please, to whom

---

[14] Perhaps the closest idea is Paul's use of ἀσυνθέτους (covenant breaker) in Rom. 1:32. The term διαθήκη only appears in Rom. 9:4 and 11:27, but the concept of covenant would raise the issue of loyalty.

[15] The same phrase appears in *Diatr.*, 4.7.1 and the similar discussion in *Diatr.*, 4.7.30-33 (31) "Take him off to prison," says the tyrant about me. "I follow, because that is part of the game." "But your head will be taken off." "And does the tyrant's head always stay in its place, and the heads of you who obey him? … (33) Oh yes, but statements like these make men despise the laws.—Quite the contrary, what statements other than these make the men who follow them more ready to obey the laws? Law is not simply anything that is in the power of a fool."

I must submit (ὑποτάσσω), whom I must obey, that is, God, and after Him, myself" (4.12.10-11). There is an inherent relationship between submission and obedience. Submission is the first stage on the way to further obedience, where submission may be the acknowledgment of power or superiority to whom obedience is owed.

The ability to pursue submission and obedience to a god despite the pressure of a tyrant is given an explanation a few discourses earlier in discourse 4.7, titled "of freedom from fear." Epictetus argues that despite the natural inclination to fear a tyrant because of swords and spears, he charges, "I have considered all this, no one has authority over me. I have been set free by God, I know His commands, no one has power any longer to make a slave of me" (4.7.17). Epictetus's admonition that the person who is set free by God cannot be enslaved by another power is in stark contrast with Paul's admonition in Rom. 6:22 about being set free from sin to be enslaved again to God himself (cf. Rom. 6:18, 8:1-3). Paul has a more limited sense of freedom as mitigated freedom to love and serve God.

The importance of this section in the *Discourses* is not only the combination of obedience to both the tyrant and a god as in 1.14.16-18 but also the combination of obedience and submission language. In this example, Epictetus combines the verbs ὑποτάσσω (to submit) and πείθω (to obey). Their order appears important: submission precedes obedience.[16] Such an example bears directly on Rom. 13:1 and Paul's admonition to submit to the governing authorities, which utilizes the same terms.

The nature of knowledge of and obedience to God also forms part of Epictetus's emphasis on moral progress. He argues that knowledge of the divine and their attributes provides a model to follow in obedience. The overall aim of Epictetus is to admonish his students to be imitators of god (2.14.13). But how does one do this? Epictetus lays out the following. Once one has acknowledged god (2.14.11), the imitation of the divine is the second stage of development. In a way reminiscent of Paul's statements in Rom. 1:19-20, Epictetus remarks on the reality of a god's existence, their provision for the world, and even the inability to hide one's thoughts or plans from the divine (2.14.11). In light of this existence, Epictetus notes that the student should "learn what the gods are like" because emulation of their character is essential to the one who wants "to please and obey them" (2.14.12). Epictetus lists several character traits, such as faithfulness. "If the deity is faithful, he also must be faithful" (2.14.13). Pleasing the divine and not incurring wrath is a staple of Greco-Roman religion, and Epictetus falls within these expectations.

In this section of the *Discourses* we have the combination of the verbs ἀρέσκω (to please) and πείθω (to persuade), indicating that obedience is tied to pleasing the divine. Of importance for our study of Romans is Paul's argument in Rom. 8:8, where those who are in the flesh and are unable to *please* God. For those in Paul's audience familiar with some elements of Stoic philosophy, this idea may have sounded familiar. Similarly, Paul posits that those in the flesh cannot please God because they cannot obey God or his laws.[17] However, the inability of those in the flesh to please God in

---

[16] Cf. *Ench.*, 31.1; *Diatr.*, 4.1.15, where in speaking of Diogenes, Epictetus states, "Nor would he have suffered another to yield them more obedience and submission."

[17] Cf. Epictetus *Diatr.*, 3.12.13, 24.43; 4.4.32; 4.12.12; to commands 1.25.14.

Paul is because the flesh is hostile to God and does not submit to the law of God (Rom. 8:7-8).

Another important example of obedience language in connection with wrath language appears in *Discourses* 3.1.37. Epictetus exhorts his students, "Come then, let us obey God, that we rest not under His wrath (θεοχόλωτος)." Although a different word, θεοχόλωτος, a combination meaning "God-anger," it seems to carry the same connotation as Paul's use of wrath in several places in Romans (1:18, 2:5, 8; 3:5; 5:9; 9:22, 12:19). Disobedience is connected to divine wrath both in Epictetus and in Paul.[18] In the *Discourses*, this disobedience is characterized as a battle with god and "the wages of this fighting against God and this disobedience (ἀπειθείας) will not be paid by 'children's children,' but by me myself in my own person" (3.24.24).[19] As mentioned above, wrath language in connection with Roman deities is not uncommon in the wider religious discourse of the Roman Empire.[20]

This section bears striking parallels to several places in Romans. First, disobedience is characterized as wages or debt, such as in Rom. 3:23; and second, disobedience is punished "in the person," as in Rom. 1:27. Further, in *Diatr.* 2.16.45, obedience is contrasted with unrighteousness and lawlessness. "It was therefore in obedience to His [god's] will that he went about clearing away wickedness and lawlessness" (see Rom. 2:8; 6:13, 17–19).[21]

Epictetus, known for his warm religious language, shows how obedience to God manifested itself in philosophical thought. Obedience to God is the primary way that obedience language is used in the *Discourses*. Epictetus's remarks on loyalties to God and the emperor are a helpful parallel for the early Christian communities and particularly for Paul's admonitions in Rom. 13:1 about submission to the governing authorities.

Obedience in Plutarch

Although we briefly treated Plutarch at the end of Chapter 3, the focus there was on select examples from Plutarch as it related to Rome's rule over the nations and the subsequent obedience they demanded. Our focus here will be broader. Plutarch is again a highly valuable resource for the study of obedience language within the first century due to his chronological proximity to the New Testament writings. The majority of obedience language in Plutarch occurs in *The Lives* and the *Moralia* as such the focus will primarily be on these texts.

Perhaps Plutarch's most famous and greatest literary achievement is his collection of *Parallel Lives*.[22] Within the *Lives*, obedience functions in various ways, and numerous

---

[18] On obedience to God in Epictetus see *Diatr.*, 1.29.29; 2.10.6-8; 3.24.95-97; 3.24.111; 3.26.29; 4.3.10; to Zeus 2.23.42. Obedience to the philosopher *Diatr.*, 3.1.16-18.
[19] Obedience to God's commands is also given the metaphor of obeying the laws of the state (*Diatr.*, 3.24.107).
[20] See Reinhard Gregor Kratz and Hermann Spieckermann, eds., *Divine Wrath and Divine Mercy in the World of Antiquity* (Tübingen: Mohr Siebeck, 2008).
[21] Epictetus is speaking of Heracles and he is described as a "friend of God."
[22] *OCD*, 1201.

individuals are signaled out for their obedience or disobedience. For example, Plutarch praises Agesilaus, the son of Archidamus king of the Lacedaemonians, for his obedience (*Ages.* 15.4). More importantly, obedience to authority is seen as a righteous or just activity and as an example for others to follow.[23] Plutarch notes, "When confronting a dangerous crisis, to be of one mind in paying obedience to an authority which is absolute, and holds the scales of justice in its own hands" (*Cam.* 18.6). Plutarch links wisdom with obedience to the authority figure that dispenses justice. Behind such logic is of course the discourse of power and justice defined in a particular way.

Likewise, in *Lycurgus*, Thales is praised for his "exhortations to obedience and harmony" (4.2), leading Plutarch to remark that "people [were] justly punished for disobeying laws" (15.2).[24] The connection between obedience and righteousness or justice is expressed and important for this study as Paul's aims in Romans are nothing less than an exhortation to obedience (Rom. 1:5). Likewise, in the second example, the ideas of just punishment for disobedience, or in Pauline terms "unrighteousness," is seen in Rom. 1:18-32.[25] This will be explored more in the subsequent chapters where obedience and righteousness are linked.

How might Plutarch align with the broad discourse of the nations and obedience that was established in the previous chapters? Several examples in the *Lives* are similar to the evidence we found in the historians for the obedience of the nations due to Rome. In his life of Caesar, Plutarch records that Caesar was successful and "overpowered them, and marched on as far as the outer sea, subduing the tribes which before were not obedient (ὑπακούω) to Rome" (12.1).[26] As was seen in the previous chapters in the historians, Rome's horizon of victory extended widely to bring the nations into obedience to themselves (cf. Rom. 1:5).[27]

Two final examples of obedience in the *Lives* merit further attention, and both revolve around the issue of obedient subjects and the character of leadership. Proper obedience for Plutarch is easily given to leaders who exercise virtue and rule justly. In *Lycurgus* 30.2, Plutarch praises Sparta for keeping subjects in obedience and establishing justice for the city. Although an ancient example, it shows for Plutarch's audience a model of just obedience.[28] By removing injustice in the form of tyranny,

---

[23] Obedience is often connected to following commands; see Plutarch, to country *Ages.* 4.2; *Ant.* 34.3; *Art.* 26.5, 35.5; *Caes.* 33.2; *Comp. Eum. Sert.* 1.1; *Demetr.* 15.1; *Dion.* 10.1; *Fab.* 4.2; *Galb.* 22.4, 22.8; *Gen. Socr.* 595B; *Lyc.* 2.3; 16.4-6 (3x); not obeying officers *Lys.* 10.5; 23.2; *Mar.* 14.4; soldiers taking oath to obey Vitellius as emperor *Marc.* 3.4; *Oth.* 4.4; *Pel.* 9.4; *Phil.* 9.8; *Phoc.* 10.5; *Pomp.* 41.1, 59.2; *Rom.* 3.4; *Sert.* 3.2; *Sol.* 8.3; *Ti. C. Gracch.* 17.4; *Tim.* 10.1.

[24] Persuasion is also tied to obedience in *Pomp.* 13.2 where Pompey seeks to persuade his soldiers to obey. This again shows the connection between the πειθ root and obedience (see Chapters 3 and 4).

[25] This is further supported in Plutarch, *Cor.* 16.3, where disobedience leads to destruction.

[26] Other examples of obedience nations are seen in Plutarch, *Cim.* 1.3, where nations obey other nations, others are persuaded to obey, and the leaders' goal is to secure "prompt obedience." See also the account in *Galb.* 4.2, where Fabius hopes that the citizens will become more submissive and obedient to his commands (cf. Rom. 13:1).

[27] A readiness to obey is seen in *Ages.* 2.1; *Arat.* 11.1; *Lyc.* 3.7 (of women); on nature of people *Praec. ger. rei publ.* 20.

[28] One should not miss that Plutarch alludes to Virgil's *Georg.* 4.2. The same line is in Seneca. Cf. Seneca, *Clem.* 4.2-3; *Ep.* 114.2.

Sparta was able to keep Hellas obedient. Both the ability to rule well on the part of the authorities and the obedience of the subjects lead to justice (cf. Rom. 6:16; 13:1).

If the Spartans are Plutarch's positive example of good governance leading to obedient subjects, the negative example occurs in his life of *Galba*. In the aftermath of the death of Nero, Plutarch remarks, "An empire has nothing more fearful to show than a military force given over to untrained and unreasoning impulses" (*Galb*. 1.3-4). Plutarch ties this fear to an untrained and disobedient military, saying, "A good commander or general can do nothing unless his army is amenable and loyal; and he [Plato] thinks that the quality of obedience, like the quality characteristic of a king, requires a noble nature and a philosophic training" (1.3).[29]

The importance of this final example from the *Lives* is the contrast formed between this period in Roman history and that of Rom. 13:1-4. Such a context shows the importance of understanding Paul's admonitions to the Roman communities in a historically sensitive manner. If Paul wrote Romans sometime between 55 and 56 CE, during the *quinquennium Neronis*, then statements such as "for rulers cause no fear for good conduct but for bad" (Rom. 13:3) make appropriate sense of the times. In a span of no less than fifteen years, the situation would be drastically changed, and Plutarch bears witness to this new situation. In the aftermath of Nero's death, with disobedient and rebellious armies, there was plenty to fear in Rome.

Plutarch's *Moralia* contains numerous examples of obedience. Several require our attention here.[30] Often the terms for obedience occur in contexts of obedience to reason or laws.[31] Obedience to God is also mentioned (*Adul. amic.* 25F), and obedience to God and reason can be combined, such as in *De Auditu*, "But you have often heard that to follow God and to obey (πείθω) reason are the same tilling" (37D).[32] Likewise, obedience occurs within the social contexts of men and women, children, and parents, as well as youth and elders.[33] Obedience to authority within the structuring of the political order is also a repeated theme.[34]

---

[29] See the further example in Plutarch, *Galb*. 22.3-4. Then their officers began to fear that their lawless spirit might issue in revolt, and one of them made this speech: "What is wrong with us, my fellow soldiers? We are neither supporting the present emperor nor setting up another. It is as though we were averse, not to Galba, but to all rule and obedience."

[30] One unique occurrence in Plutarch is his reference to a temple that some think is to obedience: "He [Corilianus], accordingly, built on the Capitoline ... the Temple of Fortuna Obsequens, which some think means 'obedient' and others 'gracious'" (*Fort. Rom.* 322F).

[31] On obeying laws see Plutarch, *Ages.* 1.2; *Amat.* 761F; *Brut.* 29.4; *Cam.* 17.4; *Cat. Min.* 8.2; *Comp. Ag. Cleom. cum Ti. Gracch.* 9.3 (2x); of on obedience to the commands of God *[Cons. Apoll.]* 111E; oracles *Gen. Socr.* 578B; *[Lib. ed.]* 7E; *Mar.* 29.4, 42.3; *Quaest. conv.* 655D; *Quaest. rom.* 55; of an inscription *Tranq. an.* 472C; *Vit. Pud.* 534E. Disobey *Fort.* 570D; *Lycg*15.2.

[32] On obeying reason see Plutarch, *Coheb. ira* 453C; training curiosity to obey reason *Curios.* 13; *Inim. util.* 90C; *Rect. rat. aud.* 26E; *Virt. mor.* 445B. Disobedient to reason *Philosophers and Men in Power* 777D; *Quaest. plat.* 1008B.

[33] Cf. Plutarch, *Sayings of Spartan Women* 242B of women; *An seni* 789E of youth; *Frat. amor.* 487C to elders (2x); *Inst. Lac.* 237D of young men to fathers.

[34] To authority see Plutarch *[Apoph. lac.]* 236E to a commander; *Inst. Lac.* 237E; *An seni* 797D of a master. To the political order see Plutarch, *Praec. ger. rei publ.* 814F, "However, the statesman, while making his native State readily obedient to its sovereigns ... [must not] bring the reproach of slavery upon their country." Cf. *Praec. ger. rei publ.* 815E. Also helpful is 816F, "It is a most excellent and useful thing to learn to obey those in authority, even if they happen to be deficient in power and reputation."

One helpful example of obedience occurs in Plutarch's essay, *Concerning Talkativeness*, where he takes Odysseus as a moral example of self-control. In building this example, Plutarch uses Homer's *Odyssey* as his source material. To emphasize self-control, Plutarch recounts the death of Odysseus's wife and his ability to withhold tears (*Od.* 19.210-12).[35] Plutarch remarks, "So full of self-control was his [Odysseus] body in every limb, and Reason, with all parts in perfect obedience and submission, [He] ordered his eyes not to weep, his tongue not to utter a sound, his heart not to tremble or bark: His heart remained enduring in obedience" (506A–B).[36]

Several important aspects of this example are worthy of comment in light of our material in Romans. First, commonplace in ancient ethical works is the use of a moral example—in this case, Odysseus. We could compare this with Paul's use of Christ as an example of obedience in Rom. 5:15-21 that forms a basis for the Roman audience's obedience. Certainly some components of being "in Christ" revolve around the idea of imitation. Second, perhaps most importantly, Plutarch's connection between obedience and the heart concerning Odysseus perhaps comes closest to Paul's praise for the Romans' obedience from the heart (6:17). Finally, this is another occurrence of obedience and submission occurring as near synonyms (cf. Rom. 13:1).

A final example will conclude our short survey of obedience in Plutarch's work. In his discourse on *Progressing in Virtue*, as part of a discussion of controlling the impulses of the body by reason, Plutarch argues that if the "irrational impulse" has "already been rendered obedient and gentle by reason" (83B) then sleep or illness will not cause the body to retreat into the irrational. Since the impulses have been rendered obedient, a habit is now formed. The process of forming the habit is particularly illuminating:

> For if the body by virtue of training is actually capable of rendering itself and its members so obedient (ὑπήκοος) to its injunctions of indifference that the eyes refrain from tears at a piteous sight, and the heart from throbbing in the midst of terrors, and the passions chastely remain unexcited and undisturbed in the presence of youthful or maidenly beauty, is it not indeed even more probable that training, by taking hold of the emotional element in the soul, will, as it were, do away with the irregularities and vagaries of our fancies and incitements, and carry its repression of them even into our slumbers? (83B–C)

Plutarch draws an analogy from training the body, something Paul is quite capable of as well (cf. Rom. 12:4; 1 Cor. 12:12; 1 Cor. 9:27). Plutarch's point appears to be that just as one can train the physical body, one can train one's impulses by reason and form habits. Of interest for our study is Plutarch's attention to making one's "members obedient," which is similar to Paul's point found in Rom. 6:12-13, 6:19; 7:5 and Paul's admonition on not obeying the body's desires and offering one's members to unrighteousness or disobedience. The striking difference between Plutarch and Paul is obvious. Whereas for Plutarch, reason is the power at work in bringing the body

---

[35] Plutarch also discusses obedience in connection with the vice of anger; see Plutarch, *Cohib. ira* 455B.
[36] The last line is a direct quote from Homer, *Od.* 20.23. On obedience of the body see Plutarch, *Garr.* 503C the tongue; *Gen. Socr.* 591E the soul; *Tu. san.* 123C; *Virt. mor.* 442D the body.

and mind into obedience, in Paul this is part of the work of the Spirit and results from having been transferred from the realm of Adam to the new realm of Christ (6:19).

Plutarch offers several helpful examples of obedience and its function in both political and philosophical contexts. His work contains similar conclusions as those of the historians and philosophers of the first century. Obedience was expected of citizens within the empire and contributed to the flourishing of a just society; likewise, disobedience resulted in punishment.

Obedience in Cicero

In turning to Cicero, we shift gears somewhat slightly as the focus shifts more properly to the inhabitants of Rome. Although the nations that Rome subjects are still in view, one receives more of an interior approach from one, if not the, leading Roman political theorist. By interior, we mean that Cicero shapes the Roman discourse for its inhabitants as much as those on the periphery. We begin with *De Republica* and Cicero's contribution to Roman political theory in the tradition of Plato's *Republic*.[37]

According to Cicero, the safety of the state depends on "the wisdom of its best men" (1.34).[38] In the selection of the "best men," Cicero argues that according to nature, "those men who are superior in virtue and in spirit should rule the weaker, but also that the weaker should be willing to obey (*pareo*) the stronger" (1.34). We see laid bare a fundamental Roman position, the strong rule the weak. Rome, not only by its military superiority but one might say also by its own, self-professed, philosophical priority, has garnered such a right. Such a starting point also reveals the incongruity of thought between Roman attitudes and Paul's pastoral and philosophical task. A discussion of weak and strong members resembles Paul's discussion of the similarly named groups in Rom. 14:1–15:13. However, this is where the similarities end. Whereas it may have been "natural" for the Roman Christians who comprised the "strong" group to overrun the weaker, the moral advice they receive is profoundly countercultural at this point.

Also notable is the role that these persons play within the larger sociopolitical landscape and in terms of decisions and actions. We might take as an example, Cicero's discussion of the promises and perils of kingship, when he notes,

> They thought that life, honor, and glory had been granted to them through the justice of their king. And the same good-will toward kings would have abided in their descendants had the true image of kingship abided; but, as you know, it was through the injustice of one man alone that this whole form of government was overthrown. (*Rep.* 1.41)

---

[37] OCD, 1558–64; E. M. Atkins, "Cicero," in *The Cambridge History of Greek and Roman Political Thought*, 477–516; David E. Aune, *The Westminster Dictionary of New Testament and Early Christian Literature and Rhetoric* (Louisville: Westminster John Knox, 2003), 97–9; C. E. W. Steel, *Cicero, Rhetoric, and Empire* (New York: Oxford University Press, 2001), 1–20; C. E. W. Steel, ed., *The Cambridge Companion to Cicero* (New York: Cambridge University Press, 2013).

[38] On obedience to wisdom see Cicero, *Phil.* 13, 3.7, "I am hearing the voice of wisdom and would obey as I would obey a god." Cf. *Resp.* 3.15.

In an analogous way, both Cicero and Paul focus on the actions that one person has on a community. In Rom. 5:1-12, it's the actions of Jesus and Adam that have bearing on humanity that is determinative of existence for others. Such similarity of course is part of the collectivist nature of the Greco-Roman world but still should not be discarded as constituting a broadly shared approach to individuals and power.

Turning to Cicero's *De Legibus*, which was a complementary volume to his *De Republica*, it laid out the laws appropriate to the ideal city. *De Legibus* begins with a discussion of law and an emphasis on right reason.[39] Law is identified with correct reason and forms the base of the relationship between humanity and the divine.[40] As a result of law, people must share justice as well (*Leg*. 1.7). According to Cicero, those who share both law and justice are members of the same commonwealth with one important addition: "If indeed they obey (*pareo*) the same authorities and powers" (*Leg*. 1.7). Authorities and powers, later described as "magistrates," are essential to the "care" of the state (*Leg*. 3.2). Obedience is key to this endeavor. Cicero notes:

> We must also instruct the citizens as to the extent of their obligation to obey (*obtempero*) them. For the man who rules efficiently must have obeyed (*pareo*) others in the past, and the man who obeys (*pareo*) dutifully appears fit at some later time to be a ruler. Thus he who obeys ought to expect to be a ruler in the future, and he who rules should remember that in a short time he will have to obey (*pareo*). And we must provide, as Charondas does in his laws, not only that the citizens be obedient (*obtempero*) and dutiful (*oboedio*) toward the magistrates, but also that they love and honor them. (*Leg*. 3.2)

Obedience is something expected of any citizen, and Cicero notes the vacillating nature of obedience and its rendering. What is fascinating about this account is how obedience prepares one for future political office. Such potential is trotted out in an almost elusive, but anticipatory matter. Cicero lays out the expectations of citizens are also worth comment. In addition to obedience, one offers love and honor as well.

The obedience expected of citizens is built on philosophical assumptions as well. Obedience to the magistrates and those in authority includes obedience to the laws.[41] Cicero notes, "Commands shall be just, and the citizens shall obey (*pareo*) them dutifully and without protest" (*Leg*. 3.3). In this comment, we see that forms of protest are deemed inappropriate to true obedience as they are viewed as an opposition. Cicero presents the "best case scenario" as he assumes that the laws are just, and that those laws

---

[39] On Roman law see Barry Nicholas, *An Introduction to Roman Law* (Oxford: Clarendon Press, 1962); O. F. Robinson, *The Sources of Roman Law: Problems and Methods for Ancient Historians* (New York: Routledge, 1997); Dennis P. Kehoe, "Law and Social Formation in the Roman Empire," in *The Oxford Handbook of Social Relations in the Roman World* (ed. Michael Peachin, New York: Oxford University Press, 2011), 144–66.

[40] On obedience to God see Cicero, *Tusc*. 1.49; *Div*. 1.53.

[41] Obedience to the Senate is often noted; see *Lig*. 7.20 (4x), 22; *Phil*. 6, 3.5, 9 (2x); 4.9; *Phil*. 7, 1.2; 4.14; 9.26 (disobedience equates to war on the Roman people); *Phil*. 13, 6.14; *Prov. cons*. 10.25; *Sest*. 63.143. Obedience to the state or officials of the state is seen in Cicero, *Leg*. 3.4, 7, 19; *Resp*. 1.36, 40 (refusal to obey magistrates); *Off*. 2.7 (tyrant).

correspond to reason (*Leg.* 3.1).[42] Just laws are required to be obeyed, and disobedience is punishable by fines, imprisonment, and lashings (*Leg.* 3.3).[43]

Such an emphasis on obedience to the magistrates and authorities along with the admonition to honor them helps us to understand the expectations placed on the citizens of Rome and those who lived within the empire. Good cities are made up of good laws and good citizens. Those in Rome were to obey, love, and honor those in authority over them.

Although writing much later, but in a world shaped by the Ciceronian ideal, Paul counsels something quite similar. The audience of Romans might have understood the admonitions in 13:1, to submit to the authorities; and 13:7, to give honor to whom honor is due as aspects of being a good citizen. These fall within the parameters of "good citizenship."[44] Although missing in Paul's admonition is "love" of such figures. Perhaps not much should be made of this, as it might be an argument from silence, but it's worth contemplating why Paul might leave out such an admonition. One might also comment that in light of Rom. 13:10, love for one another might be unique as within Cicero's construction love and obedience was to flow up the social ladder. The mutuality of Paul's commands would stand out.

Two sections of Cicero's *Tusculan Disputations* provide important examples of obedience as well. The first example comes in 2.4, where Cicero criticizes philosophers who do not obey their own teachings:

> How few philosophers are found to be so constituted and to have principles and a rule of life so firmly settled as reason requires! How few there are to think that the tenets of their school are not a display of knowledge but a law of life! To control themselves of their own will and obey (*pareo*) their own dogmas! Some of them we may see guilty of such frivolity and vanity that it would have been far better for them never to have been students.

Cicero's rebuke of his fellow philosophers for their hypocrisy bears resemblance to Paul's critique of his fellow Jewish teachers in Rom 2:1-3, 17-23.[45] Both Cicero and Paul

---

[42] Cicero offers a cosmological argument at this point:
> Nothing, moreover, is so completely in accordance with the principles of justice and the demands of Nature (and when I use these expressions, I wish it understood that I mean Law) as is government, without which existence is impossible for a household, a city, a nation, the human race, physical nature, and the universe itself. For the universe obeys God; seas and lands obey the universe, and human life is subject to the decrees of supreme Law. (*Leg.* 3.1)

[43] On obedience to the laws see Cicero, *Clu.* 53.146; *Leg.* 3.8, 13; *Inv.* 1.38; *Resp.* 3.11 (3x); *Tusc.* 4.9 (laws of a philosophical school); 5.31 (to maxims).

[44] Although Cicero's *Att.* 293 is helpful, "I see you are in favor of sending my letter to Caesar. Well, I was very much of the same opinion, especially as it contains nothing unbefitting a loyal citizen—loyal, however, as the times permit. Obedience to them is the precept of all experts on politics."

[45] See a similar idea in Cicero, *Caecin.* 18.52: "Even our authority at home will cease to exist if we allow our slave-boys to obey our orders to the letter only, without paying any attention to the meaning implied in our words."

are critical of teachers who see their schools simply as "displays of knowledge" and do not obey their own teachings.[46]

Another crucial example of obedience is Cicero's discussion of self-mastery in 2.20. Cicero moves his argument to the twofold division of the soul: "one of which is gifted with reason, while the other is destitute of it ... It is man's duty to enable reason to have rule over that part of the soul which ought to obey (*oboedio*)" (2.21.48).[47] When seeking to show how this process takes place, he uses three social metaphors: that of the master and slave, the general and solider, and the parent and son. Each of these examples provides a social context where obedience is assumed.[48] Such a conclusion is reached by Cicero, who concludes his argument, returning to the military image, "The weaker part of his soul was submissive (*pareo*) to reason in the same way that the disciplined soldier obeys the strict commander" (2.21.50).[49]

Such an example is important for several reasons. First, Cicero uses obedience (*oboedio*) and submission (*pareo*) nearly synonymously (cf. Rom. 13:1). More importantly, Cicero's examples from the domestic and military spheres reinforce the point that obedience was assumed within these contexts. Thus to evoke their imagery is to evoke the expectation of obedience as well.

Turning to Romans, slavery metaphors appear in Rom. 5–8, where the ideas of obedience to a master are not far behind. The equivalence of slavery and obedience is supported by another important passage in Cicero. In his *Paradox Stoicorum*, Cicero states:

> All wicked men, therefore, are slaves therefore! Nor is this really so startling a paradox as it sounds. For they do not mean that they are slaves in the sense of chattels that have become the property of their lords by assignment for debt or some law of the state; but if slavery means, as it does mean, the obedience (*oboedio*) of a broken and abject spirit that has no volition of its own, who would deny that all light-minded and covetous people and indeed all the vicious are really slaves? (5.35)

Cicero defines slavery as obedience and having choice revoked. Most important is the metaphorical use of the slavery language, which Cicero goes out of his way to establish. Namely, slaves are persons who are characterized by vices that control them. Such imagery and usage are quite close to Paul's discussion in Rom. 6:16-23; 7:14-20.[50]

---

[46] Cf. Cicero, *Parad.* 5.33.
> First let him curb his lusts, despise pleasures, restrain his angry temper, control his avarice, repulse all the other defilements of the mind; let him start commanding others only when he has himself left off obeying those most unprincipled masters, unseemliness and turpitude: so long as he is subservient to these, he will be altogether unworthy to be deemed not merely a commander but even a free man.

[47] On obedience to reason see Cicero, *Clu.* 58.159 (conscience); *Fat.* 11.25; *Off.* 1.23, 28, 29 (3x); *Tusc.* 2.20; 4.9, 17.

[48] Obedience in a specifically religious context is seen in Cicero, *Div.* 2.33; *Leg.* 2.8 (2x of priests); *Nat. d.* 2.3.8; *Resp.* 2.1.

[49] Obedience in military contexts is frequently seen in [*Letter to Octavian*] 10.38; (to kings); *Cat.* 4.22; *Fam.* 9.25.2; 15.1.5, 4.10; *Phil. 3* 4.8-9; *Leg. man.* 15.48 (of enemies); *Phil. 5* 11.29-30 (envoys); *Phil. 6* 2.4 (3x); *Phil. 9*, 3.6 (obedience to death); *Rab. Perd.* (to orders) 8.22; *Resp.* 1.39; 3.29; 6.11.

[50] See Dale B. Martin, *Slavery as Salvation: The Metaphor of Slavery in Pauline Christianity* (New Haven: Yale University Press, 1990), 1–49.

One final example in Cicero concludes this section. Its importance is the combination of the terms of faith, obedience, justice, and persuasion—usage not dissimilar from what will be seen with Paul. In his discussion on the importance of rhetoric and persuasion, he offers the following remark:

> Consider another point; after cities had been established how could it have been brought to pass that men should learn to keep faith (*fides*) and observe justice and become accustomed to obey (*pareo*) others voluntarily and believe not only that they must work for the common good but even sacrifice life itself, unless men had been able by eloquence to persuade their fellows of the truth of what they had discovered by reason? Certainly only a speech at the same time powerful and entrancing could have induced one who had great physical strength to submit to justice without violence. (*Inv.* 1.2.3)

Cicero envisions the task of rhetoric and persuasion as essential in bringing people to keep faith, observe justice, and obey others. The task of rhetoric is persuasion to *this* truth.[51] Such a task aligns with Rome's purpose as "the people of Rome and eternal glory for their city, which has compelled the world to obey our rule" (*Pro Murena* 22). Indeed, C. E. W. Steele concludes that Cicero's presentation of Roman acquisition of subjects was a reward to those conquered by the empire. "The Romans do not simply conquer: they make their subjects glad to have been conquered."[52] What might this mean for the inhabitants of Rome? Cicero seems to attempt to argue that rhetoric reduces the need for brute force. Something born out and not born out by Roman history. As we saw in the historians, Rome did try to compel nations to enter into treaties with them, but if this failed, then often brutal force was nearby to ensure the desired outcome. What is remarkable is how Cicero aligns keeping faith and customary obedience in an almost parallel fashion. Such a pairing reveals the complementary nature of faith and obedience.

Cicero's aims at persuading individuals to accept the truth certainly parallel Paul's aims in Romans or any philosopher or teacher for that matter. However, Paul's persuasive task is quite unlike Cicero's in one important aspect: the truth Paul presents is not something discoverable by reason. Rather, obedience and faith are tasks given to Paul by God, and ultimately, this is a justice revealed by God himself (cf. Rom. 1:16-17). However, to a different end, it is for the nations. Paul, likewise, unites the concepts of nations, obedience, justice, and rhetoric. Romans is at some level just this rhetorical program.

Cicero's work shows several examples of how obedience language was used in various kinds of discourse. Obedience to the various functions of the state, whether the Senate, the laws, or the generals, are the primary ways that obedience language is employed in Cicero's works. Cicero helps show the importance of rhetorical discourse in ordering a political society. Likewise, Cicero is particularly beneficial in regards

---

[51] Also similar is Cicero's discussion of Antony, *Ep. Brut.* 17.4, "If he remains loyal (*fide*) and obeys me."
[52] Steel, *Cicero, Rhetoric, and Empire*, 75.

to understanding how obedience is used in social metaphors that would have been drawn from everyday life, such as slavery and parent–child relationships. Finally, Cicero is quite instructive for our understanding of how obedience functioned in the construction of civic life.

Obedience in Seneca the Younger

The importance of Seneca the Younger is his proximity to Nero. More than any other writer, Seneca provides insight into Nero's reign and thus offers one of the best parallels to the period of the Roman communities with which Paul corresponds.[53] The closer we get to the writing of Romans for examples of obedience in Rome, the better case we have for overlapping narrative programs and for the plausibility of entering into the thought world of the inhabitants of the churches in Rome.

We begin with Seneca's work *De Clementia*, written around 55 or 56 CE, where he advises Nero on mercy (*clementia*). The dating of *De Clementia* and Romans should not be missed. *De Clementia* begins by reminding Nero of the immense power at his disposal (1.1.2-4). This catalog of power centers around the nations and Nero's ability to give them freedom or slavery. Seneca's opening foray showcases the central importance of Nero to the Roman Empire. The ability of a national leader to maintain safety and stability is the reason people pray and defend this "one man" (1.3-4). The desire for safety leads people to go to war on behalf of their leader.[54] Such importance is seen by Seneca's quotation of Virgil: "If safe their king, one mind to all; Bereft of him, they troth recall" (*Georg.* 4.2).[55] The safety of the nation is tied to the safety of their leader. Seneca concludes that the demise of Nero would be to the detriment of the Roman people:

> Such a calamity would be the destruction of the Roman peace, such a calamity will force the fortune of a mighty people to its downfall. Just so long will this people be free from that danger as it shall know how to submit to the rein; but if ever it shall tear away the rein, or shall not suffer it to be replaced if shaken loose by some mishap, then this unity and this fabric of mightiest empire will fly into many parts, and the end of this city's rule will be one with the end of her obedience (*pareo*). (4.2-3)

Seneca posits two dangers in this small section. The first danger is that the removal of Nero would be the removal of stability in the empire. The second danger present in the section is the disobedience of the people that would lead to the fraying of the empire

---

[53] See the helpful volume on other issues related to Paul and Seneca, Joseph R. Dodson and David E. Briones, eds., *Paul and Seneca in Dialogue* (Boston: Brill, 2017).
[54] On obedience in military contexts see Seneca, *Ep.* 59.7; 90.5; *Ira* 9.4; 18.6; [*Octavia*], 458.
[55] Seneca can also use the imagery and quotation of Virgil of the safety of a king as a metaphor for the soul; see Seneca, *Ep.* 114.2, "If the soul lose its balance, down comes all the rest in ruins. If but the king be safe, your swarm will live Harmonious; if he die, the bees revolt. The soul is our king. If it be safe, the other functions remain on duty and serve with obedience; but the slightest lack of equilibrium in the soul causes them to waver along with it."

into dissolution.⁵⁶ Seneca quite plainly indicates that the demise of obedience would result in the demise of Rome. Obedience to the various aspects of Rome's rule is the glue holding the empire together.⁵⁷ Seneca concludes that this "rein" must be moderate and that mercy is key to moderation (5.1-2).

The larger discursive point of Seneca's entire work applies to Romans. The topic of mercy appears at several important places in Romans (9:15-16, 18, 23; 11:30-31; 12:1; 15:9). Both ideas—mercy and obedience—are part of the verbal currency of the day, both in Seneca and Paul. Seneca argues that the gods are merciful (7.2, cf. Rom. 15:9) and likewise that mercy is extended to the disobedient (5.1; Rom. 11:30-31). Further, the importance of obedience for Seneca, essentially tied to the stability of Rome itself, gives proper context for understanding Paul's call for obedience in Rom. 1:5 and his admonition for the Christian communities in Rome to submit to the governing authorities (Rom. 13:1). To be disobedient is a threat to the empire. What we find is that obedience language is in the contemporary discourse of Roman culture in Paul's day and allows us an avenue into the ways the audience of Paul's letter may have perceived his call to obedience.

Slavery and obedience also occur at several places in Seneca's other works, most notably *De Beneficiis*. The importance of slavery and obedience for our study is Paul's use of the imagery to discuss the reigns of Adam and Christ in Rom. 5–6. Seneca notes the inevitability of obedience (*pareo*), from a slave as they cannot refuse or take credit, since obedience is simply what slaves do (3.19.1).⁵⁸ Seneca also notes the logical limits of a slave's obedience: "Nor, indeed, are we able to command all things from slaves, nor are they compelled to obey (*pareo*) us in all things; they will not carry out orders that are hostile to the state, and they will not lend their hands to any crime" (3.20.2). Obedience in this sense is limited by the larger authorities.

Seneca does distinguish between the slavery of the body and mind. While the former "penetrates into the whole being of a man," it is "the mind and reason, [which] are not subject to slavery, only the body" (3.20.2). He seems, somewhat naively, to assume that the mind can remain free from slavery and only the body comes under the command of a master. Of course, Seneca is not concerned and rather well unaware of the physiological and neurological impact of slavery on the human person. The incipient evil of slavery of course did affect both body and mind.

Several aspects of Seneca's discussion of slavery stand out in comparison with Romans. The equation of slavery and obedience is again highlighted by Seneca and was also maintained by Cicero and Epictetus. The invocation of the image carries the assumption of obedience. A slave obeys. Also of importance from *De Beneficiis* are the limits of obedience. Obedience ends when civic laws are transgressed or when requests

---

⁵⁶ Obedience functions several ways in Seneca's writings: Virtue: *Ep.* 67.16; *Vit. beat.* 11.3; Fate: *Ep.* 76.4; 91.5; *De Providentia*, 5.9 (of God); Nature: *Ben.* 5.9.1; *Ep.* 93.2 (2x); 99.21; 107.9; *De Constantia*, 2.1.1 (of women); *Vit. beat.* 13.2 (of virtue); God: *Ep.* 16.5, 76.4; 96.2; *Vit. beat.* 15.4; Reason: *Ep.* 90.5 (2x), 94.44; *Ira* 17.2; Mind: *Ep.* 8.5; Commands/Law: *Ep.* 94.38; *Ira*, 13.6; *Tranq.* 9.1.3, 10; Parents: *Ben.* 3.38.2; One's executioner: *Nat.* 2.59.8; Passions: *Ben.* 2.18.5; contra the Stoics, *Ben.* 4.2.1.

⁵⁷ On obedience to the emperor or his decrees see Seneca, [*Octavia*], 840, 863, *De Ira.* 20.5; *Clem.* 24.2, "The more indulgent the ruler, the better he is obeyed."

⁵⁸ Cf. Seneca, *Ben.* 3.21.2.

would be subversive to the state. Here, the authority of the state transcends the request of the master. Obedience is not blind and unyielding. Analogously, fashion, Rom. 13:1, with the idea of submission to the governing authorities, perhaps also envisions such a caveat. By instructing the Roman communities to submit—that is, obey—Paul does not mean unwavering obedience but obedience to a certain extent, namely the specific situation envisioned in 13:3-4.

We conclude this chapter with an example of obedience in Seneca's treatise *De Vita Beata*. In this moral essay, he utilizes a military metaphor to discuss obedience. In the pursuit of the "happy life," Seneca advises his brother Gallio to follow virtue (15.5). Personifying virtue, Seneca states that virtue, "like a good soldier she will submit to wounds, she will count her scars, and, pierced by darts, as she dies she will love him for whose sake she falls—her commander; she will keep in mind that old injunction, 'Follow God'" (15.6).[59] Seneca concludes, "This is the sacred obligation by which we are bound—to submit to the human lot, and not to be disquieted by those things which we have no power to avoid. We have been born under a monarchy; to obey (*pareo*) God is freedom" (15.7). In a world with limited freedom, Seneca offers a middle way. Given one's "human lot," everyone can experience freedom by obeying God.

The importance of this final example is the utilization of military imagery in moral discourse. Seneca uses the example of a soldier to explain a moral concept. Just as a soldier obeys, so must the virtuous person and the one who desires to have a happy life obey God. The significance of this section is the accessibility of such imagery for moral persuasion. Similarly, Paul likewise utilizes common Roman imagery in his persuasive discourse (cf. Rom. 6). Such a background would have been familiar to many in the Roman world and hence its potency as a metaphor would be apparent.

Although writing from different social positions, both Seneca and Paul are Roman citizens constructing discourses under the reign of Nero of Caesar. Seneca, therefore, serves as a helpful aid in understanding the historical situation at the time of the writing of Romans. Most notable is Seneca's discussion of mercy, slavery, and obedience, topics also occurring in Romans. Although there are significant differences between these concepts and how they are understood and utilized, it shows their importance at this point in the Roman Empire.

Philosophical Reflections on Obedience

From Aristotle to Seneca, obedience forms a central component of their discourses, whether in their admonitions for subjects to be good citizens or their exhortations to allow reason to dominate and provide progress in virtue. The philosophers rely on language and images from the realm of Rome's military and political program. As stated at the onset of this chapter philosophy and history were cross-pollinating endeavors with one another—both forming, supporting, and furthering conceptions of obedience. From Cicero to Epictetus, many philosophers drew on the language of

---

[59] Seneca quotes Cicero, *Fin.* 3.22.

the soldier or war as a way of talking about obedience. Along with slavery, the sphere of the military offered the best examples of obedience in the philosophers. Paul's aims are perhaps closest to the philosopher Epictetus, who offers similar arguments and examples of obedience to both rulers and deities. Historically speaking, the most beneficial works are those of Cicero and Seneca, the latter because of his proximity to Nero. These authors assist our understanding of the empire in the first century. The survey of obedience within the Greek and Latin philosophers shows that obedience language was alive and well at the time of Paul and forms an avenue for how some Roman Gentiles in Paul's audience may have been familiar with such concepts.

6

Sculpting Obedience

How would an illiterate slave perceive the contours of the obedience expected by the empire? Let us imagine that they arrived from Roman conquests in the east and had arrived on a boat in Ostia. As conquests of war, they would have been indirectly—if not directly—familiar with the proclamation that their obedience was now due to Rome and as a result of their local city or town's disobedience has been defeated and were being taken to Rome. They of course would not have access to the historical works of Polybius, Tacitus, and, of course, only passing knowledge of a philosopher. As they made their way from Ostia to the heart of Rome, what would catch their eye? As they went on errands for their master and they passed by the Campus Martius area would anything of note stand out to them? Without access to texts or public readings, how would the nonliterate residents of Rome and—in particular-those in the Roman house churches come to be acquainted with the language of the empire?[1] How did this language of obedience become ingrained and embedded in the topographical aspects of the city of Rome?

In this chapter, we shift gears to look at nonliterary sources in both Rome and the empire to see how obedience and the nations were graphically attested. The translation of the terms of obedience into pictures of obedience is important for an illiterate population. The images could be seen and understood by all who stood in their shadow. The interplay of obedience in images and inscriptions shows forth the relationship between Rome and the provinces with their expectations and reciprocations. This chapter aims to present a more fully orbed picture of obedience in the Roman world. By not only relying on literary texts but also supplementing these with nonliterary images, we gain a fuller picture of the ways obedience would be understood by some in Paul's audience.

---

[1] There is of course good historical reasons to infer and assume that illiterate groups made up the Roman house church(s). Although not named, a good possibility exists in Rom. 16:10-11 and the unnamed persons Paul mentions in the various houses of non-Christians who were most likely the masters of the unnamed persons. See Peter Lampe, *From Paul to Valentinus: Christians at Rome in the First Two Centuries* (Minneapolis: Fortress, 2003), 153–83; Scot McKnight, *Reading Romans: A Gospel of Peace in the Midst of Empire* (Waco: Baylor University Press, 2019), 2–14. See also Susan Matthew, *Women in the Greetings of Romans 16.1-16: A Study of Mutuality and Women's Ministry in the Letter to the Romans* (New York: T&T Clark, 2013), 65–113.

The *Res Gestae*

After his death, on August 19, 14 CE, Augustus had commissioned four documents to be read aloud in the Senate House by the Vestal Virgins (Suet, *Aug.* 101). One of these documents was the *Res Gestae Divi Augusti* (*RG* hereafter). Although the original is now lost, the document was to be published in bronze at the entrance to his mausoleum in the Campus Martius in Rome. Our knowledge of the document comes to us via Ancyra, the capital of Galatia, where both Greek and Latin copies of the document were affixed to the temple dedicated to Rome and Augustus. Smaller fragments of the document have also appeared in Apollonia (Latin) and Pisidian Antioch (Greek) leading some to suggest that copies were disseminated widely throughout the provinces.[2]

The *RG* is important for several reasons. First, it is one of only three sources that are contemporary to the Augustan period. Second, we possess copies of the record in both Latin and Greek.[3] For our concerns in this work, this is immensely helpful as it shows not only the translation of terms in both Latin and Greek but also conveys the importance for both the Greek- and Latin-speaking world(s). We know that the Latin original was to be displayed in Rome, but Greek copies throughout Asia Minor show the importance of the document for non-Latin-speaking regions, as the accompanying introduction to the Greek copy in Ankara explicates.[4] Third, as Karl Galinsky has argued, "It suffices to say that the *Res Gestae* is the most important historical document of the period ... it presents Augustus' own perspective on his achievements and on what he wanted to be understood as their quintessence."[5] Composed late in his life, perhaps around age seventy-five, and perhaps as early as 13 CE. The *RG* contains what Augustus wanted the wider Roman world to know about his rule. In the words of Suna Güven, the *RG* is a "monumental text" in every sense of the word.[6] As an inscription, the *RG* is monumental in that it was inscribed upon monuments in both Rome and the province of Galatia. In another sense of the word, the *RG* is monumental in that it is essentially a self-portrait of Augustus including, describing, and interpreting the events that he deemed most important.

In Rome, the placement of the *RG* in the Campus Martius was of major significance. The area known as the Campus Martius was a "monumentalized open space" that during the Republican period was increasingly filled with temples and monuments of gratitude to the gods for military victories.[7] Matthew Roller has recently reminded us, "Scholars have long recognized that the erection of public monuments in Rome, from the middle

---

[2] *OCD*, 1309.
[3] The insights of Morgan's work ought to bear on this linguistic relationship between Greek and Latin terms for obedience. She argues on the relationship between *pistis* and *fides* that "all individuals, groups, or structures which constantly employ and articulate *fides* language ... translate it with *pistis* language." See Teresa Morgan, *Roman Faith and Christian Faith: Pistis and Fides in the Early Roman Empire and Early Churches* (New York: Oxford University Press, 2015), 27.
[4] The Greek introduction differs from the Latin.
[5] Karl Galinsky, *Augustan Culture: An Interpretive Introduction* (Princeton: Princeton University Press, 1996), 10.
[6] Suna Güven, "Displaying the *Res Gestae* of Augustus: A Monument of Imperial Image for All," *JSAH* 57 (1998): 30.
[7] *OCD*, 284.

Republic into the Augustan age, was an arena of intense competition."[8] Of course, the competition for Augustus was nonexistent, but the placement of his monument, by its very nature, certainly established and furthered this aura of competition. The area included not only Augustus's massive mausoleum, which dominated the area between the Tiber and the Via Flaminia at some eighty-seven meters wide and forty meters high, but also the Pantheon (5 BCE) and the *Ara Pacis* (9 BCE). Such an area was made for visitors and, with the addition of a large park, those strolling through would not only see Augustus's mausoleum bearing the *RG* but also the enormous *Ara Pacis* and the *Horologium* (see later).[9]

It is into the monumental context that Augustus's *RG* was to be inscribed and memorialized. It comes as no surprise, therefore, that the first lines of the *RG* discuss the subjugation of the whole world under the Roman people. The process by which these nations (*gens*/ἔθνη) were subjected was, of course, by war (3.1). As Augustus states, "The foreign nations which could with safety be pardoned I preferred to save rather than to destroy. The number of Roman citizens who bound themselves to me by military oath was about 500,000" (3.1). Although obedience is not explicitly mentioned, it is clear from other historical sources that obedience was crucial to securing peace with Rome, and that destruction awaited those that would not obey (see Chapter 4).

Toward the end of the *RG*, obedience is explicitly mentioned in Augustus's recounting of his deeds. In 26.1, Augustus remarks, "I enlarged the boundaries of all the provinces of the Roman people who bordered peoples (*gens*/ἔθνη) not obedient (*non pareo*/μὴ ὑποτάσσω) to our empire." Such a line is revealing. Augustus divides his empire along the lines of obedience. The nations included in the boundaries of the Roman people are those that are obedient, while those "outside" are the ones not (yet) obedient.

This section also parallels the introduction to the *RG* and augments the subjection language that appears there. The Latin and Greek verbs are similar to what we have seen in our survey of obedience language in the literature of the Roman Empire. It should not be missed that we have the language of obedience in one of the most influential documents of the Roman Empire.

Sections 26–30 of the *RG* lay out the long list of subjected or obedient nations. This includes the Gauls, Spain, Germany, the Alps, Ethiopia, Armenia, Africa, Sicily, Macedonia, Achaea, Asia, Syria, Psidia, Pannonia, Illyricum, and Egypt. The extensive inventory of nations conveys the impressive breadth of the empire that Augustus had established. The notion of obedience made explicit in the opening statement in section 26.1 is completed by reference to the obedience of the Dacians at the end of the list. Obedience thus begins and concludes this portion of Augustus's *RG*.

In the final section of the *RG*, Augustus mentions nations such as the Parthians with whom he had "friendships." He notes that Phrates, the king of the Parthians, "sent all his sons and grandsons to me in Italy, not because he had been conquered in war, but

---

[8] Matthew Roller, "On the Intersignification of Monuments in Augustan Rome," *AJP* 134 (2013): 119.
[9] Paul Zanker, *The Power of Images in the Age of Augustus*, trans. Alan Shapiro (Ann Arbor: University of Michigan Press, 1988), 72–3.

rather seeking our friendship by means of his own children as pledges" (32). Augustus mentions that this alliance was not established by conquering Parthia in war but by Phrates seeking a "friendship." According to Augustus, this process of friendship was used by a large number of other nations that "experienced the good faith of the Roman People" (p. R. fidem/Ρωμαίων πίστεως) (32). This process should sound familiar as the exact phrases are used by Polybius and Livy who also discuss entering the Roman faith. As we saw in those contexts, obedience was essential to maintaining "good faith" with the Roman people. Disobedience was regarded as "breaking faith."

An imaginative thought experiment is needed at this point. We might imagine how a Gentile in Rome may have encountered this inscription at some point on their journey through the Campus Martius in Rome and walking past Augustus's mausoleum. What if their next stop was a Roman house church? When they would sit and hear Romans read aloud, might they catch the resonances of obedient nations common to both documents? How might Romans be heard under the shadow of the *RG*? One point of convergence would be the domains of obedience and the nations in both documents. However, while a *lord* calling for obedience would not be surprising, the nature of his rule would begin to form a contour of the juxtaposition of two very different rulers.

Examples of Obedience in Inscriptions and Monuments

Augustus's style of listing conquered or obedient nations was also used in other inscriptions and monuments throughout the Roman Empire. For example in his *Natural History*, Pliny references a triumphal monument to the Alpine victories (7–6 BCE) that had the following inscription:

> To the Emperor Caesar—The son of Caesar now deified, Augustus, Pontifex Maximus, and emperor fourteen years, in the seventeenth year of his holding the tribunal authority, the Senate and the Roman people, in remembrance that under his command and auspices all the Alpine nations which extended from the upper sea to the lower were reduced to subjection by the Roman people—The Alpine nations so subdued (*devinco*). (3.136-137)[10]

In this small inscription are forty-eight nations that had been subjected, made obedient, to Rome. The verb used to describe the subjugation of all these nations is *devinco*, which means conquered or subdued. Of note is that Pliny mentions that the twelve states of the Cottiani were not included because they had not shown hostility.[11] Judging from our surveys of the historians, when Rome met disobedience, they responded with war and defeated the various nations and tribes. When Rome encountered obedience, they

---

[10] Cf. Strabo, *Geog.* 4.6.6-9.
[11] See also *ILS* 94 and the Arch of Cottius from 9 to 8 BCE that lists several communities under the prefect of Cottius and ends with the line, "and the communities which have been subject to this prefect." Cottius was a prefect under Augustus and ruled over the Alpine regions. On the monument there are six tribes listed that also appear on the arch mentioned by Pliny above.

formed a treaty of surrender (*deditio*) and established a friendship with the nation. In this case, it is apparent that the Cottiani did not refute the advances of Rome and most likely obeyed the demands and thus were not "conquered."

The Pisan Decrees of 2 and 4 CE

A fragment from a decree from Pisa around 2 CE illuminates how colonies outside of Rome positioned themselves as obedient to Augustus and Rome.[12] On September 19, 2 CE, on hearing of the death of Augustus's son Lucius, the Pisan council issued a decree honoring Lucius Caesar. At the end of the decree are the following lines: "What the senate of the Roman people will decree about these things should be followed ... and ask him [Augustus] that it be allowed to the Julian colonists of the Loyal (*opsequenti*) Julian colony of Pisa to do and carry out all these things in accordance with this decree."[13] Greg Rowe has argued, "The Pisan decree for Lucius presents a picture of continuing loyalism in a town with a tradition of allegiance to the dynasty."[14] The Pisan self-description represents Pisa as an obedient or loyal colony. This honorific title is important as it represents the attempt of the colony to establish itself before Rome.

Two years later, at the death of Gaius Caesar, the grandson of Augustus (4 CE), the residents of Pisa would issue another decree. This time the decree would be accompanied by a monument in honor of the victorious campaigns of Gaius Caesar. In the decree, Gaius would be honored for "successfully waging war on the furthest boundaries of the Roman people, after he had carried out his state duties properly, with the most warlike and greatest peoples subdued or brought into alliance."[15] The Pisans would highlight his role as "protector of the Roman Empire and the guardian of the whole world." Gaius is praised for subduing and bringing into alliance the most powerful nations. These alliances were, of course, structured along the lines of obedience, as seen in the examples from Greek and Latin literature. This time the Pisans would go further and construct a monument to document the conquered nations. The Pisans decreed "that an arch be set up in the most frequented place of our colony decorated with the spoils of peoples subdued (*devinco*) or brought into alliance (*fides*), and that on top of it should be placed a statue of him on foot in triumphal dress, and on either side of this statue two gilded equestrian statues of Gaius and Lucius Caesars."[16]

In previous examples, literary documents portrayed the Roman victories over nations and their subsequent obedience. That which could only be heard or read before could now be seen. Now the honorific monument, the Gaius Arch, would graphically represent Roman conquest for all who had eyes to see. Both the decrees and the monument stress the loyal sentiments of the colony. The monument was a powerful

---

[12] See also the Augustan Edicts from 15 CE mentioning loyalty in M. G. L. Cooley, ed., *The Age of Augustus*, LACTOR 17 (London: LACTOR, 2008), 287–8.
[13] *ILS* 139.
[14] Greg Rowe, *Princes and Political Cultures: The New Tiberian Senatorial Decrees* (Ann Arbor: University of Michigan Press, 2002), 108.
[15] *ILS* 140.
[16] *ILS* 140.

reminder to Rome of Pisan obedience and was, at the same time, a celebration by the colony of its loyal status due to Roman victory. By being one of the first to honor Gaius, "on the map of politics, they would appear as leaders, not followers."[17]

The Oath to the Emperor

In 1899, an oath of loyalty was found on a sandstone slab in the Northern Turkish city of Paphlagonia at its capital Gangra. One of many oaths of loyalty found in the Greek East, this oath would have administered around 3 BCE, three years after the region was organized as a province (6 BCE).[18] The inscription reads as follows:

In the third year after the twelfth consulate of the emperor Augustus, the son of the divine Caesar, 6 March, at Gangra, in the marketplace: this oath was sworn by the Paphlagonians of the area and the Romans engaged in business among them.

> I swear to Zeus, Earth, Sun, all the gods and goddesses, and to Augustus himself, that I will be loyal (εὐνοέω) to Caesar Augustus, his children, and descendants all through my life, both in word, deed, and thought, holding as friends those they hold as friends and considering those as enemies whom they judge to be such, that with regard to things that concern them I will not be sparing of my body or my soul or my life or children, but will face every peril with respect to things that affect them. If there is anything that I should recognize or hear as spoken, plotted, or done contrary to this, I will report this and be an enemy of the person speaking, plotting, or doing any of these things. Whomever they judge to be enemies, I will pursue and defend against them by land and sea with arms and steel.
>
> If I should do anything contrary to this oath or fail to follow up what I have sworn, I impose a curse upon myself encompassing the destruction and total extinction of my body, soul, life, children, my entire family, and everything essential down to every successor and every descendant of mine, and may neither earth nor sea receive the bodies of my family and descendants nor bear fruit for them.
>
> The same oath was sworn by all throughout the regions in the countryside at the temples to Augustus by the altars to Augustus.[19]

This oath of loyalty to Augustus was sworn at several towns in the near region.[20] In a recent study of oaths in Greek society, Serena Connolly has drawn attention to its importance, noting, "Although the practice of swearing loyalty to rulers was nothing new in Greece and Asia Minor, the Paphlagonian oath was important because it is the first attested to a Roman emperor in the Greek East."[21] Such an oath indicates the

---

[17] Rowe, *Princes and Political Cultures*, 118.
[18] Rowe, *Princes and Political Cultures*, 193–4.
[19] *IMT* 573; *PHI* 288053; *ILS* 8781.
[20] See the denarius struck with such an oath in 16 BCE in M. G. L. Cooley, ed., *Tiberius to Nero*, LACTOR 19 (London: London School of Classical Teachers, 2011), 262. L10.
[21] Serena Connolly, "Ὀμνύω Αὐτὸν Τὸν Σεβαστόν: The Greek Oath in the Roman World," in *Horkos: The Oath in Greek Society* (ed. Alan H. Sommerstein and Judith Fletcher, Exeter: Bristol Phoenix Press, 2007), 203. She notes several other oaths such as the Baeticans to Augustus, Gaius,

importance attached to loyalty, especially given the political climate of the time with the rebellions in Parthia and Armenia. Although the specific terms for obedience we have been using do not appear in the primary text, the clear intent of the passage concerns the theme of obedience. The one swearing the oath offers their obedience to various tasks, such as refusing friendship with the enemies of Augustus, among other things. Disobedience or failing to maintain the oath of loyalty invokes an imprecatory curse on oneself, demonstrating the importance of maintaining loyalty and obedience.

Similar oaths were vowed under subsequent emperors, such as the Cyprian oath of loyalty to Tiberius.[22] In 1959, this oath inscribed on white marble was discovered in the village of Nikokleia.[23] The contents of the inscription are striking. After swearing by their own Cyprian deities, by Caesar Augustus, and Rome eternal, they swear:

> We, ourselves and our children, [swear] to harken (ὑπακούω) unto and to obey (πειθαρχέω) alike by land and sea, to regard with loyalty and to worship Tiberius Caesar Augustus, son of Augustus, with all his house, to have the same friends and the same foes as they, to propose the voting of [divine honors] to Rome and to Tiberius Caesar Augustus, son of Augustus, and to the sons of his blood, to these only, together with the other gods, and to none other at all. [If we keep this oath, may prosperity be ours; if we break it, may the opposite befall us].

Several features stand out from the oath of allegiance to Tiberius. First, the verbs ὑπακούω (to obey) and πειθαρχέω (to persuade) appear side by side showcasing their synonymous nature, as was established in Chapter 3. Second, this oath shares several important similarities to the oath to Augustus, such as swearing by the gods, the mention of loyalty in regards to the emperor, the phrase "by land and by sea," and, although broken off, the conditional blessing and curse. Third, the explicit obedience language in the oath to Tiberius helps us to understand the oath to Augustus more clearly and bears out some of the working assumptions we had with that oath. Fourth, T. E. J. Wiedemann has argued that such oaths were sworn in Rome by the Senate, the equestrian order, and the Roman people (cf. Rom. 1:5; 13:1).[24]

We should not underestimate the importance of inscriptions such as oaths and discharges. The function of this type of inscription is manifold. From the Roman point of view, it naturally solidified the terms of the agreement, both penalties and promises.

---

and Lucius. Importantly she notes that there was not a standard oath, but that it was flexible. In case her argument could be misunderstood, she notes the long history of the swearing of oaths to foreign leaders going back all the way to the Hittites (208). For example, she mentions that the Greeks swore an oath of loyalty to Flamininus and Sulla during the Roman republic (203). The point to be remembered is that this oath of loyalty is not unique to Rome or any of its emperors.

[22] *SEG* 18 578. See T. B. Mitford, "A Cypriot Oath of Allegiance to Tiberius," *JRS* 50 (1960): 75-9; Takashi Fujii, *Imperial Cult and Imperial Representation in Roman Cyprus* (Stuttgart: Franz Steiner Verlag, 2013). Other emperors include Caligula who in 37 CE received an oath of loyalty from the people from Assos (*PHI* 288053).

[23] Mitford, "Cypriot Oath of Allegiance to Tiberius," 75.

[24] *CAH* 203. An oath of allegiance (Latin) was also given to Gaius by the residents of Aritium on May 11, 37 CE. It bears similar language to the other oaths above. See *ILS* 190. Another oath to Gaius has been found in Greek in the Assus (Cooley, *Tiberius to Nero*, 187.J19d). See also the oath of the Maroneia as shown in Cooley, *Tiberius to Nero*, 247-9.M10A-C.

Second, these oaths served to ward off the threat of revolution, as the outcome of disobedience was clear for all to see. However, from the viewpoint of the swearers, it also functioned as a celebration of their inauguration into the Roman Empire. It served as a reminder of the safety and security Rome offered them and affirmed what Rome could do on their behalf.[25] In short, it was part of the process of Romanization in the provinces.[26]

Shifting to Claudius's reign we find another important piece of evidence. Claudius had inherited the continued unrest in Alexandria, Egypt, between the Jews and the local Greek residents. In an important find, a papyrus was discovered from Egypt containing a letter from Claudius to one Lucius Aemilius Rectus. This letter dates from Nov 10, 41 CE, and it was copied onto papyrus by a wealthy resident.[27] Claudius's threat to discipline the troublemakers in Alexandria bears several important elements for our study here. Claudius's annoyance with the disturbance is on full display. He remarks, "I am storing up an unyielding indignation against those who renewed the conflict" (cf. Rom 1:18-32).[28] He continues, "I tell you plainly that, unless you immediately put a stop to this destructive and mutual enmity, I shall be forced to show you what it is like when a benevolent ruler is moved to righteous indignation."[29] The threat of force is levied against the community if they fail to obey. Obedience is in view as Claudius continues with a list of demands for both sides and concludes, "If they [Alexandrian Jews] disobey, I shall proceed against them in every way as fomenting a common plague for the whole world."[30] Claudius lays out the terms for obedience. He makes clear that disobedience comes at the cost of his wrath. Paul's admonition in Rom. 13:4 comes into closer view in light of accounts such as these. Perhaps the tamping down of unnecessary disobedience might be in Paul's purview.

Examples of Obedience in the Campus Martius

A short survey of the Campus Martius is important for this study as this was the place where armies practiced their exercises and gathered for the triumphal procession that celebrated their victories. Most importantly, the Campus Martius was decorated with monuments, porticos, and temples dedicated to celebrating and thanking the gods for Roman military victories.[31] Our survey of the historical sources has noted the dominance of obedience language occurring within military contexts, whether between a general and his army or between nations engaged in battle with Rome. As such, the Campus Martius is a source of great importance for the representation of Roman victories to the masses. That such monuments could be called upon as examples

---

[25] The younger Agrippina is depicted as *securitas* on an *sestertius* from 37 to 38 CE (*RIC* Gaius 33).
[26] Connolly, "Greek Oath in the Roman World," 212.
[27] This text was brought to my attention by Cooley, *Tiberius to Nero*, 227-8.L17.
[28] E. Mary Smallwood, *Documents Illustrating the Principates of Gaius, Claudius and Nero* (London: Cambridge University Press, 1967), 370.73
[29] Smallwood, *Documents Illustrating the Principates of Gaius*, 370.79.
[30] Smallwood, *Documents Illustrating the Principates of Gaius*, 370.96.
[31] *OCD*, 284.

is shown in Cicero's *De Republica*, where Philus comments, "What is the meaning of those words of praise inscribed on the monuments of our greatest generals, 'He extended the boundaries of the empire'" (*Rep.* 3.15). The monuments and inscriptions not only communicated to the masses but also found their way into the examples and argumentation of Rome's elite. Such a resource with its temples and monuments helps communicate Roman dominance to the large swath of the illiterate population and those who might never hear or read the evidence of the previous chapters. Hence, this section will help bridge some of the gaps between the literary sources (most likely read by the elite alone) and the representation of those narratives to the public masses through inscriptions, monuments, and temples. Our focus will be on the development of the Campus Martius during the imperial period.

Reading Romans in context, we ought to remember the way in which the physical landscape of Rome would have impacted Paul's audience in Rome. These were the streets on which his audience walked, the images they would have seen, and the ideologies they would have interacted with both before and especially after having heard Romans read to them by Phoebe (Rom. 16:1). It is this audience form whom Paul would call forth the obedience and direct it to their new Lord Jesus (Rom. 1:5).

Walking north on the Via Flaminia in Rome, one would pass a series of temples, tombs, and theaters. The resident of Rome would pass by the Altar of Mars before coming to the *Ara Pacis* and the Horologium on the eastern side of the road and just before arriving at the Mausoleum of Augustus to the north.[32] Karl Galinsky's comments are instructive, in speaking of some of the monuments. He writes, "They use a concrete historical event as a starting point for illustrating, in an associative manner that is never imprecise, some wider dimensions and meanings for Augustus' rule."[33] The Campus Martius housed not only Augustus's Mausoleum bearing the *RG* (28 BCE) but also the Solarium (10 BCE) and the *Ara Pacis* (9 BCE). Also worthy of note was the Theater of Pompey, dedicated in 52 BCE. It housed fourteen statues of the nations that he had subdued.[34]

The Theater of Pompey was situated west of the Tiber River and just south of the Pantheon. The entire complex stretched some 45,000 square meters.[35] Dedicated in 52 BCE, Pompey's theater was the first "leisure complex" intended to entertain the masses of Rome.[36] The Theater of Pompey would continue to play an important role throughout the history of the empire, as is suggested by both the retainment and refurbishment of the theater by Augustus (32 BCE), Tiberius (21-37 CE), Caligula (37-41 CE), and Claudius (41 CE), and even emperors in the late empire.[37]

---

[32] The Altar of Mars was of course where many would meet to complete their military obligations.
[33] Galinsky, *Augustan Culture*, 53.
[34] The Augustan Mausoleum will not be discussed, for the *RG* (see earlier in the text).
[35] Richard C. Beacham, *Spectacle Entertainments of Early Imperial Rome* (New Haven: Yale University Press, 1999), 65-71.
[36] Beacham, *Spectacle Entertainments*, 71. He goes on to note, "After its construction and for many decades to come, architecturally speaking, Pompey's theater was the 'only show in town.'"
[37] Roland Mayer, "Impressions of Rome," *GR* 54 (2007): 158; Charmaine Gorrie, "The Restoration of the Porticus Octaviae and Severan Imperial Policy," *GR* 54 (2007): 6. New excavations have been undertaken in Rome on the theater. Cf. John R. Patterson, "The City of Rome Revisited: From Mid-Republic to Mid-Empire," *HJRS* 100 (2010): 210-32; Maria C. Gagliardo and James E. Packer, "A New Look at Pompey's Theatre: History, Documentation, and Recent Excavation," *AJA* 110

The building was much more of a theater-temple structure as at one end it had a temple to the goddess Venus Victrix (Victory).[38] The combination of this goddess with Theater of Pompey pointed to the guarantor of Pompey's victories across the Mediterranean. One part of the complex contained a huge nude statue of Pompey holding a globe representing his domination of the world.[39] Somewhere around the theater-temple complex were fourteen statues of "nations" that Pompey had conquered along with plants from those regions.[40] Mary Beard has noted that "these were presumably new commissions, personifications of the peoples conquered in his campaigns" so that their inclusion of the nations was intended to recreate the experience of Pompey's triumph for the visitors.[41] Most likely these nations were Pontus, Armenia, Cappadocia, Paphlagonia, Media, Colchis, Iberia, Albania, Syria, Cilicia, Mesopotamia, Phoenicia, Palestine, Judaea, and Arabia.[42]

In 32 BCE, during the Augustan restoration of the theater, it appears that Augustus added the "*Porticus ad nationes.*"[43] Stephen Dyson has noted that the "Porticus ad nationes became the place of dedication by governors and foreign ambassadors, suggesting an ongoing association with the provinces."[44] The subjected nations represented here became the place for future Roman foreign diplomacy.

The theater and portico complex also played an interesting role in the period most important for this study, the reign of Nero. Mary Beard again rightly notes, "The statues certainly continued to make an impression well into the Empire: Suetonius claims that, after he had murdered his mother, the emperor Nero dreamed that was he was being menaced by them; it was a nightmare that foreboded provincial uprising from the peoples whom Pompey had once conquered."[45] A group of rambunctious Gentiles in the Roman house churches then might be a cause of concern for Paul in

---

(2006): 93–122; James E. Packer, John Burge, and Maria C. Gagliardo, "Looking Again at Pompey's Theatre: The 2005 Excavation Season," *AJA* 111 (2007): 505–22. See also Suet, *Aug.* 31; *Claud.* 21; *Tib.* 47; *Cal.* 21; Tacitus, *Ann.* 3.72; Cass. Dio LX 6.8. LXII 6.1.2.

[38] The construction of Theater of Pompey represents a turning point in the building program of Rome. As Andrew Wallace-Hadrill has noted, "The Republic ... is characterised by frenetic temple building, and the Empire by secular building." See Andrew Wallace-Hadrill, "*Mutatas Formas:* The Augustan Transformation of Roman Knowledge," in *The Cambridge Companion to the Age of Augustus* (ed. Karl Galinsky, New York: Cambridge University Press, 2005), 79.

[39] Mary T. Boatwright, Daniel J. Gargola, and Richard J. A. Talbert, eds., *The Romans: From Village to Empire* (New York: Oxford University Press, 2004), 227. Augustus would move this statue out of the Senate Hall, Suetonius *Aug.* 31.5.

[40] Pliny, *Nat.* 36.41. Cf. Vitruvius, *Arch.* 5.9.1; Cicero, *Fat.* 8. The placement of the statues is debated, and the text of Pliny is corrupt and is hard to distinguish whether the statues were around the theater complex or around the statue of Pompey himself.

[41] Mary Beard, *The Roman Triumph* (Cambridge: Harvard University Press, 2007), 25. The number fourteen is also the number of nations that were led in triumph.

[42] The nations are recorded by Plutarch, *Pomp.* 45.2. Pliny the Elder writes that Varro created the fourteen statues (*Ency.* 36.41).

[43] This is mentioned in two sources: Servius, *ad Aen* 8.721; Pliny, *Nat.* 36.39. Augustus mentions the restoration of the theater in his *RG* (20.1). Cf. Lawrence Richardson, *A New Topographical Dictionary of Ancient Rome* (Baltimore: Johns Hopkins University Press, 1992), 316–17.

[44] Stephen L. Dyson, *Rome: A Living Portrait of an Ancient City* (Baltimore: Johns Hopkins University Press, 2010), 103.

[45] Beard, *The Roman Triumph*, 25. Cf. Suetonius, *Nero* 46.1; Pliny, *Nat.* 7.98.

the first century, given these realities. A desire to offset fomenting disobedience might be necessary to not draw undue attention from Roman authorities (cf. Rom. 1:5; 13:1).

Moving from north to south along the Via Flaminia, immediately after the Altar to Mars and the Temples of Isis and Serapis, and directly across from Tiberius's altar to providence (*Ara Providentia*), a visitor would come to one of the best-known features of the Campus Martius, the *Ara Pacis Augustae*.[46] In his *RG*, Augustus links the commissioning of the altar with his return from a successful three-year military campaign in Gaul and Spain (*RG* 12.2). The altar was promised in 12 BCE and dedicated three years later in 9 BCE. The honor of the altar is mentioned precisely before the closing of the doors of the Temple Janus to signify peace (*RG* 13). As Karl Galinsky comments, "The *Ara Pacis* thus is linked with the concept that peace is a result of military victories which secure the imperium Romanum on land and sea."[47] Such a connection between victory and peace is found repeatedly in ancient sources. Peace with Rome is mediated through the obedience of the conquered nations to Rome's demands. Rome is victorious when the nations obey their rule. Such is explicitly stated by Augustus himself in the *RG*.

Two panels on the eastern side of the *Ara Pacis* draw out this connection between war and victory, which lead to peace with Rome.[48] One panel contains the image of the god Mars, the god of war, but this is balanced with another panel on the northeast side of the monument that depicts the goddess Roma sitting on a pile of weapons accumulated as spoils of war where she is watching over Romulus and Remus.[49] Directly across from Roma is perhaps Pax, the goddess of peace. Supporting the identification of the woman on this panel as the goddess Pax is the comparison and contrast that would be gained from juxtaposing Roma and Venus. As Paul Zanker has noted, "The viewer was meant to read the two images together and understand the message, that the blessings of peace had been won and made secure by the newly fortified *virtus* of Roman arms."[50]

The association between peace and war in the *Ara Pacis* is carried further as directly west of the altar was the *Horologium Augusti*, an enormous sundial that was built in conjunction with the altar.[51] The *Horologium* was constructed with "obelisks brought from 'captured Egypt'; the paved ground under the feet of pedestrians was itself the sundial; and the equinoctial line on the ground passed through the *Ara Pacis* and subtended a right angle to the Mausoleum by the Tiber."[52] The sundial was built in

---

[46] The best overview of the entire monument is given by Galinsky, *Augustan Culture*, 141–55. See also the respective sections in Zanker, *The Power of Images*.
[47] Galinsky, *Augustan Culture*, 141.
[48] Even a professional association of musicians set up honorary monuments honoring the Roman Dynasty, hailing both Tiberius and Germanicus as "hailed victorious commander." See Cooley, *Tiberius to Nero*, 180-1.J12F.
[49] Philip A. G. Sabin, Hans van Wees, and Michael Whitby, eds., *The Cambridge History of Greek and Roman Warfare: Greece, the Hellenistic World, and the Rise of Rome* (New York: Cambridge University Press, 2007), 2:27.
[50] Zanker, *The Power of Images*, 175. The woman could also be identified as Venus, Italia, or Tellus as the imagery was used interchangeably by poets and artists.
[51] Elisha Ann Dumser, "The Urban Topography of Rome," in *The Cambridge Companion to Ancient Rome*, 140.
[52] *CAH* 96.

12 CE after Augustus was made Pontifex Maximus. The sundial also bore an inscription that notes that Augustus "gave this as a gift to the Sun, once Egypt had been reduced to the power of the Roman people."[53] The inscriptions on the monument were provided in Greek, apparently so that residents and visitors from the Roman East could read it.[54] As if the inscription was not enough, completing the imagery of subjection was the globe on top of the sundial symbolizing world power.[55]

The intersection of all these monuments profoundly displayed the message of victory and domination that Rome set out to construct. By capitalizing on their conquests, the monuments gave graphic depictions of their military success, a success that was dependent on the surrender and defeat of the nations. As James Harrison has pointed out, "The sundial celebrates Augustus' victory at Actium (31 BC) that secured peace in the Greek East, whereas the *ara Pacis Augustae*, strategically placed nearby, eulogises Augustus' establishment of peace in the Latin West."[56]

We might pause again to creatively imagine a Roman house church member, who had walked by the images of Mars and who would then hear Paul discuss having peace with God (Rom 5:1). Mars and Roma would be juxtaposed with God and Jesus. However, another contour of difference would be highlighted for this Gentile. Peace was obtained on the *Ara Pacis* through the bloody conquest of Roman war. The dominating images of the weapons of Mars are contrasted with Jesus and the cross. The peace Paul speaks of was obtained through the sacrifice of God himself.

The Impact of Images on a Roman Audience

The monuments serve to communicate the overarching narrative of worldwide subjection. Rome has conquered and made obedient nations from Actium to Egypt (cf. Rom. 1:5). Judging from our historical sources, these images of globes, victory, and peace collapse a much wider narrative that involved a specific process whereby the defeated nations surrendered in obedience to Rome's rule. The ability for these monuments to continue representing these aspects of Rome's rule was conditioned on the continued obedience of those defeated nations. The connection to Paul's letter to the Romans is that these inscriptions and monuments were the visuals most likely seen by the members of the house churches in Rome and formed their imaginations and understanding of obedience. This would have been the visual world they would have encountered. The concept of obedience was both a linguistic idea bantered about among the literary sources and an image that permeated the Roman landscape. The latter may have had the greatest impact on the audience of Paul's letter.

---

[53] *ILS*, 91. See also *ILS*, 103, the base of a golden statue in the Augustan forum honoring Augustus in an inscription that notes the province of Hispania was "pacified."
[54] Zanker, *The Power of Images*, 144.
[55] James R. Harrison, *Paul and the Imperial Authorities at Thessalonica and Rome: A Study in the Conflict of Ideology* (Tübingen: Mohr Siebeck, 2011), 107.
[56] Harrison, *Paul and the Imperial Authorities*, 107.

7

Reading Obedience from the Margins: Rom. 1:1-12 and 15:14–16:23

We turn now to Paul's letter to Rome. How would the book of Romans sound to a slave, a freedman, a poor stoneworker, or a migrant worker in one of the Roman house churches?[1] Let us imagine, some in Paul's audience had walked the Via Flaminia in Rome themselves and had seen the *Res Gestae* or the massive *Horologarium*. Perhaps some were from a more well-to-do household and would have heard of Rome's conquests from a public reading of a Roman historian. If the residents of Rome had sworn the oath of loyalty to Tiberius or Nero then they would be acquainted with obedience language. The topic of obedience was surely not lost on those who lived in Rome and were confronted daily with Rome's message of domination and victory, whether by literature, coins, sculptures, and inscriptions. We must not discount, either, the *lived* experience of some inhabitants of Rome—those who did not or would not adjust to life in the epicenter of Roman power. How would someone who was recently conquered perceive their world? What weight might they carry in terms of the implicit and sometimes explicit calls to obedience? Having surveyed the role of obedience within the Greco-Roman historians and philosophers, we are now in a better position to reflect on the ways that obedience would be understood by a Gentile Roman audience. Since as we have shown the topic of obedience in a letter to Rome tapped into one of the essential features of Roman discourse and rule.

As stated at the onset of this work, our second task is to trace the theme of obedience in Romans to show that it is a consistent theme throughout Rom. 1–16. Given the rhetorical features at work and the mentions of obedience in both the *exordium* and *peroration*, Paul has rhetorically signaled the importance of the obedience theme that functions as rhetorical bookends to his entire discourse. This chapter focuses on those rhetorical bookends.

These two tasks, understanding the obedience language from a Roman Gentile viewpoint and tracing the theme of obedience throughout Romans, will form a conversation as we continue in these next three chapters. Our focus in this chapter

---

[1] The most extensive treatment thus far on the sociological makeup of the early Christian Communities is now John S. Kloppenborg, *Christ's Associations: Connecting and Belonging in the Ancient City* (New Haven: Yale University Press, 2019), 97–130. See also Peter Oakes, *Empire, Economics, and the New Testament* (Grand Rapids: Eerdmans, 2020), 3–62. Such works form the basis for the ideal audience of the community who heard Paul's letter.

will be on the obedience language and imagery in the *exordium* and *peroration* sections of Romans before we turn in Chapter 8 to look at the rest of the discourse of Romans.

The Species of Rhetoric

Rhetorical argumentation was tied to specific social contexts and the audiences from which it had arisen.[2] In the case of Romans, the situation Paul envisioned was determinative of the type of rhetoric he would use. Despite all the commentaries on Romans, only a few have rhetorically analyzed the entire letter.[3] Among the rhetorical treatments, Romans is typically identified as either deliberative or epideictic rhetoric.[4] Several factors negate the possibility of Romans being epideictic rhetoric.[5]

First, praise or blame is the primary mode of reasoning in epideictic rhetoric, and Romans hardly appears to be of this sort. In Romans, Paul seeks to persuade and dissuade the Romans of certain beliefs and behavior (cf. Rom. 12–15). Second and more importantly, Witherington has noted that "a *narratio* is out of place in a piece of epideictic rhetoric, but is quite appropriate in a deliberative piece, especially when it includes travel plans."[6] It appears, then, that Romans should be understood as a piece of deliberative rhetoric that seeks to persuade the church in Rome to accept certain beliefs and behaviors. In other words, the rhetorical task is aimed at the practical obedience of this community.

---

[2] Aristotle, *Rhet.* 2.18.
[3] Debate surrounds the extent of the rhetorical analysis of the correspondences of Paul. However, this work focuses on the benefits and positive implications of rhetorical analysis. The arguments against rhetorical analysis of Paul's letters fall short. See Stanley E. Porter and Bryan R. Dryer, eds., *Paul and Ancient Rhetoric: Theory and Practice in the Hellenistic Context: Theory and Practice in the Hellenistic Context* (New York: Cambridge University Press, 2016). My work would stand in contrast and disagreement with Stanley Porter and Bryan R. Dyer, "Oral Texts? A Reassessment of the Oral and Rhetorical Nature of Paul's Letters in Light of Recent Studies," *JETS* 55 (2012): 323–41. My conclusions and assessments can be found in Jason A. Myers and Ben Witherington, "A Rhetorical Response to Stan Porter," *BBR* 26.4 (2017): 547–9.
[4] See Ben Witherington, *Paul's Letter to the Romans: A Socio-Rhetorical Commentary* (Grand Rapids: Eerdmans, 2004), 20; David E. Aune, "Romans as Logos Protreptikos," in *The Romans Debate: Revised and Expanded Edition* (ed. Karl P. Donfried, Peabody: Hendrickson, 1991), 278–98; Anthony J. Guerra, *Romans and the Apologetic Tradition: The Purpose, Genre, and Audience of Paul's Letter* (New York: Cambridge University Press, 1995); Christopher Bryan, *A Preface to Romans: Notes on the Epistle in Its Literary and Cultural Setting* (New York: Oxford University Press, 2000), 21–2.
[5] See Wilhelm Wuellner, "Paul's Rhetoric of Argumentation in Romans: An Alternative to the Donfried–Karris Debate over Romans," in *The Romans Debate: Revised and Expanded Edition* (ed. Karl P. Donfried, Peabody: Hendrickson, 1991), 134–6; Robert Jewett, "Following the Argument of Romans," in *Romans Debate*, 268; Robert Jewett, *Romans: A Commentary* (Minneapolis: Fortress, 2007), 43.
[6] Witherington, *Romans*, 20.

A Rhetorical Outline of Romans

Understanding Romans as a piece of deliberative rhetoric is a helpful way of viewing the discourse. In such a large rhetorical piece, an outline will prove helpful for grasping the big canvas on which Paul constructs this argument. Although there is of course disagreement among various rhetorical sections of the letter, the large features remain helpful, even if one might understand individual sections of the argument differently. To this end, the following rhetorical structure will be employed to frame Paul's argument and our understanding of obedience in Romans.[7]

The division of an argument is essential for its communication to an audience who will hear the letter. Rhetoric was organized around the categories of *exordium, narratio, propositio, probatio, refutatio,* and *peroratio*.[8] For this section, only the *exordium* and the *peroratio* will be analyzed.[9]

The Exordium

The rhetorical speech began with an *exordium*, which was part of the introduction. Both Cicero and the *Rhetorica Ad Herennium* begin their rhetorical speeches with an *exordium* as the first major section and do not include a separate introduction before an *exordium* is given.[10] The function of the exordium is to gain the goodwill of the audience and the "paving of the way for what follows."[11] Quintilian states, "The sole purpose of the *exordium* is to prepare our audience in such a way that they will be disposed to lend a ready ear to the rest of our speech."[12] Cicero added that the *exordium* brings the mind of the audience "into a proper condition to receive the rest of the speech by making him well-disposed, attentive and receptive."[13] In this section, an author would gain the benevolence of his audience so that they would listen to him, preparing the way for the introduction of the main themes of the speech.

In Romans, the *exordium* is found in 1:1-12.[14] Although many have noted that Paul's introduction is much longer than his typical introduction, few have taken note of Cicero who mentions this type of *exordium*. In *De Invention* 1.18.26, he notes somewhat negatively that there are six types of *exordium*; among them are the general,

---

[7] This rhetorical outline follows the one given by Jewett, *Romans*, vii–x. The subsections largely align with Frank J. Matera, *Romans* (Grand Rapids: Baker, 2010), vii–viii.

[8] Catherine Steel, "Divisions of Speech," in *The Cambridge Companion to Ancient Rhetoric* (ed. Erik Gunderson, New York: Cambridge University Press, 2009), 78.

[9] On the importance of the *propositio* and specifically with Romans in mind see Witherington, *Romans*, 47–57; Quintillian, *Inst. Or.* 4.4.2-4.

[10] Cicero, *Inv.* 1.14.19; *Rhet. Ad. Herr.* 1.3.4.

[11] Aristotle, *Rhet.*, 427.

[12] Quintilian, *Inst.*, 4.1.5.

[13] Cicero, *Inv.*, 1.15.6-7. For an overview of Cicero as a rhetor see James M. May, "Cicero as Rhetorician," in *A Companion to Roman Rhetoric* (ed. William Dominik and Jon Hall, Malden: Blackwell, 2007), 250–63; Andrew Riggsby, "Rhetoric," in *The Oxford Handbook of Roman Studies* (ed. Alessandro Barchiesi and Walter Scheidel, New York: Oxford University Press, 2010), 391.

[14] In support, Jewett, *Romans*, 99; Neil Elliott, *The Rhetoric of Romans: Argumentative Constraint and Strategy and Paul's Dialogue with Judaism* (Minneapolis: Fortress, 1990), 69–72.

Table 1 A Rhetorical Outline of Romans

Rhetorical Section	Verses and Theme
The Exordium	1:1-12 Introduction and The First Appeal to Obedience
The Narratio	1:13-15 Short Narration of Historical Events
The Propositio	1:16-17 Thesis Statement
The First Proof	1:18–4:25
Section 1	1:18-32 A Diatribe on Gentile Disobedience
Section 2	2:1-16 The Disobedience of Both Jew and Gentile
Section 3	2:17-29 Jewish Disobedience
Section 4	3:1-20 Jew and Gentile under Sin's Sway
Section 5	3:21-31 Righteousness through the Faith of Jesus
Section 6	4:1-25 Abraham: The Father of the Gentiles
The Second Proof	5:1–8:39
Section 1	5:1-21 The Kingdoms of Sin and Death and the Kingdom of Grace and Faith
Section 2	6:1-23 No Longer Obedient to Sin and Death
Section 3	7:1-25 The Dilemma of Obedience and Disobedience
Section 4	8:1-39 Obedience by Grace via the Power of the Spirit
The Third Proof	9:1–11:36
Section 1	9:1-29 The Tragedy of Israel's Disobedience
Section 2	9:30–10:21 The Failure to Exercise Obedience
Section 3	11:1-36 Israel's Disobedience Is Not Final
The Fourth Proof	12:1–15:13

Rhetorical Section	Verses and Theme
Section 1	12:1–13:15 The Obedience of Faith at Ground Level
Section 2	14:1–15:13 The Obedience of Faith towards One Another
The Peroratio	15:14–16:27
Section 1	15:14–33 Final Appeal to Obedience
Section 2	16:1-27 Final Greetings

the common, and the tedious. He explains that the tedious *exordium* "is one which is spun out beyond all need with a superabundance of words or ideas." The rules of rhetoric were, of course, elastic and easily amenable to the situation at hand, and perhaps this is what leads Paul to include such a lengthy *exordium* in Romans.

In 1:1-7, Paul not only introduces himself and his apostleship (1:1) but also begins laying the groundwork for the rest of the letter. The *exordium* also contains Paul's statement on the purpose of his apostleship: to bring about the "obedience of faith among the nations" (Rom. 1:5). In this short but densely packed section, Paul has introduced himself, his apostleship, and obedience.

The Peroratio

The last section of any speech, according to several rhetors, was what Cicero identified as the *peroration*. In Greek rhetoric, Aristotle identified this as the *epilogos* or epilogue (3.13). The later *Rhet. Ad Herr* identified it as the *conclusio*. The main function of this section was summing up arguments that had been put forth in the previous sections.[15] Whether rhetors divided their speech up into four, five, or six parts, an epilogue or conclusion was included as a way of reminding the audience of their intentions and purposes.[16]

According to Aristotle, both the *exordium* and *epilogos* are "aids to memory" (3.13.5). Correspondingly, Aristotle argues that, in the *epilogos*, "all that remains is to recapitulate what has been said" (3.19.4). Aristotle acknowledges the similarities of the *exordium* and *epilogos* and notes the frequent confusion on a rhetor's part because of their similarities. He writes, "In the exordium we should state the subject, in order that the question to be decided may not escape notice, but in the epilogue we should give a summary statement of the proofs" (3.19.4).

---

[15] This section is included by both Greek and Latin rhetors. Cf. Aristotle, *Rhet.* 3.13; Cicero, *Top.* 97-98; *Inv.* 1.14.19; *Orat.* 2.80; Quintilian, *Inst. Orat.* 3.9.1.

[16] See the helpful chart of sources in David E. Aune, *The Westminster Dictionary of New Testament and Early Christian Literature and Rhetoric* (Louisville: Westminster John Knox, 2003), 62-4.

Both Cicero and Quintillian indicate that the *peroratio* consisted of two or three parts.[17] One part of the *peroratio* was aimed at "the summing up" (*Inv.* 1.52.98). Cicero further elaborates on the nature of "summing up," indicating that this is where "matters that have been discussed in different places are brought together in one place and arranged so as to be seen at a glance in order to refresh the memory of the audience" (1.52.98). How this is accomplished is by stating the "topics" of the "most important points" that were covered (1.52.99-100). The *Rhet. Ad. Herr* also includes the *conclusio* as the final part of a speech, briefly noting that "the conclusions will be brief, in the form of a summary at the end of the discourse" (3.8-9).

The *peroration* occurs in Rom. 15:14-21 and includes a reference to the ὑπακοὴν ἐθνῶν (15:18).[18] The meaning of this phrase and its connection to obedience imagery will be discussed in the next chapter. What is clear is that we have a reference to obedience at the beginning and end of Romans proper.[19] It is certainly revealing that in Rom. 16:19, obedience is also mentioned in a second *peroration* (see Chapter 8). The rhetorical signals are clear because Paul has included a topic both at the beginning and end of this letter, indicating the importance Paul attached to the subject. Such an *inclusio* forms rhetorical bookends and alerts us to the thematic nature of obedience within Romans—a theme that has not been heard often enough but rhetorically stands on sure footing. How might we rehear Romans by paying attention to these rhetorical clues? We turn now to begin our study of obedience in Romans and show how this theme of obedience is interwoven throughout the discourse.

The Exordium: Introduction and the First Appeal to Obedience (1:1-12)

Rom. 1:5 is the first occurrence of obedience language in Romans. Obedience appears within Paul's *exordium* as the purpose for his apostleship: to bring about the obedience of faith (ὑπακοὴν πίστεως) among the nations. Two important factors must be considered; the first is more obvious than the second. As seen throughout Greco-Roman literature, obedience is the prerogative that Rome expects from the "nations" whether *amicii* or *socii*—friend or ally. As we saw in numerous examples in the historians, obedience is crucial to securing peace with Rome. The nations were expected to obey all that Rome demanded of them, no matter how outlandish the request might have seemed. Obedience was the piece that solidified Rome's republic

---

[17] The other two parts according to Cicero are *indignatio* (*Inv.* 1.53-4) and *conquestio* (*Inv.* 1.55-6). Quintilian lists exciting the feelings (*Inst. Orat.* 6.1). Cf. Cicero, *Top.* 25.98-99.

[18] The recent work of Jackson W. also misses this element, even though the first chapter of his work is interested in understanding the "framing chapters" of Romans. See Jackson W., *Reading Romans with Eastern Eyes: Honor and Shame in Paul's Message and Mission* (Downers Grove: IVP, 2019), 26–38. Obedience does not play a role in his treatment of Paul's mission or framing of the message of Romans.

[19] In agreement with Witherington viewing Rom. 16 as a "letter of recommendation" (*Romans*, 375–6).

and empire as it grew throughout the ancient world. Paul is certainly in line with the notion that nations are expected to obey.

If we compare Paul's argument in Rom. 1 to some of the conceptions that Gentiles had with obedience, one clear point of similarity for the Gentiles in the audience of Romans is the idea that nations obey. The Roman audience would have been familiar with certain aspects of this victorious tradition, especially if they had come to Rome via conquest.[20] Or as Roman citizens who had seen the imagery of conquered nations in the Campus Martius area, they would have been familiar with the idea of nations obeying Roman rule. One only needs to remember Pompey's Portico of Nations that shows how Rome viewed such nations. Certainly one aspect of Roman identity as seen through the poets, historians, and monuments was that Rome ruled the nations and expected their obedience. A call for the obedience of nations was not unusual in the Roman rhetoric both before and during the first century. One stark contrast would have been the person calling for obedience, namely a Jewish messenger, on behalf of a minority religious group. Also surprising to many would have been that the call for obedience was to follow a crucified "king."

Whether Paul's call for obedience from the nations is anti-imperial is a discussion that will be fully entered into in Chapter 8 in a discussion of Rom. 13:1-7. In light of examples of obedience being offered to various kings and lords that evidence no explicit anger or resentment against Rome and given the sprawling sociopolitical climate of the ancient world, Rome certainly needed local kings and officials to run the day-to-day operations, and obedience from the top-down allowed the empire to run smoothly. If Rom. 1:5 is read out of the context of the rest of Romans, it is possible to see anti-imperial rhetoric at work. The meaning of obedience in Rom. 1:5 must be tempered by Rom. 13:1 (see Chapter 8).[21]

The second important feature to note from our survey of obedience in the Roman historians helps solve the perennial difficulty with the grammar of the phrase ὑπακοή πίστις. The genitive construction has been no small source of debate in scholarship on Romans.[22] The solution to this grammatical problem is assisted by the evidence from the historical sources. The main ways of understanding the genitive construction ὑπακοὴν πίστεως are either as an objective, subjective, adjectival, or appositional genitive phrase.[23] The latter two options can be dismissed rather quickly, at least from historical usage. The appositional understanding is the least likely as it blurs the lines

---

[20] A similar approach is undertaken for various topics in Romans; see Paula Fredriksen, "Paul's Letter to the Romans, the Ten Commandments, and Pagan 'Justification by Faith,'" *JBL* 133 (2014): 801–8; James R. Harrison, "Paul's 'Indebtedness' to the Barbarian (Rom 1:14) in Latin West Perspective," *NovT* 55 (2013): 311–48. On immigration see the work by David Noy, *Foreigners at Rome: Citizens and Strangers* (London: Duckworth/The Classical Press of Wales, 2000).

[21] See the recent article by Matthew V. Novenson, "What the Apostles Did Not See," in *Reactions to Empire: Sacred Texts in Their Socio-Political Context* (ed. John Anthony Dunne and Dan Batovici, Tübingen: Mohr Siebeck, 2014), 55–72. The last line of his article is helpful: "If the Romans could not be bothered to take notice of the apostles, well, neither could the apostles the Romans" (72).

[22] All commentaries engage in a debate on the nature of this genitival phrase.

[23] Cranfield still provides one of the best layouts of the grammatical features and thus serves as a primary partner in this small section. See C. E. B. Cranfield, *The Epistle to the Romans: A Critical and Exegetical Commentary*, 2 vols. (Edinburgh: T&T Clark, 1980), 1:66.

between faith and obedience too much. From the historical sources that we surveyed, obedience and faith are distinguished to a large degree, and this distinction ought to be maintained with Rom. 1:5.[24]

The adjectival genitive category translates the genitive phrase as "believing obedience." From our survey, this fails to take into account the functional aspect of obedience. Belief has relatively little to do with the obedience that Rome expected, although if the phrase is translated as "faithful obedience," this is not too far from the mark of what we see in these historical sources. Continued loyalty is stressed as an outworking of entering into the faith of the Romans. However, again, maintaining a distinction between the two genitives is important as these appear to be two concepts within the Greco-Roman sources. One enters into "the faith of the Romans" and then offers obedience.

The two best options for understanding the phrase are the objective and subjective genitive categories. The objective genitive takes faith as the object of obedience and could be translated as "obedience to *the* faith," as in the sense of obedience to doctrinal concepts. Such an understanding of concepts seems to introduce a later theological sense to the terms.[25] Although Paul could have been doing this, it is not clear that his audience would have been familiar with such an attempt. The objective category could also translate the phrase as "obedience to faith" with "faith" functioning as a sense of authority or even obedience to God's faithfulness as shown in the gospel.

Of the objective understandings of the phrase, the sense of obedience to faith, or faith's authority, carries the most historical weight. This understanding incorporates the themes of authority alongside those of obedience and faith that, to a degree, reflect our evidence in the historical sources. The Roman authority as victor carries with it the demand for obedience.

The subjective genitive category takes faith as the subject of obedience and is translated either as "the obedience that faith produces" or "the obedience faith requires." Of these two options, the best translation is the latter where obedience is understood as something required by faith. Throughout the Greco-Roman sources, I showed how obedience was a functional requirement of entering into the Roman faith, as seen in Polybius and Livy. Obedience was expected by those who entered into a treaty with the Romans. Disobedience broke the treaty with Rome and was the antecedent to war. Likewise, continued loyalty or obedience to Rome resulted in receiving the blessings that Rome could provide, whether through military protection or other incentives. Furthermore, such imagery serves as the foundation for later philosophical discourse.

One aspect missing in previous treatments of the "obedience of faith" phrase was sufficient attention to the historical usage of both obedience and faith. The previous

---

[24] Also dismissed is the argument by Friedrich that "Diese für Paulus selbstverständliche verbindung von Verkündigung und Glauben würde ebenfalls dafür sprechen, ὑπακοή πίστεως Röm 15 zu übersetzen mit »Predigt des Glaubens«." Cf. Gerhard Friedrich, "Muss Hypakoē Pisteōs Röm 1:5 Mit 'Glaubengehorsam' Übersetzt Werden.," ZNW 72 (1981): 123.

[25] See also Paula Fredriksen, "Paul's Letter to the Romans, the Ten Commandments, and Pagan 'Justification by Faith'." JBL 133 (2014): 807–8.

chapters have documented the usages of obedience and faith in similar contexts and have provided insight into this grammatical construction. Among the grammatical options, the two best categories are the subjective and objective. The weight of the historical evidence in Greco-Roman sources points toward the subjective understanding that obedience is something that is required by faith.[26] The content of the obedience will be unpacked throughout Paul's discourse (cf. Rom. 6:17; 10:16; 12–16).

The call for obedience in Rom. 1:5 raises the specific issue of the identity of the recipient of this obedience. From the evidence gathered in the previous chapters, several figures called for obedience, namely emperors, generals, and from the philosophers, reason personified. Paul's call for obedience certainly involves at least two, if not three, components. First and most immediately, obedience is directed to Paul himself. Paul issues forth a call for obedience. Certainly, this is part of the orientation of the *narratio* in Rom. 1:8-15—gathering authority for himself so that he can issue commands in the latter part of his discourse (Rom. 12:1–15:33; see Chapter 8). Part of Paul's assertion of apostolic authority among the Gentiles indicates that obedience is certainly directed toward him and the issues he raises.

This is, of course, not the entire story. Paul indicates in Rom. 1:5 that the call for obedience is on behalf of the name of Jesus. Obedience to God and the gospel is also part of where their obedience is directed. In Rom. 6:17, Paul will specifically praise the Romans for "have become obedient from the heart to the form of teaching to which you were entrusted." Paul commends their obedience to the gospel. Likewise, the inverse of 6:17 is found with Israel in Rom. 10:16 where Paul indicates that some did not "obey the good news." Paul's call for the obedience of faith is certainly directed first and foremost to God and the gospel and, subsequently, to Paul himself as its apostolic herald.

But what of the other half of Paul's phrases, the obedience of *pistis*? How should the ideas of obedience affect the nature of our understanding of *pistis*? Growing evidence suggests that the translation *faith* with the minimal definition of *belief* is inadequate in light of the usage of the term in antiquity (see Chapter 1). The influential work of Teresa Morgan and a growing litany of author authors are helping the shift from understanding *pistis* as simply belief and helping to incorporate more significant concepts like faithfulness, trust, and loyalty.[27] Although it is difficult to dislodge the phrase "the obedience of faith," one must reckon with the evidence that bold phrases like the "obedience of loyalty," "trusting obedience," and "faithful obedience" strike closer to the core of usage in antiquity. In order to aid in this process, at critical places, the translation "obedience of loyalty" will be added to the traditional translation to remind us of the nuanced nature of the terms in question.

In light of the whole message of Romans, however, this good news includes the encompassing message of unity with one another (Rom. 12:1–15:33), Jew and Gentile.

---

[26] Even if one is not persuaded by the subjective treatment of the genitive construction, the historical evidence helps to rule out the appositional category.

[27] Teresa Morgan, *Roman Faith and Christian Faith: Pistis and Fides in the Early Roman Empire and Early Churches* (New York: Oxford University Press, 2015), 36–123; Nijay Gupta, *Paul and the Language of Faith* (Grand Rapids: Eerdmans), 178.

A Gentile Christian reflecting on the call for the obedience of faith/obedience of loyalty would understand and respond, aware that this call has come from God himself, and that entering into faith with God includes the corollary of obedience to his commands and his messengers (i.e., Paul). Paul, as the divinely commissioned representative of God, shares the good news, and this includes obedience to their Lord.[28] In the latter half of Romans, this is spelled concerning a very important issue, the welcoming of one another (Rom. 14:1) and fellow Jewish Christians (Rom. 16:1-7). The obedience that flows from faith/trust has this communal component. The obedience of faith/loyalty to the gospel includes the welcoming of one another (Rom. 14:1) and also the list of persons Paul mentions in Rom. 16.

The Peroratio: Final Appeal to Obedience and Final Greetings (15:14–16:27)

As mentioned in the previous chapter, the final section of a rhetorical argument was the Greek *epilogos* or the Latin *peroratio* or *conclusio*. Part of the *peroratio* was the "summing up" whereby a rhetorician reminded the audience of the key themes of his discourse in a final rousing appeal. It is worthwhile to restate Cicero's definition of a *peroration*. He says that this is where "matters that have been discussed in different places are brought together in one place and arranged so as to be seen at a glance in order to refresh the memory of the audience" (*Inv.* 1.52.98).

As most recognize, the *peroratio* in Romans is 15:14-21.[29] Relevant to our project, we have the appearance of the phrase, "to win (κατεργάζομαι) obedience from the Gentiles" (εἰς ὑπακοὴν ἐθνῶν), in 15:18 signaling the importance of the obedience theme observed throughout the discourse and appearing appropriately in the *peroration*.

The *peroration* is broken up into two unequal sections, 15:14-16 and 17-21. The first section focuses on Paul's communication strategy with Rome, while the second section focuses on the Gentile mission.[30] The themes encountered in these sections correspond

---

[28] See Joshua Jipp, *Christ Is King: Paul's Royal Ideology* (Minneapolis: Fortress, 2015), 192-3.
[29] Witherington, *Romans*, 350; Jewett, *Romans*, 902-3; Wuellner, "Paul's Rhetoric," 128-46. Although not noting the rhetorical aspects, see Matera, *Romans*, 329-30. He provides an excellent chart showing the similarities between the *exordium* and the *peroration*. Contra, Cranfield, *Romans*, 2:749, who misses the theme of obedience entirely; also Ernst Käsemann, *Commentary on Romans* (Grand Rapids: Eerdmans, 1980), 390. Fitzmyer disappointingly translates ὑπακοὴν as "commitment" (*Romans* (New York: Doubleday, 1993), 713. Entirely missing any discussion of the section or phrase is Bryan, *Preface to Romans*, 222-3; N. T. Wright, "Romans," in *The New Interpreter's Bible* (Nashville: Abingdon, 2002), 754; Phillip F. Esler, *Conflict and Identity in Romans: The Social Setting of Paul's Letter* (Minneapolis: Fortress, 2003); Thomas H. Tobin, *Paul's Rhetoric in Its Contexts: The Argument of Romans* (Grand Rapids: Baker, 2005).
[30] Stanley N. Olson, "Epistolary Uses of Expressions of Self-Confidence," *JBL* 103 (1984): 585-97. He notes, "A language pattern characteristic of Paul's letters is the expression of confidence—a first-person report or assertion that the writer's emotional state is or was one of certainty, confidence, or hope" (585). In other Hellenistic letters and speeches, expressions of self-confidence are found almost exclusively in the immediate context of apologetic or self-commendation. Further, this commendatory section is usually followed (or preceded) by a section of advice (587).

"in style and content to Rom. 1:1-12, providing a sober recapitulation of Paul's earlier argument."[31] It is the second section of the *peroration* that is most important for this study and will be the primary focus.

In 15:15, Paul reintroduces his apostolic vocation to the Gentiles and links back to 1:5 with the notion of God's calling Paul in grace. This phrase appears not only in 1:5 but also most recently in 12:3 and reiterates these themes of grace, calling, gentiles, and obedience.[32] in 15:16, Paul then characterizes his mission as a priestly vocation to present the Gentiles as an acceptable offering to God (15:16).[33] Verse 17 functions as a transition verse from the first section of the *peroration* to the second section. If the first section of the *peroration* is a summary of the authority and basis of Paul's ministry, the second section is a summary of the features and aspects of that ministry and contains the purpose for writing Romans.

One aspect that Paul chooses to highlight and recapitulate is the phrase "obedience from the nations" (ὑπακοὴν ἐθνῶν) (15:18), which is essentially a restatement of the obedience of faith (ὑπακοὴν πίστεως) of 1:5 and yet another reminder of the importance Paul placed on his mission to the Gentiles.[34] Paul elaborates that this obedience among the Gentiles, be in both word and deed, highlights the all-encompassing nature of Pauline obedience (Rom. 12:1). Such language was often used in ancient literature "as a way of summarizing all behavior or demonstrating behavioral consistency with verbal claims."[35] The theme of obedience has been a uniting feature throughout Paul's discourse. As Dunn rightly notes, "The thematic ὑπακοή (v 18) provides a thread which unites missionary impulse, theological rationale, and paraenesis (1:5; 5:19; 6:16)."[36]

Paul's repetition of his purpose in the *peroration* summarizes not only his argument in Romans but also his apostolic vocation both in Rome and in Spain on the near horizon.[37] By emphasizing the obedience of faith or obedience of loyalty, Paul pulls the Roman Christians into his apostolic orbit, aligns and corrects their local problems, and brings them into the broader context of the mission of God for the upcoming mission to Spain (15:21).

---

[31] Jewett, *Romans*, 902.

[32] I'm not as confident as Das that much can be ascertained as it regards the audience and these sections. Cf. A. Andrew Das, "'Praise the Lord, All You Gentiles': The Encoded Audience of Romans 15.7-13," *JSNT* 34 (2011): 90–110.

[33] Cf. David J. Downs, "'The Offering of the Gentiles' in Romans 15.16," *JSNT* 29 (2006): 173–86. I do not think Downs is correct, given the rhetorical aspects of a *peroration* this would be an entirely new topic to introduce. Rather in light of 15:15, Paul is referring to his mission or activity not the activity of his Gentile converts.

[34] So James D. G. Dunn, *Romans*, 2 vols. (Dallas: Word, 1988), 2:856; Jewett, *Romans*, 909; Luke Timothy Johnson, *Reading Romans: A Literary and Theological Commentary* (Macon: Smyth & Helwys, 2001), 224; Leander Keck, *Romans* (Nashville: Abingdon, 2005), 361; Colin G. Kruse, *Paul's Letter to the Romans* (Grand Rapids: Eerdmans, 2012), 539.

[35] Craig S. Keener, *Romans* (Eugene: Cascade, 2009), 175.n20.

[36] Dunn, *Romans*, 2:856. "The use of the thematic ὑπακοή is no accident: it was part of Paul's most basic conviction regarding his mission" (862).

[37] Cf. A. Andrew Das, "Paul of Tarshish: Isaiah 66.19 and the Spanish Mission of Romans 15.24, 28," *NTS* 54 (2008): 60–73. Das challenges Jewett's identification of Spain as a primary purpose of Romans.

Excursus on Romans 16

Romans does not end at 15:33. What about Rom. 16:1-25? Any discussion of Rom. 16 must take into account the varied and complicated textual tradition that lay behind the letter before addressing the particulars of Rom. 16.[38] This work follows the work of Harry Gamble and accepts the authenticity of the entire chapter. Romans 16 represents a letter of recommendation where Paul names and greets twenty-six individuals in Rome.[39] Witherington correctly identifies the social force of such a greeting. He argues that it aimed to "create a new social situation in Rome, overcoming the obstacles to unity and concord dealt within chs. 14–15."[40] We are reminded that it is those issues in Rom. 12:1–15:33 where Paul expects the Gentiles to exercise the obedience of faith.

After greeting numerous individuals in Rome, Paul includes one final admonition in 16:17-21 in a second *peroratio*.[41] Paul advises this recently mentioned group to avoid those who would cause more discord or continue much of the same discord referenced in 14:1–15:13. Paul then states in 16:19 that "your obedience is known to all," a phrase that echoes Rom. 1:8, where the previous reference was to their faith that was proclaimed "in the whole world."[42] Such similar phrasing between 1:8 and 16:19 shows once again the close nature of ὑπακοή and πίστις or, to put it in a more Pauline way, the obedience of faith/trust (ὑπακοή πίστις). Dunn's comments are worth full quotation:

> This closing echo of Paul's introductory remarks right back at the beginning of the letter (1:5, 8) is no accident. It shows how readily Paul can sum up the meaning and force of the gospel in terms of "obedience" and so confirms for the last time

---

[38] Harry Y. Gamble, *The Textual History of the Letter to the Romans: A Study in Textual and Literary Criticism* (Grand Rapids: Eerdmans, 1977). Harry Gamble's work still sets the precedent for accepting a full sixteen-chapter letter, and most studies in Romans have followed his work. Witherington comments, "In other words, the textual problems need not affect our assessment of vv. 1-23" (*Romans*, 377). Few today doubt that authenticity of the sixteen-chapter form of Romans, although there is debate as to where the final doxology (vv. 25-27) appeared in the original form. See Karl P. Donfried, "A Short Note on Romans 16," in *Romans Debate*, 44–52; Bruce M. Metzger, *A Textual Commentary on the Greek New Testament*, 2nd ed. (Stuttgart: UBS, 2006), 471–7; D. C. Parker, *An Introduction to the New Testament Manuscripts and Their Texts* (New York: Cambridge University Press, 2008), 270–4; Kurt Aland and Barbara Aland, *The Text of the New Testament: An Introduction to the Critical Editions and to the Theory and Practice of Modern Textual Criticism*, trans. Erroll F. Rhodes, 2nd ed. (Grand Rapids: Eerdmans, 1989), 294–7; Richard N. Longenecker, *Introducing Romans: Critical Issues in Paul's Most Famous Letter* (Grand Rapids: Eerdmans, 2011), 16–30. For the commentators see Käsemann, *Romans*, 409; Dunn, *Romans*, 2:884; Fitzmyer, *Romans*, 55-67; Peter Stuhlmacher, *Paul's Letter to the Romans: A Commentary*, trans. S. J. Hafemann (Louisville: Westminster John Knox, 1994), 244–6; Wright, *Romans*, 761, 767–8; Witherington, *Romans*, 375–7; Keck, *Romans*, 27, 368; Keener, *Romans*, 182; For arguments against see Jewett, *Romans*, 985; J. K. Elliott, "The Language and Style of the Concluding Doxology to the Epistle to the Romans," *ZNW* 72 (1981): 124–30.

[39] Such practice was common; see Keener, *Romans*, 184, cites *P. Oxy.* 114.16-18; 1296.9-19; Cicero, *Att.* 6.3; Fronto, *Verum Imp.* 2.6.

[40] Witherington, *Romans*, 380. Also see his four issues of rhetorical effect on pages 381–2.

[41] Contra Jewett, *Romans*, 986-8, I do not think this is an interpolation. Wuellner's comments are very helpful ("Paul's Rhetoric of Argumentation," 136–9).

[42] See Christoph W. Stenschke, "Your Obedience Is Known to All (Rom 16:19): Paul's References to Other Christians and Their Function in Paul's Letter to the Romans," *NovT* 57 (2015): 251–74.

the importance Paul places on a faith which works out in a daily discipline under Christ's lordship ("obedience," v 19 = "serving Christ," v 18)—as a faith, that is, in full continuity with the obedience of faith which characterized the witness of the scriptures.[43]

Further, in context, Paul contrasts the obedience of this group with those who cause "dissensions and offenses" to the teaching (16:17-18; cf. 6:17).[44] Such a contrast provides further confirmation for understanding Rom. 14:1–15:33 as places where Paul expects the Roman community to exercise the obedience of faith/loyalty.[45] We ought not to miss, either, that the Gentile acceptance of these Jewish Christians mirrors the inverse of Israel's opportunity and subsequent disobedience in Rom. 9–11, where they were disobedient to God and the gospel by not including the Gentiles within the scope of God's worldwide encompassing righteousness for all (Rom. 10:4). The Gentiles are now presented in Rom. 16 with their opportunity to be all-embracing. Paul's command "to welcome" the list of people he references indicates a specific component of the trusting obedience that Paul wants them to exercise.

In 16:25-27, Paul concludes with a doxology.[46] The doxology contains numerous parallels to the previous contents of the letter, most notably the introduction in 1:2-15.[47] One of the most important echoes is the reference to the obedience of faith in 16:26, which appears as the final subject of the final lines of Romans. The obedience of faith is the mystery that was disclosed and made known to the Gentiles.[48] Among the last words heard by the Romans is the obedience of faith, indicating the importance of the phrase and the last item Paul wanted his audience to remember.

---

[43] Dunn, *Romans*, 2:907.
[44] Stuhlmacher, *Romans*, 252-3. Cf. Bryan, *A Preface*, 231.
[45] Contra Dunn, *Romans*, 2:901, who states, "The dangers addressed are not those of 14:1–15:6."
[46] The textual history of this section is complicated as it appears in several places in the manuscripts. This section follows the recommendation of Metzger, "while recognizing the possibility that the doxology may not have been part of the original form of the epistle, on the strength of the impressive manuscript evidence the Committee decided to include the verses at their traditional place in the epistle" (*A Textual Commentary on the Greek New Testament*, 476-77.) Commentators accepting the doxology are Keener, *Romans*, 192; Stuhlmacher, *Romans*, 256; Katherine Grieb, *The Story of Romans: A Narrative Defense of God's Righteousness* (Louisville: Westminster John Knox, 2002), 146; Witherington, *Romans*, 400; Wright, *Romans*, 768; Cranfield, *Romans*, 2:208-9; Douglas J. Moo, *The Epistle to the Romans* (Grand Rapids: Eerdmans, 1996), 936-7. Cf. Larry W. Hurtado, "The Doxology at the End of Romans," in *New Testament Textual Criticism: Its Significance for Exegesis: Essays in Honor of Bruce M. Metzger* (ed. E. J. Epp and G. D. Fee, Clarendon: Oxford University Press, 1981), 185-99; Don Garlington, "The Obedience of Faith in the Letter to the Romans: Part 1," *WTJ* 52 (1990): 201-24; I. Howard Marshall, "Romans 16:25-27—an Apt Conclusion," in *Romans and the People of God: Essays in Honor of Gordon D. Fee on the Occasion of His 65th Birthday* (ed. Sven Soderlund and N. T. Wright, Grand Rapids: Eerdmans, 1999), 170-84. Rejecting are Käsemann, *Romans*, 409; Dunn, *Romans*, 2:912-7; Fitzmyer, *Romans*, 753; Jewett, *Romans*, 998; Donfried, "A Short Note on Romans 16," 44-52; Byrne, *Romans*, 461-2. Although even Jewett notes, "The list of those favoring interpolation is about as long as that of defenders of its authenticity as a Pauline creation designed for the end of chapter" (*Romans*, 998).
[47] See the excellent chart in Keener, *Romans*, 192; and Matera, *Romans*, 330. Cf. Stuhlmacher, *Romans*, 256, "This section corresponds to 1:1-7 and is likewise formulated with great care." Contra Cranfield, *Romans*, 1:5-11, who argues this is post-Pauline; Dunn, *Romans*, 2:916-7.
[48] Cf. Cranfield, *Romans*, 2:812; Wright, *Romans*, 769; Matera, *Romans*, 347.

Conclusion on Rhetorical Bookends

The placement of obedience, both in the *exordium* and the *peroratio*, rhetorically indicates Paul's concern for this as a theme of his argument. Previous studies have not drawn out this theme to its full extent as has been done in this chapter. In Rom. 1:5, Paul declares his purpose to bring about "the obedience of faith among the nations." Our survey of the Roman historians offered new insight into how to translate the genitival phrase "the obedience of faith" (ὑπακοὴν πίστεως) in light of the Greek and Latin usage. As well, Paul's conclusion in 15:14–16:27 indicates the importance of obedience by reference to it in the *peroration*(s) of Romans, where rhetors repeated the important themes they wanted their hearers to remember. The rhetorical inclusion of obedience language signals Paul's intention of his purpose as stated in 1:5. Specifically, Rom. 15:7-29 represents the highest confluence of the term ἔθνος in Romans and is the further explanation of Paul's purpose in Rom. 1:5. Paul concludes one of his most important letters with a final reference to the obedience of faith in the final sentences of Romans (16:26), thus indicating the primary importance of obedience for Paul and the Roman audience. Having established the rhetorical concerns and Paul's intention to discuss obedience as a purpose of Romans, we are now attuned to hear this melody throughout the letter.

8

Reading Obedience in the Argumentation in Romans

In this chapter, our goal is to continue our effort to trace the obedience theme in the major rhetorical sections of Romans outside the *exordium* and the *peroration* (1:16–15:33) and reflect on the ways that Gentiles in Paul's audience would understand his obedience language.[1] It is important to remember again that topic of obedience in a letter to Rome tapped into one of the essential features of Roman discourse and rule. So in returning to the original question, what would it look like to sit in the Roman audience? Reminded again of Peter Oakes's work on the makeup of a house church, how would Gentiles from various backgrounds and statuses—craftsmen, slaves, family members, and dependents—in the city of Rome hear and understand the emphasis on obedience in this section of the discourse?

The Propositio: Thesis Statement (1:16-17)

We ought to ask at the beginning what connection does Paul make between obedience and two important topics within Romans—the gospel (εὐαγγέλιον) and righteousness (δικαιοσύνη)? Such an issue immediately confronts a reading of obedience in Romans. Turning to the thesis statement in 1:16-17, we must ask what relationship does Paul's purpose in 1:5 have with the *propositio* in 1:16-17?[2] What does obedience have to do with the grand themes?

Two issues in the latter sections of Romans help illuminate the connection between 1:5 and 1:16-17. Although they anticipate our argument in those sections, it is

---

[1] The rhetorical outline is adapted from Robert Jewett, *Romans: A Commentary* (Minneapolis: Fortress, 2007).
[2] On the importance of the *propositio* see Katherine Grieb, *The Story of Romans: A Narrative Defense of God's Righteousness* (Louisville: Westminster John Knox, 2002), 138; Ben Witherington, *Paul's Letter to the Romans: A Socio-Rhetorical Commentary* (Grand Rapids: Eerdmans, 2004), 47–50; Thomas H. Tobin, *Paul's Rhetoric in Its Contexts: The Argument of Romans* (Grand Rapids: Baker, 2005), 104–5; Craig S. Keener, *Romans* (Eugene: Cascade, 2009), 25–7. Surprisingly not identified by Neil Elliott, *The Rhetoric of Romans Argumentative Constraint and Strategy and Paul's Dialogue with Judaism* (Minneapolis: Fortress, 1990), 80–2. Contra Lucian Legrand, "Rm 1.11-15 (17): Proemium or Propositio?," *NTS* 49 (2003): 566–72. He argues, "La propositio de la lettre aux Romains commence donc en 1.11 et se prolonge jusqu'au v. 17."

important to mention some details in passing. First, in 10:16, Paul reports negatively that Israel did not obey the gospel. Paul directly connects obedience and the gospel. Second, Paul's admonition in 1:17, quoting Habakkuk 2, is that the righteous one will live by faith/faithfulness.[3] This link is important as Paul explicitly connects obedience and righteousness in Rom. 6:16 in his *synkrisis* of the first and last Adam, stating that one is a slave to what one obeys, whether sin, resulting in death or "obedience resulting in righteousness" (ὑπακοή εἰς δικαιοσύνη).

In 6:1-23, Paul indicates that the righteous one is the person who enslaves himself or herself to obedience.[4] Living by faith entails living a life of obedience to the gospel. Jewett rightly notes, "The major point in the thesis statement, that the gospel is God's means of restoring righteous control over a disobedient creation, dovetails with Paul's understanding of his mission to extend that reign."[5] The obedience of faith/trust showcases the extent of God's power at work in the gospel. Thus, Paul's admonition to bring about the obedience of faith/trust relates directly to his thesis statement in 1:16-17.[6]

The First Proof: A Diatribe on Gentile Disobedience (1:18-32)

While obedience is not explicitly mentioned in the rest of 1:18-32, something more sinister takes center stage. Disobedience occupies a leading role. Rom. 1:18-32 contains Paul's second "apocalyptic reveal." In 1:17, the righteousness of God was apocalyptically revealed, but now it is the wrath of God that is being unveiled.[7] What follows in 1:18-32 is a series of Gentile vices that Paul groups under the main themes of ἀσέβεια (ungodliness) and ἀδικία (unrighteousness).[8]

Paul's invective catalogs the ways that humanity has been unrighteous *through* acts of disobedience.[9] In view are disobedient acts that result from "suppressing" the truth (1:18). The inventory of Gentile disobedience is the outworking of ἀδικία.

---

[3] Noting the importance of Hab. 2:4 for Rom. 1:1-5 is Stephen L. Young, "Romans 1.1-5 and Paul's Christological Use of Hab. 2.4 in Rom. 1.17: An Underutilized Consideration in the Debate," *JSNT* 34 (2012): 277–85.
[4] So Witherington, *Romans*, 48. "The focus in this discourse is both on God's faithfulness and on humans who have faith and live out the obedience of faith."
[5] Jewett, *Romans*, 138. Cf. Keener, *Romans*, 29–30. Keener on verse 17: "The term *pistis* includes the sense of 'faithfulness'—loyalty and allegiance" (29).
[6] Robert Matthew Calhoun, *Paul's Definitions of the Gospel in Romans 1* (Tübingen: Mohr Siebeck, 2011), 147–92.
[7] On the importance of apocalyptic in Romans see the recent edited volume, Beverly Roberts Gaventa, ed., *Apocalyptic Paul: Cosmos and Anthropos in Romans 5-8* (Waco: Baylor University Press, 2013).
[8] For the Jewish parallels such as the *Wisdom of Solomon* see Witherington, *Romans*, 63. Hans-Joachim Eckstein, "'Denn Gottes Zorn Wird Von Himmel Her Offenbar Werden': Exegetische Erwägungen Zu Röm 1:18," *ZNW* 78 (1987): 87.
[9] Entirely unpersuasive is the reading by Douglas A. Campbell, *The Deliverance of God: An Apocalyptic Rereading of Justification in Paul* (Grand Rapids: Eerdmans, 2009), 542–7. He suggests that Rom. 1:18-32 is "speech in character" from the opponents of Paul. In fact, such an overemphasis on this permeates the entire work and thus makes interaction difficult given the starting premises.

Disobedience explicitly appears in the list in Paul's description of children who are disobedient (ἀπειθής) to parents in 1:30.[10] Is this a tenuous link? Jewett has drawn proper attention to the fact that this wrath is being "revealed against" the very group Paul focuses on for their obedience of faith/trust. Both are ongoing processes.[11] We should not miss the fact that, immediately after Paul signals his intention to bring about the "obedience of faith" among the Gentiles, he cites a long list of ways Gentiles disobey. Rom. 1:18-32 is backward referencing to Rom. 1:5 by showing the drastic situation of disobedience among the nations.[12]

Of importance for the audience at the end of this section of Paul is the relationship between disobedience and wrath. Such a conceptual link between disobedience and wrath was readily identified in the previous sections (Chapters 3-6). Disobedience provokes the wrath of Rome, both globally and locally. Various nations faced destruction as a result of Rome's wrath toward their disobedience, and this was documented and illustrated in Roman imagery throughout Rome (Chapter 6). Members of the audience who reflected on these images would readily understand the connection between disobedience and wrath. Disobedience in Rome by its citizens was also met with resistance and was a threat to the stability of Rome. As we saw in Dionysius of Halicarnassus, the Plebians' disobedience at various stages in the history of Rome provoked punishment.

A point of comparison would be established with the audience and their previous understanding of disobedience provoking wrath. However, a contrast would be emerging in the continuing argument Paul is making whereby the audience may be surprised that disobedience and wrath need not be the final outcome. Highly unlike their previous conceptions of obedience and disobedience, new pathways are opened up through the obedience of one man (Rom. 5-6).

The Disobedience of Both Jew and Gentile (2:1-16)

Paul shifts his argument in 2:1 to a diatribe style in castigating a fellow Jewish teacher who fails to live up to the demands they expect from others (2:1-5).[13] In 2:6, Paul states,

---

[10] Both Senecas discuss obedience. Seneca the Elder noted, "Remember, fathers expected absolute obedience from their children and could punish recalcitrant children even with death" (*Con.* 1.2). While Seneca the Younger noted, "I obeyed my parents; I deferred to their authority, whether it was fair or unfair or even harsh; I showed myself compliant and submissive" (*Ben.* 3.38.2). Both cited in Jewett, *Romans*, 188.

[11] Jewett, *Romans*, 151. See also Epictetus who mentions disobedient people (*Discourses* 3.11.1); also in Witherington, *Romans*, 70.

[12] Also noting this backward reference but to Rom. 1:8-17 is Nijay Gupta, "Human Idolatry and Paul as Faithful Worshipper of God: Reconnecting Romans 1:18-32 to 1:8-15 (Via 1:16-17)," *NeoT* 46 (2012): 29-40.

[13] On diatribe see David E. Aune, *The Westminster Dictionary of New Testament and Early Christian Literature and Rhetoric* (Louisville: Westminster John Knox, 2003), 127. Boyarin's comments are helpful: "Paul has essentially produced a sermon to which many if not most Pharisaic preachers … could have and would have assented" (92). He goes on, "Insofar as Paul is simply attacking hypocrisy, then, there is nothing in his preaching that is foreign to the prophets or indeed the Rabbis" (93). Cf. Daniel Boyarin, *A Radical Jew: Paul and the Politics of Identity* (Berkeley: University of California Press, 1994), 92-3. For an alternative view that Paul is engaging a Gentile via his

"God will give to each person according to what he has done," quoting Prov. 24:12 with a slight change of the verbs to reflect a future situation.[14] The contrast with the previous section (2:1-5) that focused so strongly on "the teacher" is the shift in verse six, universalizing the argument to include the Roman audience in the diatribe.[15]

The importance of the outworking of God's judgment is the contours of that judgment. We will take these in reverse order. In 2:8-9, the focus is on disobedience, and Paul indicates two actions: disobeying (ἀπειθέω) the truth and obeying (πείθω) unrighteousness. These references to obedience and disobedience are important as they are formed from the πείθω root, similar to our evidence from the Roman historians and philosophers. What is most striking about the disobedience is the result. Disobedience to the truth (most likely rejecting the gospel) results in incurring God's wrath.

From Rom. 1:5, the nations have been summoned to a new obedience to their true and rightful king, who is Lord (Rom. 1:3-4).[16] Disobedience to this Lord is met with the same outcomes that we saw in the Roman historians, that is, disobedience provokes wrath.[17] As Dunn has noted, this wrath should not be sharply distinguished from the wrath described in 1:18-32 that was a strong summary of disobedience.[18]

The surrounding verses, although not explicitly mentioning obedience, contribute to the theme of obedience that Paul is establishing. Rom. 2:7-10 revolves around two groups: one is explicitly described as disobedient (2:8-9) and the other is, of course, the inverse or contrast, established in verse eight by the δὲ (but), those who are obedient.[19]

---

diatribe see Runar Thorsteinsson, *Paul's Interlocutor in Romans 2* (Stockholm: Almqvist and Wiksell, 2003); Rafael Rodriguez, *If You Call Yourself a Jew: Reappraising Paul's Letter to the Romans* (Eugene: Cascade, 2014).

[14] Jewett, *Romans*, 204, root the future tense verbs as a quotation of Ps. 61:13b (LXX).

[15] Oda Wischmeyer, "Römer 2.1-24 Als Teil Der Gerichtsrede Des Paulus Gegen Die Menschheit," *NTS* 52 (2006): 374. She also rightly notes that this is not anti-Jewish polemic. Gathercole goes too far in suggesting that in 2:1-11 Paul uses categories: "Not only that are thoroughly Jewish, but also that *could be only Jewish* (italics original)." Cf. Simon J. Gathercole, *Where Is Boasting: Early Jewish Soteriology and Paul's Response in Romans 1-5* (Grand Rapids: Eerdmans, 2002), 198. Contrast with Leander Keck, *Romans* (Nashville: Abingdon, 2005), 74.

[16] Joshua Jipp, *Christ Is King: Paul's Royal Ideology* (Minneapolis: Fortress, 2015), 212–32. Jipp offers a helpful situating of the righteousness language within ancient political kingship discourse. However, a weakness in Jipp's overall excellent argument is the failure to connect the obedience of the Messiah to the forthcoming obedience of his people. He states, "For Paul, the Messiah *is the only one who is righteous, faithful, and obedient* (italics original)" (215). What this entirely misses is the Pauline vocation of the obedience of faith among the nations, which as will be shown issues forth from their allegiance to their obedient Messiah. Much of Jipp's chapter only tangentially touches on a Greco-Roman context for kingship. Also, Matthew Thiessen, *Paul and the Gentile Problem* (New York: Oxford University Press, 2016), 126.

[17] Jewett draws attention to this dyad in the LXX, Josephus, and pagan magical curses but not the Greco-Roman historians. Cf. Jewett, *Romans*, 207.

[18] Dunn, *Romans*, 1:92. Dunn goes onto mention the difference as,

> The only difference is that the process of divine retribution is already in clear evidence among the Gentiles (1:18–32, particularly 18–27), whereas the too-confident Jew is simply storing it up for the future, for the day of final judgment. In that day such a one will be surprised to find that he has stored up not treasures of good (Tob 4:9–10), but treasures of divine wrath!

Likewise Johnson notes that obedience and disobedience continues the line of thought from Rom. 1:18-32. See Luke Timothy Johnson, *Reading Romans: A Literary and Theological Commentary* (Macon: Smyth & Helwys, 2001), 38; Keck, *Romans*, 77.

[19] So agrees Ernst Käsemann, *Commentary on Romans* (Grand Rapids: Eerdmans, 1980), 60.

The obedient group frames the disobedient in this section (2:7 and 2:10). Paul's description of this "obedient" group is more elaborate as he describes them as those who are "patiently doing good" (2:7) and, three verses later, as "everyone who does good" (2:10). The second description, represented by the present middle participle ἐργαζομένῳ (from ἐργάζομαι; "to do, to work"), stresses the continuous nature of obedience. A contrast is formed, therefore, with obedience related to "the good" and disobedience related to "evil." The two groups are given as the ultimate contrast between good and evil, built on the concepts of obedience and disobedience. A moral connotation is thus inherent to Paul's discussion.

The use of the phrase "to the Jew first and then the Greek," which is repeated twice (2:9-10), links this entire section back to the thesis statement of Rom. 1:16-17. The concepts of obedience and disobedience are integrated closely with the topics of gospel, righteousness, and Jew/Gentile. Obedience and disobedience come to characterize both groups.

The importance of this section for a Roman audience is highlighted not only through the themes of judgment and obedience but also in the outcomes. If we carry through the contrast from verses 8 to 9, obedience includes obeying the truth and obeying righteousness. The result of this obedience is "glory, honor, and peace," three highly prized Roman values.[20] The connection between glory and obedience was highlighted in the reign of Tiberius by Tacitus in Annals 6.8 who used the phrase "the glory of obedience (*obsequium*)." Because these are three highly prized Roman values inscribed in texts and enshrined in the imagery of the Roman world, a Gentile audience would see familiar concepts of obedience at work between their previous understanding and Paul's point in Rom. 2:8-11.

The contrast between obedience and disobedience is the result of opposing outcomes. While disobedience provokes the wrath of God, obedience secures peace (2:10). Rom. 2:11 concludes with the rhetorical maxim that there is no favoritism with God. Similar to our survey, friendship with Rome does not entail a privileged position that can somehow usurp obedience or undercut Rome's demands. Such confusion was evident in Polybius's description of the Aetolians who misunderstood what "faith" meant for the Romans (*Hist.* 20.9.10-12). Friend and foe alike must be obedient to Rome's demands or face wrath. Analogously, some in the audience of the book of Romans may have had similar thoughts from this section, as God himself does not show favoritism, and obedience and disobedience carry consequences.

In 2:12, Paul references the issue of the law (νόμος) for the first time in Romans.[21] He shifts his argument slightly from a general discussion of obedience and disobedience

---

[20] Witherington, *Romans*, 81.
[21] On Paul and the law see E. P. Sanders, *Paul and Palestinian Judaism* (Minneapolis: Fortress, 1977); Heikki Räisänen, *Paul and the Law*, 2nd ed., vol. 29 (Tübingen: J. C. B. Mohr (Paul Siebeck), 1987); N. T. Wright, "The Law in Romans 2," in *Paul and the Mosaic Law* (ed. James D. G. Dunn, Grand Rapids: Eerdmans, 2008), 131–50; James D. G. Dunn, "Paul and the Torah: The Role and Function of the Law in the Theology of Paul the Apostle," in *The New Perspective on Paul* (Grand Rapids: Eerdmans, 2008), 447–68; Brian S. Rosner, *Paul and the Law: Keeping the Commandments of God* (Downers Grove: IVP, 2013); Hans Hübner, *Law in Paul's Thought*, ed. John Riches, trans. James C. G. Greig (Edinburgh: T&T Clark, 1984); Brendan Byrne, "The Problem of Nomos and the Relationship with Judaism in Romans," *CBQ* 62.2 (2000): 294–309; Frank Thielman, *Paul & the Law: A Contextual Approach* (Downers Grove: IVP, 1995); Thomas R. Schreiner, *The Law and Its*

to the specific issue of obedience and disobedience to the law (2:12-29). To this extent, the two groups are first described indirectly as those who are without law or lawless and those under or in the law. The identity of the latter group is easily identifiable as Jews. The identity of the first group, the ἀνόμως (without law or lawless), has caused great debate. While it is clear that those who are ἀνόμως are Gentiles, the precise identity of these Gentiles, as either pagans or Christian Gentiles, has served as a *crux interpretum* for the passage as a whole.[22]

The debate concerning the exact identity of this group would take us too far from our goal in this chapter.[23] Our attention will be directed toward how Paul describes this group vis-á-vis the Jews, rather than whom Paul describes. Particular comments on this passage will have a bearing on the specific identity of this Gentile group.

Paul begins this argument on law, obedience, and righteousness by contrasting the hearers (ἀκροατής) of the law (νόμος) with those who do (ποιητής) the law. It is this latter group that will be declared righteous (δικαιόω) on the last day (2:13). The situation envisaged is eschatological, as the future passive verb indicates. It is important to note that this reinforces the idea made clear in 2:7 that those who "work the good" will receive eternal life.[24]

In both 2:13 and 2:14, the primary emphasis is on the verb ποιέω (to do). It is those that "do the law" in 2:13 or 2:14 who "do the things required by the law" that will be justified in the eschatological scenario Paul envisions (2:13, 16). The clear sense of ποιέω in this context is obedience. The hearers of the law are not contrasted with those who disobey the law but rather with those who hear *and* obey. Obedience is contrasted with the "mere hearers" of the law. Regardless of how we identify the basis of this Gentile obedience, that is, natural law or the new covenant, the emphasis is on obedience to a form of law. This is certainly the case when we see where Paul proceeds with his argument in the next verses.

Jewish Disobedience (2:17-29)

In Rom. 2:17-29, Paul returns to the first group, leaving behind the generic identity marker of "hearers of the law" and replacing it with the more explicit Ἰουδαῖος (Judeans). In contrast to Rom. 1:18-32 that listed general Gentile vices, Rom. 2:21-23 is a shortlist of Jewish vices described in terms of nomistic violations, or what Simon Gathercole has termed "phenomenological evidence."[25] Similar in some ways

---

Fulfillment: A Pauline Theology of Law (Grand Rapids: Baker, 1993); N. T. Wright, *The Climax of the Covenant: Christ and the Law in Pauline Theology* (Philadelphia: Fortress, 1991).

[22] For a more recent short survey of the interpretive options and a short bibliography, cf. Jewett, *Romans*, 212–13. For a robust defense of the Christian Gentile view see Wright, "Romans," 436–43.

[23] I have written on this topic. Cf. Jason A. Myers, "Who Are Those Who Do the Law? A Critical Analysis of Gentiles, Righteousness, and Justification in Romans 2:14-15" (Grand Rapids Theological Seminary, 2010).

[24] See the creative, yet unpersuasive thesis by Jane Heath, "The Righteous Gentile Interjects (James 2:18-19 and Romans 2:14-15," *NovT* 55 (2013): 272–95.

[25] Gathercole, *Where Is Boasting?*, 211.

to Cicero's *Tusc. Disp.* 2.4, Paul critiques vices such as hypocritical teaching, stealing, adultery, and robbing temples.

How we understand 2:21-23 hinges on how we translate the term Paul uses to describe the vices. The term that requires attention is παράβασις, often translated into English as "breaking" the law. However, the noun παράβασις often refers to disobedience.[26] Law is something that sets a boundary for behavior and that has authority to do so. Thus, following the law is recognizing this boundary and adapting behavior to it while breaking the law is rejecting this boundary and going beyond it. This adherence to or going beyond a boundary fits with the concept of obedience as acceptance of an external authority and submission to that authority in one's behavior. There is an explicit contrast of these stances toward the law just a few verses later in Rom. 2:27 between those who "keep the law" and those who "break (παραβάτην) the law."

The primary thrust of Paul's argument is on the disobedience of certain Jews in light of their national identity. Paul quotes Isa. 52:5 precisely at this point to reaffirm Israel's vocation as a light unto the nations. Paul indicates that Jewish disobedience results in the misuse of God's name among the nations, the very nations of Paul's apostleship in Rom. 1:5 for obedience "on behalf of his name." Paul has juxtaposed the disobedience of *the* nation of Israel with his prerogative of bringing about obedience among the nations.

In 2:25-27, Paul reiterates similar themes found in the previous section. So far, Paul's argument has moved progressively in concentric circles. As Dunn has noted, "The argument has narrowed from a vaguely defined 'doing good,' through the more specific 'doing the law,' and now to the single issue of circumcision."[27] Paul drives home the point of the importance of Jewish obedience by singling out circumcision, perhaps the most identifiable Jewish marker of identity.[28]

According to Paul, disobedience, in a sense, undoes the physical marks of circumcision (2:25). Paul again uses the terminology of "breaking" to indicate disobedience. This notion is familiar in light of Livy and Dionysius Halicarnassus's description of disobedience as "breaking faith." In contrast to disobedience, obedience is mentioned twice with two different verbs for "keeping" (φυλάσσω in 26 and τελέω in 27). The law is described as being "regarded (λογίζομαι) as circumcision," foreshadowing Paul's argument in Rom. 4. James Dunn rightly notes again, "In view of the important role filled by λογίζεσθαι from 3:28 through chap. 4, the word will be pregnant with significance as the focus steadily narrows to the *Christian* Gentile as such."[29]

Paul's comparison throughout Rom. 2:13-27 revolves around the twin themes of obedience and disobedience. Obedience serves as a new identity marker that identifies one's place within the eschatological situation now inbreaking in Paul's community. The overall arc of Paul's argument in 1:18–2:27 is on the impartiality of God in both

---

[26] BDAG, 758.
[27] Dunn, *Romans*, 1:120.
[28] See Gen. 17:9-14; 1 Macc. 1:48, 2:46; 2 Macc. 6:10; Josephus, *Ant.* 13.257-8; Keener, *Romans*, 49–50.
[29] Dunn, *Romans*, 1:123.

judgment and salvation. The clear emphasis lands on the importance of obedience and disobedience as impartial arbiters of identity, whether Jew or Gentile.

Jew and Gentile under Sin's Sway (3:1-20)

In Rom. 3:1, Paul carries forward his discussion on circumcision by focusing on the benefit to the circumcised. Given Paul's previous statements in 2:25-29, the argument raises the validity of circumcision, to which he must offer an answer. In this chapter, Paul will continue his task of showing the impartiality of God's righteous judgment on humanity, both Jew and Gentile. Paul's argument in Rom. 3 will focus on the Jewish side of the equation. The similarities between Rom. 3 and Rom. 9–11 ought not to be missed as they revolve around the key issue of divine faithfulness contrasted with Jewish infidelity.

Obedience language does not explicitly appear in the sections of 3:1-20 or 3:21-31. As mentioned in the introduction, the goal is to show how the theme of obedience works its way through Romans. As was also mentioned, certain passages will have to be argued for in context. This applies to Romans 3. Although obedience is not specifically highlighted, it is certainly looming in the background at various points in these sections. Certainly, Paul's discussion of ἀπιστία (unfaithfulness), ἀδικία (unrighteousness), and ἁμαρτία (sin) all point toward the domain of disobedience. Paul's *cento* in 3:10-18 also drives home the point of human disobedience.

The discussion in 3:21-30 will immediately be contrasted in the next section of the discourse with the character of Abraham (4:1-25). Abraham is presented as a paragon of faithfulness, preparing the way for Paul's discussion of Adam and Christ and the climactic section of obedience in Romans. Rom. 3:1-20 and 3:21-31 then prepare us for Paul's argument in the next several sections of his discourse. To briefly summarize the next argument in this discussion, 3:1-20 and 3:21-31 point toward the inverse of the obedience of faith, namely the infidelity of disobedience.

In Rom. 3:3, Paul poses the rhetorical question, "What if some were unfaithful? Will their faithlessness nullify the faithfulness of God?" In this diatribe section, Paul poses a series of "probing questions" to his interlocutor, one of which in verse three proves relevant to this argument. The interpretation of the section hinges on the understanding of the noun ἀπιστία. Specifically, does ἀπιστία mean "unbelief" or "unfaithful?"[30] A bifurcation of the meanings is certainly not helpful as both emphases are present. Witherington offers one explanation concerning the identity of these unfaithful ones, referencing Rom. 15:31 and the "disobedient ones in Judea" as those who not only rejected the Christ but also the Gentile mission.[31] First, as Witherington has suggested, if the identity of the ἀπιστία are the disobedient ones of Rom. 15:1, then both belief and actions are present as not only did some fail to believe Jesus was the Christ, but this resulted then in disobedience and failure to carry out the Gentile mission.

---

[30] *BDAG*, 103.
[31] Witherington, *Romans*, 93.

The meaning of ἀπιστία is connected to the preceding verse of Rom. 3:2 and Israel being "entrusted" with the words of God. Shedding some light on the matter is the second half of Rom. 3:3, where God will remain faithful (πίστις) despite the lack of ἀπιστία on behalf of Israel. Faith in this context does not mean belief—as if God would not continue to "believe" the promises—but focuses on the actions of God to remain true to his promises, that is, that he continues to "do" what he said he would do.

It is within this context above, then, that we understand the ἀπιστία of "some" Jews (3:1) who have failed to act consistently with the oracles of God. This is not in the sense that they have not believed in God's words, although this certainly is not excluded, but that they have not acted in obedience to those words, specifically to fulfill their divine vocation (cf. Rom. 2:13-16). Interestingly, BDAG includes Rom 3:3 underneath the category of being "unfaithful." It notes that this means "lacking a sense of obligation" and cites as an example the disloyal soldiers in Xenophon's *Annals* 2.6.19.[32]

Third, the context of 3:5-18 bears out further evidence to take ἀπιστία to denote conduct rather than belief. The combination of the negated nouns ἀπιστία and ἀδικία points in this direction as well, as does the subsequent *cento* of verses from the Psalms in verses 3:13-18 that focus on actions such as cursing and murder (3:15).

As we saw in the survey of Roman historians the linkage between a nation's faithfulness to Rome was tied to Rome's faithfulness to their treaty. Disobedience provided just cause for the breaking of a treaty and war with Rome. What may have struck a Roman audience member in the house churches would be the faithfulness of God to his treaty/covenant with Israel despite their unfaithfulness. Perhaps if some community members had come to Rome as prisoners of war, they might be all too well aware of the consequences of being unfaithful or disobedient to a superior force. Indeed in some ways, what might have stood out, in particular, was the mercy inherent to such faithfulness. Thus Paul may be slightly hinting at his argument to come in Rom. 11:30-32.

In Rom. 3:5, Paul reintroduces the notion of ἀδικία, last mentioned in 2:8 and most famously in 1:18.[33] The noun ἀδικία often refers to acts of wrongdoing or behavior that can be characterized as disobedience.[34] The combination of both the negated ἀπιστία and ἀδικία shows the interplay between the failure to believe and the notion of disobedience, with the negated noun ἀδικία bearing the functional aspect of disobedience. For Paul, the terms faithful/unfaithful and righteous/unrighteous are parallel ideas, as Rom. 3:3 and 3:5 demonstrate.[35] Paul introduces both 3:3 and 3:5 with a marker of condition (εἰ), both verses are posed as questions that receive negative answers, both involve wordplays on the πιστ and δικ- roots, and both appear in similar constructions as shown below:

---

[32] BDAG, 103.
[33] ἀδικία is mentioned in Rom. 1:18, 29; 2:8; 3:5; 6:13; 9:14.
[34] BDAG, 20.
[35] In agreement is Dunn, *Romans*, 134.

Rom. 3:3 and 3:5

ἡ ἀπιστία αὐτῶν τὴν πίστιν τοῦ θεοῦ (3:3)
Will their faithlessness nullify the faithfulness of God?

ἡ ἀδικία ἡμῶν θεοῦ δικαιοσύνην (3:5)
Our injustice serves to confirm the justice of God.

Finally, in this short section of 3:10-18, Paul quotes a powerful set of OT passages to round out his argument. This catena of verses from the LXX is introduced in the typical Pauline way with "just as it is written" functioning rhetorically as an in-artificial proof that strengthens his previous argument. The negative aspect of the argument is roundly made through the fourfold use of the negative (οὐ) in 3:10-12 and six times in the broader context of 3:10-18.

The summary of the negative indictment is equally shown by the quotation of Eccl. 7:20, "there is no one on earth who is righteous, no one who does what is right and never sins" (NIV), in Rom. 3:10 that demolishes the presupposed distinction between the righteous and the unrighteous that some in the audience might have assumed.[36] By incorporating Eccl. 7:20 and righteousness, Paul has tied this section of his argument back into the thesis statement of Rom. 1:16-17. The next three Old Testament quotations in 3:11-12 are rhetorically structured with a similar introduction of "there is no one / not" followed by a substantive participle, stressing the parallel nature of the three clauses that explicate the head quote of Ecclesiastes.

Paul's argument that none are righteous is rounded out by the three parallel clauses from Ps. 13:2-3 (LXX) where no one "understands" or "seeks" God and all have "turned away." Finally, a general indictment concludes this minor section, where Paul notes that "no one shows goodness" (Rom. 3:12b). The combination of righteousness in 3:10 with goodness or kindness in 3:12 carries through the notion of righteousness as not only one's righteous standing before God but also as the moral imperative of justice (similar to Mic. 6:8).[37] The emphasis on "good" then allows Paul to pivot and introduce the next series of quotations that focus on actions. Rom. 3:13-18 includes another seven citations that focus on various parts of the body, thus bringing unity to the condemnation. As Fitzmyer has noted, "The connotation of such elements is that all parts of a human being are involved in sin ... and [have] participated in evil."[38] The rhetorical function of such indictments is to indicate that from "head to toe," humanity has engaged in sin, or since these quotations are mostly from the Psalms, all have disobeyed the way that leads to life (Psalm 1).[39]

---

[36] Following Dunn, *Romans*, 1:149.
[37] Cranfield comes close to this idea but does not connect Rom. 3:10 to 3:12. See C. E. B. Cranfield, *The Epistle to the Romans: A Critical and Exegetical Commentary*, 2 vols. (Edinburgh: T&T Clark, 1980), 1:192.
[38] Joseph A. Fitzmyer, *Romans* (New York: Doubleday, 1993), 334.
[39] On the concept of sin in Romans see Matthew Croasmun, *The Emergence of Sin: The Cosmic Tyrant in Romans* (New York: Oxford University Press, 2017).

Disobedience is the prime leitmotif of the section that culminates in the final indictment that "all have fallen short of the glory of God" (3:23), thus summing up Paul's long argument begun in Rom. 1:18 emphasizing the negative implications of the thesis statement in Rom. 1:16-17. The entire section of 1:18-3:20 revolves around the disobedience of both Jews and Gentiles, although each has disobeyed in their unique ways. Thomas Tobin rightly directs the reader's attention to the fact that the entire argument of 1:18-3:20 is "temporally or historically oriented" by noting that Rom. 3:21 emphasizes the changing of the times, "But now."[40] Although the past *aeon* was one characterized by rampant and trenchant disobedience that Paul categorizes as unrighteous, a new *aeon* of righteousness has been unveiled (3:21). The shifting of the times introduces what Paul will explicate in Rom. 5-8, but first, he must discuss the character of Abraham.

At this point in the discourse, if we were able to "sit in the audience" and attempt to understand how Gentiles would have heard Paul's discourse two notable issues of comparison and contrast stand out. In 1:18-3:23, the thematic emphasis has been on the disobedience of humanity and God's righteous judgment. Two similar notions would offer both a profound comparison and contrast for a Gentile audience. First, disobedience resulting in punishment would be well understood, as we previously stated. However, Paul's statement about "justice" or "righteousness" for those who were disobedient would have been surprising (3:21-24), particularly the element of hope that was accompanied such a statement. Destruction and defeat is not the final note of Paul's argument nor the story of the Gentiles. Rather than bearing their punishment or destruction, the offer of hope through a crucified Lord (3:25) would have been startling for Gentiles in Paul's audience.

Abraham: The Father of the Gentiles (4:1-25)

Turning to the final section of Paul's first rhetorical proof in Romans, we end with an appeal to Abraham (Rom. 4:1-25) that has long puzzled scholars and commentators.[41] Specifically, Abraham's position and purpose in the broader context of 1:13-4:25 is debated. Abraham is seen to some as the classic example of justification by faith employed by Paul to illustrate his theological point.[42] Others perceive a more sociological emphasis and see Abraham employed to theologically underpin Paul's mission to the Gentiles and explain how Jews and Gentiles can form one unified

---

[40] Tobin, *Paul's Rhetoric*, 123. Cf. Johannes Woyke, "'Einst' Und 'Jetzt' in Röm 1-3? Zur Bedeutung Von Nyni De in Röm 3,21," *ZNW* 92 (2001): 185-206.

[41] For the grammatical issues of 4:1 see Richard B. Hays, "'Have We Found Abraham to Be Our Forefather according to the Flesh?' A Reconsideration of Rom 4:1," *NovT* 27 (1985): 76-98. See also Michael Cranford, "Abraham in Romans 4: The Father of All Who Believe," *NTS* 41 (1995): 71-88; Andrew Kimseng Tan, *The Rhetoric of Abraham's Faith in Romans 4* (Atlanta: SBL, 2018).

[42] As examples Brendan Byrne, *Romans* (Collegeville: Liturgical, 2007), 140-3; F. F. Bruce, *Romans: Revised Edition* (Grand Rapids: Eerdmans, 1986), 140-5; Thomas R. Schreiner, *Romans* (Grand Rapids: Baker, 1998), 212; Gathercole, *Where Is Boasting*, 232-4; Douglas J. Moo, *The Epistle to the Romans* (Grand Rapids: Eerdmans, 1996), 225; Käsemann, *Romans*, 105; J. A. Ziesler, *Paul's Letter to the Romans* (Philadelphia: Trinity International, 1989), 120-1.

community.⁴³ Further, some scholars identify 4:1-25 as a backward reference to 1:18-32, where Abraham's obedience is the antithesis of the disobedient Gentiles of 1:18-32.⁴⁴ If Abraham is meant to contrast Gentile disobedience in 1:18-32, then the obedience of Abraham is certainly in view, namely his obedience to believe or trust in God's promises in Gen. 15.

Paul does not recount the entire story of Abraham, but only selective portions of the Abrahamic narrative, specifically focusing on the "timing" of the blessing.⁴⁵ The timing of the event(s) is theologically important for Paul. Several phrases are used in Rom. 4 that are pertinent for our discussion of the theme of obedience in Romans. The first is the genitive construction "the righteousness from/of faith" in 4:11 and the second is the promise of the nations to Abraham repeated twice—implicitly in Rom. 4:11, 16 and explicitly in Rom. 4:17-18.

A quick search of the nouns that precede or follow faith (πιστις) in Romans reveals that only a few persons or ideas dominate Paul's modification of faith language.⁴⁶ Apart from the obedience of faith phrases (Rom. 1:5; 16:26), the noun faith is modified by the faith of/in Jesus (Rom. 3:22, 26), the faith of Abraham (Rom. 4:16), and law or principle (Rom. 3:27). The only other instance of faith being modified by another genitive is in 4:13 and 10:6 with righteousness (δικαιοσύνης). To put this in another way, apart from persons, both obedience and righteousness are the two main ways of modifying faith in Romans. So how exactly does the obedience from/of faith and the righteousness from/of faith relate to one another? Getting ahead of ourselves a bit, it is critical to remember that in the following sections obedience and faith will be linked in both Rom. 5:19 and Rom. 6:16.

Concerning the relationship of these phrases, it is important to note that these genitive constructions have the same social domain of the nations/Gentiles. Rom. 4:13-25 is focused on the promise of blessing coming to the Gentiles (Rom. 4:17-18, 1:5). The genitive constructions, obedience from/of faith, and the righteousness from/of faith form a triad of faith, righteousness, and obedience. Connecting these ideas is the notion of the "promise language" to Abraham. God's promise to Abraham is the theological underpinning for Paul's apostolic mission. As Paul indicates, it is because Abraham is the father of us *all* (4:16) and the promise to inherit the *world* (4:13) that this promise serves as the theological rationale for the inclusion of the Gentiles.⁴⁷ It

---

⁴³ As examples: Jewett, *Romans*, 307; Paul J. Achtemeier, *Romans* (Louisville: Westminster John Knox, 1985), 77–9; Stanley K. Stowers, *A Rereading of Romans: Justice, Jews, and Gentiles* (New Haven: Yale University Press, 1997), 227–9. Cf. Nancy Calvert-Koyzis, *Paul, Monotheism and the People of God: The Significance of Abraham Traditions for Early Judaism and Christianity* (New York: T&T Clark, 2004); Richard J. Bautch, "An Appraisal of Abraham's Role in Postexilic Covenants," *CBQ* 71 (2009): 42–63; Gregory C. Bradley, "Abraham as the Jewish Ideal: Exegetical Traditions in Sirach 44:19-21," *CBQ* 70 (2008): 66–81.

⁴⁴ Edward Adams, "Abraham's Faith and Gentile Disobedience: Textual Links between Romans 1 and 4," *JSNT* 65 (1997): 47–66; C. K. Barrett, *The Epistle to the Romans: Revised Edition* (Peabody: Hendrickson, 1991), 98; Käsemann, *Romans*, 125; Fitzmyer, *Romans*, 388; Dunn, *Romans*, 1:221; Johnson, *Reading Romans*, 79.

⁴⁵ See the helpful work by Ronald Hendel, *Remembering Abraham: Culture, Memory, and History in the Hebrew Bible* (New York: Oxford University Press, 2005).

⁴⁶ On faith in Romans see Ben C. Dunson, "Faith in Romans: The Salvation of the Individual or Life in Community?," *JSNT* 34 (2011): 19–46.

⁴⁷ On the uniqueness of Paul highlighting inheriting "the world," cf. Keck, *Romans*, 126.

is this storied theology that allows Paul to indicate that his apostolic purpose is to bring about the obedience of faith among those very people of Abraham's promise and inheritance.[48]

The relationship of obedience and righteousness is, therefore, drawn along mutual lines of thought. Both obedience and righteousness come, not from the law (Rom. 4:13) but by or through faith. Abraham's righteousness came not through his observance of the Mosaic law but through his belief or trust (πιστεύω) that God is the one "who gives life to the dead and calls into existence the things that do not exist" (4:17). Likewise in 4:24, Paul draws a direct line between Abraham's belief in bringing dead things to life to his Gentile audience who also believe "like Abraham" in life coming back from the dead in the person of Jesus who was raised from the dead. Abraham's belief is also his trust, believing not only what God says but also "trusting" God, evidenced by action consistent with that belief.[49] Luke Timothy Johnson rightly stresses, "Responding in trust and obedience to *this* action [God's resurrection of Jesus] of the living God now represents the possibility of having 'faith like Abraham's.'"[50] In Paul's thought, both righteousness and obedience flow from faith. This case will be made in the next section when Paul indicates that the obedience of Jesus results in the "many" being made righteous (5:19).

Romans 4 also offers us another important consideration with its fourfold repetition of nation language (4:11, 16, and 17-18). The nations are referenced implicitly in both 4:11 and 4:16. In verse 11, the phrase "ancestor of all who believe without being circumcised" functions as a long description for the shorter ἔθνος (nations).[51] In 4:16, the use of πᾶς (all) indicates not only those "of the law" but also those not under the law, referring indirectly to the ἔθνος. The two direct references to ἔθνος appear in 4:17-18, where Paul cites Gen. 17:5 (LXX) where Yhwh changes Abram's name to Abraham and states, "I have made you the father of many nations," which Paul follows up with a direct quote of Gen. 15:5 (LXX). Dunn argues that the "many nations" would most obviously refer to "the rapidly growing Gentile mission."[52] Following Dunn, Jewett draws on the broader horizon of Romans and connects this to Paul's "project of the mission to the end of the known world, Spain."[53] By connecting the divine promises to Abraham to the "nations," Paul has linked his apostolic mission with that of divine undertaking. Paul finds his place calling for the obedience of faith among those very nations that God had promised to Abraham.

---

[48] On Paul's storied worldview, cf. Ben Witherington, *Paul's Narrative Thought World: The Tapestry of Tragedy and Triumph* (Louisville: Westminster John Knox, 1994); Bruce W. Longenecker, *Narrative Dynamics in Paul: A Critical Assessment* (Louisville: Westminster John Knox, 2002); James D. G. Dunn, *The Theology of Paul the Apostle* (Grand Rapids: Eerdmans, 1998), 18; N. T. Wright, *Paul and the Faithfulness of God*, 2 vols. (Minneapolis: Fortress, 2013), 1:456–537. For the importance of these "stories" in Romans see Grieb, *The Story of Romans*.
[49] On resurrection themes in Romans see J. R. Daniel Kirk, *Unlocking Romans: Resurrection and the Justification of God* (Grand Rapids: Eerdmans, 2008).
[50] Johnson, *Reading Romans*, 80.
[51] Johnson, *Reading Romans*, 75.
[52] Dunn, *Romans*, 1:217.
[53] Jewett, *Romans*, 333; Keck, *Romans*, 131.

Such an invocation of nation language ties into a theme that Paul has been developing from 1:5 onward and will conclude at 16:26.[54] The first and final occurrences of "nations" language in Romans are connected to the theme of obedience. To recall such language at this point harkens back to Paul's initial usage of ἔθνος and their obedience as the aim of his apostleship (Rom. 1:5). The discussion of the nations at various points in Romans is as much about their inclusion as it is their purpose within God's plans for the world. Restating the point, Paul argues not only for Gentile inclusion in Romans but also for their theological and teleological purpose of obedience as indicated by Rom. 1:5 and 16:26.

If we return to our approach of reading Romans from a Gentile point of view, we must ponder how a Gentile audience would have heard this portion of Paul's argument. The person of Abraham represents for Gentiles their inclusion into God's mission in the world. The use of persons as moral examples was a common ancient practice, and this would have been familiar to Gentiles in Paul's audience. In our previous sections, notable figures such as Julius Caesar, generals, and soldiers, as well as Odysseus, are held up as examples to follow, specifically for their obedience. Part of this ethical discourse could have been familiar to many in Paul's audience. Also similar would have been the idea of Abraham responding in faith and obedience. Such a parallel structure of thought was also seen throughout the historians where one enters into faith and then offers obedience. Some preconceptions Gentiles may have had that would have been different from Paul's argument certainly include the content of that faith—namely, faith in God raising Jesus from the dead (4:24).

The Second Proof: 5:1–8:39

Rom. 5:1-2 forms an appropriate rhetorical *transitio* from the preceding section of 4:1-25 and introduces subsequent themes that will appear through 8:39. The *Rhetorica Ad Herrenium* indicates that the *transitio* is "a figure which briefly recalls what has been said, and likewise briefly sets forth what is to follow."[55] Paul's *transitio* includes references to righteousness and faith that look back to the previous chapter, while the references to the topics of grace, hope, and glory look forward to the themes of subsequent sections. Rom. 5:1-21 represents the theological foundation of Paul's call for the obedience of faith (1:5).

Together Rom. 5:1-21 and 6:1-23 form the climax of obedience language in Romans. Both Rom. 5:19 and Rom. 6:16 explicitly refer to obedience and disobedience (ὑπακοή and παρακοή). However, like ascending and descending a great precipice, Paul mounts his argument in several critical stages. To carry the metaphor farther, if Rom. 5:19 and 6:16 represent the dual peaks of the obedience language, then Rom. 5:1-17, 19-21 and Rom. 6:1-15 and 17-23 are the flanks.

It is also important, at this stage of the argument, to be mindful of our survey of the Greco-Roman historians and philosophers. Their use of imagery and language informs

---

[54] Rom. 1:5, 13; 2:14, 24; 3:29; 4:17-18; 9:24, 30; 10:19; 11:11-13, 25; 15:9-12, 16, 18, 27; 16:4, 26.
[55] *Rhet. Her.* 4.26.35. Noted by Jewett, *Romans*, 346.

our understanding of these passages from a Roman Gentile viewpoint. Witherington correctly draws attention to this Roman background in Rom. 5, when he notes that Paul

> argues in terms a Gentile could readily understand and identify with. The language of peace, reconciliation, and the pacification of enemies would be familiar to those in Rome used to hearing the honorific propaganda about the emperor and his accomplishments, vis-á-vis the Pax Romana.[56]

The following section seeks to highlight further examples alluded to by Witherington.

The Kingdoms of Sin and Death and the Kingdom of Grace and Faith (5:1-21)

First, notice at the outset of Rom. 5:1 that we have a pattern similar to that which was identified in the historians. In 5:1, those that have been established in right standing before God by "faith" now have "peace" with God.[57] The structure of logic parallels similar patterns in the Greco-Roman historians, such as Polybius and Livy, as seen in the previous chapters. Such a structure would have been familiar to a Roman audience.[58]

Applying this pattern of faith–peace–obedience, which we saw in the historians to Rom. 5:1-2, Paul's audience was previously objects of God's wrath (Rom. 1:18) because of their disobedience. Now, by entering into faith, they have peace and are saved from God's wrath (Rom. 5:9). Similar to the Roman treaties, entering into the faith of the Romans was the prerequisite for peace. The progression between wrath, faith, and peace would certainly have been very familiar to some in Paul's audience who may have come to Rome as conquered peoples.[59] Paul's argument would have been reminiscent of what some Gentiles thought about when they thought about the obedience of the nations.

---

[56] Witherington, *Romans*, 131.
[57] On the textual and grammatical issues of 5:1 see Frank J. Matera, *Romans* (Grand Rapids: Baker, 2010), 125-6.
[58] Jonathan Bersot has rightly reflected on the logical argument of Rom. 5:1-11 and the audience's understanding, noting that, le texte paulinien suggère que les premiers lecteurs de l'épître aux Romains devaient accepter la thèse de la péricope sans difficulté, celle-ci faisant référence à des préacquis implicites. En effet, si cette thèse avait été nouvelle pour les destinataires du texte, du moins pour ce qu'en connaissait l'auteur, celui-ci se serait donné la peine de développer la question. See Jonathan Bersot, "La Paix Avec Dieu, Passage De La Justification À La Réconciliation: Observations Structurelles Et Narratives En Romains 5,1-11," *Science et Esprit* 62 (2010): 125-42. Although he is focusing on the relationship between justification by faith and peace, his question is appropriate to our own task.
[59] See Peter Lampe, *From Paul to Valentinus: Christians at Rome in the First Two Centuries* (Minneapolis: Fortress, 2003), 153-83. Cf. Klaus Haacker, *Der Brief Des Paulus an Die Römer* (Leipzig: Evangelische Verlagsanstalt, 1999), 126; Jeffrey B. Gibson, "Paul's 'Dying Formula': Prolegomena to an Understanding of Its Import and Significance," in *Celebrating Romans: Template for Pauline Theology* (ed. Sheila E. McGinn, Grand Rapids: Eerdmans, 2004), 20-41. Gibson draws attention to dying formulas used in not only Jewish sources but also military contexts between commanders and soldiers (36-7). So also Witherington, *Romans*, who draws out that this was the language of the "pacification efforts of the Roman emperor" (134).

Many commentators note that Paul has in mind the OT concept of *šālôm*, but this still misses the component of how a Roman audience would have been familiar with peace language as residents of the *Pax Romana*—through a lord that achieved peace through victories (*Res Gestae* 13).[60] Peace was a benefit given to Rome's allies or friends as a result of entering into their faith and obedience (Rom 1:5).[61] This peace of course would begin to contrast with Paul's understanding, as God's offer of peace is not just to "friends" but as seen previously to enemies.

Rom. 5:3-11 focuses on the theme of reconciliation. However, we do not want to miss the broader scope here and in the following section. At a structural level, we have the reconciliation of God's enemies in Rom. 5:3-11, followed by a discussion of obedience in 5:19. Reconciliation from enemy status to obedient "subjects" of God's kingdom follows a similar Roman pattern of treaty-making. Groups that were previously enemies of Rome are now "obedient" *amicii* or *socii* of Rome. One point of notable contrast for a Gentile audience familiar with the ideological program of Rome would have been the idea of "having hope" as this might be a novel concept for a Roman audience.

In 5:10-11, we have the expansion and explanation of the phrase "we have peace with God" from 5:1. The description of "enemies" is a continuation of Paul's characterization of the previous state of his audience who was ungodly (5:6), sinners (5:8), and now enemies (5:10). The piling up of terms showcases the continuity between them, all of which include the concept of disobedience. Contrary to Roman expectations, this Lord dies *for* his enemies rather than going to war against them. Paul anticipates such an unexpected turn of events based on his parenthetical statement in 5:7. Such a counterrevolutionary idea would not have been lost on an audience saturated with the discourse of an empire that brought peace through victory over their enemies. A point of tension emerges with a Pauline conception of obedience in Romans and previous understandings of Roman Gentiles and the relationship with obedience. If obedience in their experience was a coerced obedience on pain of war and death, this obedience is not coerced but responsive to divine favor and reconciliation.

Reconciliation is effected through the death of God's own son, which leads to salvation (5:10).[62] Jewett rightly notes that the reconciliation language is drawn from "spheres of conflict, in which warring groups, quarreling citizens ... make peace."[63] Such a background to this language, combined with the absence of any OT quotations in this section, lends credence to reading Romans from a Gentile point of view. It seems clear that Paul intended to use terms his Gentile audience would have been familiar with. The current stage of Paul's argument is that of a contrast between what God did while his creation was "weak," "sinners," and "enemies," but anticipating that

---

[60] For the Jewish background, cf. Fitzmyer, *Romans*, 395.
[61] Interestingly, Cranfield draws attention numerous times to being "God's friends" but without any recourse to the Greco-Roman background (*Romans*, 1:256-8).
[62] Jens Schröter, "Der Heilstod Jesu—Deutungen Im Neuen Testament," *Luther* 84 (2013): 139-58.
[63] Jewett, *Romans*, 364. Although the suggestion of Hengel and Hahn that Paul drew this language from the Greco-Roman ruler cult seems overdrawn (noted by Jewett). On the broader theological concept of reconciliation see the still excellent work by Ralph P. Martin, *Reconciliation: A Study of Paul's Theology* (Atlanta: John Knox, 1981).

there is "much more" to come. This language anticipates his next argument in Rom. 5:15-21 and also in Rom. 6:1-23 and 8:1-39.

Rom 5:12-21 is a small *synkrisis* between two people and two alternate actions.[64] The *synkrisis* revolves around the two persons of Adam and Christ and their corresponding actions of transgression and the "grace-gift."[65] Paul's accounting of sin's origin occupies the argument in the first half of this section (5:17) with a dominant emphasis on the Adam side of the equation. Paul focuses on Adam's sin, trespass, and resulting judgment of death that has extended to all mankind (5:15). In 5:15, Paul introduces Christ into his argument, focusing on the grace and gift of God. The gulf between Adam and Christ is extended in 5:15-21. Paul reaches the "climax of his comparison" in verse 19 when he specifically focuses on the disparate actions of Adam and Christ—their disobedience and obedience.[66] Don Garlington has noted the parallelism of verses 18–19, where the "trespass" of Adam in verse 18 is replaced by the "disobedience" of Adam in verse 19. Likewise, the "act of righteousness" (δικαίωμα) of Christ in verse 18 is replaced by "obedience" (ὑπακοή) of Christ in verse 19.[67]

In 5:19, we have two explicit references to obedience and disobedience. Adam's sin and transgression are now identified clearly as an act of disobedience. Paul sets up his antithetical parallelism with the two nearly identical phrases: "through the disobedience of one man" and "through the obedience of one man." The argument put forth in 5:12-18 has now been reduced to its essence for Paul, namely the acts of disobedience and obedience.[68]

For a Gentile audience, the notion that one person's actions could lead to a grave result for many has clear parallels in a nation's representatives before Rome. Throughout the sources, the rulers of various territories hold this type of decision-making power. Their actions have the ability to affect a large number of people. One example is the relationship between King Philip of Macedon and Rome, highlighted by Polybius, where he notes that Rome demanded, "If he [Philip] acted so, they added, he might consider himself at peace with Rome, but if he refused to obey the consequences would be the reverse" (16.27.3). Paul's concept of sin and grace seems to share a similar framework. That such background may be in play is supported by Paul's use of "βασιλεύω" (to rule) in 5:17 where he focuses on death "ruling or reigning" as a result of Adam's disobedience. Jewett draws attention to the fact that the Latin equivalent of this term would be *regnere* that "implies irresistible coercive power."[69]

Although not relying on Greco-Roman background, Käsemann bears out the implication of the evidence we showed in the previous chapter, whereby "ruling

---

[64] Helpful is Ryan S. Schellenberg, "Does Paul Call Adam a 'Type' of Christ? An Exegetical Note on Romans 5, 14," *ZNW* 105 (2014): 54–63.
[65] On the rhetorical features of a *synkrisis*, cf. Witherington, *Romans*, 141–2. Contra Tobin, *Paul's Rhetoric*, 184, who argues that Rom. 5:18-21 is a comparison between equals.
[66] Fitzmyer, *Romans*, 421.
[67] Don Garlington, *Faith, Obedience, and Perseverance: Aspects of Paul's Letter to the Romans* (Eugene: Wipf & Stock, 2009), 103.
[68] Rightly noted by Michael J. Gorman, *Cruciformity: Paul's Narrative Spirituality of the Cross* (Grand Rapids: Eerdmans, 2001), 107–9.
[69] Jewett, *Romans*, 377.

powers ... implicate all people individually and everywhere determine reality as destiny."[70] One person's actions resulting in two different outcomes are a frequent refrain of the Greco-Roman sources, where a representative such as a king or ambassador carries the power to either obey or disobey Rome's requests. The result is either peace and life or wrath and destruction for an entire community. Perhaps such concepts and imagery would be familiar to a Roman audience.

We have a similar example from the philosophers (Cicero, *De Repub.* 1.4). For Paul, these representatives of the human race are Adam and Christ. Through Adam's disobedience, the "many" were made sinners—or, in other words, became objects of God's wrath.[71] The opposite is true for Christ; his obedience leads to life and the removal of wrath (Rom. 5:9).

In 5:19, Paul explicitly connects obedience and righteousness. Christ's obedience opens up the channel for "many" to be made righteous, reflecting the righteousness language used in the thesis statement of 1:16-17. We see the interplay between obedience and faith in Paul's thought world and, as such, Rom. 5:19 brings us again to the obedience of faith (Rom. 1:5).[72] We should not miss the fact that by "many" Paul means both Jews and Gentiles. The logic of Paul's argument is that through the obedience of Christ, the Gentiles will be made righteous and now able to pursue the obedience of faith. Paul's argument about Christ anticipates the next stage of his argument in 6:16 about those "in Christ." For Paul, the person of Christ serves as not only the basis and reality of the righteous life but also its forming pattern as we will see in Rom. 6:1-23.

Paul's argument in Rom. 5:1-21 bears several notable similarities to how Gentiles encountered obedience language in their day-to-day lives. The argument in this section would have resonated with his Gentile audience. The structure of thought that moves from wrath-faith-peace-obedience would have been a familiar refrain for those familiar with Rome's history and their dealings with various nations. Our research in Chapters 3–4 bore out this theme repeatedly. Second, Paul's introduction of two figures (Adam and Christ) with the ability to affect the outcomes of entire peoples also parallels the decision-making power of a nation's representatives before Rome. Third, the movement from being an enemy to being reconciled members of a group was an often repeated action by Rome. One notable contrast for a Gentile audience, however, would have been that God has enacted this reconciliation through the death of his own son (5:10). If one remembers the images of conquering from Rome's landscape (Chapter 6), nations are shown in the defeated positions. In Paul's discourse, God

---

[70] Käsemann, *Romans*, 150. Witherington likewise notes some similar features (*Romans*, 144).
[71] See Günter Röhser, "Paulus Und Die Herrschaft Der Sünde," *ZNW* 103 (2012): 84–110. He argues,

> Der griechische Begriff für »Sünder« (ἁμαρτωλός) kommt in den Briefen des Paulus nur selten vor, jedoch sind zentrale Aussagen mit ihm verbunden. In Röm 5,19 kommt das Sündenverhängnis zur Sprache, welches in der UnausWeichlichkeit des Sündigens für alle Menschen aufgrund des Ungehorsams Adams besteht und »die Vielen« als »Sünder« hingestellt, d.h. sie zu Sündern gemacht hat, die dieses auch durch ihr eigenes Tun und Wollen beständig ratifizieren (vgl. 5,12; s.u. in Abschn. 2). (84)

[72] On the vocabulary of faith in Romans, cf. Jean-Noël Aletti, *God's Justice in Romans: Keys for Interpreting the Epistle to the Romans* (Rome: Gregorian & Biblical Press, 2010), 103–14.

himself through Christ assumes the defeated position for the sake of the world. Rather than conquering and defeating disobedient persons, this Lord dies for his enemies. Such a point offers a profound moment when Gentile members in Paul's audience would see the stark contrast to any previously held notions of not only obedience but also the nature of God himself. The noncoercive nature of God's power on behalf of his enemies might be the most shocking difference a Gentile audience would notice having heard this section.

No Longer Obedient to Sin and Death (6:1-23)

Beginning in Rom. 6:1, Paul must now confront some of the logical implications and explain the realities of this new "reign" (βασιλεύω) being exercised through Jesus Christ (5:21). Paul's argument shifts from a discussion of the disobedience, sin, transgression, and wrath that "reigned" from Adam that dominated 5:1-21, whereby he only briefly introduced the concepts of Christ, grace, and obedience (5:18-21), to focus now on this new reign "in Christ." For his Gentile audience, Rom 6:1-23 focuses on the inverse of the type of life that was described in 1:18-32.[73] C. K. Barrett has rightly noted the importance of obedience in 6:1-23. He states that Paul wants "to show that obedience has a place in the system of grace and faith ... indeed, it would not be wrong to say that the whole of ch. vi is an attempt to vindicate that place."[74]

One of the persistent social metaphors that Paul will use to describe this transition from being "in Adam" to being "in Christ" is the imagery of being set free from slavery. Slavery is part of Paul's self-description in Rom. 1:1 as a "slave of Jesus Christ," so it should not be surprising that this imagery plays a prominent role.[75] The social language of slavery is incorporated throughout the rhetorical section. Paul will use the language of slavery—δουλεύω (to serve), κυριεύω (to master), δοῦλος (slave/servant), ἐλευθερόω (to set free)—alongside obedience language, such as ὑπακούω (to obey) and ὑπακοή (obedience). As James Dunn has noted, "Paul would not have cherished the image of believer as 'slave' if he had not also embraced its corollary: the slave obeys."[76] The theme of obedience is included as a corollary of Paul's discussion and usage of slavery language.

The first reference to obedience in this section occurs in 6:12 after Paul's conclusion that the believer has died to "sin" by being crucified with Christ through baptism (6:3-4). Now that the believer has been transferred from the realm of Adam, death, sin, and disobedience, the believer is now under the rule of Christ marked by life, righteousness, and obedience. In light of this new reality, one is to be "dead to sin," but alive to God. This new "life in God" can no longer be marked by obedience to the former ruler, so Paul exhorts those in his audience to no longer obey sin's desires

---

[73] So also Stowers, *Rereading Romans*, 256.
[74] Barrett, *Romans*, 123. He also rightly connects this to Rom. 1:5.
[75] This point is highlighted by Phillip F. Esler, *Conflict and Identity in Romans: The Social Setting of Paul's Letter* (Minneapolis: Fortress, 2003), 220.
[76] Dunn, *Theology of Paul*, 635. Although Dunn is certainly wrong that obedience was a little-known word at Paul's time as our previous chapters have shown this is unsustainable.

(6:12) and confirms the same negative assessment of disobedience expressed in 1:18-32 and the forthcoming opportunity for obedient actions in 14:1–15:13. This also bears a striking similarity to the concepts in the philosophers, such as Epictetus, where he indicates that obedience is tied to pleasing the divine (*Disc.* 2.14.11-13).

Such a transfer of allegiance—where obedience is directed to one's new ruler and their aims or desires—would have been familiar to many in Rome, whether citizens or conquered subjects, although especially the latter. Those conquered by Rome would have been aware of the requirements to enter into the new reign of Rome where obedience was paramount to maintaining that new relationship. A nation's previous goals and aims were by necessity now aligned with the directives of Rome. The formerly independent nation would have to lay aside its desires as a new reign had begun. One might also note that this is a feature that is more readily explained by Greco-Roman sources than the Hebrew Bible.

Gentiles in Paul's audience could be tempted to think that this new freedom in Christ meant no longer having to obey (see Rom. 6:1) and could express the same sort of shock or dismay as the Aetolians had in their interactions with Rome. In Chapter 3, we showed how various groups could misinterpret their relationship with Rome and begin to think that their continued obedience was no longer necessary. Gentiles in Paul's audience may have been under the same assumptions, whereby now having entered into faith with God, their obedience was optional. The idea that obedience could curry favoritism was not out of the question. There would be both a comparison and a contrast with Gentiles hearing Paul's argument, where like Rome, Paul also envisions continued obedience to this Lord, despite the new relationship recently established.

Paul's terms in Rom. 6:13 evoke Roman imagery as well. Paul instructs those in Rome to refrain from using their bodies as "weapons" for unrighteousness (ἀδικία) or disobedience (Rom. 1:18-32) and to present themselves as "weapons" for righteousness/obedience.[77] Again, obedience and disobedience are integral to the argument Paul is making. His use of "weapon" language invokes a Roman military context as well. As Jewett has pointed out, "Rome used its weapons to dominate others and, if they refused to be subjugated, to destroy them."[78] The imagery would have been familiar to anyone who had visited Augustus's mausoleum and seen the image of Mars sitting on top of a pile of weapons. The war imagery is carried further by the contrast of presenting one's body (cf. Rom. 12:1) either as "of sin" or to God as "instruments of righteousness" (Rom. 6:13b).[79]

The idea of laying down one's weapons was paramount in the examples of the Roman historians of those nations who submitted to Rome. Failing to lay down one's weapons was cause for termination of the peace treaty. Analogously, here in 6:13, one's body is now given over to God himself in obedience (cf. Rom. 12–15). Similar military imagery was also employed in moral discourses as seen in the works of the

---

[77] Stowers, *Rereading Romans*, 255–6, also notes this point.
[78] Jewett, *Romans*, 410.
[79] Witherington draws attention to the noun ὅπλον, noting that these were often spears carried in a Greek army known as the *hoplites* (*Romans*, 163).

philosophers (Chapter 5). The corollary of Paul's argument is that if an individual is using his body in service to sin, he is taking up arms against God himself.

Roman imagery pervades this verse and would have been familiar to a Roman audience or anyone who walked along the Via Flaminia in Rome. We noted previously that one of the large structures that dominated the Roman landscape was the *Ara Pacis* that contained an image of Roma sitting on top of a pile of weapons. Such imagery may have been part of a Gentile's previous notions about weapons and familiar imagery to draw upon during Paul's discussion in 6:13. Likewise, the war imagery of Paul's statement about using one's "members" in service of disobedience comes in stark contrast to the requirement of laying down one's weapons in the historical sources. Indeed, previously we showed how taking up arms was equivalent to breaking a treaty and declaring war against Rome. Such illustrative images would have been familiar to those within the shadow of numerous images throughout Rome.

In 6:14, Paul personifies sin as he had done in the previous section, where sin is pictured as formerly reigning as a "lord" with the subject being obedient to its master.[80] Paul wants to make clear that this new transfer of lordship (from Sin to Christ) does not include the corollary that obedience is no longer necessary (6:15). One is reminded of the confusion on behalf of the Aetolians who thought that by submitting to Rome they would get better bargaining conditions when only unconditional surrender was acceptable to Rome. Paul seems to be dispelling a similar type of confusion, whereby some in his audience may have thought that "not being under law" afforded them the freedom to do whatever they wished (6:14). They are reminded that their new Lord requires obedience as well. The imagery used in this section, whether in a military context or a slavery context, all conveys the same effect. As Dunn has noted, "Whether the image is that of slave-owner (vv. 16–18), of king ... or of military force ... the effect is the same—acknowledgment of a superior power and authority to whom the only proper response is submission and obedience."[81]

According to Paul, obedience is the mark of every person in his audience. The only question is the object to which that obedience is directed—either their former *kurios* of Sin, leading to death, or the new reigning *kurios* Christ, leading to righteousness (6:16). Obedience serves as a primary identity marker to indicate the lordship under which one lives. As Michael Gorman has rightly identified, "In Romans 6, death to sin in baptism leads to life in Christ (6:1–11), and life in Christ is a life of obedience (6:12–23)."[82] Paul connects obedience and righteousness, thus tying the theme of obedience to the thesis statement of Romans.

In 6:17, Paul signals through the use of the imperfect ἦτε (from εἰμί, to be) that his audience's status as slaves to sin is something in the past (also see 7:5-6). Rather out

---

[80] The personification of concepts would have been familiar to a Roman audience, used to the personification of virtues such as peace, concord, fortune, and victory.
[81] Dunn, *Romans*, 1:337.
[82] Gorman rightly connects this to Paul's purpose in 1:5 (*Cruciformity*, 32). The recent work of Jean-Sébastian Viard also sheds light on 6:15-23. Although Viard notes correctly that freedom is not the focal point of the section, he wrongly concludes that obedience is not one of the main topics of the section. See Jean-Sébastien Viard, "Obéissance Ou Liberté? Redécouverte Structurelle De Rm 6,15-23," *ScEs* 54 (2002): 351.

of profound gratefulness to God (perhaps in contrast to his profound agony in Rom. 9:1-5), Paul declares that the Roman community members "have become obedient from the heart to the form of teaching to which you were entrusted" (6:17).[83] At a moment where one would expect Paul to use a *pist-* root to emphasize this audience's belief, he emphasizes their obedience.[84] He can characterize them now as "slaves of righteousness" or, in the terms of Rom. 6:16, obedient to righteousness. Indeed, as Matthew Thiessen concludes, "his claim that his readers now obey ... matches the response that he believes his apostleship was ordained to engender among the gentiles—obedience."[85]

The parallelism between 6:16 and 6:18 indicates that for Paul slavery and obedience go together. Again, Dunn offers insightful comments: "The use of ὑπακοῆς here is surprising and striking, since θεοῦ or equivalent would seem to be more appropriate. It must be the consequence of the close association between the two ideas, slavery and obedience, which dominate these two verses."[86] Or as Wright has noted, obedience functions "as another synecdoche for the entire grace/righteousness sphere."[87] Paul's audience is made up of those who have been transferred from the realm of sin, death, and disobedience to the new realm in Christ, which is marked by righteousness and obedience. Obedience corresponds to Rom. 1:17, as these are the "righteous who will live by faith" in conformity with the righteousness of God (Rom. 1:16-17).

Rom. 6:20-23 concludes the major portion of Paul's argument thus far on those who are "in Adam" and those who are "in Christ." Paul indicates such a transference through the paradoxical imagery of "you have been freed from sin and enslaved to God" (6:22). For Paul, human reality is a bounded experience—an experience bound by obedience, whether to God or Sin, and one that results in life or death, respectively.

The slavery language used in this section gives us an excellent opportunity to reflect on how a Gentile audience would encounter such imagery. If studies of ancient slavery are any indication, anywhere between one-third and two-thirds of the Roman population were slaves or former slaves, and thus this imagery and language of slavery would have been quite potent.[88] The experience of obedience would have been a practical

---

[83] The content of Paul's phrase is a notoriously debated issue. I follow those who see this as some type of oral tradition regarding the Jesus tradition. Cf. Dunn, *Romans*, 1:343–4; Fitzmyer, *Romans*, 449–50; Byrne, *Romans*, 206; Peter Stuhlmacher, *Paul's Letter to the Romans: A Commentary*, trans. S. J. Hafemann (Louisville: Westminster John Knox, 1994), 95. Contra Jewett, *Romans*, 418–19, who identifies 17b as interpolation by later authors.

[84] Gorman, *Cruciformity*, 133.

[85] Thiessen, *Paul and the Gentile Problem*, 45.

[86] Dunn, *Romans*, 1:342.

[87] Wright, *Romans*, 544.

[88] Peter Garnsey, *Ideas of Slavery from Aristotle to Augustine* (New York: Cambridge University Press, 1996), 1–22; Peter Garnsey and Richard Saller, *The Roman Empire: Economy, Society, and Culture* (Los Angeles: University of California Press, 1987), 107–24; Robert Knapp, *Invisible Romans* (Cambridge: Harvard University Press, 2011), 125–69; John K. Goodrich, "From Slaves of Sin to Slaves of God: Reconsidering the Origin of Paul's Slavery Metaphor in Romans 6," *BBR* 23 (2013): 509–30; Leonhard Schumacher, "Slaves in Roman Society," in *The Oxford Handbook of Social Relations in the Roman World* (ed. Michael Peachin, New York: Oxford University Press, 2011), 589–608. See also Keener, *Romans*, 81, for a list of important ancient sources on this subject.

reality for most, if not all, of Paul's audience in Rome.[89] The daily reality of obedience to some higher authority—whether a master, patron, or ultimately the empire—was not something that would quickly fade. In the previous chapters, we noted that one of the main domains for obedience language was with slaves. Philosophers frequently drew upon slavery imagery. Epictetus uses similar language of being "enslaved to God" while Cicero calls "wicked men" slaves (*Parad.* 5.35). Likewise, when nations were subjected to Rome, many of them became slaves. Thus Gentiles sitting "in the audience" would sadly all too well understood the implications of obedience. What might not have been as familiar was to Gentiles was the language of slavery to sin, although slavery to the vices was a familiar notion. Further, Paul's paradoxical image of being "set free" to be "enslaved to God" may also have confounded some Gentiles' conceptions of obedience.

The Dilemma of Obedience and Disobedience (7:1-25)

Rom. 7:1-25 begins a new subsection of Paul's argument in the unfolding argument of Rom. 5:1-8:39. The new portion of the argument is signaled rhetorically through Paul's use of the diatribe style with a question to his interlocutor, "Do you not know" (7:1). The discussion of law comes right after Paul effectively showed that obedience to God is paramount (Rom. 6:15-23). Paul turns to a much more specific example, one of crucial importance given the Jew–Gentile relationship in Rome. Specifically, what about obedience to the law?[90] Paul must engage in a two-pronged conversation. On one hand, he must continue his emphasis on obedience from 6:1-23, while at the same time not insisting on obedience to the Mosaic law (7:1-6).[91]

Over the next two sections, 7:7-25 and 8:1-39, Paul will lay out two very dissimilar arguments. In short, Rom. 7:7-25 spells out the reality of an "in Adam" type existence, while Rom. 8 envisions an "in Christ" existence.[92] This is not only communicated rhetorically through the use of *prosopopoeia* in Rom. 7 as a "speech in character" utilizing the voice of Adam but also through the argument devoid of references to the Spirit in 7:1-25. This is in contrast to the plethora of Spirit language in 8:1-39.[93] Paul is not comparing two similar types of stories but two divergent pictures of reality. One corollary of this rhetorical feature is that the voice of Adam represents the world of sin, death, and disobedience. As such, one expects the argument in Rom. 7:7-25 to be

---

[89] A short search of the language of eternal life in Romans indicates the linked relationship obedience has with eternal life. Most notably in Rom. 2:7 but also 5:21; 6:22-23.

[90] Contra Christopher Bryan, *Preface to Romans: Notes on the Epistle in Its Literary and Cultural Setting* (New York: Oxford University Press, 2000), 138, to some degree, I think this is a more specific example of the obedience conversation rather than a "broader question."

[91] Jacob Thiessen, "Paulinische Versus Jüdische Und Hellenistische Anthropologie? Zur Frage Nach Dem Verständnis Von Römer 7,7-25," *EuroJTh* 21 (2012): 26.

[92] To illustrate the differences between the transference from the realm of Adam to the realm of Christ, Paul employs an analogy from marriage law (7:1-6). The Augustan legislation on marriage would have been familiar to many in Rome and might form part of the purpose of Paul's inclusion of such imagery. One should note the differences between Roman and Jewish law on marriage. Cf. *OCD*, 928–9; Keener, *Romans*, 85–6. However, one must be careful as Paul is offering a metaphor and it should not be pressed too literally. Paul is not expounding a legal case in the present context.

[93] Cf. Witherington, *Romans*, 179–206; Jewett, *Romans*, 441–5.

more focused on disobedience rather than obedience, which will be the focus of Rom. 8:1-39.[94]

Paul's last extended argument on the law occurred back in Rom. 2:12-27, but now the law appears again in Rom 7:1-25.[95] The discussion of law necessarily involves the concepts of obedience and disobedience. As Neil Elliott has pointed out, "The everbinding force of Law ... compels obedience to the 'lord' or 'dominion' one has chosen to serve (7.2, cf. 6:16) and it releases from that compulsion the one who through death has left one dominion 'with the result of becoming obligated to another.'"[96]

Through the use of νόμος (law) and ἐντολή (commandment), Paul invokes a discussion of obedience in a similar way to the slavery language. The inclusion of legal language carries with it the notion that a law must either be obeyed or disobeyed. In Rom. 7, the line of argument Paul pursues is one of disobedience, although he certainly stresses the "inability" of an individual rather than the "intentionality" (cf. Aristotle, *Pol.* 2.5.14). Rom 7:7-25 is part of the Adamic framework. As part of the Adamic framework, it is included underneath the rubrics of sin, death, and disobedience in Paul's symbolic world.

Intersecting this line of thought of sin making one unable to pursue the good, the moral tradition of philosophy also reckoned with the role the passions played in a battle with reason. Helpful for understanding one avenue for the philosophical underpinnings of Paul's statements in this section is the wonderful works of Emma Wasserman.[97] She has analyzed the language and rhetoric of middle-Platonic discourse about the death of the soul and notes several points of comparison with Paul discussion in Rom. 7 and sin's power over humanity. She has noted that several philosophers, such as Plato, Plutarch, Galen, and Philo, discuss the topic of "extreme immorality" (compare with 1:18-32) and argues that reason experiences "utter defeat at the hand of passions and appetites, represented as sin."[98] The rhetorical and literary similarities stem from a "rich moral tradition that ... contests self-contradiction in the form of a dramatic monologue."[99] The conclusion of her work suggests that Rom. 7:7-25 is not about the possibility of choice but the totalizing power of sin and death.[100] However, even granting the totality of sin and death, Susan Eastman reminds us, "Within this

---

[94] Cf. L. Ann Jervis, "'The Commandment Which Is for Life' (Romans 7.10): Sin's Use of the Obedience of Faith," *JSNT* 27 (2004): 193–216.

[95] Thirty-one percent of the occurrences of νόμος appear in Rom. 7 (23/74). The second highest percentage is Rom 2. with 26 percent (19/74).

[96] Elliott, *Rhetoric of Romans*, 245. I am inclined with others to take this reference to "law" throughout the section more generally, rather than as a specific reference to the Mosaic Law.

[97] Emma Wasserman, "The Death of the Soul in Romans 7: Revisiting Paul's Anthropology in Light of Hellenistic Moral Psychology," *JBL* 126 (2007): 793–816. See further Emma Wasserman, *The Death of the Soul in Romans 7: Sin, Death, and the Law in Light of Hellenistic Moral Psychology* (Tübingen: Mohr Siebeck, 2008). She draws parallels between Plato, Plutarch, Galen, and Philo and their discussion of "extreme immorality" to show how the mind/reason is devastated by the passions that are represented as sin.

[98] Wasserman, "The Death of the Soul in Romans 7," 794.

[99] Wasserman, "The Death of the Soul in Romans 7," 814.

[100] Similar conclusions are reached by Susan Eastman, *Paul and the Person: Reframing Paul's Anthropology* (Grand Rapids: Eerdmans, 2017), 109–25.

situation human actors are not simply passive victims, but rather are both captive and complicit."[101]

In 7:23, Paul reintroduces military language similar to what we saw in 6:13 where one's body was used as a weapon in unrighteousness.[102] Now at 7:23, Paul relates the internal "war" of the in-Adam type life. Jewett notes the importance of the military language for Paul's Roman audience, as some were either slaves or former slaves. He rightly notes, as our evidence in Chapters 3-5 showed, that defeat by Rome was followed by enslavement or death in most circumstances.[103] The language of enslavement and captivity again points to the inferred obedience demanded therein. Although obedience and disobedience language do not explicitly appear in Rom. 7:1-25, the contours of the argument are shaped around such notions and form an integral part of Paul's discussion.[104]

Returning to our framework of reading Romans from a Gentile point of view, how would they have experienced this section? They might be reminded again of the slavery language and imagery that dominated the previous section and continued to be a primary image in this part of Paul's discourse. Further, Paul's introduction of the law and the issue of obedience in Rom 7:1-25 might also have sounded familiar as philosophers debated the connection between obedience and law (both civic and moral). As seen in the previous chapters, Paul and Aristotle express frustration at the inability of persons to fulfill the law (*Pol* 2.5.14). At the civic level, Rome was a city full of laws and Gentiles would have understood that obedience to these laws was paramount. Additionally, some Gentiles in Paul's audience who had pursued moral progress only to experience defeat along the way may have resonated deeply with the lamentations of the "I" in Rom. 7. However, some of their expectations may have been confronted and challenged by the degree of futility that Paul ascribes to the "flesh" and its ability to do "the good."

Obedience by Grace via the Power of the Spirit (8:1-39)

Rom. 8:1-39 is an explication of how Paul's thesis statement (1:16-17) about the δικαιοσύνη θεοῦ (righteousness of God) is truly seen as working God's power unto salvation.[105] Rom. 8:1-4 serves as a climax in Paul's argument that those "in Christ" are no longer under condemnation, but set free from the law of sin and death, which had been the focus of Paul's argument from 5:1 to 7:25.[106] Whereas Rom. 7:7-25

---

[101] Eastman, *Paul and the Person*, 111. See also Matthew Croasmun, *The Emergence of Sin: The Cosmic Tyrant in Romans* (New York: Oxford University Press, 2017), 22-51.
[102] Barrett, *Romans*, 133, also draws attention to 7:11 and ἀφορμή that was often used in military contexts to denote the origin of a war.
[103] Jewett, *Romans*, 470-1; so also Keener, *Romans*, 94-5.
[104] One should note similarities in language between Chapters 6 and 7 including death and slavery. See Dunn, *Romans*, 367.
[105] Helpfully pointed out by Wright, *Romans*, 575.
[106] On the notorious issue of the identification of the law at work here, cf. Stuhlmacher, *Romans*, 118; Wright, *Romans*, 576-7; Dunn, *Romans*, 1:423-4; Fitzmyer, *Romans*, 482; Cranfield, *Romans*, 1:374-8; Bryan, *Preface to Romans*, 145-6.

focused on the reign of sin and death that characterizes those who were "in Adam," Paul shifts gears in the section of 8:1-39 to discuss the other half of his archetypal *synkrisis*: those who are "in Christ" and the subsequent characterization of this group with the language of "spirit" and "life."[107] Käsemann is right that in light of 7:1-25, "it is not accidental that v. 2 sets all that follows under the heading of liberation."[108] Paul's continued usage of slavery language is evident in his description of those who are in Christ as "set free" (ἐλευθερόω) in 8:2.[109] An interesting parallel to this freedom language is seen in Cicero. He states, "Then what is freedom? The power to live as you wish. Who actually lives as he wishes if not the one ... who submits to the law not out of fear but honors and obeys it because he believes it is advantageous" (*Parad.* 34).[110] Paul likewise signals this new obedience is brought about by being set free from the powers of sin and death and by being invigorated by life according to the Spirit.

The decree in Rom. 8:1 that there is no longer condemnation links 8:1 back to the only previous reference to condemnation (5:16-18) and the two figures of Adam and Christ.[111] Wright notes, "The clue is to remind ourselves, not for the first time, that we are still watching the unfolding of the Adam/Christ contrast in 5:12-21."[112] In 5:12-21, condemnation (κατάκριμα) was mediated to "all" through the one person of Adam (5:18) through his act of disobedience, or what Paul labels "transgression" (5:16). According to Paul, the logical link is as follows: Adam—disobedience/transgression—condemnation—death to all humanity. The inverse of this story is Christ—obedience/righteous act—righteousness—life for all humanity.

Several contrasts are at work in 5:16-18. Paul contrasts Adam's transgression with Christ's "one righteous act." Likewise, the outcome of Adam's disobedience resulted in condemnation for all in 5:18, whereas Christ's obedience led to righteousness leading to life for all in 5:18. Christ's obedient action undoes and outdoes Adam's disobedient action. Therefore, in 8:1, when Paul argues that there is no condemnation for those "in Christ" he invokes these previous parallel stories and their operating actions of obedience and disobedience.[113] Stated more specifically, behind the decree of "no condemnation" stands Christ's obedience.[114]

In Rom. 8:4, Paul emphasizes that those who walk according to the Spirit have the "just requirement of the law fulfilled" in them. The noun δικαίωμα appears five times

---

[107] On the placement of Rom. 8 in the structure of Romans see Tobin, *Paul's Rhetoric*, 251-6.
[108] Käsemann, *Romans*, 215.
[109] On ways to take the dative phrase ἐν Χριστῷ Ἰησοῦ in 8:1 see Fitzmyer, *Romans*, 482. I am inclined to the instrumental understanding. Cf. Eduard Lohse, "Ὁ Νόμος Τοῦ Πνεύματος Τῆς Ζωῆς: Exegetische Anmerkungen Zu Röm 8:2," in *Neues Testament Und Christliche Existenz* (ed. Hans Dieter Betz and Luise Schottroff, Tübingen: J. C. B Mohr (Paul Siebeck), 1973).
[110] As quoted in Jewett, *Romans*, 482.
[111] Such use of figures are part of the overall deliberative strategy at work in this section of the discourse. See Quintilian, *Inst. Or.* 3.8.61-36; Witherington, *Romans*, 208.
[112] Wright, *Romans*, 574; Keener, *Romans*, 99.
[113] On the coherence of Rom. 5-8, cf. Nils Alstrup Dahl, *Studies in Paul: Theology for the Early Christian Mission* (Minneapolis: Augsburg, 1977), 70-94.
[114] Certainly the reference to κατέκρινεν τὴν ἁμαρτίαν ἐν τῇ σαρκί in 8:3 refers to Christ's act of obedience on the cross. So Wright, *Romans*, 574.

within the letter to the Romans, twice in the singular and three times in the plural form. The occurrence in 1:32 is important for our discussion of the term in 8:4.[115]

Excursus on δικαίωμα

The first occurrence of δικαίωμα appears in 1:32 at the climax of Paul's diatribe against abhorrent Gentile behavior. This is where Paul notes that the Gentiles "know God's decree (δικαίωμα)" yet praise those who do not practice it. In Chapter 1, δικαίωμα appears to represent a moral aspect of God's law. This stands in contrast to the practices in 1:18-32 and results in a decree of death. In the subsequent section of 1:29-31, Paul provides a vice list of immoral behaviors of Gentiles that stands under the "wrath of God" (1:18). God's δικαίωμα appears in contrast to the list of behaviors Paul describes in 1:29-31 that result in death (cf. 8:2, 10-13).

Reading 1:18-32 alongside the argument Paul unpacks in 5:1-8:39, the list of behaviors Paul describes in 1:18-32 falls under the Adamic state of being and is the epitome of "walking according to the flesh" (cf. Gal. 5). While this instance is not found in direct relationship to law, it best reflects the usage in 8:4, where Paul refers to a single aspect of God's law without further explanation.

The usage of δικαίωμα in Rom. 8:4 is similar to the usage in 1:32, although this time Paul qualifies δικαίωμα with the law. Rom. 8:4 appears to be the inverse of 1:32. Those who "walk according to the Spirit" have the δικαίωμα of God "fulfilled" in them. When Paul refers to the "just requirement of the law" in 8:4, he is referring to the realm of moral behavior as described in the law that was "rebelled against" in 1:18-32 but is now fulfilled or completed in those who have the Spirit.

The relationship between Rom. 1:32 and Rom. 8:4 is important as it represents the positive and negative responses to God's δικαίωμα. δικαίωμα in Rom. 8:4 should be taken as the behavior that corresponds to God's righteousness as found in the law—or in other words, a life that is lived in obedience to God's intention.[116] From 8:4 onward, this is the life that is characterized by those who "walk according to the Spirit" and thus their lives correspond to God's intent in giving the law. Sanders rightly states, "Living in the Spirit results in obeying the law."[117] The lives of those "the law have been fulfilled in" are characterized in opposition to the litany of descriptions found in 1:29-31. Therefore, they respond in obedience rather than rebellion to God's decree.[118]

---

[115] The third usage and fourth usage of δικαίωμα in 5:16, 18 reflect the definition provided by Aristotle in his *Nicomachean Ethics*. Aristotle defines δικαίωμα as "rectification of an act of injustice." Within Paul's argument in Rom. 5, clearly Paul is setting up a contrast between competing "works" or "acts." Specifically the acts of Adam and Christ, with the acts of Adam leading to sin and death and the acts of Christ reversing or setting to right the acts of Adam and leading to righteousness and life (Rom. 5:18).

[116] So Charles H. Talbert, *Romans* (Macon: Smyth & Helwys, 2002), 204.

[117] E. P. Sanders, *Paul, the Law, and the Jewish People* (Philadelphia: Fortress, 1983), 105.

[118] Perhaps there is no difference for Paul between the τὸ δικαίωμα τοῦ θεοῦ (Rom. 1:32), τὸ ἔργον τοῦ νόμου (Rom. 2:15), τὰ δικαιώματα τοῦ νόμου (Rom. 2:26), γράμματος (Rom. 2:27), τὰ λόγια τοῦ θεοῦ (Rom. 3:2), and τὸ δικαίωμα τοῦ νόμου (Rom. 8:4). All these occurrences refer to the same semantic category, namely God's law. This, however, does not mean that Paul cannot stress certain aspects of the law, such as the penal character in 1:32 or the positive aspects in 2:14-15, 26, and 8:4.

Rom. 8:1-11 is Paul's continuing argument (*probatio*) concerning the Spirit and the life of those "in Christ." Several important terms are linked with the Spirit and flesh language of this section. Paul links the terms of death and hostility to the "flesh" and "life and peace" to the Spirit (Rom. 8:6).[119] These terms are reminiscent of Paul's language in Rom. 5:1–6:23 and continue his comparison between the two figures of Adam and Christ. The reference to peace in 8:6 harkens back to Rom. 5:1 and the new peace with God established through Christ, whereas the flesh is "at war" with God and deemed "hostile" in 8:7. Such a confluence of obedience and disobedience along with peace and war language is now seen in a fresh light by the evidence from the Roman historians. A verity of persons hearing this section for this first time might reflect on such experiences in light of Paul's argument here.

Paul will argue that the flesh is hostile to God because it does not "submit" (ὑποτάσσω) to God's law. The verb ὑποτάσσω in the middle reflexive position carries the sense of voluntary submission, usually rendered to a superior authority.[120] We find a similar formulation in the Roman peace treaties from our survey of the Greco-Roman historians, where obedience or submission to a higher authority results in the cessation of war or hostilities (Chapters 3–4). The inverse of Paul's logic in Rom. 8:7 is that those of the Spirit *can* obey God's law as indicated in Rom. 8:4. Obedience or disobedience to God's law results in either hostility or peace.[121] In contrast to some Roman understandings of forced or coerced obedience, God gives the gift of the Spirit to enable the obedience that leads to peace. Also one might add that a contrasting element is that the punishment of disobedience has been taken by God himself as well in the death of his son.

As Paul's argument continues, he issues two contrasting conditional clauses in 8:13, indicating, as Cranfield has noted, that "life and death are presented as the consequences of the alternative ways."[122] Paul warns his audience that those who continue to live according to the flesh, that is, hostile and disobedient to God's law, will end in death (Rom. 8:13). Continued disobedience to God's gracious activity results in destruction. Conversely, the one who lives by the Spirit receives life, whereby fulfilling the just requirement of the law, namely obedience.

If we reflect on our Gentile audience again, many could see a comparison with Paul's argument where disobedience leads to death and obedience to life, with similar outcomes for obedience and disobedience as we saw with peace treaties with Rome. In those sources, disobedience to Rome results in destruction and death, whereas obedience results in peace and, ultimately, life (temporally speaking, of course). Gentiles aware of Rome's interactions with the nations would not have been surprised

---

Pressing a great distinction between these categories or terms may be to distinguish to a greater degree than Paul himself may have differentiated.

[119] For θάνατος see Rom 1:32; 5:10, 12, 14, 17, 21; 6:3-5, 9, 16, 21, 23; 7:5, 10, 13, 24; 8:2, 6, 38. For ζωή see Rom 2:7; 5:10, 17–18, 21; 6:4, 22–23; 7:10; 8:2, 6, 10, 38; 11:15. For εἰρήνη see Rom 1:7; 2:10; 3:17; 5:1; 8:6; 14:17, 19; 15:13, 33; 16:20.

[120] *BDAG*, 1042. Submission language appears here for the first time in Romans but is used four times in the remainder of Romans (Rom. 8:7, 20; 10:3; 13:1, 5).

[121] Grieb, *Story of Romans*, 77, is helpful at this point but only points to the Jewish traditions on "holy war" and neglects the Roman background.

[122] Cranfield, *Romans*, 1:394.

by such a framework as this was shown repeatedly in the historians of Rome's rise to power. Indeed many of Paul's audience were from peoples conquered by Rome and would personally understood this all too well. Certainly, the imagery of Mars on the *Ara Pacis* drove home the imagery of Rome's prowess and destructive capability. Quite surprising to many Gentiles would be that a "spirit" would aid one in obeying the requirements of a law. Further that God himself would aid his subjects in obedience would starkly contrast the demands Rome made of its subjects without any help at all.

At the end of 8:1-39, Paul's triumphant conclusion contains two important terms for the consideration of this work on obedience as a theme of Romans. Like an intricate tapestry, Paul has continued weaving together key themes throughout the work. First, in Rom. 8:28, Paul famously states that "all things work together for the good for those who love God and are called (κλητός) according to purpose."[123] The adjective κλητός is important as it only occurs three other times in Romans (Rom. 1:1, 6-7).[124] In Rom. 1:1, the adjective κλητός is applied to Paul himself, and in Rom 1:6-7, it is applied to Paul's audience. In Rom. 1:6, Paul includes his Roman audience as those who are "called" to belong to Jesus Christ; this group is "among them." The relative pronoun "those" is a backward referent to 1:5 concerning the Gentiles to whom Paul is called to bring about the obedience of faith/loyalty. The reference to calling in 8:28 links his powerful conclusion to the beginning of the discourse and the obedience of faith. Additionally, we should not miss that this is the first reference to the word "purpose" in Romans and that it dovetails with Paul's explicit purpose in Rom. 1:5.[125]

Second, in Rom. 8:37, Paul includes himself in the group described as conquerors. Fitzmyer is right to categorize this entire section as one where "Paul utters a cry of victory." But what type of victory cry might be uttered here than a battle cry?—although such victory is stridently countercultural, as they are conquerors through the death of their leader.[126] The love of Jesus, evidenced by his death on the cross, is the climactic event that secures the "complete victory" for those in the Roman audience. Rather than victory through the conquest of others, we have victory through the conquered by the death of that conquered one.

We should not miss the profound contrast with the relationship between obedience and victory for Gentiles who had come from pagan backgrounds. For Gentiles in Paul's audience, those led by the Spirit, they now have complete victory, through a defeated figure who was obedient (Rom. 5:18; 8:1)! The notions of victory through defeat may have been quite unlike what some Gentiles had previously encountered. For Paul's audience in Rome, victory comes not through "Victoria" but through their crucified Lord who has inaugurated a new reign of peace through his own death. Jesus's own obedience to death leads to victory. Victory through defeat, despite one's obedience, would have confounded previous conceptions of what obedience secures.

---

[123] Witherington rightly notes that "His" is not in the text (*Romans*, 227). Interestingly Cranfield refers to a number of patristic commentators who understood the "called" to refer to a smaller group who "meet the divine call with obedience" (*Romans*, 1:430).
[124] Noted by others such as Jewett, *Romans*, 528; Keener, *Romans*, 108n.42.
[125] The calling language also anticipates the next major discussion in Rom. 9-11.
[126] Fitzmyer, *Romans*, 481. Although speaking of Rom. 8:1 it applies equally here.

The key to this victory for the Roman audience is living according to the Spirit. Such victory imagery would have certainly been important for Paul's Roman audience. As seen in Chapter 6, the themes of victory and conquest dominated the landscape of Rome. As one walked along the *via Flaminia*, one could not help but be impressed by such a massive array of victory symbols. Rome's victories over the nations were often celebrated, not only through Roman literature but also through architecture and coins that would have been important for any resident or visitor to Rome (see Chapter 6). Paul's discussion of conquering and victory here calls into question just what constitutes true victory.

The Third Proof: 9:1–11:36

In Rom. 9:1–11:36, Paul begins the third proof of his argument (*probatio*) on the righteousness of God.[127] Cranfield rightly orients us toward this major transition in the discourse stating, "There are very many features of chapters 1 to 8 which are not understood in full depth until they are seen in the light of chapters 9 to 11—the characterization of the scope of Paul's apostleship by εἰς ὑπακοὴν πίστεως ἐν πᾶσιν τοῖς ἔθνεσιν in 1:5."[128] Rom. 9:1–11:36 is not an aside to the statement about his own identity in Rom. 1:5 but an integral part as "Paul's own role and vocation become topics within the story."[129]

The unfaithfulness of Israel, represented most poignantly by their disobedience, places a profound question before Paul and his audience, a question that has been "simmering" throughout the letter.[130] Asked squarely, does the disobedience of Israel call into question the "power of God" to bring about the obedience of the nations?[131] As Peter Stuhlmacher notes, "Paul is concerned with the very life nerve of his mission and with the question of the faithfulness of God."[132] If the obedience of one nation was not accomplished, what hope (a key Pauline term) is there for the Gentiles?

---

[127] This section is far from an afterthought as many now point out; see Witherington, *Romans*, 237; Fitzmyer, *Romans*, 541; Krister Stendahl, *Paul among Jews and Gentiles: And Other Essays* (Minneapolis: Fortress, 1976), 4; Keck, *Romans*, 223–6; Barrett, *Romans*, 164; Byrne, *Romans*, 281–4. Cf. Klaus Haacker, "Das Thema Von Römer 9-11 Als Problem Der Auslegungsgechichte," in *Between Gospel and Election: Explorations in the Interpretation of Romans 9–11* (ed. Florian Wilk, J. Ross Wagner, and Frank Schleritt, Tübingen: Mohr Siebeck, 2010), 55–72; Mark Reasoner, "Romans 9-11 Moves from Margin to Center, from Rejection to Salvation: Four Grids for Recent English-Language Exegesis," in *Between Gospel and Election*, 73–90.

[128] Cranfield, *Romans*, 2:445. He also cites the use of κλητός in 1:6 and 7, God's promises in Rom. 4, the golden chain of 8:29-30, and the ἐκλεκτῶν θεοῦ of 8.33 as a "only a few examples." See also Christoph Stenschke, "Römer 9-11 Als Teil Des Römerbriefs," in *Between Gospel and Election*, 197–226.

[129] Wright, "Romans," 624. Interestingly Wright notes that self-references of Paul in the early parts of Rom. 9 invoke Paul's self-introduction in 1:8-17; however, he does not mention Rom. 1:5.

[130] Matera, *Romans*, 211. Cf. Bruce W. Longenecker, "Different Answers to Different Issues: Israel, the Gentiles, and Salvation History in Romans 9–11," *JSNT* 36 (1989): 95–123.

[131] As Johannes Munck concluded long ago, "The salvation of the Gentiles and of Israel are inseparable" (*Paul and the Salvation of Mankind* (Richmond: John Knox, 1959), 44).

[132] Stuhlmacher, *Romans*, 144.

It is to these types of questions that Paul must offer a *refutatio* on behalf of God himself. Rom. 9:1-11:36 is nothing other than a defense of the faithfulness and righteousness of God despite the continued disobedience (of some) of Israel. It is also an argument *for* the possibility of the obedience of faith among the nations. Both questions invoke one another in this section.

Given Paul's defense of the faithfulness of God vis-á-vis the unfaithfulness of Israel, it is not surprising that Rom. 9:1-11:36 is his most scripturally saturated argument.[133] If Paul is responding to his question posed in 9:6—"Has the word of God failed?"—it should not surprise us that Paul uses several citations of that "word" as proof, hence all the OT quotations.[134] Therefore, we should not be surprised that the contours and logic of the passage are not amenable to a Roman understanding of obedience.[135]

A small reminder is in order. The goal is not to read every occurrence of obedience in light of Greco-Roman usage but to acknowledge the theme of obedience (or disobedience) that occurs *throughout* the discourse. Neil Elliott's comments on Rom. 9:1-33 are thought-provoking. He says, "The sovereignty of Israel's Lord is not like the caprice of Zeus."[136] Even without direct reference to Roman conceptions of obedience, we should not miss the contrast that Gentiles with pagan origins would have seen between their former gods and the God of Israel. One particular difference a Gentile audience would see with God's treatment of Israel is the extension of mercy at their disobedience. As we saw in Chapters 3-4 with the historians, Rome met disobedience with destruction and wrath. Throughout Rom. 9:1-11:36, there is an optimistic tone whereby there is still hope for a remnant of Israel's restoration. The God of Israel's long-suffering patience, seen throughout this section, highlights that the obedience expected is returned to a gracious and merciful figure. Such ideas would have contrasted with a Gentile's understanding of both Rome and their former deities.

In light of the audience issues in Romans, J. Ross Wagner proposes, "In these chapters, the apostle carefully constructs for his Gentile hearers a negative identity as outsiders with respect to God's elect people Israel."[137] The rhetorical feature of this long argument is to pose the question to his Gentile audience: In light of God's grace and mercy, how will you respond? Will you exercise the obedience of faith or not? Paul then offers a short rehearsal of Israel's story of disobedience.

---

[133] See Witherington, *Romans*, 237. Indeed some 31 percent of all of Paul's citations of scripture in the undisputed letters occur in Rom. 9-11. Cf. Fitzmyer, *Romans*, 539; Richard B. Hays, *Echoes of Scripture in the Letters of Paul* (New Haven: Yale University Press, 1993); Stanley E. Porter and Christopher D. Stanley, eds., *As It Is Written: Studying Paul's Use of Scripture* (Atlanta: Society of Biblical Literature, 2008); Craig A. Evans and James A. Sanders, eds., *Paul and the Scriptures of Israel*, vol. 83 (Sheffield: Sheffield Academic Press, 1993); Richard B. Hays, *The Conversion of the Imagination: Paul as Interpreter of Israel's Scripture* (Grand Rapids: Eerdmans, 2005).

[134] Cf. Tobin, *Paul's Rhetoric*, 339.

[135] Although see Stowers proposal of how Greek Gentile hearers would have understood Rom. 11. Cf. Stowers, *Rereading Romans*, 314-15.

[136] Elliott, *Rhetoric of Romans*, 266.

[137] J. Ross Wagner, "'Not from Jews Only, but Also from the Gentiles': Mercy to the Nations in Romans 9-11," in *Between Gospel and Election*, 420.

The Tragedy of Israel's Disobedience (9:1-29)

In 9:1-5, Paul attempts to offset his next arguments concerning the unrighteousness and disobedience of Israel.[138] Paul's aim in this section seems to have two intended effects. First, Paul wants to ward off anti-Semitic sentiments on behalf of his Roman congregation.[139] Second, Paul is also refuting contentions that the failure of Israel places a massive question mark on God's faithfulness to the Gentiles. Florian Wilk has argued, rightly, that this section revolves around the contradiction of nations flocking to Israel's God despite Israel's rejection of their salvation.[140] Paul's aim in Rom. 9:1–11:36 is directly connected to his thesis statement in Rom. 1:16-17. Jewett rightly notes:

> In this sense, the thesis of Rom 9–11 is a direct expression of the main thesis of Rom 1:16-17 concerning the gospel as the "power of God" capable of setting right the entire world. The failure of Israel to respond to the gospel appears to invalidate this main thesis.[141]

In Rom. 9:7-8, we have another discussion of Abraham and the flesh that mirrors the previous argument in Rom. 4:1-25. Paul juxtaposes one group, the "flesh," with another group, the "children of the promise" (Rom. 9:8). Paul uses Israel's history, through the choosing of Isaac instead of Ishmael, to establish his distinction between the two groups. Simply being "born of" Abraham is not a guarantee of the divine promises therein. Paul's juxtaposition of "flesh" and "promise" sheds a negative light on the flesh component, evoking his previous discussion in Rom. 5:1–6:25.[142] In this light, we should not miss that Paul simply replaces "Spirit" with the word "promise." As a corollary, Paul's previous discussion of disobedience as a characteristic of the σάρξ (flesh) cannot be far removed from this conversation about the "true descendants." For Paul, some descendants have more in common with Adam than Abraham.

Paul connects his argument about Abraham's descendants with the issue of calling. We encounter "calling" language twice in 9:1-29.[143] The first occurrence appears in 9:7, in Paul's quotation of Gen. 21:12 with the passive "called." This bears out Paul's point: the promises rest, not on the actions of individuals but on the God who calls and promises. The children who are called in 9:7 are also counted in 9:8 as the true "seed" of Abraham. God issues forth a call that comes to fruition. The same God who calls light out of darkness, who calls forth children from barren wombs, who calls forth a family from Abraham, also calls forth an apostle (Rom. 1:1) with yet another call, this time

---

[138] On the arrangement of Rom. 9–11 see the helpful article by Jean-Noël Aletti, *God's Justice*, 159–81.
[139] See Witherington, *Romans*, 237; Elliott, *Rhetoric of Romans*, 262; Wright, *Romans*, 623; Keener, *Romans*, 135. Käsemann, *Romans*, 260, rightly reminds that this is not a dialogue with the Jews.
[140] Florian Wilk, "Rahmen Und Aufbau Von Römer 9–11," in *Between Gospel and Election*, 227–54.
[141] Jewett, *Romans*, 574. So also Aletti, *God's Justice*, 163; Wright, *Romans*, 621–2. Stowers, *Rereading Romans*, 286, connects Rom. 9-11 as a response to Rom. 2:17-5:11.
[142] Aletti, *God's Justice*, 204, shows a strong connection between Rom. 8 and Rom. 9 with similar repeated themes and frameworks. Cf. Boyarin, *A Radical Jew*, 57–85.
[143] On the rarity of calling language in Romans see καλέω 4:17; 8:30; 9:7, 12, 24–26; κλητός 1:1, 6-7; 8:28 and our discussion in Chapter 6, pp. 52–3. On the use of Hosea by Paul see David I. Starling, *Not My People: Gentiles as Exiles in Pauline Hermeneutics* (Berlin: De Gruyter, 2011), 107–66.

for the obedience of faith among the nations (Rom. 1:5-6).[144] Paul's discussion of Jacob, Esau, and Pharaoh (Rom. 9:13-18) offers further specific examples of Paul's emphasis on the divine will and calling of God, and are poignant examples of disobedience.

We should not miss how Gentiles in the audience would understood Paul's selection of certain individuals, like Jacob, Esau, and Pharaoh, as negative examples of disobedience. Similar to both the historians and the philosophers (Chapters 3–5), it was helpful to put forth models, both positive and negative, to illustrate one's point. One might compare the usage of such figures in Livy's account of the general Popilius and his disobedient actions (42.9.1-6). There certainly was a degree of correspondence between how some Gentiles may have thought about these figures and grasped the rhetorical usage of such figures—do not be like them!

The second occurrence of calling resurfaces in Rom. 9:24-26 with Paul's quotation of Hosea 2, where he argues that the Gentile Christians are part of God's "people."[145] Such an emphasis would be drawn out by the awkwardness of the phrase "including us whom he has called" that, as Dunn has noted, "would have to be taken slowly and with emphasis."[146] The calling of Gentiles into God's family is under the domain of Paul's apostolic vocation that includes the purpose of obedience (1:5). Rom. 9:24-26, therefore, serves as Paul's missional rationale for seeking the "obedience of faith" among the Gentiles.

Further, in 9:26, Paul indicates that these "not my people" are "sons and daughters of the living God." That resounds with reverberations from Paul's discussion of adoption as God's children through the Spirit in 8:14-23. In 9:27-29, Paul concludes the first sweep of his argument in response to his question in 9:6 concerning whether or not the divine word had failed. The answer is no. In 9:29, Paul envisions a worldwide realization of God's promises that reaffirms the faithfulness of the divine word and promise (Isa. 10:22-23).[147]

The Failure to Exercise Obedience (9:30–10:21)

In 9:30–10:21, Paul moves on to address the issue of Israel's failure to *obey* the gospel.[148] The section of 9:30-33 is a "decisive turning point" as it sums up the discussion so far and introduces the key themes of the next section.[149] Cranfield rightly notes the

---

[144] Gaventa highlights the creation aspect of the calling and the connection to Rom. 1:18-32. See Beverly Roberts Gaventa, "On the Calling-into-Being of Israel: Romans 9:6-29," in *Between Gospel and Election*, 255–70.

[145] On the issue of Paul's wording in his quotation of Hos. 2:25 and that he changed it from "say" to "call" see Cranfield, *Romans*, 2:498–500; Jewett, *Romans*, 600; Dunn, *Romans*, 2:571. Dunn comments, "The καλέσω is almost certainly Paul's insertion: it sustains his main thematic emphasis" (571). So also Keener, *Romans*, 121n.18; Johnson, *Reading Romans*, 164–5.

[146] Dunn, *Romans*, 2:570. Cf. Haacker, *Die Römer*, 197. Haacker argues this section "Hier vollzieht sich ein gleitender Übergang zu einem neuen Thema."

[147] On the difficulty of this wording see Cranfield, *Romans*, 2:501–2. On Paul's use of Isaiah see J. Ross Wagner, *Heralds of the Good News: Isaiah and Paul "in Concert" in the Letter to the Romans* (Boston: Brill, 2002).

[148] We should be mindful of E. P. Sanders's note that Rom. 9:30-33 is the beginning of an argument that concludes in 10:21. See Sanders, *Paul, the Law*, 37.

[149] Stuhlmacher, *Romans*, 152.

relationship between 9:1-29 and 9:30-33: "Both the nature of Israel's disobedience and the nature of the Gentile's obedience need to be defined more closely ... in vv. 30-33, Paul gives this necessary definition in summary form."[150] At this point, Paul reintroduces the discussion of Gentiles, faith, and righteousness and connects this section to his *propositio* in Rom. 1:16-17.

In Rom. 9:30, Paul begins with a rhetorical question, "what then are we to say" (see Rom. 4:1; 6:1; 7:7; 8:31; and 9:14, 30)? In verses 30-33, we have the tight and ironic argument that some Gentiles received righteousness, although not intending to pursue it, while despite their pursuit, Israel has not found righteousness.[151] In 9:32, Paul poses the obvious question in his audience's mind: "Why not?" Paul's response is one of the common refrains of Romans, faith. Paul emphasizes that the law was not pursued from or by faith. Such a phrase is important in Romans and corresponds to the second half of the thesis statement of 1:17, The righteous one will live by faith/faithfulness.[152]

We should not neglect the role that obedience plays in these "pursuits." Previously in Rom. 6:18, Paul argued that obedience leads to righteousness. Gentiles now, through the acceptance of Christ through faith, can offer themselves as slaves to obedience leading to righteousness. Paul's statements in Rom. 9:30-31 then fall into place. Paul is most likely referencing Rom. 1:18-32 when he states that the Gentiles did not pursue righteousness (Rom. 9:30). Similarly, the inference then is that even though Israel "pursued" righteousness, in the sense of obedience to the law, they were not able to obtain it. Dunn is right to note, "It is not the 'pursuing' which Paul criticizes but how that was understood."[153] Paul's critique of (some of) Israel is that they did not pursue it by faith (9:32; cf. 2:17-29). This failure parallels the "in-Adam" type description of Rom. 7:7-25. For Paul, Christ is the fulfillment or *telos* of the *nomos* (10:4). By rejecting Christ, some of his kinsmen failed to obtain the righteousness to which the law points, namely Christ.[154]

These micro-stories of Israel and the Gentiles culminate around the issue of faith, evoking Paul's argument in Rom. 5:1 and following. Obedience leads to righteousness and disobedience leads to unrighteousness, but it is only the obedience of faith that can both pursue and obtain righteousness. The obedience that flows from the faith in Jesus as Lord invokes the changing of stories from Adam—death—sin—disobedience to Christ—the Spirit—life—obedience.

Paul's argument throughout Rom. 9:1-33 provided opportunities for Gentiles in his audience to reflect on the message of obedience and disobedience in light of their previous understanding of these categories. One aspect of Paul's argument that would

---

[150] Cranfield, *Romans*, 2:504.
[151] Contra Schleritt, this is not intentionally formulated in an incongruous manner. See Frank Schleritt, "Das Gesetz Der Gerechtigkeit. Zur Auslegung Von Römer 9,30-33," in *Between Gospel and Election*, 271-98.
[152] On the importance of this theme in Romans see 1:17; 3:26, 30; 4:16; 5:1; 9:30, 32; 10:6; 14:23. Matera is correct that this is not a disparagement of the law but the starting point (*Romans*, 241–2). Also making this point is Bryan, *Preface to Romans*, 165.
[153] Dunn, *Romans*, 2:581; Sanders, *Paul, the Law*, 36–43. Contra Colin G. Kruse, *Paul's Letter to the Romans* (Grand Rapids: Eerdmans, 2012), 395–6.
[154] Witherington, *Romans*, 259; Tobin, *Rhetoric of Romans*, 341–2; Dunn, *Romans*, 2:594; Cranfield, *Romans*, 2:512.

have been quite unlike their previous understanding was God's mercy to those who were disobedient (Rom. 9:16). From the historians, the notion of disobedient nations was a common refrain in those sources and typically resulted in their punishment or destruction. In the reign of Claudius, Dio's record of the conquering of Britannia showed that mercy is extended to the obedient, not the disobedient (*R. H.* 62b.11.2). For some Gentiles, this may explain why they could assume that God was finished with this disobedient nation. Israel had disobeyed, end of the story. God should move on to more obedient nations. Paul's continuing argument, drawing on his own story, might have confounded some expectations of Gentiles "in the audience" who would be surprised at the nature and level of mercy that Israel's God extends to his disobedient people.

Rom. 10:1-4 is a parallel explanation of Paul's statements in Rom. 9:30-33 and the continuation of his argument that runs through 10:21. Paul continues his discussion of Israel, the law, and righteousness that recapitulates the previous discussion in 3:19-22. In 10:3, we are reintroduced to the language of the thesis statement of 1:16-17 and the righteousness of God. In a point that Paul will explain over the next several verses, he argues that in Israel's ignorance of the righteousness from God, they sought to establish their own righteous standard. Within the context of 10:13, it appears Israel failed to pursue a righteousness for "all." Their own righteousness, consequently, is something excluding Gentile inclusion. In 10:3, Paul characterizes Israel's activity as failing to submit (ὑποτάσσω).

Understanding "submission" in 10:3 hinges on the meaning of ὑποτάσσω (which will reappear in 13:1). The understanding of this term is greatly aided by Cynthia Kittredge's excellent study of the relationship between ὑπακούειν (to obey) and ὑποτάσσω (to submit). She has demonstrated from the literary evidence of Paul's contemporaries that the two words

> do not have substantially different meanings ... the quantity of evidence from these contemporary authors [suggest] that Paul ... uses both words to designate "obedience" as a feature of relationships of subordination. The claim that the two verbs have different meanings is not supported by contemporary Greek literature.[155]

The importance of her study for the analysis of Rom. 10:3 is that it highlights another instance of obedience and disobedience language within Romans. To translate ὑποτάσσω in 10:3 in light of the linguistic evidence then is to understand that, in establishing their own righteousness, Israel disobeyed or did not submit to God's righteousness.

If we reflect on how some Gentiles might have understood Rom. 10:3, we might be surprised at the degree of continuity they would have with Paul's thought on the ignorance of Israel not submitting or obeying God's righteousness. Throughout the historians (Chapters 3–4) we showed that one crucial aspect of a relationship with

---

[155] Cynthia Briggs Kittredge, *Community and Authority: The Rhetoric of Obedience in the Pauline Tradition* (Harrisburg: Trinity Press International, 1998), 51. Contra Jewett who argues that this verb in the middle does not imply obedience (*Romans*, 618).

Rome was submission or obedience to all of Rome's demands. There was no example of nations allowed to define their terms of obedience. The group in a superior position laid out the terms for obedience. Likewise, some Gentiles may have seen the futility of Israel trying to define righteous standards on their terms and how this would equate to not submitting or obeying God's demands.

The issue at the end of the argument in Rom. 9:1-33 is that God has included a people within the scope of salvation that Israel had written out of the story. Paul explains in 10:1-3 how this took place. By defining righteousness too narrowly around Jewish identity markers, (some of) Israel had failed to obey God's world-encompassing righteousness (cf. Rom. 3:29). This point is proven in Rom. 10:4 when Paul states that through Christ, and the end of the law, so that "there may be righteousness for everyone who believes," with the stress falling on the everyone or all. The goal of the law is righteousness. This, Paul and his kinsmen would have agreed on.[156] George Howard rightly notes that Rom. 10:4 means that the "very *aim* and *goal* [of the law] was the ultimate unification of the nations under the God of Abraham according to the promise."[157]

Paul ends this small portion of his argument by signaling the thesis statement, where "to all" is another way of saying both Jew and Gentile. Reading Rom. 10:4 alongside Rom. 6:16 and 1:5, Paul has laid the theological groundwork for the possibility of his stated purpose in Rom. 1:5, for the obedience of faith for the nations.

In Rom. 10:5-13, Paul continues with the theme of righteousness he established in 9:30-10:4.[158] In 10:5-13, Paul again utilizes *prosopopoeia* whereby it is the "righteousness of faith" that speaks a "word of warning from Deuteronomy" (Rom. 10:6-8).[159] The phrase "the righteousness that comes from faith" echoes the former use of this phrase by Paul (1:17; 3:26, 30; 4:16; 5:1; 9:30, 32).[160] According to this interpretation, Rom. 10:5 and 6 are not antithetical; Paul is not citing Moses versus the "righteousness by faith."[161] Paul appears to be allowing the "righteousness of faith" to

---

[156] Here I follow Jewett and others as seeing τέλος as goal and not "end." He cites as support Plutarch, *Princ. iner.* 780e ("Now justice is the goal of law, but law is the work of the ruler, and the ruler is the image of God who orders everything") (*Romans*, 619). See Friedrich Avemarie, "Israels Rätselhafter Ungehorsam. Römer 10 Als Anatomie Eines Von Gott Provozierten Unglaubens," in *Between Gospel and Election*, 299–320.

[157] George Howard, "Christ the End of the Law: The Meaning of Romans 10:4ff," *JBL* 88 (1969): 336. So also Thomas C. Rhyne, "Nomos Dikaiosynēs and the Meaning of Romans 10:4," *CBQ* 47 (1985): 486–99. Contra John Paul Heil, "Christ, the Termination of the Law (Romans 9:30-10:8)," *CBQ* 63 (2001): 484–98.

[158] On the use of Lev. 18:5 in Rom. 10:5 see Nicole Chibici-Revneanu, "Leben Im Gesetz: Die Paulinische Interpretation Von Lev 18:5 (Gal 3:12; Röm 10:5)," *NovT* 50 (2008): 105–19. A novel view is Chibici-Revneanu's point that, "In Rom 10:5 hingegen stellt Paulus dem 'Menschen im Gesetz' aus Lev 18:5 das 'Gesetz (bzw. eher Gebot) im Menschen'" (119), although powerful rhetorically, misses the point by assuming a distinction between the theological outlooks of Lev and Deut.

[159] Stowers, *Rereading Romans*, 309. Although see the recent work, Matthew W. Bates, *The Hermeneutics of the Apostolic Proclamation: The Center of Paul's Method of Scriptural Interpretation* (Waco: Baylor University Press, 2012), 225–32. He argues for a prosopological exegesis of Rom. 10:5 and 6-8, although he seems to set this against a rhetorical reading of *prosopopoeia*.

[160] Jewett, *Romans*, 625.

[161] On this relationship see Akio Ito, "The Written Torah and the Oral Gospel: Romans 10:5-13 in the Dynamic Tension between Orality and Literacy," *NovT* 48 (2006): 234–60.

follow up Moses's statement taken from Deut. 30:11-14.[162] This is, of course, to confirm the conclusion in Rom. 10:4 that Christ is the *telos* of the law leading to righteousness, not away from it! The citation of Deuteronomy concerning righteousness personified shows that this "righteousness by faith" is consistent with God's previous revelation.[163] The similarity between the righteousness of faith and the obedience of faith is noted by Brian Rosner: "Paul reads Deuteronomy as affirming that the presence of God's word in the community of God's people empowers the obedience of faith."[164]

The theme of faith and obedience is highlighted extensively within the section of 10:6-17. This is seen in the fact that the *pist-* root is used ten times and in the explicit reference to disobedience in Rom. 10:16 and 21.[165] This emphasis on the *pistis* vocabulary contrasts dramatically with Paul's argument about the disobedience of (some of) Israel.

Paul's theme of faith and obedience would have sounded quite familiar to some of the previous understanding Gentiles may have had concerning obedience. Throughout the historians, such as Polybius and Livy, we established the paradigm of entering into faith with Rome and the importance of continued obedience thereafter. Gentiles who reflected on (some of) Israel who had heard God's message and yet still responded with disobedience may have been shocked. The contrast between Paul's emphasis on faith and some of Israel's disobedience could naturally lead some Gentiles to understand why God "could" reject Israel if he wanted. A Gentile's previous notion, informed by Rome's treatment of disobedient nations, provides a framework for how they might expect God to act as well. Truly shocking would be the response of Paul to this disobedience in 11:1, which we will discuss below.

In this third and final unit of 10:14-21, Paul focuses on Israel's disobedience to the gospel and ultimately their disobedience toward God himself. Paul again highlights the connection between the gospel and obedience. Paul uses the corollary of Israel's disobedience to defend the notion that God's word has not failed (9:6).

In 10:16, we have clever wordplay on the role of hearing.[166] Paul reports that Israel has not "obeyed" (ὑπακούω) the "report" (ἀκοή). After laying out the importance of preaching, hearing, believing, and calling in 10:14-15, Paul highlights the one point where the link in the chain was broken: obedience to what was "heard." In Paul's formulation, Israel has been preached to through the prophets (Isaiah and Joel), they have heard God's word, but they have failed to obey the "report."[167] The quotations in 10:11-13 echo Paul's thesis statement through the linguistic parallels of belief (1:16; 10:11), shame (1:16; 10:11), Jew and Greek (1:16; 10:12), all (1:16; 10:11), and salvation terms (1:16; 10:13).

---

[162] On the role of Moses in 9-11 see Michel Quesnel, "La Figure De Moïse En Romains 9-11," *NTS* 49 (2003): 321-35.
[163] So Wagner, *Heralds*, 160; Wright, *Romans*, 662; Matera, *Romans*, 249; Keener, *Romans*, 126. Contra those who see a contrast: Fitzmyer, *Romans*, 589; Byrne, *Romans*, 317,
[164] Rosner, *Paul and the Law*, 141.
[165] Rom. 10:6, 8-11, 14, 16-17.
[166] However, C. Bryan's translation "not all have listened to the good news' (10:16a) is too weak. See Bryan, *Preface to Romans*, 176.
[167] This is not "Christian preaching." Contra Käsemann, *Romans*, 295.

In 10:16, Paul connects the gospel and obedience, linking obedience to his thesis statement in 1:16-17. Paul is left bewildered, like the prophet Isaiah, that some of his people have not responded in obedience to God's message.[168] Both Isaiah and Paul's proclamations share a "fundamental correspondence." Paul is not just looking retroactively at a prefiguration of his ministry in Isaiah, but as Wagner has shown, "Isaiah remains a living voice for Paul, one who speaks alongside the apostle as an authoritative witness to the gospel."[169]

Rom. 10:16 also shows the correspondence for Paul between "faith and obedience" as obeyed in 10:16a is paralleled with believed in 10:16b. Some are surprised that Paul did not utilize "faith" in 10:16a.[170] Rather, 10:16 shows the interplay between faith and obedience in Paul's mind, most dramatically represented in the apostolic purpose— the obedience of faith. We should not miss the parallels between Rom. 10:16 and 1:5. While Paul laments his own people's disobedience, he is the apostle to the Gentiles *for* the obedience of faith, which has been, up to this point, quite successful.[171]

From the standpoint of the Christian Gentiles in the Roman house churches, this is not their position. They are quite unlike Israel at this point in Paul's argument, for they have responded with the obedience of faith and were praised for it (Rom. 1:7). As stated previously, Gentile obedience contrasted with (some of) Israel's disobedience could easily lend itself to a presumed arrogance for their position and a disdain for those who had been disobedient. In our survey of the primary source material (Chapters 3–5), obedience was courted and rewarded by Rome with numerous benefits, and disobedience was met with punishment or destruction. We ought to be reminded of Livy's account of colonies that were thanked before the Senate (27.10.8-10). The colonies publicly thanked were those that were obedient, while those that were disobedient were "silently passed over" (27.10.10). Such an emphasis on disregarding disobedient peoples could have informed how some Gentiles would treat those who were obedient and disobedient.

Paul must now propose a solution to this dilemma of Gentile obedience, on the one hand, and the disobedience of his people to the message of the gospel, on the other. Paul removes two major possible objections to his argument in 10:18-21.[172] He rejects two notions, first that perhaps Israel has not heard. According to Paul's quotation of Ps. 19:4 in Rom. 10:18, they did. He also dismisses the possibility that they did not understand. According to Deut. 32:21 and Isa. 65:1, quoted in Rom. 10:19-20, they have.

We should notice again the global scope of Paul's argument as highlighted in his quotation of Ps. 19:4, "to all the earth" and "the ends of the world." Paul argues that the gospel message has always included this worldwide vision. The inclusion of obedient Gentiles is not a novel thought but one prophesied by Moses, the psalmist, and the

---

[168] Wagner, *Heralds*, 179.
[169] Wagner, *Heralds*, 179–80.
[170] Moo, *Romans*, 665. Keck, *Romans*, 259, notes the surprise as well.
[171] Jewett rightly notes, "The choice of ὑπακούειν also resonates with the missionary goal of eliciting 'obedience of faith' in 1:5 and the 'obedience of the Gentiles' in 15:18." See Jewett, *Romans*, 641.
[172] Sanders rightly reminds that this is part of the larger argument building from 9:30. See Sanders, *Paul, the Law*, 37.

prophet Isaiah.[173] Paul has mounted a very effective argument drawing on the main corpora of Israel's scriptures: the law, the writings, and the prophets. The rhetorical point seems to indicate that "all the scriptures" bear witness to this point.[174]

Paul concludes this portion of his argument with a two-pronged quotation of Isa. 65:1-2 that uniquely summarizes Paul's dilemma: Gentile obedience and Israel's disobedience. Wagner argues that the two questions in Rom. 10:18-19 echo the challenge of Israel's unbelief in Isa. 40:1-2.[175] He also asserts that the similarities between Paul's dual questions about hearing and knowing address Isaiah's questions to Israel once again.[176] Paul's questions reflect Isaiah 40 and are aimed at the "moral nature of knowing ... these are not idle inquiries, but challenges to respond in faith and obedience."[177] In Isaiah, Paul finds a mirror image of his ministry: a disobedient Israel juxtaposed with the discovery and reception of the gospel message by those that did not seek it, the Gentiles. Just as Isaiah experienced an Israel that questioned and disobeyed God's message of salvation, Paul finds himself at similar crossroads.

The argument in Rom. 10:1-21 ends on the emphatic note of Israel's disobedience. We should not miss the unintended rhetorical effect of Paul's message thus far. As mentioned above, the Gentiles in Paul's audience are certainly not in this precarious position. Indeed, a juxtaposition exists between the disobedient people (Rom. 10:21) and the obedience of the Gentiles (Rom. 1:5) and, more specifically, the forthcoming obedience from the Gentiles (15:18). Cranfield likewise notes that the words "disobedience" and "stubborn" in verse 21 "may not unfairly be regarded as expressing the direct opposites to the obedience of faith."[178] The Gentiles in the Roman house churches responded to the gospel message with the obedience of faith representing the "nations" prophesied through the scriptures that would respond positively to the gospel.

Paul's statements could indirectly play into the Gentile pride and anti-Semitic sentiments within the Roman house churches.[179] This is why Paul moves to his discussion of the root and the branches in Romans 11 as a means of offsetting this possible but unintended consequence of his narrative defense of God's faithfulness to his word in 9:6–10:21.

Israel's Disobedience Is Not Final (11:1-36)

In Rom. 11:1-2, Paul takes up another possible objection in his ongoing defense of God's faithfulness.[180] This time the question directly proceeds from the previous context of

---

[173] Quesnel, "La figure de Moïse en Romains 9-11," 334.
[174] Also Dunn, *Romans*, 2:634.
[175] Wagner, *Heralds*, 181.
[176] Wagner, *Heralds*, 182-3. Indeed as he points out γινώσκω and ἀκούω only appear in parallel questions in Isaiah 40 in the entirety of the LXX.
[177] Wagner, *Heralds*, 187-8.
[178] Cranfield, *Romans*, 2:541. Cf. Stuhlmacher, *Romans*, 160.
[179] Too strong is Stowers, *Rereading Romans*, 312, where he suggests that this section is a "dark riddle ... a snare designed to catch gentiles in their own arrogant presumption."
[180] On the organization of the chapter and its relationship within 9-11 see "Rm 11–Its Arrangement and Interpretation," in Aletti, *God's Justice*, 213-40.

10:18-21. If Israel has rejected God, has God now rejected Israel?[181] In other words, since Israel has disobeyed, has God rejected them in favor of accepting the obedient Gentiles? Such pressing matters are raised and refuted in this section in response to what was surely a pressing question. This would have been a topic of discussion in Roman house churches as well as in the early Christian missionary movement as a whole, especially given the tide of Gentile obedience that had been crashing on the shores of the early church.[182] Paul gives a flat-out rejection in the strongest terms by invoking himself as proof that God has not rejected Israel (11:1). Paul not only appeals to himself as evidence but also mounts other in-artificial proofs through the quotations of scripture in this section.[183]

Perhaps most shocking to a Gentile audience, accustomed to the Roman pattern of obedience and disobedience seen in Chapters 3-4, would have been that Israel's disobedience does not result in outright rejection and destruction. As mentioned above, Paul's response that even despite Israel's disobedience, God would remain true to his promises would appear shocking and quite unlike how some Gentiles might have expected God to act. Given the role disobedience played in Roman relationships with other nations, disobedience was met with wrath, punishment, and destruction. The disobedience of Israel noted in this context could easily prompt many Gentiles to tacitly assume that God would reject Israel for its disobedience and provoke his wrath. The twist for Gentile listeners is that God extends further mercy to a disobedient people group. The injustice of Israel's killing God's messengers (Rom. 11:3-5) is met only by the equally shocking response of God's grace (11:5). It is worth remembering how Rome responded to the Varian disaster (Dio, *Hist.* 56) when the Germanic tribes killed Varus. Gentiles familiar with these recent events would be quite astounded at a God who responded in grace and mercy even at the death of his messengers.

Paul returns to the theme of stumbling in 11:11 (last mentioned in 9:32-33) but this time indicates that Israel's stumbling has resulted in salvation for the Gentiles, utilizing an argument *a minore ad maius*.[184] In 11:11, Paul mentions Israel's singular "transgression," which most likely refers to their act of disobedience in 10:16 and their refusal to obey the gospel.[185] The result of this stumbling and hardening is that salvation now comes to the Gentiles, and as in 10:19, the purpose is jealousy. Therefore, Paul states, Israel's current status and state is temporary and for a divine purpose. Certainly

---

[181] See "Paul and the People of Israel," in W. D. Davies, *Jewish and Pauline Studies* (Philadelphia: Fortress, 1984), 130–52.

[182] Jewett, *Romans*, 671, rightly connects the rhetorical questions in 11:11, 12, 15, and 24 to the Gentile mission. Cf. Boyarin, *A Radical Jew*, 201–6.

[183] So Witherington, *Romans*, 264. "The proof he gives immediately is himself." Cf. Cranfield, *Romans*, 2:544; Keener, *Romans*, 130; Fitzmyer, *Romans*, 603. Stuhlmacher, *Romans*, 164, draws attention to Prisca and Aquila, Andronicus, and Junia as other examples.

[184] Witherington, *Romans*, 267.

[185] So Cranfield, *Romans*, 2:555–6. Although he goes on to note that he sides with Barth and that this could possibly signify Jewish rejection of Jesus as Messiah. Also Wright, *Romans*, 680. Contra Dunn who states, "It is not necessary to specify more closely what 'trespass' Paul had in mind" (*Romans*, 2:654).

Israel's "stumbled state" is not permanent. Paul alludes to this in 11:12 when he speaks of their inclusion.[186]

Gentiles in the audience who reflected on Paul's discourse at this point may also have been surprised at the outcome of restoration or "inclusion" (11:12). The notion that disobedience might work toward the good may have seemed a foreign concept to most Gentiles that saw the aftermath of disobedience in the defeated cities. Such imagery was displayed throughout Rome in the monuments and imagery that decorated the Roman landscape (cf. Campus Martius—Chapter 6) in light of the Roman themes of victory through conquest (cf. *Res Gestae*). One area of both continuity and discontinuity with how Gentiles thought about obedience would have occurred with Paul's notion that defeat or failure results in something positive in 11:12. At first, such a statement may have sounded very similar to how some Gentiles may have thought about the defeat of other nations. Certainly, in Rome, the defeat of various nations contributed to the "riches" of Rome, both in the form of tribute payments, slaves, and the grandeur of Roman dominance. However, the next clause of 11:12, whereby restoration of a defeated group result in even "more" might have been a puzzling thought for some Gentiles.

In 11:13, Paul specifically addresses Gentiles in the audience, "Now I am speaking to you Gentiles" and reiterates his apostolic vocation in 11:13, before embarking on his extensive metaphor of the olive tree.[187] As Paul turns to specifically address the Gentile Christians in the Roman house churches, he reminds them that he is the apostle *to them*, highlighted through the emphatic use of εἰμι ἐγώ (I am).[188] The last time Paul invoked his apostolic role was in 9:24-26 that echoed Rom. 1:1 and 1:5.

In 11:13, Paul again reminds them of his "ministry," one that sought to bring about the obedience faith (1:5). Such an echo of his apostolic vocation comes right on the heels of Israel's disobedience or transgression (11:12).[189] In this sense, 11:13-14 is an expansion of Rom. 1:5, placing it in its broader theological context. The obedience

---

[186] See Richard H. Bell, *The Irrevocable Call of God: An Inquiry into Paul's Theology of Israel* (Tübingen: Mohr Siebeck, 2005). See also the discussion in Fitzmyer, *Romans*, 611; Davies, *Jewish and Pauline Studies*, 153-63.

[187] Many now take this as the beginning of a new section. See Barrett, *Romans*, 211-12; Dunn, *Romans*, 2:650-1; Witherington, *Romans*, 242-3. Contra, Cranfield, *Romans*, 2:558. For audience issues see Chapter 2. On the olive tree metaphor see Rainer Schwindt, "Mehr Wurzel Als Stamm Und Krone: Zur Bildrede Vom Ölbaum in Röm 11,16-24," *Bib* 88 (2007): 64-91. He notes, "Die Reflexion auf die Wurzel als die für Juden wie Heiden grundlegende Bezugsgröße verankert die göttlichen Verheißungen in dem vormosaischen, 'gesetzesfreien' Gotteswort, das über die Väter zu einer unwiderbringlichen Heilszusage an alle Völker der menschheitsgeschichte eingepflanzt wurde" (91). Cf. Phillip F. Esler, "Ancient Oléculture and Ethnic Differentiation: The Meaning of the Olive-Tree Image in Romans 11," *JSNT* 26 (2003): 103-24.

[188] Jewett, *Romans*, 678-9, rightly points out that Paul's phrase lacks the definite article, thus placing "his task alongside other and implies that service to the cause of the Jewish mission is a generic obligation of every Gentile apostle."

[189] Wagner, "Mercy to the Nations," 426. On the jealousy motif see Richard H. Bell, *Provoked to Jealousy: The Origin and Purpose of the Jealousy Motif in Romans 9-11* (Tübingen: J. C. B. Mohr (Paul Siebeck), 1994); Jean-Noël Aletti, "Interpreting Romans 11:14: What Is at Stake?," in *Celebrating Paul: Festschrift in Honor of Jerome Murphy-O'connor, O.P., and Joseph A. Fitzmyer, S.J.* (ed. Peter Spitaler, Washington, DC: Catholic Biblical Association of America, 2011), 245-64. See also Stuhlmacher, *Romans*, 174, who interestingly connects this section to Paul himself "who was once conquered by the obedience of faith on the road to Damascus."

of faith/loyalty looms in the background with the discussion of Israel's disobedience. Given the progression of Paul's argument, he reminds his Gentile audience of the necessity of their obedience to the gospel (intimating his next argument in Rom. 12:1–15:33), lest they end up in a precarious position like Israel (11:20-21).[190]

In 11:30-32, Paul explicitly mentions disobedience four times in three verses. The first occurrence of disobedience language in verse 30 highlights the disobedience (ἀπειθέω) of the Gentiles, most likely referring back to 1:18-32. However, as Paul indicates, and we should note, disobedience was their former status. Indeed, the Gentiles and Israel have "switched places" regarding disobedience, perhaps reflecting an active sense of the Gentiles exercising the obedience of faith from Rom. 1:5 in the present context, as Paul stated himself directly in Rom. 1:7.[191] The next three instances of disobedience in 11:30-32 all refer to Israel's disobedience.[192] Similar to 3:23, God consigns all to "disobedience" again so that he might show impartial treatment to all.[193]

In light of the theme of disobedience that dominates this section, and reflecting on Paul's previous argument in Rom. 5:1–8:39, Israel finds itself paradoxically within the Adamic realm marked by disobedience. The Gentiles are marked by the inverse, the obedience of faith (Rom. 1:5).[194] Dunn rightly notices such an emphasis and deserves full quotation:

> The emphasis on disobedience … in this final summary formulation is certainly intended to recall not simply 10:21, but also once again the Adamic disobedience expressed in the earlier climax of 5:12-21 by means of the synonym παρακοή (5:19; cf. 2:8) and the preferred antonym ὑπακοή (so also 10:16). Note also that Paul sums up his own mission in terms of bringing Gentiles to "the obedience of faith" (1:5; 15:18; also 16:26). The choice of ἀπείθεια to sum up the epoch of Adam in its continuing effect on Israel even in the epoch of Christ is therefore deliberate: it reinforces the thematic unity of the letter and underlines the fact that the eschatological tension of this overlap of the epochs period is not simply an individual experience (chaps. 6-8) but afflicts whole nations as such.[195]

---

[190] Contra Tobin *Paul's Rhetoric*, 363, who argues, "Paul is not directly addressing the Gentile members of the Roman community in 11:13-24."

[191] Keener, *Romans*, 139. So also, Dunn, *Romans*, 2:695. Contra, Michael Wolter, "Apokalyptik Als Redeform Im Neuen Testament," *NTS* 51 (2005): 171–91. Wolter argues that Paul has an unsolvable problem, "Paulus kann sich aus dieser Aporie nur befreien, indem er apokalyptisch redet" (184).

[192] On the translation of the dative phrases see Bryan, *A Preface to Romans*, 193.

[193] Wagner, *Mercy to the Nations*, 425, rightly highlights that the similarities in this short section break down as the Gentiles never take the place as "Israel's benefactors." Robert Jewett also rightly notes that "mercy" in a Roman context was only reserved for the worthy among captives and enemies (*Romans*, 711). Cf. Keener, *Romans*, 133, for a comparison of Israel and the role of Christ in Rom. 5; Käsemann, *Romans*, 317; Tobin, *Paul's Rhetoric*, 362; Dunn, *Romans*, 2:677; Christopher Zoccali, "'And So All Israel Will Be Saved': Competing Interpretations of Romans 11.26 in Pauline Scholarship," *JSNT* 30 (2008): 289–318.

[194] Contra Jason A. Staples, "What Do the Gentiles Have to Do with 'All Israel'? A Fresh Look at Romans 11:25-27," *JBL* 130 (2011): 371–90. Staples argues that "Paul sees the ἐκκλησία in full continuity with Israel" (388).

[195] Dunn, *Romans*, 2:687–8.

Paul concludes his sweeping argument from Rom. 9:1–11:36 and ties the subpoints of his argument to the issue of disobedience and, by implication, obedience. Certainly, Gentiles within the Roman house churches would be on full alert as their arrogance and presumption risk their own "standing" (11:21-24). However, by putting Israel's disobedience on full display, Paul intimates his next major argument in Romans. In the next section, he will raise several current issues within the house churches, many of which revolve around Jew/Gentile issues, such as table fellowship between the weak and the strong. One of the rhetorical implications of Rom. 9:1–11:36, with its focus on Israel's disobedience, is that the Gentiles should not presume that their status is secure. In the next major section, they too will be called on to exercise obedience to God's plan.

The Fourth Proof: (12:1–15:13)

In Rom. 12:1–15:13, Paul turns to the critical issues within the Roman house churches.[196] This section provides the Roman house churches with their opportunities to respond to the gospel and to exercise the obedience of faith as it relates to God's mission. We are reminded that in in Rom. 1:17, Paul quoted Habakkuk and stated the righteous one will live by faith/faithfulness. It is these aspects of righteous living that Paul will now sketch out for the Roman communities. Stanley Stowers has noted that 12:1–13:15 "serve as a positive reversal and counterpoint to the programmatic criticism of the gentile peoples in 1:18–32."[197]

If accepted, then just as 1:18-32 characterized the Gentiles as disobedient and rebellious, 12:1–15:13 open up a new avenue for the obedience and faithfulness of the Gentiles to the gospel. Through their obedience, Rom. 12:1–15:13 is how the righteousness of God will become visible to the world around them.[198] Or as Cranfield rightly notes, "The life, which, according to 1.17, is the destiny of the man who is righteous by faith, is a life of obedience to God."[199]

---

[196] On the issue of Rom. 12–15 to the whole letter, see the foundational work of Paul S. Minear, *The Obedience of Faith: The Purposes of Paul in the Epistle to the Romans* (Naperville: SCM, 1971). A very "grounded" and helpful reading of this section is offered by Peter Oakes, *Reading Romans in Pompeii: Paul's Letter at Ground Level* (Minneapolis: Fortress, 2009), 98–126. Cf. Jeremy Moiser, "Rethinking Romans 12–15," *NTS* 36 (1990): 571–82; Mark Reasoner, "The Theology of Romans 12:1-15:13," in *Pauline Theology*, 287–99; A. J. M. Wedderburn, *The Reasons for Romans* (Edinburgh: T&T Clark, 1988). See also the relevant articles in *The Romans Debate*.

[197] Stowers, *A Rereading of Romans*, 317. On the connections between Rom. 1:18-32 and Rom. 12 see Keck, *Romans*, 293; Johnson, *Reading Romans*, 190; Seyoon Kim, "Paul's Common Paraenesis (1 Thess. 4–5; Phil. 2–4; and Rom. 12–13): The Correspondence between Romans 1:18-32 and 12:2, and the Unity of Romans 12–13," *TynB* 62 (2011): 109–40.

[198] Stuhlmacher, *Romans*, 186.

[199] Cranfield, *Romans*, 2:592; Matera, *Romans*, 283–4; Wright, "Romans," 704; Keck, *Romans*, 290. Barrett notes, "Obedience well summarizes the following words" he is referring to Rom. 12:1. See Barrett, *Romans*, 212.

The Obedience of Faith at Ground Level (12:1–13:15)

Rom 12:1 is tightly linked to the previous section of 9:1–11:36 through the language of mercy, especially 9:15-23 and 11:30-32.[200] Other linguistic links to previous sections are seen through the use of the verb "present" (6:13, 16, 19) and body language (6:6, 12; 7:4, 24; 8:10-11, 13, 23). In 6:1-23, Paul introduced the new life offered through the second Adam and described this existence as one of slavery to righteousness and a life of obedience.[201] It is no surprise, then, that as Paul turns to the issues where the Romans must make decisions and choose to exercise the obedience of faith, that Rom. 6 would be looming in the background. Rom. 6:1-23 provided some of the most explicit references to obedience and established the theological groundwork for that obedience.

To rehearse our stated aim(s), obedience forms a main theme *throughout* Romans. Using the language of Rom. 6:1-23, Rom. 12:1–15:13 provides opportunities for those in Rome who have been freed from sin (6:7) to now present their bodies and members as instruments *for* righteousness (6:13, 16). The previous section of Rom. 9:1–11:36 was characterized by the disobedience of Israel. As Paul turns to address the crucial issues dividing the Roman house churches, the previous discussion of disobedience is not far removed from view. God's mercies should prompt the community to respond in obedience to God's plan(s). The practical outcome or content of Paul's call for obedience in Rom. 1:5 is Rom. 12:1–15:13, where the Gentiles are given opportunities to exercise the obedience of faith.[202]

The context of this obedience in Romans should not be missed. From Rom. 5:1 onward, the Roman Christians are those who have experienced "peace with God" and removal of hostilities under their new Lord, Jesus Christ. As slaves to God, they offer themselves as a sacrifice in obedience to the will of God (12:2) as expressed in the elaborations of Rom. 12:1–15:21. The dynamic change in their relationship with God correlates to the community as well.[203] Those who have entered into faith with God are now empowered and are expected to demonstrate obedience.

---

[200] Despite the tendency of some in Pauline studies to see the ethical sections of Paul's letters as "detached" or a "grab bag," Dunn rightly sees the intimate connection between Rom. 1–11 and 12–15; "chaps. 12–15 follow naturally from and constitute a necessary corollary to the overall argument of chaps. 1–11; they should not be regarded as a piece of standard paraenesis [sic] which has no direct material or thematic connection with what has gone before and could have been discarded or wholly reordered without loss" (*Romans*, 2:705). Cf. Stowers, *Rereading Romans*, 317-19; Wright, "Romans," 700; Käsemann, *Romans*, 323-4; Fitzmyer, *Romans*, 637-9.

[201] Likewise Fitzmyer, *Romans*, 637; Tobin, *Paul's Rhetoric*, 388.

[202] Esler, *Conflict and Identity*, 307. Esler is right to some extent that Rom. 12–13 is an attempt by Paul of "recategorization" or the "development of a common ingroup identity." However, he limits this to the two areas of faith in Christ and the influence of the Holy Spirit. He misses that there is also a common obedience that would have been particularly important for Jewish Christians and Gentiles to unite around. Noting this common obedience is James W. Thompson, *Moral Formation According to Paul: The Context and Coherence of Pauline Ethics* (Grand Rapids: Baker, 2011), 166-73.

[203] Cf. Tobias Nicklas and Herbert Schlögel, "Mission to the Gentiles, Construction of Christian Identity, and Its Relation to Ethics according to Paul," in *Sensitivity towards Outsiders: Exploring the Dynamic Relationship between Missions and Ethics in the New Testament and Early Christianity* (ed. Jakobus (Kobus) Kok et al., Tübingen: Mohr Siebeck, 2014), 325. They note, "The relationships to other members of the community had to become determinative for behavior."

Reflecting again on Paul's Gentile audience, we should not be surprised that the premise of faith and obedience relates well to the Greco-Roman sources on obedience. Some Gentiles in the audience may have had such conceptions in mind. The intent of Paul is very close to Witherington's summarizing statements on Rom. 12:1-21. He writes, "Paul's appeal is for the people of the Roman house churches to become *subjects* (emphasis mine), to follow the way of the King, the way of the cross."[204] As "subjects" of Rome, such a framework of "faith and obedience" would be familiar (see Chapters 3-6). Gentile members in Paul's audience upon hearing this framework would see degrees of continuity with how they had thought about obedience previously. For example, in the historians, one enters into faith and then offers continued obedience. Paul's admonition, however, in 12:2-3 to not be conformed to the world or to think more highly about oneself, would warn Gentile members to not allow their obedience to be a basis for presuming arrogance or superiority over those who had been previously disobedient (cf. 11:17-24, 30-32).

As Paul defines his "moral vision" for the communities, he draws attention to this new eschatological scenario (vis-á-vis Rom. 5:1–8:39). As Witherington has rightly noted again, it is "a new and eschatological situation in which the Spirit of God has been fully poured out, enabling God's people to press on to the 'obedience of faith.' "[205] Likewise, Cranfield rightly titles this section, "The obedience to which those who are righteous by faith are called (12:1–15:13)."[206] In summary, Rom. 12:1–15:13 are specific areas where the Roman Christians—both Jew and Gentile—can unite to exercise the obedience of faith/loyalty.

In Rom. 12:1, Paul persuades the audience to present their bodies as a sacrifice (θυσία) that is alive, holy, and pleasing to God.[207] The cultic context, both Jewish

---

[204] Witherington, *Romans*, 298.
[205] Witherington, *Romans*, 283. Also, Dunn, *Romans*, 2:705. Matera then rightly titles this section, "Love and Obedience in the New Age." See Matera, *Romans*, 283.
[206] Cranfield, *Romans*, 2:592. This makes the monographs on the "obedience of faith" that do not deal with these sections all the more surprising and in turn were one prompt for the thesis of this monograph. Cf. Don Garlington, *The Obedience of Faith: A Pauline Phrase in Historical Context* (Tübingen: J. C. B. Mohr (Paul Siebeck), 1991); James C. Miller, *The Obedience of Faith: The Eschatological People of God, and the Purpose of Romans* (Atlanta: SBL, 2000).
[207] The beginning of Paul's persuasive discourse has engendered no small debate as it surrounds his use of Παρακαλῶ. Since Bultmann, Paul's admonition has been understood as theologically motivated persuasion intended to establish his ethics on a basis of authority. Jewett has argued, relying on the work of Carl Bjerkelund on Παρακαλῶ, that the term was prominent in diplomatic correspondence between allied groups, where commands might prove offensive. Our survey of obedience language in the Greek sources also noted that the πείθω root was often used in contexts where one was not just "persuaded" but also "persuaded to obey." In such contexts, the verb was used to obtain compliance or obedience to the decisions of a superior authority. Jewett cites King Ptolemy II writing to Miletus (P.Milet. 1.3. #139). Such usage comports with Paul's position of authority as apostle *to* the Gentile and his purpose (1:5). Παρακαλῶ is an appropriate choice for Paul's task whereby he is advising a community he has not founded or met, yet balanced with his own authority and purpose for the obedience of the Roman community. Cf. Rudolf Bultmann, "Das Problem Der Ethik Bei Paulus," *ZNW* 23 (1924): 123–40; Victor P. Furnish, *Theology and Ethics in Paul* (Louisville: Westminster John Knox, 2009), 224–7; Carl J. Bjerkelund, *Parakalô: Form, Funktion Und Sinn Der Parakalô-Sätze in Den Paulinischen Briefen* (Oslo: Universitetsvorlaget, 1967). Noted by Cranfield, *Romans*, 2:597–8; Käsemann, *Romans*, 326; Fitzmyer, *Romans*, 639; Johnson, *Reading Romans*, 189; Jewett, *Romans*, 726. Contra Matera, *Romans*, 283, that the function of persuasion is to "encourage people to do what they already know they ought to do."

and Greco-Roman, of Rom. 12:1 has often been noted through the use of sacrificial language in the section.[208] Paul's use of "present" in 12:1 echoes language in 6:13-19, where he instructed believers to "present" their members for righteousness. In 6:1-23, Paul has in mind not only "members" but entire bodies (6:13).[209] Reading 6:13 and 12:1 together, Paul is advocating that this presentation of their bodies is an act of obedience.

The priestly/cultic setting of sacrifice in 12:1 will reappear in 15:16, where Paul characterizes his ministry in similar terms, and obedience is explicitly mentioned in 15:18 as part of his purpose.[210] Such a context supports the reading we have put forward here, namely that their sacrifice is and involves an act of obedience. This first act of worship, marked by obedience, is forward-looking. It is intended to carry through the rest of the sections so that the Roman Christians will carry through the obedience of faith with the issues that arise in the next several sections, assisted by a transformed and renewed mind (12:2). Witherington rightly notes that the worship in view here "is an act of submission ... if one does what this verse says, then it follows that one has committed herself to obeying the commandments and exhortations that follow."[211]

One act of obedience leading to continued obedience was repeatedly shown in the Greco-Roman sources documenting obedience (Chapters 3-4). Gentiles reflecting on the notion of continued obedience would see a correspondence between Rome's demand for continued obedience of the nations and Paul's desire for the community to continue to exercise obedience to his various directives. In both Polybius, Livy, and Tacitus, continued obedience was a constant refrain throughout their descriptions of a nation's response to Rome. Roman peace was built on the notion of continued obedience. Paul's admonition to present their bodies as a sacrifice functions as an act of obedience that issues forth continued obedience to the instructions that follow. One point of discontinuity that some Gentiles may have had with the expectation to obey was the content of that obedience, although some of Paul's admonitions would have been shared with other philosophers, such as patience in suffering (12:12) and living in harmony (12:16). Several of the admonitions in Rom. 12:1-15:13 would have required obedience to countercultural norms, such as associating with the lowly (12:16) and not repaying evil for evil (12:17). Obedience to these directives may not have aligned with Gentile assumptions about obedience in a Greco-Roman context.

Rom 12:3-21 provides numerous issues of community life where Paul wants this community to pursue unity through their common obedience.[212] These maxims

---

[208] Jewett, *Romans*, 727-8.
[209] Also Dunn, *Romans*, 709; Halvor Moxnes, "Quest for Honor and the Unity of the Community in Romans 12 and in the Orations of Dio Chrysostom," in *Paul in His Hellenistic Context* (ed. Troels Engberg-Pedersen, Edinburgh: T&T Clark, 1994), 217.
[210] Noted by Jewett, *Romans*, 729; Matera, *Romans*, 288; Johnson, *Reading Romans*, 190; Keener, *Romans*, 143.n4.
[211] Witherington, *Romans*, 285.
[212] The importance and parallels of these issues in the Greco-Roman world are noted by Keener, *Romans*, 147-51. Cf. Walter T. Wilson, *Love without Pretense: Romans 12.9-21 and Hellenistic-Jewish Wisdom Literature* (Tübingen: J. C. B. Mohr, 1991); Dieter Zeller, "Pauline Paraenesis in Romans 12 and Greek Gnomic Wisdom," in *Greco-Roman Culture and the New Testament: Studies*

consist of some of Paul's ethical admonitions along with what is most likely some of the oral Jesus tradition (12:14-21).[213] Paul's rationale for his ethical authority and desired obedience is linked to his apostleship through the "grace given to me language." He is referencing Rom. 1:5 and 15:15 (cf. 9:24-26; 11:13) where Paul indicates the basis for his authority to bring about obedience among the nations. The grace language invokes Paul's apostleship, one that is aimed at the obedience of faith among the nations, to persuade and compel certain courses of action within the Roman communities. In short, Paul is indicating that, given his task of bringing about the obedience of faith among the nations, Rom. 12:3-15:13 are the places where he would like to see the obedience of faith/loyalty exercised.

The maxim of 12:21 stands out in light of our reading Romans from a Roman Gentile point of view.[214] Paul's admonition not to be overcome by evil but to overcome evil with good reverberates with the overtones of the Roman conquests and allows us an excellent opportunity to reflect on this section in light of the Greco-Roman evidence (Chapter 6). Some Gentiles in the Roman house churches would have been familiar with the numerous monuments to the Roman goddess Victoria, the Campus Martius, or the building along the *via Flaminia* (see Chapter 6), and with the inscriptions and coins that documented the subduing of the nations by the Romans. Such images, combined with the other sources in Chapters 3-4, proclaim the oft-repeated theme: Roman victory brings peace, and the requirements of both Roman victory and the attainment of peace are continued obedience. If victory was key to the *Pax Romana*, it was the continued obedience of the nations that maintained this peace. Jewett rightly notes that Paul here offers a "subtle interaction with the Roman cultural context."[215] However, there was nothing "subtle" about Paul's interaction/ Paul's words to the Roman congregation(s) appear strikingly countercultural to a culture dominated by power and violence, yet his exhortation presented the Roman congregation(s) with another opportunity to exercise the obedience of faith/loyalty.

In an antagonistic culture of honor and shame, one's reputation hung in the balance. Such obedience could lead to self-abasement and may not have cohered with how some Gentiles thought about obedience. Further, conquering language was usually ripe with reverberations of violence, as seen in the historians and Rome's typical response to disobedient peoples. Paul's commands would require a reevaluation for some Gentiles of their previous conceptions of obedience and cultural norms.

Rom. 13:1-7 has been subjected to an ever-increasing array of interpretations. These range from political servitude to anti-imperial resistance literature meant to subvert imperial programs. Rom. 13:1-7 is a problematic passage in the history of its

---

Commemorating the Centennial of the Pontifical Biblical Institute (ed. Frederick E. Brenk and David Aune, Leiden: Brill, 2012), 73–86.

[213] On this issue see the work of Michael Thompson, *Clothed with Christ: The Example and Teaching of Jesus in Romans 12:1–15:13* (Eugene: Wipf & Stock, 2011); Craig L. Blomberg, "Quotations, Allusions, and Echoes of Jesus in Paul," in *Studies in the Pauline Epistles: Essays in Honor of Douglas J. Moo* (ed. Matthew S. Harmon and Jay E. Smith, Grand Rapids: Zondervan, 2014), 129–43.

[214] See again the helpful work of Oakes, *Reading Romans*, 123–6. Contra Kent L. Yinger, "Romans 12:14-21 and Nonretaliation in Second Temple Judaism: Addressing Persecution within the Community," *CBQ* 60 (1998): 74–96.

[215] Jewett, *Romans*, 779.

reception.[216] The passage also has a direct bearing on one aspect of our work, namely the issue of whether Paul's call for obedience is anti-imperial. One's interpretation of Rom. 13:1-7 has a direct impact on the implications of the obedience theme in Romans.[217]

More recently, political readings of Paul have struggled to understand Rom. 13:1-7 when compared to other passages in Paul where it is argued that he is countering an imperial ideology with the gospel of Jesus Christ.[218] Rom. 13:1-7 on a prima facie level argues the exact opposite point of an anti-imperial reading of Paul. Indeed, many commentators have struggled with the placement of these verses within a political reading of Paul, characterizing this passage as the "Achilles' heel" of all anti-imperial readings of Paul.[219] Several issues need to be examined to understand the "appropriateness" of Rom. 13:1-7 within the discussion of Romans. These are: (1) the historical situation of Romans and (2) precision in regards to the particulars of Rom. 13:1-7.

---

[216] Indeed even the very integrity of the section has been challenged, but Cranfield's defense of the integrity of the passage within the overarching section still persuades (*Romans*, 2:651–5). The problematic reception of Rom. 13:1-7 has been highlighted by South African theologians among others. See Jean-Noël Aletti, "La Soumission Des Chrétiens Aux Autorités En Rm 13,1-7: Validité Des Arguments Pauliniens?," *Bib* 89 (2008): 457–76; Jan Botha, *Subject to Whose Authority? Multiple Readings of Romans 13* (Atlanta: Scholars Press, 1994); Jan Botha, "Creation of New Meaning: Rhetorical Situations and the Reception of Romans 13:1-7," *JTSA* 79.2 (1992): 24–37. Keener provides an excellent excursus on "Church and State" (*Romans*, 155–6).

[217] The early church fathers struggled with Rom. 13:1-7. See Gerald Bray and Thomas C. Oden, eds., *Ancient Christian Commentary on Scripture: Romans*, vol. New Testament 6 (Downers Grove: IVP, 1998), 312–17.

[218] See Chapter 1 for full bibliography as well as works of Christopher D. Stanley, *The Colonized Apostle: Paul through Postcolonial Eyes* (Minneapolis: Fortress, 2011); Richard A. Horsley, ed., *Paul and Politics: Ekklesia, Israel, Imperium, Interpretation* (Harrisburg: Trinity Press International, 2000); Richard A. Horsley, *Paul and the Roman Imperial Order* (Harrisburg: Trinity Press International, 2004); Richard A. Horsley, *Paul and Empire: Religion and Power in Roman Imperial Society* (Harrisburg: Trinity Press International, 1997); John Dominic Crossan, "Paul and Rome: The Challenge of a Just World Order," *USQR* 59 (2005): 6–20; Marcus J. Borg and John Dominic Crossan, *The First Paul: Reclaiming the Radical Visionary behind the Church's Conservative Icon* (New York: HarperOne, 2009). Others have looked to the notions of hybridity and constraints on Paul as a "subjected" person that limit the potential for what Paul *could* actually envision. See John W. Marshall, "Hybridity and Reading Romans 13," *JSNT* 31 (2008): 157–78; Neil Elliott, *The Arrogance of Nations: Reading Romans in the Shadow of the Empire* (Minneapolis: Fortress, 2008), 152–8. Jewett has issued a correction to his own argument about Rom. 13; see Robert Jewett, "Reinterpreting Romans 13 within Its Broader Context," in *Celebrating Paul*, 265–74.

[219] Seyoon Kim, *Christ and Caesar: The Gospel and the Roman Empire in the Writings of Paul and Luke* (Grand Rapids: Eerdmans, 2008), 36. It should be noted that while Kim notes that this passage is the "Achilles' heel" for anti-imperial readings, Kim's arguments fail at several points and are less than convincing. A much better critique is offered by John M. G. Barclay, "Paul, Roman Religion, and the Emperor. Mapping the Point of Conflict," in *Pauline Churches and Diaspora Jews* (Tübingen: Mohr Siebeck, 2011), 345–62. Also, Christopher Bryan, *Render to Caesar: Jesus, the Early Church, and the Roman Superpower* (Oxford: Oxford University Press), 2005, 77–94; Scot McKnight and Joseph B. Modica, eds., *Jesus Is Lord, Caesar Is Not: Evaluating Empire in New Testament Studies* (Downers Grove: IVP, 2013), 146–65.

The Historical Situation: The Golden Age of Nero

Nero's ascension as emperor was heralded as the "dawn of the golden age."[220] His rise to power and early years of his reign were a sharp contrast to the dark and murderous reign of Claudius. When he was named emperor in 54 CE, Nero promised positive relationships with the Senate and the army.[221] Although Nero's ascension was not completely free of bloodshed—the deaths of Silanus and Britannicus come to mind—it was noted by poets and historians to be the dawn of a new age. In a poem after the death of Claudius and before the ascension of Nero, the poet Diodorus Siculus notes:

> Clemency has commanded every vice that wears the disguise of peace to betake itself afar: she has broken every maddened sword-blade ... Peace in her fulness shall come; knowing not the drawn sword ... right will come in fullest force; a kinder god will renew the former tradition and look of the Forum and displace the age of oppression.[222]

The emphasis on peace and distancing from the sword was a cardinal characteristic of the early Neronian principate. Later sources referred to the early rule of Nero as the *quinquennium Neronis*, the first five years of Nero's rule, marked by peace and moderation of his desires.[223] Nero's early reign was so revered that Tacitus makes a direct comparison between Nero and Augustus.[224] This would quickly end in 59 CE in what began as a power struggle with Agrippina and ended in her matricide.[225] The tyrannical and despotic reign of Nero was about to begin. The five years of peace were quickly shattered and forgotten as a result of his later monstrous reign that eventually led up to the Civil War of the Flavians and the tumultuous year of 69 CE.

It is specifically in light of this *quinquennium Neronis* that we can begin to understand Rom. 13:1-7.[226] If Romans was written during these five years, then Paul's instructions seem all the more fitting, especially Rom. 13:3, where Paul states that

---

[220] Vasily Rudich, *Political Dissidence under Nero: The Price of Dissimulation* (New York: Routledge, 1993), 4. Cf. Edward Champlin, *Nero* (Cambridge: Belknap Press of Harvard University Press, 2003); Miriam T. Griffin, *Nero: The End of a Dynasty* (New Haven: Yale University Press, 1985), 37–66; Anthony A. Barrett, Elaine Fanthem, John C. Yardley, eds., *The Emperor Nero: A Guide to the Ancient Sources* (Princeton: Princeton University Press, 2016), 22–40.

[221] Mary T. Boatwright, Daniel J. Gargola, and Richard J. A. Talbert, eds., *The Romans: From Village to Empire* (New York: Oxford University Press, 2004), 332.

[222] *Library of History* 1.59-64, 69–73.

[223] Martin Goodman, *The Roman World: 44BC–AD180* (New York: Routledge, 1997), 56. See also David Shotter, *Nero* (New York: Routledge, 1997), 14–24.

[224] Tacitus, *Ann.* 13.5.

[225] Goodman, *Roman World*, 56.

[226] William L. Lane, "Social Perspectives on Roman Christianity during the Formative Years from Nero to Nerva: Romans, Hebrews, and 1 Clement," in *Judaism and Christianity in First-Century Rome* (ed. Karl P. Donfried and Peter Richardson, Grand Rapids: Eerdmans, 1998), 196–244. Cf. James D. G. Dunn, "Romans 13.1-7—a Charter for Political Quietism?," *Ex Auditu* 2 (1986): 55–68; William S. Campbell, "The Rule of Faith in Romans 12:1-15:13," in *Pauline Theology*, 264–8. Also, Witherington, *Romans*, 305–8, Bryan, *A Preface to Romans*, 205.

the "governing authorities" are of no fear for those who do right.[227] If Romans was written after the *quinquennium*, then Paul's statements were quite out of touch with the situation of the Christians in Rome. The end of Nero's reign would strongly contradict Paul's statement in 13:3.

Our material from the previous chapter on the philosophers is important at this juncture. Troels Engberg-Pedersen offers a very helpful comparison to the Stoic writer Seneca's treatment of Nero that offers a helpful parallel to Paul:

> At the time and place of the writing of these two texts there was a conventional view of the good, divinely installed ruler to which one might appeal without further ado—and then use the appeal for one's own purposes. To say that this view was conventional is not to suggest that "people did not believe it." On the contrary, the view was probably generally accepted, otherwise, the appeal would have had no point.[228]

Witherington likewise states, "He [Paul] could in good faith exhort his audience to pay their taxes and do their civic duties and live at peace with their neighbors because there was a widespread hope, and not only in Rome, that Nero would keep the peace and govern wisely, fairly, and justly."[229] Such features are also assumed in the philosophers like Epictetus and Seneca.

Indeed, Gentiles in Paul's audience hearing Paul's directives to submit to rulers who are no cause for fear bear out a similar understanding of just government offered by Aristotle, Cicero, and Seneca the Younger. If some Gentiles in the audience were familiar with any of the major philosophical groups in Rome, admonitions to just rule would not have appeared surprising. One aspect that may not have cohered with some Gentiles preconceived notions of obedience would have been the admonition not to resist authority. As seen in the historians (particularly Livy and Tacitus), the plebeian groups were highlighted several times for their disobedience to Rome's laws. Further, the Augustan legislation on marriage was met with great resistance in Rome. Paul's admonition to be "good citizens" could have surprised those in his audience who tended toward subversion or animosity toward Rome. Obeying Paul's directives

---

[227] For the importance of the cultural milieu for interpretation see Bruce W. Winter, *Seek the Welfare of the City: Christians as Benefactors and Citizens* (Grand Rapids: Eerdmans, 1994), 4–5.

[228] Troels Engberg-Pedersen, "Paul's Stoicizing Politics in Romans 12-13: The Role of 13.1-10 in the Argument," *JSNT* 29 (2006): 169. Likewise, Fitzmyer, *Romans*, 665; Bryan, *Preface to Romans*, 206–7.

[229] Witherington, *Romans*, 306. Furthermore, Paul comments only on one side of the conversation, that of the subjects' responsibility to legitimate governments. There is no indication with 13:1-7 of a discussion of government ordering or political theory. In the words of Käsemann, Paul is "silent about possible conflicts and the limits of earthly authority" (*Romans*, 354). Likewise Jewett aptly states, "Romans 13:1-7 was not intended to create the foundation of a political ethic for all times and places in succeeding generations" (*Romans*, 786). One should not go as far as Carter in his article where he detects Pauline irony. Carter's points are too subtle for a historic or modern audience to grasp. He even states that Paul was unaware of his own words. "Paul's words are pregnant with a significance of which he was unaware." Cf. T. L. Carter, "The Irony of Romans 13," *NovT* 46 (2004): 209–28. On the issue of taxation at this time, cf. Stuhlmacher, *Romans*, 200–1; Bryan, *A Preface to Romans*, 207; Keener, *Romans*, 154–5; Thomas M. Coleman, "Binding Obligations in Romans 13:7: A Semantic Field and Social Context," *TynB* 48 (1997): 307–27.

to submit may not have been met with wholehearted approval at "ground level" in Rome. The issue of taxation was fraught with contention and contained the potential for revolt as seen in Judea. Paul's directive to obey in this regard may have proved difficult for some in the Roman house churches who thought that their new obedience to God could carry the corollary of disobedience to Rome.

We will now move into a discussion of the particulars in Rom. 13:1-7. With the following context and the aims of this work in mind, our primary focus will be on the meaning of subjection to the authorities (13:1). Specifically, what is the relationship between submission (ὑποτάσσω) and obedience (ὑπακούω)?[230] As already mentioned, our understanding of the relationship between ὑπακούω and ὑποτάσσω has been greatly aided by the excellent, although too infrequently cited work by Cynthia Briggs Kittredge, *Community and Authority: The Rhetoric of Obedience in the Pauline Tradition*.[231] She has shown that, in the textual evidence from Epictetus, Dionysius of Halicarnassus, Philo, and Josephus, the two words

> do not have substantially different meanings ... the quantity of evidence from these contemporary authors [suggest] that Paul ... uses both words to designate "obedience" as a feature of relationships of subordination. The claim that the two verbs have different meanings is not supported by contemporary Greek literature.[232]

For example, she notes a passage in Epictetus where he remarks, "Nor would he have suffered another to yield them more obedience and submission."[233] She notes that although Epictetus uses the ὑποτάσσω root less frequently than the ὑπακούω root, "the meaning of the passive sense of the word [ὑποτάσσω] appears to overlap with the meaning of ὑπακούειν in that one who subjects oneself to another is also one who would obey that one."[234] In summing up the usage of obedience in Philo, Kittridge notes, "To be subjected (ὑποτάσσεσθαι) is not used in contexts where there is a choice. Rather, it describes where one fits in the order of creation or where one is *subjected to a political or military ruler* (emphasis mine)."[235]

Alongside her insights from the ancient philosophers, we marshaled our evidence in the previous chapters that showed the synonymous nature between obedience and submission in the Greco-Roman historians and the philosophers. For example, in his

---

[230] An older generation of commentators saw ὑποτάσσω as equivalent to "obey." See William Sanday and Arthur C. Headlam, *The Epistle to the Romans* (Edinburgh: T&T Clark, 1902), 365; Barrett, *Romans*, 254. Wright, "Romans," 720, comes the closest in saying that to be subject does not necessarily mean obey, "though that will usually follow."

[231] See previous discussion on pages 10–11 of this chapter.

[232] Kittredge, *Community and Authority*, 51. Contra Jewett who argues that this verb in the middle does not imply obedience (*Romans*, 618). There certainly were other alternatives to blind obedience that still entailed the necessity to obey. See Cranfield, *Romans*, 2:660–3; Käsemann, *Romans*, 351–2; Fitzmyer, *Romans*, 665; Matera, *Romans*, 294.

[233] Epictetus, *Diss.*, 4.1.154.

[234] Kittridge, *Community and Authority*, 43.

[235] Kittridge, *Community and Authority*, 47. Cf. Bruno Blumenfeld, *The Political Paul: Justice, Democracy and Kingship in a Hellenistic Framework* (New York: T&T Clark, 2003), 389–95. Blumenfeld draws comparisons between Paul's political outlook and that of the Hellenistic political thinking, particularly that of the Pythagoreans.

Roman Antiquities, Dionysius of Halicarnassus compares previous empires to Rome and castigates the Persians for failing to reduce various nations to "submission" (1.2.2). Likewise, the Macedonians are castigated for they did not "subjugate (ὑπήκοος) every country and every sea" (1.2.4). In light of the historical evidence of the synonymous nature between ὑπακούω and ὑποτάσσω, readings of Rom. 13:1 that posit a sharp distinction between obedience and submission cannot be upheld.

Paul's admonition to submit to the governing authorities means that the Christians in Rome are to obey those in authority over them.[236] However, we need to connect Paul's remarks in 13:1 with Paul's stated purpose in 1:5. Whatever Paul means by the obedience of faith or loyalty, in light of 13:1, it cannot mean disobedience to the ruling authorities.[237] Paul does not envision the obedience of faith as something inherently antithetical to the obedience due to the Roman emperor.[238] It is at this point that we must keep in mind the specific historical situation in which Paul is writing, referred to above, as there were certainly times coming when disobedience would need to be exercised.[239] We ought to remember also that the philosophers debated similar allegiances and obedience (cf. Epictetus, *Disc.* 1.14.16-18).

Paul's purpose for obtaining the obedience of faith, if read apart from Rom. 13:1, might indicate a revolutionary stance; however, when combined with Rom 13:1, it tempers and contours Paul's call for obedience among the nations.[240] As Christopher Bryan has cogently argued, Paul's view of the Roman Empire aligns with the Hebrew prophetic tradition, whereby "it accepts and holds as legitimate Roman authority; on the other it leaves Roman authority in principle open to prophetic challenge where and whenever it as claimed too much for itself or betrayed the purposes for which it was instituted."[241]

Remembering our aim of reading these sections of Romans in light of a Gentile audience, the implications for those in Paul's audience who had come from a subjected background would have been manifold. First, since Rome demanded obedience as a surety of continued peace, most would have been familiar with this requirement of obedience. Perhaps some had heard of the disastrous results that disobedience had for those who did not submit to Rome and its commands.[242] For some in Paul's audience,

---

[236] Keener also notes that "ancient writers often addressed the topic of societal relationships to the state" and lists several ancient examples. See Keener, *Romans*, 152; Engberg-Pedersen, "Paul's Stoicizing Politics," 163–72.

[237] See Pierre Debergé, "Romains 13,1-7: De La Soumission Requise À La Désobéissance Possible?," *BLE* 108 (2007): 289–314.

[238] Elliott does conclude that Paul understands "obedience as subjection, including subjection to the present governing authorities." However, this does stand at odds with his statements in the early part of the chapters about the counter-imperial nature of the ὑπακοὴν πίστεως. Elliott attempts to mitigate this tension by appealing that Paul suffers "ideological constraints" as Paul replaces one "*kyriarchal*" program for another. However this explanation is not persuasive. See Elliott, *Arrogance of Nations*, 56.

[239] Aletti, "La soumisson," 475.

[240] Although not discussing the obedience of faith, cf. Dorothea H. Bertschmann, "The Good, the Bad and the State—Rom 13.1–7 and the Dynamics of Love," *NTS* 60 (2014): 232–49.

[241] Bryan, *Render to Caesar*, 79. Also, Stuhlmacher, *Romans*, 201–2; Matera, *Romans*, 294, Tobin, *Paul's Rhetoric*, 397.

[242] Agreeing is Bryan, *A Preface to Romans*, 206, who notes the reference to the "sword" in 13:4 as "reference to the general life-and-death power of the Roman imperium." Cf. A. N. Sherwin-White, *Roman Society and Roman Law in the New Testament* (Oxford: Clarendon, 1963), 8–11.

this may have been one of the most nonrevolutionary statements within the letter, for this was the day-by-day mode of operation for those living in the city and certainly abroad, had they come from the provinces. Such a correspondence between obedience and submission may have been quite similar to some Gentiles' assumptions about obedience.

The counterpoint could also be made that Paul's admonition to submit may have been an unlikely notion for some Gentiles who thought that their obedience to God meant the dismissal of Rome's authority or outright opposition to Rome itself. Paul's admonition in 13:2 would certainly close off the potential for subversive activity had some Gentiles in Paul's audience thought that their obedience to Christ or the gospel put them in opposition with Rome. Subversive activity was often associated with the *collegia*. Perhaps Paul's intention here is to avoid any misunderstanding with this new association.[243] Such apprehension could have been on Paul's radar given the recent return of the Jews from Claudius's expulsion. Paul's continued argument in 13:2-4 aligns with the historical evidence in Chapters 3-4 of this work, whereby resistance in the form of disobedience to Rome's rule or authority resulted in punishment and possibly destruction, although such features probably were not novel thoughts to those living in Rome in full view of the architecture of victory that surrounded them (Chapter 6). The implications of Paul's command may have surprised some Gentiles disaffected with Rome's rule.[244]

The dichotomy of reward for good works and punishment for evil is a common Greco-Roman ideal of government, although emperors during certain periods may have caused people to question this basic assumption. Given the historical setting of this passage, Paul's assessment of the Roman Empire is neutral. Bruno Blumenfeld notes, "Paul's vocal approval of taxation (13.6-7) is perhaps his most overt consent to the existing political regime."[245] Likewise, Paul's statement in 13:3 of "praise for good conduct" was not hollow as Bruce Winter has pointed out in his research on public honoring. Winter writes, "Epigraphic evidence clearly demonstrates along with literary evidence that not only did rulers praise and honour those who undertook good works which benefited the city. ... they promised likewise to publicly honour others who would undertake similar benefactions in the future."[246]

Finally, Rom. 13:1-7 must be placed within the broader discourse of the Pauline mission. As Luke Timothy Johnson argues, Paul might have seen the empire as an enabler of the Christian mission.[247] Paul's attribution of the "governing authorities" as "the servant of God" further highlights the positive aspects of the empire.[248] Johnson's

---

[243] Also Keener, *Romans*, 152-3; Tobin, *Paul's Rhetoric*, 399; Edwin A. Judge, "The Social Pattern of the Christian Groups in the First Century," in *Social Distinctives of Christians in the First Century: Pivotal Essays by E. A. Judge* (ed. David M. Scholer, Peabody: Hendrickson, 2008), 1-56.

[244] Thus the ambiguity of κρίμα in 13:2 ought to be retained. Käsemann makes similar comments regarding "wrath" in verse 4 (*Romans*, 358). Contra Matera, *Romans*, 295.

[245] Blumenfeld, *Political Paul*, 391.

[246] Bruce W. Winter, "The Public Honouring of Christian Benefactors: Romans 13:3-4 and 1 Peter 2:14-15," *JSNT* 34.1 (1988): 87. Although Witherington notes some objection to Winter's conclusions. Cf. Witherington, *Romans*, 313-14; Jewett, *Romans*, 825.

[247] Johnson, *Reading Romans*, 199.

[248] For Paul's uses of the terms elsewhere see Rom. 13:4; 15:8; Eph. 3:7; Col. 1:25. See also Josephus, *Ant.* 9.55; *J.W.* 4.626.

statements on the Christian mission carry important weight. We must not speak of "empire" in broad strokes but recognize the nuances each emperor brought to the empire. There may have been times, in light of 13:1-7, where the empire was neutral in its relationship to the early Christian movement. This situation probably changed after the fires in Rome. Certainly, the writing of the book of Revelation indicates that times were coming when the empire would be bitterly hostile to the Christian movement.[249] The historical situation of Paul, situated in a relatively positive period of Roman rule and at the onset of a new Spanish mission, cannot be forgotten in discussing Rom. 13:1-7. The limits for the interpretation of Rom. 13:1-7 are the Pauline mission.[250]

To carry these statements further to the purpose in this work, Paul's apostolic task is securing the obedience of faith among *all* the nations to "Jesus Christ our Lord" (1:4-5). In light of Rom. 13:1-7, the Roman Christians' obedience to the governing authorities is essential in the Pauline mission to call forth the obedience of the nations beyond Rome. Stated conversely, the disobedience of the Christians in Rome to the governing authorities runs the risk of inhibiting Paul's mission to call for the obedience of faith among the nations. Bruno Blumenfeld notes, "Paul's genius was to create a parallel state that posed no immediate threat to the existing political structure, the Roman state."[251] The obedience of the Gentiles in Rome to the governing authorities is connected to the broader Pauline mission of obedience among *all* the nations.

In 13:8-14, Paul continues his discourse. We have a reintroduction of the law, last referenced in Rom. 10:5 and now referenced for the final time (13:8).[252] In this section, there is a striking similarity to Paul's argument in Rom. 8:1-4.[253] What Rom. 8:1-4 implied, 13:9-10 begins to explicitly state. When someone obediently loves one's neighbor, they fulfill the law. The social context of such love is certainly driven home by the threefold repetition in the section to "love one another/other" and forms a contrast between the act of obedience to love and the disobedient actions mentioned in the next section (13:11-14).[254]

For Gentiles in Paul's audience, the connection between obedience and love would appear unusual and surpass their previous expectations of obedience, although the topic of law was prominent in Roman discourse, particularly obedience to laws. The unique Early Christian emphasis on obedience to the law as a sign of love for one another could have prompted new reflection for some Gentiles in the audience on the nature of their obedience. Obedience as seen in the philosophers (Chapter 5) was connected to just laws and a well-running polis or the pursuit of virtue. Paul's

---

[249] See Achtemeier, *Romans*, 205.
[250] Philip P. Towner, "Romans 13:1-7 and Paul's Missiological Perspective," in *Romans and the People of God: Essays in Honor of Gordon D. Fee on the Occasion of His 65th Birthday* (ed. Sven K. Soderlund and N. T. Wright, Grand Rapids: Eerdmans, 1999), 150–1.
[251] Blumenfeld, *Political Paul*, 389.
[252] Dunn, *Romans*, 2:782. "As his readers would soon realize, these are the last references to the law in the letter as a whole. They therefore fulfill a crucial role: they would reassure that Paul's gospel was not antinomian—on the contrary, he counts fulfillment of the law as something important."
[253] Wright connects this section to not only 8:1-4 but also 2:17-29; 3:27-31; and 10:5-11 (*Romans*, 724).
[254] Cranfield rightly titles the section of 13:11-14 as "The Eschatological Motivation of Christian Obedience." He goes on to state, "Throughout chapters 12 and 13 it [obedience] is assumed." See, Cranfield, *Romans*, 2:679.

admonition in 13:10, although not contrary to those expectations, would still provide a new notion for his Roman audience. This is especially true in the mutuality of the command between persons of various social status and class. While love and obedience was often expected to flow upward toward those of higher rank or power, the inverse was certainly not always true.

A contrast appears between the fulfillment of the law in 13:8-10 and the "works of darkness" (τὰ ἔργα τοῦ σκότους) in 13:12-14. Most notable is how the list of actions in 13:12-14 parallels the ideas expressed in 1:18-32 and 6:12-13, 16-18.[255] In 1:18-32, these disobedient actions are listed as examples of pagan disobedience. Gentiles who practiced these things were the objects of God's wrath. The inner-textual link to 6:1-23 in this section is even more prominent. In the switch from the first Adam to the second Adam, those in Rome were to present their bodies as slaves to obedience and to turn away from those evil practices of disobedience. Likewise, we see in 13:12-14 that those in Rome are to "put off" the deeds of darkness—here actions of disobedience—and put on the "armor of light" (cf. 6:13).[256]

Paul's admonition to "put on" the weapons of light in verse 12 is paralleled by the similar admonition to "put on the Lord Jesus Christ" in verse 14. Putting on the weapons of light is the same as putting on Christ.[257] In light of 6:13-16, with the language of "weapons," we are again connected to our theme of obedience and disobedience. Said another way, by "putting on Christ" the individual Christian actively puts away the list of vices in 13:13 and now operates in a new realm of obedience as indicated in 13:8-10 (cf. Rom. 8:1-4). This is supported by the relationship between the list of commands in 13:8-10 and the vices of 13:13, that is, to be in discord or jealousy is not to fulfill but rather to disobey the command to "not covet" or to love one's neighbor. Paula Fredricksen rightly grasps the Pauline logic at work when she notes that these "'righteoused' pagans, spirit-filled, enabled by their commitment to Christ and, through him, to God, act 'righteously' toward others in community."[258] She continues, "This is what Paul meant by 'justification by faith.'"[259] More accurately, this is what Paul means by the obedience of faith/loyalty.

The language in 13:12 of weapons as a metaphor again connects Paul's argument to a militaristic context of war, conquest, and victory—a background familiar to at least some in Paul's audience. Gentiles in Paul's audience could readily draw on such images from the Campus Martius and the numerous monuments throughout Rome that depicted such images. Dunn rightly notes that "the idea of 'putting on weapons' sounds somewhat stilted to us, but like the similar phrase 'to be in arms,' it is a natural idiom (Herodotus 1.13; 7.218; LSJ, ὅπλον III.6); what is clearly in view is dressing

---

[255] Also noted by Cranfield, *Romans*, 2:686; Stuhlmacher, *Romans*, 213; Fitzmyer, *Romans*, 683; Keener, *Romans*, 158–9; Tobin, *Paul's Rhetoric*, 404.
[256] Wright, *Romans*, 722.
[257] The language is often associated with the Greek moralists such as Plutarch or Demosthenes. See Jewett, *Romans*, 823.
[258] Paula Fredriksen, "Paul's Letter to the Romans, the Ten Commandments, and Pagan 'Justification by Faith,'" *JBL* 133 (2014): 808.
[259] Fredriksen, "Paul's Letter to the Romans," 808. See also her more recent *Paul: The Pagans' Apostle* (New Haven: Yale University Press, 2017), 117–22.

for battle, being fitted-out with the full panoply of war (weapons and armor; cf. Eph 6:11)."[260]

Laying down arms or weapons is part of the treaty language and was one of the first aspects of obedience that Rome demanded of conquered nations. Contrary to some Gentile expectations, Paul's admonition to "put on the weapons of light" would result in the building up of the community, rather than the tearing down of one another in destruction. Obedience to this command would result in the furthering of life within the community, rather than contributing to its destruction. Some Gentiles may have been surprised at such a paradoxical image.

The entire section of 13:8-14 revolves around the new possibility of obedience (cf. Rom. 5:1–8:39). By putting on Christ, or to use the language of Rom. 5:1–6:23, by being "in Christ," the Christians in Rome are prompted to leave the Adamic realm of sin, death, and disobedience, as seen in the deeds of darkness, and live and operate in the new realm of obedience offered through Christ, the second Adam.[261]

By way of summary, in Rom. 13:1-14 Paul admonishes and exhorts his audience to practice the obedience of faith both outside the community (Rom. 13:1-7) and within the fragmented communities in Rome (Rom. 13:8-14). This section spells out one component of the content of the obedience of faith. Obedience to these issues is framed not only by Paul's discussion of the new reality in Christ (Rom. 5:1–6:23) but also by the broader Pauline mission to bring about the obedience of faith among the nations. Both obedience in the local context(s) of the Roman house churches and the broader context(s) of the empire are key to securing that mission.

Paul's admonition in 13:14 to make no provision for the flesh sets the groundwork for the following issues that arise in 14:1–15:1 with the strong and the weak.[262] The disputes that plague the Roman house church(es) are again the places where Paul desires the Roman Christians to exercise the obedience of faith/loyalty. Stan Stowers notes the internal coherence of Rom. 1–11 and Rom. 12–15: "If 1–11 finds its focus on God's righteousness being made good through Christ's faithfulness ... then 12–15 sketches an ethic of community based on the principle of faithfulness."[263] The only addition to Stowers's statement is to say that in these sections Christ's faithfulness is seen through his act of obedience (5:19). Likewise, the new community's ethic and obedience are based on Christ's obedience, having undone the powers of sin and death. The new community's ethic of obedience is based upon their faith in Jesus or, in

---

[260] Dunn, *Romans*, 2:788.
[261] So Cranfield, *Romans*, 2:688; Fitzmyer, *Romans*, 683; Stowers, *Rereading Romans*, 320; Dunn, *Romans*, 2:792.
[262] The identity of each group is strongly debated; see the works of Minear, *The Obedience of Faith*, 8–17; Campbell, "Rule of Faith," 259–86; Mark Reasoner, *The Strong and the Weak: Romans 14.1–15.13 in Context* (New York: Cambridge University Press, 1999); Mark D. Nanos, *The Mystery of Romans: The Jewish Context of Paul's Letter* (Minneapolis: Fortress, 1996), 85–165; Francis Watson, *Paul, Judaism, and the Gentiles: A Sociological Approach* (New York: Cambridge University Press, 1986), 175–81. Cf. Cranfield, *Romans*, 690–8; Dunn, *Romans*, 797–800; Stuhlmacher, *Romans*, 219–21; Wedderburn, *The Reasons for Romans*, 44–9. See the helpful and cautious article by John M. G. Barclay, "Faith and Self-Detachment from Cultural Norms: A Study in Romans 14-15," *ZNW* 104 (2013): 192–208.
[263] Stowers, *Rereading Romans*, 318. Although I disagree with Stowers's emphasis on faithfulness as adaptability.

terms of Paul's purpose, the obedience of faith (1:5). Such an ethic is seen through the multiple imperatives that color this section.

The Obedience of Faith toward One Another (14:1–15:13)

Rom. 14:1–15:13 contains thirteen imperatives, rightly highlighted by Robert Karris.[264] By reading the imperatives in light of Rom. 1:5, Paul desires the obedience of faith be exercised regarding the following issues: welcoming one another (14:1), not despising the one who does not eat everything (14:3), being fully convinced in one's mind concerning holy days (14:5), not passing judgment on one another (14:13), not destroying a brother or sister by food (14:15), not letting good be spoken of as evil (14:16), pursuing peace (14:19), not destroying a brother or sister by food (mentioned for the second time in 14:20), not judging oneself by what one approves (14:22), pleasing one another (15:2), and finally receiving one another (15:7). The issues presented in 14:1–15:13 expound on the central theme quite acutely: What does obedience look like when applied to the issues of food, Sabbath-keeping, and communal relationships?[265] Perhaps no other issues were more important for the unity of these communities.[266]

Rom. 14:1-23 is dominated by occurrences of the terms for Lord and "lording" or ruling language, which appear some ten times in this short section (Rom. 14:4, 6, 8, 11, 14) and carry the connotation of obedience. The lordship language combined with Paul's identification of servant in 14:4 carries forward the theme of obedience. By including both the strong and the weak under the same Lord, Paul has sidelined the presumption and arrogance of both groups.[267] Both the strong and the weak are under the same Lord and owe their obedience, not to one another's opinions or attitudes but to their Lord to whom they are ultimately accountable (14:12). Thus, Paul's conclusion that "we are the Lord's" in 14:8 indicates that their obedience is directed to that end.

In 14:11, Paul's citation of Isa. 45:23 points to the global and missional scope of his apostolic vision.[268] Paul places the disputes and quarrels from 14:1 within this larger missional context. Not only are the Romans—who are currently dividing—representatives of those from "every tongue," but their ability to resolve these disputes is key to the furthering of this global purpose, one that closely aligns with Paul's goal to bring about the obedience of faith/loyalty among "all the nations" (1:5).[269] The quotation

---

[264] Robert J. Karris, "Romans 14:1–15:13 and the Occasion of Romans," in *The Romans Debate: Revised and Expanded Edition* (ed. Karl P. Donfried, Peabody: Hendrickson, 1991), 65–84. Although I strongly disagree with Karris's conclusions that Rom. 14–15 has nothing to do with the specific situation in Rome.

[265] On the various issues surrounding food and vegetarianism in the ancient world see the very helpful section by Keener, *Romans*, 161. Footnotes 2–8 offer an extensive number of primary sources.

[266] See Oakes, *Reading Romans*, 161–2.

[267] See Witherington, *Romans*, 335; Matera, *Romans*, 312.

[268] Wagner, *Heralds*, 336–40.

[269] Keener rightly connects the Isaianic passage in context, noting that this section emphasizes "that God is the only savior and source of righteousness, even for Gentiles." See Keener, *Romans*, 166. As does Käsemann, *Romans*, 373; Wagner, *Heralds*, 336–7.

of Isaiah uses the imagery of "knees bowed" that invokes the notion of obedience or obeisance. As Dunn has noted, such a quotation would have a dual effect serving as a "reminder to Jewish Christians that God's final purpose had always embraced the Gentiles; and to Gentile Christians that their conversion was one of submission to the one God proclaimed by Israel and its scriptures."[270] From 14:11, it is "all" knees that will bow (obedience) and "all" tongues that will praise (nations). In short, we have another implicit reference to the obedience of faith/loyalty among the nations as Paul's global mission unfolds, dependent upon the obedience of faith of these Roman communities to resolve their disputes.

Of particular importance for this study is Paul's final appeal in 14:23 that "whatever does not proceed from faith is sin," a phrase repeated twice for emphasis.[271] The phrase "of or from faith" appears at several critical junctures. Indeed, as Barclay suggests, it is a "leitmotif" within the letter (Rom. 1:17; 3:26, 30; 4:16; 5:1; 9:30, 32; 10:6; 14:23) and most importantly connects 14:23 back to the thesis statement of 1:16-17.[272] Such language echoes and encapsulates not only the Adamic existence that was marked by unrighteousness and disobedience (Rom. 6:1-23) but more recently characterized Israel's pursuit of righteousness (10:6). Paul's argument that all actions not flowing from faith are regarded as sin or disobedience relates well to Paul's programmatic phrase in Rom. 1:5 about obedience flowing from faith. To fail to operate in faith is to be led into sin and disobedience, characteristics of the "in-Adam" type of life. The urgent appeal of Paul in this section is that to cause a "weaker" member to sin is to prevent them from exercising the obedience of faith. Similarly, preventing another member from exercising the obedience of faith runs counter to the thesis of Romans where Paul adamantly declares that faithful living is the goal (1:17).

Paul's discussion of the "weak and the strong" offers an important place for Gentiles to reflect on how obedience and one's decision relate to one another. We should not forget that Cicero remarked on the weak and the strong (*Rep.* 1.34, Chapter 5) and comes to the opposite conclusion of Paul in 15:1. Cicero argued that the weak should obey the stronger. Both 14:1 and 15:1 offer places for the Gentiles to reconsider what their strong status means and how they will exercise obedience in these delicate matters. For Gentiles formed and shaped by a culture that praised the strong and demeaned the weak, Paul's admonition to use choices and direct one's obedience toward those who were weaker would have been quite unlike some Gentiles' previous notions of obedience.

---

[270] Dunn, *Romans*, 2:809-10. Bert-Jan Peerbolte only grasps part of the issue, "In a number of passages, Paul interprets the past state of the followers of Christ as one of submission. They served idols ... they submitted themselves to the powers of the cosmos. Now, Paul considers them liberated by Christ" (222). Rather in light of Rom. 6:16, submission is still an aspect of the Gentiles new identity in Christ. See Bert-Jan Lietaert Peerbolte, "Morality and Boundaries in Paul," in *Sensitivity towards Outsiders*, 209-25.

[271] The meaning of the clause is debated. See Fitzmyer surveys from the patristics (*Romans*, 699-700); Cranfield, *Romans*, 2:728-9; Barrett, *Romans*, 267; Dunn, *Romans*, 2:829; Käsemann, *Romans*, 378-80; Jewett, *Romans*, 872; Matera, *Romans*, 319-20; Barclay, "Faith and Self-Detachment," 195-8.

[272] Barclay, "Faith and Self-Detachment," 195. Barclay also rightly stresses that the same definition should be maintained for *pistis*. See Dunn, *Romans*, 2:828-9; Wright, "Romans," 732-3.

In his final argument, Paul begins the first of two conclusions (15:1-6; 8-13) on the note of obligation.²⁷³ The idea of obligation, represented by the verb ὀφείλω and the noun ὀφειλέτης, refers to the person(s) who are under moral or social obligation.²⁷⁴ This "ethic of reciprocity" is found throughout the letter, not only Paul's apostolic vision (1:14) but also with the Spirit (8:12) and the community life (13:8).²⁷⁵ The notion of obligation or duty carries with it the notion of obedience.²⁷⁶ According to Paul, this response to "owe" the "weak ones" or "powerless ones" is the obedience of faith that springs from the gracious gift of God and fulfills the law (Rom. 13:8) by acting in Christlikeness toward one's neighbor (15:2). Rom. 15:1-2 is a recapitulation of Rom. 13:8 (cf. Cicero on the weak and the strong in Chapter 5).

For Gentiles in Paul's audience, his admonition to take care of and welcome those weaker is profoundly countercultural moral advice. Numerous depictions throughout Rome (see Chapter 6) portrayed the defeated nations in positions of weakness. Often they were depicted "under foot" of the stronger Romans. Such a cultural assumption that Roman dominance shown through its strength over weaker neighbors may have influenced some Gentile assumptions in the Roman house church(es). Likewise in the philosophers, we saw similar notions that those who are weaker ought to obey those who are superior or stronger (cf. Aristotle, *Pol.* 8.3.45). Despite the tendency of the strong to overrun the weak, Paul counters such notions with the opposite idea. The strong in the Roman house church(es) may have expected the weaker to obey them and their inclinations regarding food and sabbath issues. Paul's admonitions might have confounded Gentile expectations concerning these issues and assumptions.

Paul's second conclusion (15:7-13) along with the peroration (15:14-21) is dominated by a discussion of the Gentiles. The larger context of Rom. 15:7-29 represents the highest confluence of the term ἔθνος in Romans, appearing ten times in this short section.²⁷⁷ The importance of such frequency is that Paul's discussion of Gentiles here comprises 16 percent of the occurrences of the term in the NT, nearly 20 percent of the occurrences within the Pauline epistles, and over one-third of the occurrences in Romans.²⁷⁸ Most importantly for Romans, in light of his purpose (1:5), this is the most explicit discussion of the Gentiles in Romans. In light of such heavy usage of ἔθνος (nations) language, Rom. 15:7-29 provides one of Paul's most detailed explanations of the Gentile mission. The importance of 15:17-29 is also marked by the inclusion of the explicit reference to obedience in 15:18 and the parallels to Rom. 1:3-14 occurring in the section. In light of these similarities, it appears that 15:7-13, 14-21 unpacks Rom. 1:5 and, therefore, Paul's understanding of his apostolic calling and mission for obedience (1:5).

The last lines of argumentation in Romans revolve around the issue of Paul's mission to the Gentiles. Paul begins his final argument, through yet another imperative,

---

[273] Witherington, *Romans*, 341; Keck, *Romans*, 349; Wright, *Romans*, 744.
[274] BDAG, 742-3.
[275] Jewett, *Romans*, 876.
[276] Cranfield, *Romans*, 2:730.
[277] The next highest frequency is the section of 11:1-36 with three occurrences (11:11-13)
[278] ἔθνος occurs explicitly 162 times in the NT, 54 times in the Pauline epistles (all thirteen letters), and 29 times in Romans.

for both Jew and Gentile in Rome, to "welcome one another" (15:7). Paul roots his argument in a widely held ancient ethic of reciprocity, where "Christ's acceptance of the believer forms the basis for the obligation to accept a fellow believer."[279] Such reception, thoroughly Christological (just as Christ has welcomed you), aims at the unity of the Roman congregations, something Paul regards as part of the "the promises" (Rom. 4:13-14, 16, 20; 9:4, 8-9; 15:8) on behalf of the "truth of God" (15:8).[280] Christ becomes the *exemplar* of God's faithfulness to both Israel and the promises.[281] Cranfield rightly detects an allusion to obedience, noting that "behind the use of the word διάκονος here is … His ministry of teaching and healing—apparently with the deliberative intention of obeying God's will."[282] Christ again serves as the example of obedience for the community and the type of obedience Paul expects from his audience on *behalf* of one another (cf. 8:29, Phil. 2:5).[283]

In 15:9, the Gentiles glorify God for his "mercy," a key theme in Rom. 9 and the direct inverse of Rom. 1:21. Likewise, 15:9 draws a sharp contrast with those who suppress the truth in 1:18. If Rom. 1:18-32 was a list of Gentile disobedience rooted in their suppression of the truth and failure to give glory to God, Rom. 15:9 displays the inverse whereby the Gentiles now glorify God and, implicit in the logic, offer their obedience. Thus 15:8-9 is connected not only to Paul's apostolic mission in 1:5 but also to the thesis of Rom. 1:16-17.

Rom. 15:9-12 extends and grounds Paul's final argument with an appeal to an in-artificial proof through his citation of Ps. 17:50 (Ps. 18 MT); 117:1 (15:9, 11); Deut. 32:43 (15:10); and Isa. 11:10 (15:12). As in 10:18-21, where Paul cited the Psalms, Deuteronomy, and Isaiah, his point is that all scriptures—the law, the prophets, and the writings—bear witness to his point, with the catchword being "The Gentiles."[284] Craig Keener rightly identifies this section as the "rhetorical climax and his most compelling exegetical case for Gentile inclusion."[285] The catena of quotations fleshes out Paul's previous point in 15:4 where he states that scripture functions as an active voice for the Christian community.[286] Indeed, the last quote in the catena ends on the note of "hope," aligning precisely with the point of the instruction in 15:4.

---

[279] Reasoner, *Strong and the Weak*, 194; Jewett, *Romans*, 889.
[280] See the discussion in Thomas Söding, "Verheißung Und Erfülling Im Lichte Paulinischer Theologie," *NTS* 48 (2001): 146–70; Jan Lambrecht, "The Confirmation of the Promises: A Critical Note on Romans 15,8," *ETL* 78 (2002): 156–60. Lambrecht notes that the phrase ἀληθείας θεοῦ is best understood as faithfulness (157), contra Söding (167).
[281] See Terence L. Donaldson, *Paul and the Gentiles: Remapping the Apostle's Convictional World* (Minneapolis: Fortress, 1997), 96–100. He rightly notes that this section, although inclusive of Gentiles, is "explicitly and strikingly Israel-centered."
[282] Cranfield, *Romans*, 2:741.
[283] Käsemann, *Romans*, 381–2; Dunn, *Romans*, 2:846; Fitzmyer, *Romans*, 706.
[284] Stuhlmacher, *Romans*, 232. Cf. Käsemann, *Romans*, 386; Cranfield, *Romans*, 2:746; Dunn, *Romans*, 2:853. Not persuasive is Scot Hafemann, "Eschatology and Ethics: The Future of Israel and the Nations in Romans 15:1-13," *TynB* 51 (2000): 161–92. Hafemann attempts to find unity in the passages cited rather than through the term "Gentiles."
[285] Keener, *Romans*, 172. Such was an effective rhetorical maneuver and cited so by Keener (Cicero, *Quinct.* 25.78-80).
[286] Hays, *Echoes of Scripture*, 70–3.

Part of Paul's appeal to scripture not only provides the rationale for Gentile inclusion (15:10-12) but also the envisioning of his task and vocation (15:9). Jewett somewhat rightly concludes that 15:9 is the "most precise correlation with the missional purpose of Romans" but fails to see that it is the broader context of 15:9-12 where Paul's apostolic mission from Rom. 1:5 is given its fullest explanation.[287] Dunn is closer to the point when he notes, "The final scripture, from Paul's favorite prophet (Isa. 11:10), fittingly ties together again the thought of the Jewishness of Jesus (the Davidic Messiah) and of the risen Christ, hope of the nations—an effective recall of the themes of the letter's opening paragraph (1:2-5)."[288]

In 15:9, Paul quotes Ps. 17:50 (LXX) as a description of his vocation and broader mission. Paul sees his mission within the horizon of the Psalmist's desire to confess Yahweh among the nations. Most important is the immediate context of Paul's quotation of Psalm 17 that includes the obedience of the nations to the Messiah, which aptly summarizes the obedience of faith. Such a quotation also anticipates and reveals the logic at work in Paul's quotation from Isa. 11:10 in Rom. 15:12. Both the quotations of Ps. 17 and Isa. 11:10 reveal the substructure of obedience at work. Matthew Novenson has noted that "the psalm admits of use by authors, like Paul, who have in mind one or another latter-day χριστός κυρίου, to whom the Gentiles are to be subjected."[289] The Gentiles offer their obedience to the root of Jesse who rises to "rule" over the Gentiles. Paul's role, invoked by these quotations, is one of the eschatological heralds who call the Gentiles to the obedience of faith/loyalty in the Messiah.[290]

Paul's final quotation from Isa. 11:10 in 15:12 is particularly important and serves as the linchpin to his argument in its final stage. Paul uses Isaiah to speak of Jesus as the prophesied one who comes from the root of Jesse, "who rises to rule the Gentiles." The idea of ruling over nations entails the idea of obedience, as the context of Isa. 11:10 indicates. The full context of Isa. 11 (LXX) includes the notion of obedience (ὑπακούω), specifically of the Ammonites to Israel.[291] Paul can rightly appeal to this concept through his use of Isaiah. Paul's use of these texts is poignantly captured by Novenson: "It is no accident that the two chapters in the Greek Bible that include references to the ὑπακοή των εθνών, both of which are specifically 'messianic' textual units."[292]

Even though Paul quotes from the OT, Gentiles in Paul's audience would have additional avenues to reflect on the language of obedient nations. As was shown in

---

[287] Jewett, *Romans*, 894; Dunn, *Romans*, 2:848, Witherington, *Romans*, 343. Correspondingly, the nations are envisioned from Deut. 32:43 and Ps. 117:1 as rejoicing μετὰ τοῦ λαοῦ αὐτοῦ (15:10), again stressing Paul's point of mutual reception and welcome (15:9).

[288] Dunn rightly notes the importance of 1:5 for the final quotation (*Romans*, 2:853). On the importance of the resurrection for Romans see Kirk, *Unlocking Romans*.

[289] Matthew V. Novenson, "The Jewish Messiahs, the Pauline Christ, and the Gentile Question," *JBL* 128 (2009): 370-1. This is one of only two instances of Gentiles and obedience in the LXX, the other being Isa. 11:10.

[290] Wagner, *Heralds*, 310-13, makes similar points; however, Psalm 17 does not refer to the Messiah or Christ. So I disagree; Paul does not "read this psalm as words of the Christ" but Paul does read them as words indicative of his own vocation. So Käsemann, *Romans*, 370, contra Cranfield, *Romans*, 2:745; Wright, *Romans*, 748.

[291] Novenson, "The Jewish Messiahs," 371.

[292] Novenson, "The Jewish Messiahs," 371.

previous chapters, Gentiles familiar with the Roman themes of victory, nations, and domination would clearly understand the appeal to offer obedience to one who rules. Familiarity with such images and notions came not only from the historians but also from the urban landscape of Rome itself full of monuments documenting such features. One thinks of the Horologium where the nation of Egypt was portrayed as "subjected." One profound point of reflection for Gentiles' previous notions of obedience would have been the difference between the rule of Rome and the rule of the root of Jesse. The striking feature would be: "Christ died for his enemies rather than subjugating them by force."[293] As mentioned several times throughout these sections, Paul's use of Christ's death upends normal Roman/Gentile expectations about the true nature of victory and strength. One immediate corollary for a Gentile understanding of obedience would be that one now offers obedience not out of fear of death and destruction. Obedience in this new Christian context is in light of the death of Christ himself for those who were estranged, hostile, and enemies (cf. Rom. 5:6-10). Such motivations for obedience would have been quite dissimilar to some Gentiles' preconceptions of why one obeys within a Roman context.

Paul ends his final argument with a concluding word about the inclusion of the Gentiles into this new "hope" that confirms the eschatological vision of a united community. There is reason to hope because of Paul's apostolic mission to bring about the obedience of faith among the nations. Wright comes to that same conclusion: "The letter comes full circle, back to Paul's original self-introduction as the servant of God, the apostle of the Messiah and his gospel."[294] As Paul concludes his argument in Romans, we return to Paul's apostolic vocation and mission, "the obedience of faith among all the nations" (Rom. 1:5).

---

[293] Jewett, *Romans*, 896. Similar anti-imperial concerns are noted by Witherington, *Romans*, 344.
[294] Wright, *Romans*, 745.

9

Conclusion

This monograph began by showing the lacuna in Romans' scholarship concerning the Greco-Roman language of obedience. We noted how most research has been undertaken to understand what Paul *meant* by the obedience of faith, but that few have looked at the pertinent Greco-Roman literature to construct a background for how a Gentile audience would understand the language of obedience. Our project aimed to shed fresh light on the phrase "the obedience of faith" by studying the Greco-Roman use of obedience language prior to and during the first century. In particular, this study showed how Gentile Christians in Rome would not have heard this phrase as odd or alien to their conceptual world as the topic of obedience in a letter to Rome tapped into one of the essential features of Roman discourse and rule. The aim was to highlight the importance of obedience in Roman by situating the use of obedience language within the broader Greco-Roman discourse to understand how a Gentile audience might perceive the call to and emphasis on obedience in a moral discourse like Romans. Finally, we also sought to show how the rhetorical features of the letter identify obedience as a main theme of Romans. We have shown how obedience finds its place in every major section of the letter. A final summary shows the way obedience functions in the letter as a whole.

Tracing Obedience through Romans

In Rom. 1:5, Paul declares his purpose to bring about the obedience of faith among the nations. After this declaration, Paul includes a list of vices in 1:18-32 that flow from the disobedience of unfaithfulness or unrighteousness on the part of the Gentiles. Paul's opening introduction, with his desire for obedience among the Gentiles, is immediately countered with the drastic disobedience among the Gentiles. This obedience is directed toward Paul himself as the divinely commissioned messenger of God (Rom. 1:1-5).

Beginning in 2:1-16, Paul's discussion of obedience and disobedience widens to focus on Jews and Gentiles. In 2:8-9, obedience is initially shown negatively with the group that disobeys the truth and obeys unrighteousness and results in the outcomes of wrath and peace. We noted that the framework of obedience, which results in peace, and disobedience, which results in wrath, was similar to the evidence we saw present in the Greco-Roman historians and the treaties Rome established with other nations. Paul concludes his argument in this section by focusing on the nature of "true circumcision" that shows itself in an obedient posture toward God's will and in obedient actions. Of primary importance is the eschatological context of obedience that reveals who will be declared in the right, whether Jew or Gentile (cf. 2:13-16).

Rom. 3:1-20 and 3:21-31 is Paul's rebuttal to his own perceived indictment that circumcision may have no value. Although we mentioned that obedience does not explicitly appear in these sections, disobedience is certainly present throughout Paul's argument, especially through his use of ἀπιστία, ἀδικία, and ἁμαρτία. Through Paul's use of the Psalms and Ecclesiastes, he emphasizes the disobedience of humanity that has entrapped both Jews and Gentiles. Somewhat anticipating his argument with Adam in Rom. 5:1-6:23 humanity falls drastically short of the obedience of faith. Rom. 3:1-31 highlights the disobedience of infidelity that characterizes the human race.

Rom. 4:1-25 continues Paul's discussion of obedience through the character of Abraham who serves as the inverse of Gentile disobedience in Rom. 1:18-32. The invocation of Abraham allows Paul to discuss Abraham's identity in relationship to God's blessing that came, not as a Jew through circumcision but through uncircumcision. Paul's discussion of Abraham's blessing for the nations ties his argument back into his purpose vis-á-vis the nations in Rom. 1:5, namely their obedience. The importance of this argument for Paul's audience is they must also exercise a faith that both believes and obeys or, to put it another way, they must exercise the obedience of faith.

Rom. 5:1-21 starts the second major argument of Romans. Together the sections of Rom. 5:1-21 and 6:1-23 represent the climax of obedience language in Romans. The discourse of 5:1-21 utilizes an important structure that bears several similarities to the evidence we examined in the Greek and Latin sources. Specifically, we noted Paul's structure of faith, peace, and obedience. The notions of peace would also have been very familiar to those in Rome as residents in the heart of the *Pax Romana*. Paul's contention that reconciliation results in obedience to a new Lord would also have been a familiar idea to those who had been brought to Rome as conquered subjects. In 5:18-19, we have specific occurrences of obedience and disobedience. Christ and Adam form a rhetorical *synkrisis*, where Christ's obedience forms the basis for the obedience of faith among the nations.

Rom. 6:1-23 carries the discussion of obedience further through Paul's use of slavery language and the implicit notion of obedience. If 5:1-21 emphasized the disobedience of Adam and its ramifications, 6:1-23 emphasizes the form and pattern of Christ as an example of obedience. Paul argues that obedience is a nonnegotiable in both the reigns of Adam and Christ. The question now is: to whom is one's obedience directed? Similar to other Greco-Roman sources, obedience was not optional. Despite the transference of rulers, obedience is integral to the reign of both. Paul's use of slavery language also functions powerfully as an image of obedience, one that his audience would have been intimately familiar with. The climax of obedience language is that this obedience leads to righteousness (Rom. 6:16) and thus links obedience with the thesis statement of Rom. 1:16-17.

The placement of the argument in 7:1-25 within Paul's unfolding argument in Rom. 5:1-8:39 is centered on the life lived outside Christ and devoid of the Spirit. Using the categories he established in Rom. 5:1–6:23, Paul spells out the ramifications of Adam's story, one that was characterized by sin, death, and disobedience. Although obedience and disobedience language do not explicitly appear within this section, the entire section is colored with the language of disobedience as part of the Adamic story that Paul is narrating.

Rom. 8:1-39 is the conclusion of the second major argument in Paul's discourse. In contrast to Rom. 7:1-25, Rom. 8:1-39 introduces us to the Spirit and the new reality of obedience offered through the death of Christ. Rom. 8:1-39 is organized around the themes of liberation and victory. The section has important links to Paul's previous discussion in Rom. 5:1–6:23, specifically, that behind the decree of "no condemnation" stands Christ's ultimate act of obedience (5:16-18; 8:1). Also important for our discussion of obedience is the term δικαίωμα that not only links Rom. 8:4 back to the Gentile vices of Rom. 1:18-32 but also issues the new possibility of obedience on behalf of those who walk according to the Spirit. In contrast to those Gentiles who did not obey the δικαίωμα of God, these Gentiles now walk by the Spirit and "fulfill the just requirement" and further represent the fulfillment of Paul to bring about the obedience of faith among all the nations (Rom. 1:5). Finally, Paul's climactic conclusion at the end of Rom. 8:38-39 finished with the Roman theme of victory. Those who by the power of the Spirit are obedient secure a victory that leads to life and peace.

In Rom. 9:1–11:36, Paul mounts a third argument centered on the defense of the righteousness of God that was called into question by Israel's disobedience. Given Paul's purpose of obedience among the nations, the dramatic disobedience of Israel places a profound question mark on the implications for the obedience of the Gentiles, namely God's power to bring about their obedience (1:17). Part of Paul's task in these sections is to also defend against the notion that Israel's disobedience caused God to reject Israel in favor of the Gentiles who are "now" obedient. One of the rhetorical effects in this section is to pave the way for Rom. 12:1–15:13 where Paul instructs those in Rome to exercise the obedience of faith in response to God's vision for a unified community, in unified purpose, and unified mission. Israel's disobedience serves as a stark reminder to this community and their need to be obedient.

In Rom. 12:1–15:13, Paul turns to the critical issues that face this Roman community, namely internal and external threats to unity. As we have shown, these final sections of Romans flesh out the obedience of faith in the practical matters of communal life and are integral to Paul's future mission. Paul calls for obedience, not only to external realities such as submission to the Roman Empire but also concerning internal issues such as the list of imperatives (14:1–15:13) that revolve around issues of communal relationships such as food and the Sabbath. The obedience of faith finds its specific expression with these issues in the Roman house churches.

Common Themes

Throughout this study, we have focused on the importance of obedience, both in the Greco-Roman sources and in Paul's letter to the Romans. We are now in a position to offer some of the common emphases that we have seen throughout our study by way of summary.

First, obedience is a frequent topic in ancient literature and nonliterary sources. Our surveys of the related Greco-Roman literature provided evidence that obedience was a frequent topic among Greek and Romans both preceding Paul, contemporary with him, and subsequently after this period. The topic of obedience in a letter to Rome tapped into one of the essential features of Roman discourse and rule. Obedience was connected to Roman identity and its global rule. Nations from all across the empire must have been familiar with Rome's rhetoric of obedience from the republic through the empire. Certainly, those in Rome were familiar with the language of obedience that dominated their discourse and dotted their urban landscape. Obedience language centered on Rome's relationships with other nations or territories and was essential to the peace of the Roman Empire. When Paul calls for the obedience of faith/loyalty, it is language his audience would understand.

Second, given the historical and political realities of obedience, this became a topic for philosophers within the Greek and Roman world to reflect upon. The nature of good cities and citizenship provided the needed impetus for reflections on obedience. Obedience to reason in the pursuit of virtue was also a common refrain. The philosopher Epictetus perhaps provides the closest analogy to Paul in his reflections on obedience to Caesar and obedience or loyalty to other callings. Certainly within this spectrum of obedience to rulers, a variety of views existed. Paul's discourse on obedience to governing authorities reflects the importance of obedience in the time of Paul and his contemporaries.

Third, we highlighted the fact that the historical and philosophical discourses on obedience interacted and overlapped. Frequently, obedience language and imagery provided the basis for philosophical reflection on the "proper" citizen or pursuit of the virtues. Likewise, the philosophical reflection on obedience contributed to a well-run city and provided an impetus for good citizens and soldiers to obey their superiors. Both sources, historical and philosophical, bore witness to the importance of obedience in the first century.

The language and rhetoric of obedience come to bear, of course, on the aim of this work and on Paul's stated goal of his apostleship to bring about the obedience of the nations. Paul's language of obedience in Romans would have been heard in the light of Roman rhetoric about obedience and would have suggested not merely continued submission to the Roman governing authorities (Rom. 13:1-7) but a higher and prior obedience to God in Christ. Gentiles in Paul's audience, who notably came from a broad swath of society, would have had multiple avenues to reflect on obedience language in their various vocations.

The logic and argument of obedience in Romans at various points would have appeared quite similar to what some Gentiles may have already thought about obedience, particularly with the structure of wrath, faith, peace, and obedience. However, at other points—most poignantly with hope and reconciliation of the disobedient—Paul's argument about obedience would have confounded normal Roman expectations concerning obedience (see the summative list at the end of Chapter 8 for specific issues). If we take our examples of a slave, a freed person, a craftsman, or an immigrant worker, each of these persons in the house churches would have experienced the language, imagery, and concept of obedience before Paul's call for obedience in Rom. 1:5. As a slave, the notion that slaves obey would have been all too apparent for some members of Paul's audience. If some in Paul's audience had been conquered and brought to Rome as slaves, they would have been intimately aware of the concept of Roman victory and peace built on the notion of continued obedience. Anyone walking the streets of Rome and noticing the monumental architecture, such as along the *via Flaminia*, would have been confronted daily with the Roman images of victory, subjugation, and obedience. Numismatic and inscriptional evidence bears witness to these features as well. The topic of obedience in a letter to Rome tapped into one of the essential features of Roman discourse and rule. It should not be surprising, in light of our survey of the Greco-Roman evidence, that in a letter to Rome, Paul would stress obedience of as it was an essential aspect of Roman vision and identity.

The nature of the relationship between obedience and faith/loyalty was raised throughout the works both in ancient literature and in Romans. From the evidence gathered it is clear that obedience is not equal to faith, but that they exist in close relationship. It was clear from the Greco-Roman literature that entering into faith with Rome entailed following through with obedience, thus the two elements are distinguished. Obedience was something that could be demonstrated to evidence one's faith or commitment to a Roman treaty. Likewise, disobedience could show the inverse and provoke a breaking of the treaty. Either way, what was expected was that obedience from the conquered nations to Rome was paramount.

Turning to the evidence within Paul's letter to Rome, such a pattern also emerged. Most clearly, Paul's apostleship was to bring about obedience that flows from the faith or relationship with God. Obedience is expected. *Pistis* in these contexts looks much more like faithfulness and loyalty. Such could also be demonstrated in explicitly obedient language (Rom. 5:1–6:23) such as presenting one's body in obedience or in more enigmatic language such as putting off the deeds of darkness (13:13). Further, historic disobedience could be pointed to (Rom. 9:1–11:36) as evidence. Paul likewise sees a differentiation between faith and obedience. A robust conclusion of this study is that obedience matters to Paul. No longer can obedience be seen in juxtaposition to faith or loyalty to God but part and parcel of that faithfulness and allegiance. Further, this has immense ramifications for the Jewishness of Paul and Paul's gospel. Rather than seeing obedience versus faith, Paul aligns these together and does not offer some alternative that involves just believing versus obeying. Such a conclusion that Paul is only interested in belief would fall far from the meaning of Paul's gospel and apostolic calling.

To come full circle, this monograph sought to understand the obedience of faith from the perspective of its audience: Gentile Christians in Rome. One of the primary contributions of the Greco-Roman literature is the confluence of *obedience* and *nations* language that consistently appears in the sources. Obedience was an essential feature of Roman discourse and rule. Previous works that had addressed the notion of obedience from Jewish literature would not be as attuned to this connection for a Roman audience. Likewise, the array of notions that a Gentile would have from conflict to juxtaposition are not fully explained by recourse to Jewish literature alone. Although that literature informs Paul's understanding, it still remains incomplete for how the term of obedience would be understood. This work has widened the frame of reference and, when combined with previous works, offers a more fully substantiated and descriptive portrait of obedience in Romans and the Roman world.

Appendix

List of Terms for Obedience

Greek (bold terms used in Chapters 3 and 5)[1]

πείθομαι; πειθαρχέω:	to submit to authority or reason by obeying—"to obey."
εὐλαβέομαι:	to obey, with the implication of awe and reverence for the source of a command
ἀκούω; ἐπιδέχομαι:	to listen or pay attention to a person, with resulting conformity to what is advised or commanded—"to pay attention to and obey."
ὑπακούω; ὑπακοή, ῆς f; εἰσακούω:	to obey on the basis of having paid attention to—"to obey, obedience."
ὑπήκοος, ον:	(derivative of ὑπακούω "to obey") pertaining to being obedient—"obedient."
ἀναπληρόω; ἀποπληρόω:	to conform to some standard as a means of demonstrating its purpose—"to obey, to conform to, to submit to."
ὑποτάσσομαι; ὑποταγή, ῆς f; ὑπείκω:	to submit to the orders or directives of someone—"to obey, to submit to, obedience, submission."
φυλάσσω; τηρέω; τήρησις, εως f:	to continue to obey orders or commandments—"to obey, to keep commandments, obedience."
τελέω:	to obey as a means of fulfilling the purpose of a rule or standard—"to obey, to keep."
δογματίζομαι:	(derivative of δόγμα "law, rule," 33.333) to conform to rules and regulations—"to obey rules."
δικαιόω:	to conform to righteous, just commands—"to obey righteous commands."
ἀπειθέω; ἀπείθεια, ας f:	unwillingness or refusal to comply with the demands of some authority—"to disobey, disobedience."

---

[1] List derived from Louw and Nida, 36.12–36.30.

ἀπειθής, ές:	(derivative of ἀπειθέω[a] "to disobey") pertaining to being continuously disobedient—"disobedient."
προάγω:	to go beyond established bounds of teaching or instruction, with the implication of failure to obey properly—"to go beyond bounds, to fail to obey."
ἀνυπότακτος, ον:	(derivative of ὑποτάσσομαι "to obey") pertaining to being rebelliously disobedient—"disobedient, rebellious."
παρακούω; παρακοή, ῆς f παραιτέομαι:	to refuse to listen to and hence to disobey—"to refuse to listen, to refuse to obey, disobedience."
παραβαίνω; παράβασις, εως f; παρανομέω; παρέρχομαι:	to act contrary to established custom or law, with the implication of intent—"to disobey, to break the law, to transgress, disobedience, transgression."
παραβάτης, ου m:	(derivative of παραβαίνω "to disobey, to break the law") a person who customarily breaks or disobeys the law—"transgressor."
λύω:	the failure to conform to a law or regulation, with a possible implication of regarding it as invalid—"to break (a law), to transgress."

Latin (**bold terms used in Chapter 4**)[2]

oboedienta	obedience
oboedio *(ira)*	to obey
oboedientea	obediently
obtempreratio	obedience
obtempero	to obey
obsequium	obedience
obsequor	to obey
obsequens	obedient
obsequiter	compliant
audio	hear/heed
audiens	hear/heed
auris	give ear
observāre	to observe, obey
parēre	to obey
curāre	to attend to, take care of

---

[2] List derived from Cassell's Latin Dictionary with the assistance of Dr. Joe Dongell.

Bibliography

Achtemeier, Paul J. *Romans*. Louisville: Westminster John Knox, 1985.
Adams, Edward. "Abraham's Faith and Gentile Disobedience: Textual Links between Romans 1 and 4." *JSNT* 65 (1997): 47-66.
Agamben, Giorgio. *The Time That Remains: A Commentary on the Letter to the Romans*. Translated by Patricia Dailey. Stanford: Stanford University Press, 2005.
Aland, Kurt, and Barbara Aland. *The Text of the New Testament: An Introduction to the Critical Editions and to the Theory and Practice of Modern Textual Criticism*. Translated by Erroll F. Rhodes. 2nd ed. Grand Rapids: Eerdmans, 1989.
Aletti, Jean-Noël. *God's Justice in Romans: Keys for Interpreting the Epistle to the Romans*. Rome: Gregorian & Biblical Press, 2010.
Aletti, Jean-Noël. "Interpreting Romans 11:14: What Is at Stake?" In *Celebrating Paul: Festschrift in Honor of Jerome Murphy-O'connor, O.P., and Joseph A. Fitzmyer, S.J.*, edited by Peter Spitaler, 245-64. Washington, DC: Catholic Biblical Association of America, 2011.
Aletti, Jean-Noël. "La Soumission Des Chrétiens Aux Autorités En Rm 13,1-7: Validité Des Arguments Pauliniens?" *Bib* 89 (2008): 457-76.
Aletti, Jean-Noël. "L'authorité Apostolique De Paul. Théorie Et Pratique." In *L'apôtre Paul: Personnalité, Style Et Conception Du Ministère*, edited by Albert Vanhoye, xiii, 474. Leuven: Leuven University Press, 1986.
Algra, Kiempe, Jonathan Barnes, Jaap Mansfeld, and Malcolm Schofield, eds. *The Cambridge History of Hellenistic Philosophy*. New York: Cambridge University Press, 2008.
Anderson, Graham. *Sage, Saint, and Sophist: Holy Men and Their Associates in the Early Roman Empire*. New York: Routledge, 1994.
Anderson, R. Dean. *Ancient Rhetorical Theory and Paul*. Rev. ed. Leuven: Peeters, 1999.
Ando, Clifford. *Imperial Ideology and Provincial Loyalty in the Roman Empire*. Berkeley: University of California Press, 2000.
Ashcroft, Bill, Gareth Griffiths, and Helen Tiffin. *The Empire Writes Back: Theory and Practice in Post-Colonial Literatures*. 2nd ed. London: Routledge, 2002.
Atkins, E. M. "Cicero." In *The Cambridge History of Greek and Roman Political Thought*, edited by Christopher Rowe and Malcolm Schofield, 477-516. New York: Cambridge University Press, 2006.
Augustus, P. A. Brunt, and J. M. Moore. *Res Gestae Divi Augusti: The Achievements of the Divine Augustus*. London: Oxford University Press, 1967.
Aune, David E. "Romans as Logos Protreptikos." In *The Romans Debate: Revised and Expanded Edition*, edited by Karl P. Donfried. Peabody: Hendrickson, 1991.
Aune, David E. *The Westminster Dictionary of New Testament and Early Christian Literature and Rhetoric*. Louisville: Westminster John Knox, 2003.
Avemarie, Friedrich. "Israels Rätselhafter Ungehorsam. Römer 10 Als Anatomie Eines Von Gott Provozierten Unglaubens." In *Between Gospel and Election: Explorations in*

the Interpretation of Romans 9–11, edited by Florian Wilk, J. Ross Wagner, and Frank Schleritt, 299–320. Tübingen: Mohr Siebeck, 2010.

Aymer, Margaret P. "Empire, Alter-Empire, and the Twenty-First Century." *USQR* 59 (2005): 140–6.

Barclay, John M. G. "Faith and Self-Detachment from Cultural Norms: A Study in Romans 14–15." *ZNW* 104 (2013): 192–208.

Barclay, John M. G. *Jews in the Mediterranean Diaspora: From Alexander to Trajan (323 BCE–117 CE)*. Los Angeles: University of California Press, 1996.

Barclay, John M. G. *Obeying the Truth: Paul's Ethics in Galatians*. Minneapolis: Fortress, 1991.

Barclay, John M. G. *Paul and the Gift*. Grand Rapids: Eerdmans, 2015.

Barclay, John M. G. "Paul, Roman Religion, and the Emperor. Mapping the Point of Conflict." In *Pauline Churches and Diaspora Jews*, 345–62. Tübingen: Mohr Siebeck, 2011.

Baronowski, Donald Walter. *Polybius and Roman Imperialism*. London: Bristol Classical Press, 2011.

Baronowski, Donald Walter. "Polybius on the Causes of the Third Punic War." *CP* 90 (1995): 16–31.

Barr, James. *The Semantics of Biblical Language*. London: Oxford University Press, 1961.

Barram, Michael D. *Mission and Moral Reflection in Paul*. New York: Peter Lang, 2006.

Barrett, C. K. *The Epistle to the Romans: Revised Edition*. Peabody: Hendrickson, 1991.

Barrett, C. K. *On Paul: Aspects of His Life, Work and Influence in the Early Church*. Edinburgh: T&T Clark, 2003.

Barth, Karl. *The Epistle to the Romans*. Translated by E. C. Hoskyns. Oxford: Oxford University Press, 1968.

Bates, Matthew W. *The Hermeneutics of the Apostolic Proclamation: The Center of Paul's Method of Scriptural Interpretation*. Waco: Baylor University Press, 2012.

Bates, Matthew W. *Salvation by Allegiance Alone: Rethinking Faith, Works, and the Gospel of Jesus the King*. Grand Rapids: Baker, 2017.

Bauman, Richard A. *Impietas in Principem: A Study of Treason against the Roman Emperor with Special Reference to the First Century A.D.* München: Beck, 1974.

Beacham, Richard C. *Spectacle Entertainments of Early Imperial Rome*. New Haven: Yale University Press, 1999.

Beard, Mary. *The Roman Triumph*. Cambridge: Harvard University Press, 2007.

Beard, Mary, John A. North, and S. R. F. Price. *Religions of Rome*. 2 vols. New York: Cambridge University Press, 1998.

Beker, J. Christiaan. *Paul the Apostle: The Triumph of God in Life and Thought*. Philadelphia: Fortress, 1980.

Bell, Richard H. *The Irrevocable Call of God: An Inquiry into Paul's Theology of Israel*. Tübingen: Mohr Siebeck, 2005.

Bell, Richard H. *Provoked to Jealousy: The Origin and Purpose of the Jealousy Motif in Romans 9–11*. Tübingen: J.C.B. Mohr (Paul Siebeck), 1994.

Bénétreau, Samuel. *L' Epitre De Paul Aux Romains: Tome 1*. Seine: Édifac, 1996.

Bersot, Jonathan. "La Paix Avec Dieu, Passage De La Justification À La Réconciliation: Observations Structurelles Et Narratives En Romains 5,1–11." *Science et Esprit* 62 (2010): 125–42.

Bertschmann, Dorothea H. "The Good, the Bad and the State—Rom 13.1–7 and the Dynamics of Love." *NTS* 60 (2014): 232–49.

Best, Ernest. *The Letter of Paul to the Romans*. Cambridge: Cambridge University Press, 1967.
Best, Ernest. *Paul and His Converts*. Edinburgh: T&T Clark, 1988.
Bhabha, Homi K. *The Location of Culture*. London: Routledge, 1994.
Bingham, Sandra. *The Praetorian Guard: A History of Rome's Elite Special Forces*. Waco: Baylor University Press, 2013.
Bitzer, L. "The Rhetorical Situation." *PR* 1 (1968): 1–18.
Bjerkelund, Carl J. *Parakalô: Form, Funktion Und Sinn Der Parakalô-Sätze in Den Paulinischen Briefen*. Oslo: Universitetsvorlaget, 1967.
Blackwell, Ben, John K. Goodrich, and Jason Maston, eds. *Reading Romans in Context: Paul and Second Temple Judaism*. Grand Rapids: Zondervan, 2015.
Blomberg, Craig L. "Quotations, Allusions, and Echoes of Jesus in Paul." In *Studies in the Pauline Epistles: Essays in Honor of Douglas J. Moo*, edited by Matthew S. Harmon and Jay E. Smith, 129–43. Grand Rapids: Zondervan, 2014.
Blumenfeld, Bruno. *The Political Paul: Justice, Democracy and Kingship in a Hellenistic Framework*. New York: T&T Clark, 2003.
Boatwright, Mary T., Daniel J. Gargola, and Richard J. A. Talbert, eds. *The Romans: From Village to Empire*. New York: Oxford University Press, 2004.
Boers, Hendrikus. *The Justification of the Gentiles: Paul's Letters to the Galatians and Romans*. Peabody: Hendrickson, 1994.
Bolt, Peter, and Mark Thompson. *The Gospel to the Nations: Perspectives on Paul's Mission*. Downers Grove: IVP, 2000.
Bolton, David L. "Who Are You Calling 'Weak'? A Short Critique on James Dunn's Reading of Rom 14,1–15,6." In *The Letter to the Romans*, edited by Udo Schnelle, 595–616. Leuven: Peeters, 2009.
Borg, Marcus J., and John Dominic Crossan. *The First Paul: Reclaiming the Radical Visionary behind the Church's Conservative Icon*. New York: HarperOne, 2009.
Botha, Jan. "Creation of New Meaning: Rhetorical Situations and the Reception of Romans 13:1–7." *JTSA* 79, no. 2 (1992): 24–37.
Botha, Jan. *Subject to Whose Authority? Multiple Readings of Romans 13*. Atlanta: Scholars Press, 1994.
Bowers, William Paul. "Studies in Paul's Understanding of His Mission." PhD dissertation, Cambridge University, 1976.
Boyarin, Daniel. *A Radical Jew: Paul and the Politics of Identity*. Berkeley: University of California Press, 1994.
Brändle, Rudolf, and Ekkehard W. Stegemann. "The Formation of the First 'Christian Congregations' in Rome in the Context of Jewish Congregations." In *Judaism and Christianity in First-Century Rome*, edited by Karl P. Donfried and Peter Richardson, 117–27. Grand Rapids: Eerdmans, 1998.
Bray, Gerald, and Thomas C. Oden, eds. *Ancient Christian Commentary on Scripture: Romans*. Vol. New Testament 6. Downers Grove: InterVarsity Press, 1998.
Brinton, A. "Situation in the Theory of Rhetoric." *PR* 14 (1981): 234–48.
Brodd, Jeffrey, and Jonathan L. Reed, eds. *Rome and Religion: A Cross-Disciplinary Dialogue on the Imperial Cult*. Atlanta: SBL, 2011.
Bruce, F. F. *Romans: Revised Edition*. Grand Rapids: Eerdmans, 1986.
Brunt, P. A. *Roman Imperial Themes*. New York: Oxford University Press, 1990.
Bryan, Christopher. *A Preface to Romans: Notes on the Epistle in Its Literary and Cultural Setting*. New York: Oxford University Press, 2000.

Bryan, Christopher. *Render to Caesar: Jesus, the Early Church, and the Roman Superpower*. Oxford: Oxford University Press, 2005.
Bultmann, Rudolf. "Das Problem Der Ethik Bei Paulus." *ZNW* 23 (1924): 123–40.
Burton, Paul J. *Friendship and Empire: Roman Diplomacy and Imperialism in the Middle Republic (353–146 BC)*. New York: Cambridge University Press, 2011.
Byrne, Brendan. "The Problem of Nomos and the Relationship with Judaism in Romans." *CBQ* 62, no. 2 (2000): 294–309.
Byrne, Brendan. *Romans*. Collegeville: Liturgical, 2007.
Calhoun, Robert Matthew. *Paul's Definitions of the Gospel in Romans 1*. Tübingen: Mohr Siebeck, 2011.
Campbell, Douglas. *The Deliverance of God: An Apocalyptic Rereading of Justification in Paul*. Grand Rapids: Eerdmans, 2009.
Campbell, Douglas A. *The Quest for Paul's Gospel: A Suggested Strategy*. New York: T&T Clark, 2005.
Campbell, J. B. *The Emperor and the Roman Army, 31 Bc–Ad 235*. New York: Oxford University Press, 1984.
Campbell, William S. "The Rule of Faith in Romans 12:1–15:13." In *Pauline Theology*, edited by David M. Hay and E. Elizabeth Johnson. Minneapolis: Fortress, 1995.
Cancik, Hubert, and Helmuth Schneider. *Brill's New Pauly: Encyclopaedia of the Ancient World*. 16 vols. Boston: Brill, 2002.
Carter, T. L. "The Irony of Romans 13." *NovT* 46 (2004): 209–28.
Carter, Warren. *The Roman Empire and the New Testament: An Essential Guide*. Nashville: Abingdon, 2006.
Carter, Warren. "Vulnerable Power: The Roman Empire Challenged by the Early Christians." In *Handbook of Early Christianity: Social Science Approaches*, edited by Anthony J. Blasi, Jean Duhaime, and Paul-André Turcotte, 453–88. New York: AltaMira Press, 2002.
Champlin, Edward. *Nero*. Cambridge: Belknap Press of Harvard University Press, 2003.
Chaplin, Jane D., and Christina Shuttleworth Kraus, eds. *Oxford Readings in Classical Studies: Livy*. New York: Oxford University Press, 2009.
Chibici-Revneanu, Nicole. "Leben Im Gesetz: Die Paulinische Interpretation Von Lev 18:5 (Gal 3:12; Röm 10:5)." *NovT* 50 (2008): 105–19.
Ciampa, Roy E. "Paul's Theology of the Gospel." In *Paul as Missionary: Identity, Activity, Theology, and Practice*, edited by Trevor J. Burke and Brian S. Rosner, 180–92. Edinburgh: T&T Clark, 2011.
Cohick, Lynn H. "Philippians and Empire: Paul's Engagement with Imperialism and the Imperial Cult." In *Jesus Is Lord, Caesar Is Not: Evaluating Empire in New Testament Studies*, edited by Scot McKnight and Joseph B. Modica, 166–82. Downers Grove: IVP, 2013.
Cole, Spencer. *Cicero and the Rise of Deification at Rome*. New York: Cambridge University Press, 2013.
Coleman, Thomas M. "Binding Obligations in Romans 13:7: A Semantic Field and Social Context." *TynB* 48 (1997): 307–27.
Comfort, Philip Wesley. *New Testament Text and Translation Commentary*. Carol Stream: Tyndale 2008.
Connolly, Serena. "Ὁμνύω Αὐτὸν Τὸν Σεβαστόν: The Greek Oath in the Roman World." In *Horkos: The Oath in Greek Society*, edited by Alan H. Sommerstein and Judith Fletcher, 203–16. Exeter: Bristol Phoenix Press, 2007.

Cook, J. A. "Augustus: Power, Authority, Achievement." In *The Cambridge Ancient History: The Augustan Empire, 43 B.C.–A.D. 69*, edited by Alan K. Bowman, Edward Champlin, and Andrew Lintott, X, 113–46. Cambridge: Cambridge University Press, 1996.

Cranfield, C. E. B. *The Epistle to the Romans: A Critical and Exegetical Commentary*. 2 vols. Edinburgh: T&T Clark, 1980.

Cranford, Michael. "Abraham in Romans 4: The Father of All Who Believe." *NTS* 41 (1995): 71–88.

Croasmun, Matthew. *The Emergence of Sin: The Cosmic Tyrant in Romans*. New York: Oxford University Press, 2017.

Crossan, John Dominic. "Paul and Rome: The Challenge of a Just World Order." *USQR* 59 (2005): 6–20.

Dahl, Nils Alstrup. *Studies in Paul: Theology for the Early Christian Mission*. Minneapolis: Augsburg, 1977.

Damon, Cynthia. "The Trial of Cn. Piso in Tacitus' Annals and the 'Senatus Consultum De Cn. Pisone Patre': New Light on Narrative Technique." *AJP* 120 (1999): 143–62.

Das, A. Andrew. *Paul and the Jews*. Peabody: Hendrickson, 2003.

Das, A. Andrew. "Paul of Tarshish: Isaiah 66.19 and the Spanish Mission of Romans 15.24, 28." *NTS* 54 (2008): 60–73.

Das, A. Andrew. "'Praise the Lord, All You Gentiles': The Encoded Audience of Romans 15.7-13." *JSNT* 34 (2011): 90–110.

Das, A. Andrew. *Solving the Romans Debate*. Minneapolis: Fortress, 2007.

Davies, Glen N. *Faith and Obedience in Romans: A Study in Romans 1–4*. Sheffield: JSOT Press, 1990.

Davies, W. D. *Jewish and Pauline Studies*. Philadelphia: Fortress, 1984.

Davies, W. D. *Paul and Rabbinic Judaism: Some Rabbinic Elements in Pauline Theology*. London: SPCK, 1948.

Debergé, Pierre. "Romains 13,1-7: De La Soumission Requise À La Désobéissance Possible?" *BLE* 108 (2007): 289–314.

Deichgräber, Reinhard. "Gehorsam Und Gehorchen in Der Verkündigung Jesu." *ZNW* 52 (1961): 119–22.

Dodson, Joseph R., and David E. Briones., eds. *Paul and Seneca in Dialogue*. Boston: Brill, 2017.

Donaldson, Terence L. *Judaism and the Gentiles: Jewish Patterns of Universalism (to 135 CE)*. Waco: Baylor University Press, 2008.

Donaldson, Terence L. *Paul and the Gentiles: Remapping the Apostle's Convictional World*. Minneapolis: Fortress, 1997.

Donfried, Karl P. "Paul's Jewish Matrix: The Scope and Nature of the Contributions." In *Paul's Jewish Matrix*, edited by Thomas G. Casey and Justin Taylor. Rome: Gregorian & Biblical Press, 2011.

Donfried, Karl P., ed. *The Romans Debate: Revised and Expanded Edition*. Peabody: Hendrickson, 1991.

Donfried, Karl P. "A Short Note on Romans 16." In *The Romans Debate: Revised and Expanded Edition*, edited by Karl P. Donfried. Peabody: Hendrickson, 1991.

Donfried, Karl P., and Peter Richardson, eds. *Judaism and Christianity in First-Century Rome*. Grand Rapids: Eerdmans, 1998.

Downs, David J. "'The Offering of the Gentiles' in Romans 15.16." *JSNT* 29 (2006): 173–86.

Downs, David J. *The Offering of the Gentiles: Paul's Collection for Jerusalem in Its Chronological, Cultural, and Cultic Contexts*. Tübingen: Mohr Siebeck, 2008.
Dunn, James D. G. *Beginning from Jerusalem*. Vol. 2 Christianity in the Making. Grand Rapids: Eerdmans, 2009.
Dunn, James D. G. *The Cambridge Companion to St. Paul*. New York: Cambridge University Press, 2003.
Dunn, James D. G. "The New Perspective on Paul." *BJRL* 65 (1983): 95–122.
Dunn, James D. G. "The New Perspective on Paul." In *The New Perspective on Paul*, 99–120. Grand Rapids: Eerdmans, 2008.
Dunn, James D. G. "Paul and Justification by Faith." In *The Road from Damascus: The Impact of Paul's Conversion on His Life, Thought, and Ministry*, edited by Richard N. Longenecker, 85–101. Grand Rapids: Eerdmans, 1997.
Dunn, James D. G. "Paul and the Torah: The Role and Function of the Law in the Theology of Paul the Apostle." In *The New Perspective on Paul*, edited by James D. G. Dunn, 447–68. Grand Rapids: Eerdmans, 2008.
Dunn, James D. G. *Romans*. 2 vols. Dallas: Word, 1988.
Dunn, James D. G. "Romans 13.1-7—a Charter for Political Quietism?" *ExAud* 2 (1986): 55–68.
Dunn, James D. G. *The Theology of Paul the Apostle*. Grand Rapids: Eerdmans, 1998.
Dunson, Ben C. "Faith in Romans: The Salvation of the Individual or Life in Community?" *JSNT* 34 (2011): 19–46.
Dyson, Stephen L. *Rome: A Living Portrait of an Ancient City*. Baltimore: Johns Hopkins University Press, 2010.
Eastman, Susan. *Paul and the Person: Reframing Paul's Anthropology*. Grand Rapids: Eerdmans, 2017.
Eckstein, Hans-Joachim. "'Denn Gottes Zorn Wird Von Himmel Her Offenbar Werden': Exegetische Erwägungen Zu Röm 1:18." *ZNW* 78 (1987): 74–89.
Ehrensperger, Kathy. *Paul and the Dynamics of Power: Communication and Interaction in the Early Christ-Movement*. New York: T&T Clark, 2007.
Ehrensperger, Kathy, and J. Brian Tucker, eds. *Reading Paul in Context: Explorations in Identity Formation: Essays in Honour of William S. Campbell*. New York: T&T Clark, 2010.
Elliott, Neil. *The Arrogance of Nations: Reading Romans in the Shadow of the Empire*. Minneapolis: Fortress, 2008.
Elliott, Neil. *Liberating Paul: The Justice of God and the Politics of the Apostle*. Maryknoll: Orbis, 1994.
Elliott, Neil. *The Rhetoric of Romans: Argumentative Constraint and Strategy and Paul's Dialogue with Judaism*. Minneapolis: Fortress, 1990.
Elliott, Neil, and Mark Reasoner. *Documents and Images for the Study of Paul*. Minneapolis: Fortress, 2011.
Elliott, Susan M. "Reflections on 'New Testament and Roman Empire.'" *USQR* 59 (2005): 172–6.
Engberg-Pedersen, Troels, ed. *Paul and the Stoics*. Louisville: Westminster John Knox, 2000.
Engberg-Pedersen, Troels, ed. *Paul in His Hellenistic Context*. Edinburgh: T&T Clark, 1994.
Engberg-Pedersen, Troels, ed. "Paul's Stoicizing Politics in Romans 12–3: The Role of 13.1-10 in the Argument." *JSNT* 29, no. 2 (2006): 163–72.

Erdkamp, Paul, ed. *The Cambridge Companion to Ancient Rome*. New York: Cambridge University Press, 2013.
Erskine, Andrew. "How to Rule the World: Polybius Book 6 Reconsidered." In *Polybius and His World: Essays in Memory of F. W. Walbank*, edited by Bruce Gibson and Thomas Harrison, 496. New York: Oxford University Press, 2013.
Esler, Phillip F. "Ancient Oléïculture and Ethnic Differentiation: The Meaning of the Olive-Tree Image in Romans 11." *JSNT* 26 (2003): 103–24.
Esler, Phillip F. *Conflict and Identity in Romans: The Social Setting of Paul's Letter*. Minneapolis: Fortress, 2003.
Evans, Craig A., and James A. Sanders, eds. *Paul and the Scriptures of Israel*. Vol. 83. Sheffield: Sheffield Academic, 1993.
Fantin, Joseph D. *The Lord of the Entire World*. Sheffield: Sheffield Academic, 2011.
Fee, Gordon D., Sven Soderlund, and N. T. Wright. *Romans and the People of God: Essays in Honor of Gordon D. Fee on the Occasion of His 65th Birthday*. Grand Rapids: Eerdmans, 1999.
Fiorenza, Elizabeth Schüssler. "Empire and Christian Studies." *USQR* 59 (2005): 131–9.
Fitzmyer, Joseph A. *Romans*. New York: Doubleday, 1993.
Flower, Harriet I. *The Cambridge Companion to the Roman Republic*. New York: Cambridge University Press, 2006.
Fornara, Charles W. *The Nature of History in Ancient Greece and Rome*. Berkeley: University of California Press, 1983.
Fredriksen, Paula. *Paul: The Pagan's Apostle*. New Haven: Yale University Press, 2017.
Fredriksen, Paula. "Paul's Letter to the Romans, the Ten Commandments, and Pagan 'Justification by Faith.'" *JBL* 133 (2014): 801–8.
Friedrich, Gerhard. "Muss Hypakoē Pisteōs Röm 1:5 Mit 'Glaubengehorsam' Übersetzt Werden." *ZNW* 72 (1981): 118–23.
Friesen, Steven J. "Normal Religion, or, Words Fail Us: A Response to Karl Galinsky's 'the Cult of the Roman Emperor: Uniter or Divider?'" In *Rome and Religion: A Cross-Disciplinary Dialogue on the Imperial Cult*, edited by Jeffrey Brodd and Jonathan L. Reed, 23–6. Leiden: Brill, 2011.
Friesen, Steven J. *Twice Neokoros: Ephesus, Asia, and the Cult of the Flavian Imperial Family*. New York: Brill, 1993.
Fujii, Takashi. *Imperial Cult and Imperial Representation in Roman Cyprus*. Stuttgart: Franz Steiner Verlag, 2013.
Furnish, Victor P. *The Moral Teachings of Paul*. Nashville: Abingdon, 1979.
Furnish, Victor P. *Theology and Ethics in Paul*. Louisville: Westminster John Knox, 2009.
Gagliardo, Maria C., and James E. Packer. "A New Look at Pompey's Theatre: History, Documentation, and Recent Excavation." *AJA* 110 (2006): 93–122.
Galinsky, Karl. *Augustan Culture: An Interpretive Introduction*. Princeton: Princeton University Press, 1996.
Galinsky, Karl. *The Cambridge Companion to the Age of Augustus*. New York: Cambridge University Press, 2005.
Galinsky, Karl. "The Cult of the Roman Emperor: Uniter or Divider?" In *Rome and Religion: A Cross-Disciplinary Dialogue on the Imperial Cult*, edited by Jeffrey Brodd and Jonathan L. Reed, 1–22. Leiden: Brill, 2011.
Gamble, Harry Y. *The Textual History of the Letter to the Romans: A Study in Textual and Literary Criticism*. Grand Rapids: Eerdmans, 1977.

Garlington, Don. *Faith, Obedience, and Perseverance: Aspects of Paul's Letter to the Romans*. Eugene: Wipf & Stock, 2009.

Garlington, Don. *The Obedience of Faith: A Pauline Phrase in Historical Context*. Tübingen: J. C. B. Mohr (Paul Siebeck), 1991.

Garlington, Don. "The Obedience of Faith in the Letter to the Romans: Part 1." *WTJ* 52 (1990): 201–24.

Garnsey, Peter. *Ideas of Slavery from Aristotle to Augustine*. New York: Cambridge University, 1996.

Garnsey, Peter, and Richard Saller. *The Roman Empire: Economy, Society, and Culture*. Los Angeles: University of California Press, 1987.

Gathercole, Simon J. "A Law Unto Themselves: The Gentiles in Romans 2.14-15 Revisited." *JSNT* 85 (2002): 27–49.

Gathercole, Simon J. *Where Is Boasting: Early Jewish Soteriology and Paul's Response in Romans 1–5*. Grand Rapids: Eerdmans, 2002.

Gaventa, Beverly Roberts, ed. *Apocalyptic Paul: Cosmos and Anthropos in Romans 5–8*. Waco: Baylor University Press, 2013.

Gaventa, Beverly Roberts. "On the Calling-into-Being of Israel: Romans 9:6-29." In *Between Gospel and Election: Explorations in the Interpretation of Romans 9–11*, edited by Florian Wilk, J. Ross Wagner, and Frank Schleritts, 255–70. Tübingen: Mohr Siebeck, 2010.

Gaventa, Beverly Roberts. *Our Mother Saint Paul*. Louisville: Westminster John Knox, 2007.

Gaventa, Beverly Roberts. "Reading for the Subject: The Paradox of Power in Romans 14:1–15:6." *JTI* 5 (2011): 1–12.

Gaventa, Beverly Roberts. *When in Romans: An Invitation to Linger with the Gospel According to Paul*. Grand Rapids: Baker, 2016.

Georgi, Dieter. *Theocracy in Paul's Praxis and Theology*. Translated by David E. Green. Minneapolis: Fortress, 1991.

Gibbon, Edward. *The History of the Decline and Fall of the Roman Empire*. Vols. 1–6. New York: Penguin, 1996.

Gibson, Jeffrey B. "Paul's 'Dying Formula': Prolegomena to an Understanding of Its Import and Significance." In *Celebrating Romans: Template for Pauline Theology*, edited by Sheila E. McGinn, 20–41. Grand Rapids: Eerdmans, 2004.

Goodman, Martin. *The Roman World: 44BC–AD180*. New York: Routledge, 1997.

Goodrich, John K. "From Slaves of Sin to Slaves of God: Reconsidering the Origin of Paul's Slavery Metaphor in Romans 6." *BBR* 23 (2013): 509–30.

Gorman, Michael J. *Apostle of the Crucified Lord: A Theological Introduction to Paul and His Letters*. Grand Rapids: Eerdmans, 2004.

Gorman, Michael J. *Cruciformity: Paul's Narrative Spirituality of the Cross*. Grand Rapids: Eerdmans, 2001.

Gorman, Michael J. "What Did Paul Think God Is Doing about What's Wrong?" In *The New Cambridge Companion to St. Paul*, edited by Bruce W. Longenecker. New York: Cambridge University Press, 2020.

Gorrie, Charmaine. "The Restoration of the Porticus Octaviae and Severan Imperial Policy." *GR* 54 (2007): 1–17.

Grieb, Katherine. *The Story of Romans: A Narrative Defense of God's Righteousness*. Louisville: Westminster John Knox, 2002.

Griffin, Miriam T. *Nero: The End of a Dynasty*. New Haven: Yale University Press, 1985.

Gruen, Erich S. "Augustus and the Making of the Principate." In *The Cambridge Companion to the Age of Augustus*, edited by Karl Galinsky, xvii, 407. New York: Cambridge University Press, 2005.

Gruen, Erich S. *The Hellenistic World and the Coming of Rome*. 2 vols. Berkeley: University of California Press, 1984.

Guerra, Anthony J. *Romans and the Apologetic Tradition: The Purpose, Genre, and Audience of Paul's Letter*. 1st pbk. ed. New York: Cambridge University Press, 1995.

Gupta, Nijay. "Human Idolatry and Paul as Faithful Worshipper of God: Reconnecting Romans 1:18-32 to 1:8-15 (Via 1:16-17)." *Neot* 46 (2012): 29–40.

Gupta, Nijay. *Paul and the Language of Faith*. Grand Rapids: Eerdmans, 2020.

Güven, Suna. "Displaying the *Res Gestae* of Augustus: A Monument of Imperial Image for All." *JSAH* 57 (1998): 30–45.

Haacker, Klaus. "Das Thema Von Römer 9–11 Als Problem Der Auslegungsgechichte." In *Between Gospel and Election: Explorations in the Interpretation of Romans 9–11*, edited by Florian Wilk, J. Ross Wagner, and Frank Schleritt, 55–72. Tübingen: Mohr Siebeck, 2010.

Haacker, Klaus. *Der Brief Des Paulus an Die Römer*. Leipzig: Evangelische Verlagsanstalt, 1999.

Hafemann, Scot. "Eschatology and Ethics: The Future of Israel and the Nations in Romans 15:1-13." *TynB* 51 (2000): 161–92.

Harding, Mark, and Alanna Nobbs, eds. *All Things to All Cultures: Paul among Jews, Greeks, and Romans*. Grand Rapids: Eerdmans, 2013.

Harrill, J. Albert. "Paul and Empire: Studying Roman Identity after the Cultural Turn." *EC* 2 (2011): 281–311.

Harrison, James R. "Paul among the Romans." In *All Things to All Cultures: Paul among Jews, Greeks, and Romans*, edited by Mark Harding and Alanna Nobbs, 143–76. Grand Rapids: Eerdmans, 2013.

Harrison, James R. *Paul and the Imperial Authorities at Thessalonica and Rome: A Study in the Conflict of Ideology*. Tübingen: Mohr Siebeck, 2011.

Harrison, James R. "Paul's 'Indebtedness' to the Barbarian (Rom 1:14) in Latin West Perspective." *NovT* 55 (2013): 311–48.

Haynes, Holly. *The History of Make-Believe: Tacitus on Imperial Rome*. Berkeley: University of California Press, 2003.

Hays, Richard B. *Echoes of Scripture in the Letters of Paul*. New Haven: Yale University Press, 1993.

Hays, Richard B. " 'Have We Found Abraham to Be Our Forefather according to the Flesh?' A Reconsideration of Rom 4:1." *NovT* 27 (1985): 76–98.

Heath, Jane. "The Righteous Gentile Interjects (James 2:18-19 and Romans 2:14-15." *NovT* 55 (2013): 272–95.

Heil, John Paul. "Christ, the Termination of the Law (Romans 9:30-10:8)." *CBQ* 63 (2001): 484–98.

Hellerman, Joseph H. *Reconstructing Honor in Roman Philippi: Carmen Christi as Cursus Pudorum*. New York: Cambridge University Press, 2005.

Hendel, Ronald. *Remembering Abraham: Culture, Memory, and History in the Hebrew Bible*. New York: Oxford University Press, 2005.

Hester, James D. "The Rhetoric of Persona in Romans." In *Celebrating Romans: Template for Pauline Theology*, edited by Sheila E. McGinn. Grand Rapids: Eerdmans, 2004.

Hofius, Otfried. *Paulusstudien*. 2 vols. Wissenschaftliche Untersuchungen Zum Neuen Testament. Tübingen: Mohr, 1989.
Holdsworth, Ben. "Reading Romans in Rome: A Reception of Romans in the Roman Context of Ethnicity and Faith." PhD dissertation, Durham University, 2009.
Hölkeskamp, Karl-Joachim. *Senatus Populusque Romanus: Die Politische Kultur Der Republik: Dimensionen Und Deutungen*. Wiesbaden: Franz Steiner Verlag, 2004.
Hornblower, Simon, and Antony Spawforth. *The Oxford Classical Dictionary*. 3rd ed. New York: Oxford University Press, 1999.
Horsley, Richard A. *Paul and Empire: Religion and Power in Roman Imperial Society*. Harrisburg: Trinity Press International, 1997.
Horsley, Richard A. ed. *Paul and Politics: Ekklesia, Israel, Imperium, Interpretation*. Harrisburg: Trinity Press International, 2000.
Horsley, Richard A. ed. *Paul and the Roman Imperial Order*. Harrisburg: Trinity Press International, 2004.
Hose, Martin. "Cassius Dio: A Senator and Historian in the Age of Anxiety." In *A Companion to Greek and Roman Historiography*, edited by John Marincola, 441–6. Malden: Blackwell, 2007.
Howard, George. "Christ the End of the Law: The Meaning of Romans 10:4ff." *JBL* 88 (1969): 331–7.
Hultgren, Arland J. *Paul's Letter to the Romans: A Commentary*. Grand Rapids: Eerdmans, 2011.
Hurtado, Larry W. "The Doxology at the End of Romans." In *New Testament Textual Criticism: Its Significance for Exegesis: Essays in Honor of Bruce M. Metzger*, edited by E. J. Epp and G. D. Fee, 185–99. Clarendon: Oxford University Press, 1981.
Hurtado, Larry W. "Paul's Christology." In *The Cambridge Companion to St. Paul*, edited by James D. G. Dunn. Cambridge: Cambridge University Press, 2003.
Ito, Akio. "The Written Torah and the Oral Gospel: Romans 10:5-13 in the Dynamic Tension between Orality and Literacy." *NovT* 48 (2006): 234–60.
Jeffers, James S. "Jewish and Christian Families in First-Century Rome." In *Judaism and Christianity in First-Century Rome*, edited by Karl P. Donfried and Peter Richardson, 128–50. Grand Rapids: Eerdmans, 1998.
Jennings, Theodore W. *Outlaw Justice: The Messianic Politics of Paul*. Stanford: Stanford University Press, 2013.
Jervis, L. Ann. "'The Commandment Which Is for Life' (Romans 7.10): Sin's Use of the Obedience of Faith." *JSNT* 27 (2004): 193–216.
Jewett, Robert. "Ecumenical Theology for the Sake of Mission: Romans 1:1–17 + 15:14–16:24." In *Pauline Theology*, edited by David M. Hay and E. Elizabeth Johnson, 3, 89–108. Minneapolis: Fortress, 1995.
Jewett, Robert. "Following the Argument of Romans." In *The Romans Debate: Revised and Expanded Edition*, edited by Karl P. Donfried. Peabody: Hendrickson, 1991.
Jewett, Robert. "Reinterpreting Romans 13 within Its Broader Context." In *Celebrating Paul: Festschrift in Honor of Jeromy Murphy-O'connor, O.P., and Joseph A. Fitzmyer, S.J.*, edited by Peter Spitaler, 265–74. Washington, DC: CBA, 2011.
Jewett, Robert. "Romans." In *The Cambridge Companion to St. Paul*, edited by James D. G. Dunn, 91–104. New York: Cambridge University Press, 2003.
Jewett, Robert. *Romans: A Commentary*. Minneapolis: Fortress, 2007.
Jipp, Joshua, *Christ Is King: Paul's Royal Ideology*. Minneapolis: Fortress, 2015.
Johnson, Luke Timothy. *Among the Gentiles: Greco-Roman Religion and Christianity*. New Haven: Yale University Press, 2009.

Johnson, Luke Timothy. *Reading Romans: A Literary and Theological Commentary*. Macon: Smyth & Helwys, 2001.

Johnson, Luke Timothy. "Transformation of the Mind and Moral Discernment in Paul." In *Contested Issues in Christian Origins and the New Testament: Collected Essays*, 255-76. Boston: Brill, 2013.

Johnson, William A. *Readers and Reading Culture in the High Roman Empire: A Study of Elite Communities*. Classical Culture and Society. New York: Oxford University Press, 2010.

Johnson, William A., and Holt N. Parker. *Ancient Literacies: The Culture of Reading in Greece and Rome*. Classical Culture and Society. New York: Oxford University Press, 2009.

Jr., Eugene H. Lovering, and Jerry L. Sumney, eds. *Theology and Ethics in Paul and His Interpreters: Essays in Honor of Victor Paul Furnish*. Nashville: Abingdon, 1996.

Judge, Edwin A. *Social Distinctives of Christians in the First Century: Pivotal Essays by E. A. Judge*. Edited by David M. Scholer. Peabody: Hendrickson, 2008.

Judge, Edwin A. "The Social Pattern of the Christian Groups in the First Century." In *Social Distinctives of Christians in the First Century: Pivotal Essays by E. A. Judge*, edited by David M. Scholer, 1-55. Peabody: Hendrickson, 2008.

Karris, Robert J. "Romans 14:1-15:13 and the Occasion of Romans." In *The Romans Debate: Revised and Expanded Edition*, edited by Karl P. Donfried, 125-7. Peabody: Hendrickson, 1991.

Käsemann, Ernst. *Commentary on Romans*. Grand Rapids: Eerdmans, 1980.

Käsemann, Ernst. *Essays on New Testament Themes*. Philadelphia: Fortress, 1982.

Käsemann, Ernst. *Perspectives on Paul*. Philadelphia: Fortress, 1971.

Kaster, Robert A. *Emotion, Restraint, and Community in Ancient Rome*. New York: Oxford University Press, 2005.

Keck, Leander. "'Jesus' in Romans." *Journal of Biblical Literature* 108 (1989): 443-60.

Keck, Leander. "On the Ethos of the Early Christians." *JAAR* 42 (1974): 435-52.

Keck, Leander. *Romans*. Nashville: Abingdon, 2005.

Keener, Craig S. *Romans*. Eugene: Cascade, 2009.

Keesmaat, Sylvia C. "Reading Romans in the Capital of the Empire." In *Reading Paul's Letter to the Romans*, edited by Jerry L. Sumney, 47-64. Atlanta: SBL, 2012.

Keesmaat, Sylvia C., and Brian J. Walsh. *Romans Disarmed: Resisting Empire, Demanding Justice*. Grand Rapids: Brazos, 2019.

Kehoe, Dennis P. "Law and Social Formation in the Roman Empire." In *The Oxford Handbook of Social Relations in the Roman World*, edited by Michael Peachin, 144-66. New York: Oxford University Press, 2011.

Kennedy, George A. "Genres of Rhetoric." In *Handbook of Classical Rhetoric in the Hellenistic Period 330 B.C.-A.D. 400*, edited by Stanely E. Porter, 43-50. New York: Brill, 1997.

Kennedy, George A. *New Testament Interpretation through Rhetorical Criticism*. Chapel Hill: University of North Carolina, 1984.

Kennedy, George A. *Progymnasmata: Greek Textbooks of Prose Composition and Rhetoric*. Atlanta: SBL, 2003.

Kim, Seyoon. *Christ and Caesar: The Gospel and the Roman Empire in the Writings of Paul and Luke*. Grand Rapids: Eerdmans, 2008.

Kim, Seyoon. *Paul and the New Perspective*. Grand Rapids: Eerdmans, 2002.

Kim, Seyoon. "Paul as an Eschatological Herald." In *Paul as Missionary: Identity, Activity, Theology, and Practice*, edited by Trevor J. Burke and Brian S. Rosner, 9–24. Edinburgh: T&T Clark, 2011.

Kim, Seyoon. "Paul's Common Paraenesis (1 Thess. 4–5; Phil. 2–4; and Rom. 12–13): The Correspondence between Romans 1:18-32 and 12:2, and the Unity of Romans 12–13." *TynB* 62 (2011): 109–40.

Kirk, J. R. Daniel. *Unlocking Romans: Resurrection and the Justification of God*. Grand Rapids: Eerdmans, 2008.

Kittredge, Cynthia Briggs. *Community and Authority: The Rhetoric of Obedience in the Pauline Tradition*. Harrisburg: Trinity Press International, 1998.

Klauck, Hans-Josef. *The Religious Context of Early Christianity: A Guide to Graeco-Roman Religions*. Minneapolis: Fortress, 2003.

Kloppenborg, John S. *Christ's Associations: Connecting and Belonging in the Ancient City*. New Haven: Yale University Press, 2019.

Knapp, Robert. *Invisible Romans*. Cambridge: Harvard University Press, 2011.

Koester, Helmut. "Νόμος, Ἀγάπη, and Χαρίσματα in Paul's Writings." In *Celebrating Paul: Festschrift in Honor of Jerome Murphy-O'connor, O.P., and Joseph A. Fitzmyer, S.J.*, edited by Peter Spitaler, 233–44. Washington, DC: Catholic Biblical Association of America, 2011.

Koortbojian, Michael. *The Divinization of Caesar and Augustus: Precedents, Consequences, Implications*. New York: Cambridge University Press, 2013.

Krimmer, Heiko. *Römerbrief*. Stuttgart: Hánssler-Verlag, 1983.

Kruse, Colin G. *Paul's Letter to the Romans*. Grand Rapids: Eerdmans, 2012.

Lambrecht, Jan. "The Confirmation of the Promises: A Critical Note on Romans 15,8." *ETL* 78 (2002): 156–60.

Lampe, Peter. *From Paul to Valentinus: Christians at Rome in the First Two Centuries*. Minneapolis: Fortress, 2003.

Lampe, Peter. "The Roman Christians of Romans 16." In *The Romans Debate: Revised and Expanded Edition*, edited by Karl P. Donfried. Peabody: Hendrickson, 1991.

Lane, William L. "Social Perspectives on Roman Christianity during the Formative Years from Nero to Nerva: Romans, Hebrews, and 1 Clement." In *Judaism and Christianity in First-Century Rome*, edited by Karl P. Donfried and Peter Richardson, 196–244. Grand Rapids: Eerdmans, 1998.

Lavan, Myles. *Slaves to Rome: Paradigms of Empire in Roman Culture*. New York: Cambridge University Press, 2013.

Legrand, Lucian. "Rm 1.11-15 (17): Proemium or Propositio?" *NTS* 49 (2003): 566–72.

Lendon, J. E. *Empire of Honour: The Art of Government in the Roman World*. New York: Oxford University Press, 1997.

Lohse, Eduard. "Ὁ Νόμος Τοῦ Πνεύματος Τῆς Ζωῆς: Exegetische Anmerkungen Zu Röm 8:2." In *Neues Testament Und Christliche Existenz*, edited by Hans Dieter Betz and Luise Schottroff, 279–87. Tübingen: J. C. B Mohr (Paul Siebeck), 1973.

Long, A. A. *Epictetus: A Stoic and Socratic Guide to Life*. New York: Oxford University Press, 2002.

Longenecker, Bruce W. "Different Answers to Different Issues: Israel, the Gentiles, and Salvation History in Romans 9–11." *JSNT* 36 (1989): 95–123.

Longenecker, Bruce W. *Eschatology and Covenant: A Comparison of 4 Ezra and Romans 1–11*. Sheffield: JSOT Press, 1991.

Longenecker, Bruce W. *In Stone and Story: Early Christianity in the Roman World*. Grand Rapids: Baker, 2020.

Longenecker, Bruce W. *Narrative Dynamics in Paul: A Critical Assessment*. 1st ed. Louisville: Westminster John Knox, 2002.
Longenecker, Bruce W. "Socio-Economic Profiling of the First Urban Christians." In *After the First Urban Christians: The Social-Scientific Study of Pauline Christianity Twenty-Five Years Later*, edited by Todd D. Still and David G. Horrell, 36–59. New York: T&T Clark, 2009.
Longenecker, Richard N. *Introducing Romans: Critical Issues in Paul's Most Famous Letter*. Grand Rapids: Eerdmans, 2011.
Lopez, Davina C. *Apostle to the Conquered: Reimagining Paul's Mission*. Minneapolis: Fortress, 2010.
Luttwak, Edward. *The Grand Strategy of the Roman Empire from the First Century A.D. to the Third*. Baltimore: Johns Hopkins University Press, 1976.
MacMullen, Ramsay. *Enemies of the Roman Order: Treason, Unrest, and Alienation in the Empire*. Cambridge: Harvard University Press, 1966.
MacMullen, Ramsay. *Roman Social Relations: 50 B.C. to A.D. 284*. New Haven: Yale University Press, 1974.
MacMullen, Ramsay. *Romanization in the Time of Augustus*. New Haven: Yale University Press, 2000.
Magda, Ksenija. *Paul's Territoriality and Mission Strategy: Searching for the Geographical Awareness Paradigm behind Romans*. Tübingen: Mohr Siebeck, 2009.
Maier, Harry O. *Picturing Paul in Empire: Imperial Image, Text, and Persuasion in Colossians, Ephesians, and the Pastoral Epistles*. New York: Bloomsbury, 2013.
Malherbe, Abraham J. "Antisthenes and Odysseus, and Paul at War." In *Paul and the Philosophers*, 91–120. Minneapolis: Fortress, 1989.
Malherbe, Abraham J. *Moral Exhortation, a Greco-Roman Sourcebook*. Philadelphia: Westminster, 1986.
Malherbe, Abraham J. *Paul and the Philosophers*. Minneapolis: Fortress, 1989.
Marincola, John, ed. *A Companion to Greek and Roman Historiography*. Vol. 1. Malden: Blackwell, 2007.
Marshall, I. Howard. "Romans 16:25-27—an Apt Conclusion." In *Romans and the People of God: Essays in Honor of Gordon D. Fee on the Occasion of His 65th Birthday*, edited by Sven Soderlund and N. T. Wright, 170–84. Grand Rapids: Eerdmans, 1999.
Marshall, John W. "Hybridity and Reading Romans 13." *JSNT* 31 (2008): 157–78.
Martin, Dale B. *Slavery as Salvation: The Metaphor of Slavery in Pauline Christianity*. New Haven: Yale University Press, 1990.
Martin, H. J. "Mars." In *Brill's New Pauly: Encyclopaedia of the Ancient World*, edited by Hubert Cancik and Helmuth Schneider, 8. Boston: Brill, 2002.
Martin, Ralph P. *Reconciliation: A Study of Paul's Theology*. Atlanta: John Knox, 1981.
Matera, Frank J. *Romans*. Grand Rapids: Baker, 2010.
May, James M. "Cicero as Rhetorician." In *A Companion to Roman Rhetoric*, edited by William Dominik and Jon Hall, 250–63. Malden: Blackwell, 2007.
Mayer, Roland. "Impressions of Rome." *GR* 54 (2007): 156–77.
McGing, B. C. *Polybius' Histories*. New York: Oxford University Press, 2010.
McKnight, Scot, and Joseph B. Modica, eds. *Jesus Is Lord, Caesar Is Not: Evaluating Empire in New Testament Studies*. Downers Grove: IVP, 2013.
McKnight, Scot, and Joseph B. Modica, eds. *Reading Romans Backwards: A Gospel of Peace in the Midst of Empire*. Waco: Baylor University Press, 2019.

Meeks, Wayne A. *The First Urban Christians: The Social World of the Apostle Paul.* New Haven: Yale University Press, 1983.

Meeks, Wayne A. *The Moral World of the First Christians.* Philadelphia: Westminster, 1986.

Meeks, Wayne A. "Understanding Early Christian Ethics." *JBL* 105 (1986): 3–11.

Mehl, Andreas. *Roman Historiography: An Introduction to Its Basic Aspects and Development.* Translated by Hans-Friedrich Mueller. Malden: Wiley-Blackwell, 2011.

Metzger, Bruce M. *A Textual Commentary on the Greek New Testament.* 2nd ed. Stuttgart: UBS, 2006.

Miles, Richard. *Rivaling Rome: Carthage.* First paperback ed. Rome the Cosmopolis. Edited by Catharine Edwards and Greg Woolf. New York: Cambridge University Press, 2006.

Millar, Fergus. *The Roman Empire and Its Neighbours.* London: Weidenfeld & Nicolson, 1967.

Miller, Chris. "The Book of Galatians: Gentiles Are Not under the Mosaic Law." Dallas Theological Seminary, 1997.

Miller, James C. *The Obedience of Faith: The Eschatological People of God, and the Purpose of Romans.* Atlanta: SBL, 2000.

Minear, Paul S. *The Obedience of Faith: The Purposes of Paul in the Epistle to the Romans.* Naperville: SCM, 1971.

Mitford, T. B. "A Cypriot Oath of Allegiance to Tiberius." *JRS* 50 (1960): 75–9.

Moiser, Jeremy. "Rethinking Romans 12–15." *NTS* 36 (1990): 571–82.

Moles, J. L. "Livy's Preface." In *Oxford Readings in Classical Studies: Livy*, edited by Jane D. Chaplin and Christina Shuttleworth Kraus. New York: Oxford University Press, 2009.

Moo, Douglas J. *The Epistle to the Romans.* Grand Rapids: Eerdmans, 1996.

Moo, Jonathan. "Romans 8:19-22 and Isaiah's Cosmic Covenant." *NTS* 54, no. 1 (2008): 74–89.

Moore, Stephen D. "Paul after Empire." In *Paul the Colonized Apostle: Paul through Post-Colonial Eyes*, edited by Christopher D. Stanley, 9–23. Minneapolis: Fortress, 2011.

Morgan, Teresa. *Roman Faith and Christian Faith: Pistis and Fides in the Early Roman Empire and Early Churches.* New York: Oxford University Press, 2015.

Morris, Leon. *The Epistle to the Romans.* Grand Rapids: Eerdmans, 1988.

Moxnes, Halvor. "Quest for Honor and the Unity of the Community in Romans 12 and in the Orations of Dio Chrysostom." In *Paul in His Hellenistic Context*, edited by Troels Engberg-Pedersen, 203–30. Edinburgh: T&T Clark, 1994.

Moyise, Steve. *Paul and Scripture: Studying the New Testament Use of the Old Testament.* Grand Rapids: Baker, 2010.

Munck, Johannes. *Paul and the Salvation of Mankind.* Richmond: John Knox, 1959.

Murphy-O'Conner, Jerome. *Paul: A Critical Life.* Oxford: Oxford University Press, 1996.

Myers, Jason A. *Voices and Views on Paul: Exploring Scholarly Trends.* Downers Grove: IVP, 2020.

Myers, Jason A. "Who Are Those Who Do the Law? A Critical Analysis of Gentiles, Righteousness, and Justification in Romans 2:14-15." Grand Rapids Theological Seminary, 2010.

Myers, Jason A., and Ben Witherington. "A Rhetorical Response to Stan Porter." *BBR* 26, no. 4 (2017): 547–9.

Nanos, Mark D. *The Mystery of Romans: The Jewish Context of Paul's Letter.* Minneapolis: Fortress, 1996.

Nicholas, Barry. *An Introduction to Roman Law.* Oxford: Clarendon Press, 1962.

Nicklas, Tobias, and Herbert Schlögel. "Mission to the Gentiles, Construction of Christian Identity, and Its Relation to Ethics according to Paul." In *Sensitivity towards Outsiders: Exploring the Dynamic Relationship between Missions and Ethics in the New Testament and Early Christianity*, edited by Jakobus (Kobus) Kok, Tobias Nicklas, Dieter T. Roth, and Christopher M. Hays, 324–39. Tübingen: Mohr Siebeck, 2014.

Nicolet, Claude. *Space, Geography, and Politics in the Early Roman Empire*. Ann Arbor: University of Michigan Press, 1991.

Noreña, Carlos F. *Imperial Ideals in the Roman West: Representation, Circulation, Power*. Cambridge: Cambridge University Press, 2011.

Novenson, Matthew V. "The Jewish Messiahs, the Pauline Christ, and the Gentile Question." *JBL* 128 (2009): 357–73.

Novenson, Matthew V. "What the Apostles Did Not See." In *Reactions to Empire: Sacred Texts in Their Socio-Political Contexts*, edited by John Anthony Dunne and Dan Batovici, 55–72. Tübingen: Mohr Siebeck, 2014.

Noy, David. *Foreigners at Rome: Citizens and Strangers*. London: Duckworth with the Classical Press of Wales, 2000.

O'Brien, Peter T. *Gospel and Mission in the Writings of Paul: An Exegetical and Theological Analysis*. Grand Rapids: Baker, 1995.

Oakes, Peter. "Contours of the Urban Environment." In *After the First Urban Christians: The Social-Scientific Study of Pauline Christianity Twenty-Five Years Later*, edited by Todd D. Still and David G. Horrell, 21–35. New York: T&T Clark, 2009.

Oakes, Peter. *Empire, Economics, and the New Testament*. Grand Rapids: Eerdmans, 2020.

Oakes, Peter. *Reading Romans in Pompeii: Paul's Letter at Ground Level*. Minneapolis: Fortress, 2009.

Olson, Stanley N. "Epistolary Uses of Expressions of Self-Confidence." *JBL* 103 (1984): 585–97.

Orlin, Eric M. *Foreign Cults in Rome: Creating a Roman Empire*. New York: Oxford University Press, 2010.

Oropeza, B. J. *Jews, Gentiles, and the Opponents of Paul: Apostasy in the New Testament Communities*. Eugene: Cascade, 2012.

Oschsenmeier, Erwin. *Mal, Souffrance Et Justice De Dieu Selon Romains 1–3: Étude Exégétique Et Théologique*. New York: Walter de Gruyter, 2007.

Oschsenmeier, Erwin. "Romans 1,11-12: A Clue to the Purpose of Romans?" *ETL* 83 (2007): 395–406.

Osgood, Josiah. *Claudius Caesar: Image and Power in the Early Roman Empire*. New York: Cambridge University Press, 2011.

Packer, James E., John Burge, and Maria C. Gagliardo. "Looking Again at Pompey's Theatre: The 2005 Excavation Season." *AJA* 111 (2007): 505–22.

Parke-Taylor, George H. "A Note on 'Εἰς Ὑπακοὴν Πίστεως' in Romans I.5 and Xvi. 26." *Expository Times* 55 (1943-4): 305–6.

Parker, D. C. *An Introduction to the New Testament Manuscripts and Their Texts*. New York: Cambridge University Press, 2008.

Patterson, John R. "The City of Rome Revisited: From Mid-Republic to Mid-Empire." *HJRS* 100 (2010): 210–32.

Peachin, Michael, ed. *The Oxford Handbook of Social Relations in the Roman World*. New York: Oxford University Press, 2011.

Peerbolte, Bert-Jan Lietaert. "Morality and Boundaries in Paul." In *Sensitivity towards Outsiders: Exploring the Dynamic Relationship between Missions and Ethics in the New Testament and Early Christianity*, edited by Jakobus (Kobus) Kok, Tobias Nicklas, Dieter T. Roth, and Christopher M. Hays, 209-25. Tübingen: Mohr Siebeck, 2014.

Pelling, Christopher. "The Greek Historians of Rome." In *A Companion to Greek and Roman Historiography*, edited by John Marincola, 1. Malden: Blackwell, 2007.

Pesch, Rudolf. *Römerbrief*. Würzburg: Echter Verlag, 1985.

Peterson, David G. "Maturity: The Goal of the Mission." In *The Gospel to the Nations: Perspectives on Paul's Mission*, edited by Peter Bolt and Mark Thompson, 185-204. Downers Grove: IVP, 2000.

Polaski, Sandra Hack. *Paul and the Discourse of Power*. Sheffield: Sheffield Academic Press, 1999.

Porter, Stanely. "Paul Confronts Caesar with the Good News." In *Empire in the New Testament*, edited by Stanley E. Porter and Cynthia Long Westfall. Eugene: Pickwick, 2011.

Porter, Stanley E. "Did Paul Have Opponents in Rome?" In *Paul and His Opponents*, edited by Stanley E. Porter. Atlanta: SBL, 2005.

Porter, Stanley E. *Paul and His Theology*. Boston: Brill, 2006.

Porter, Stanley E. "Paul's Theology of the Gospel." In *Paul as Missionary: Identity, Activity, Theology, and Practice*, edited by Trevor J. Burke and Brian S. Rosner. Edinburgh: T&T Clark, 2011.

Porter, Stanley E., and Bryan R. Dyer. "Oral Texts? A Reassessment of the Oral and Rhetorical Nature of Paul's Letters in light of Recent Studies." *JETS* 55 (2012): 323-41.

Porter, Stanley E., and Bryan R. Dyer, eds. *Paul and Ancient Rhetoric: Theory and Practice in the Hellenistic Context: Theory and Practice in the Hellenistic Context*. New York: Cambridge University Press, 2016.

Porter, Stanley E., and Christopher D. Stanley, eds. *As It Is Written: Studying Paul's Use of Scripture*. Atlanta: SBL, 2008.

Potter, David. "Old and New in Roman Foreign Affairs: The Case of 197." In *Imperialism, Cultural Politics, and Polybius*, edited by Christopher John Smith and Liv Mariah Yarrow, xiv, 351. New York: Oxford University Press, 2012.

Potter, David. "The 'Tabula Siarensis,' Tiberius, the Senate, and the Eastern Boundary of the Roman Empire." *ZPE* 69 (1987): 269-76.

Price, S. R. F. "The Place of Religion: Rome in the Early Empire." In *The Cambridge Ancient History: The Augustan Empire, 43 B.C.-A.D. 69*, edited by Alan K. Bowman, Edward Champlin, and Andrew Lintott, X, 812-47. Cambridge: Cambridge University Press, 1996.

Punt, Jeremy. "The New Testament and Empire: On the Importance of Theory." *Studia Historiae Ecclesiasticae* 37 (2011): 91-114.

Punt, Jeremy. "'Pauline Agency in Postcolonial Perspective: Subverter of or Agent for Empire?'" In *The Colonized Apostle: Paul through Postcolonial Eyes*, edited by Christopher D. Stanley, 53-61. Minneapolis: Fortress, 2011.

Quesnel, Michel. "La Figure De Moïse En Romains 9-11." *NTS* 49 (2003): 321-35.

Raaflaub, Kurt A., and Adalberto Giovannini. *Opposition Et RéSistances à L'empire D'auguste à Trajan: Neuf ExposéS Suivis De Discusssions*. Vandœuvres-Genève: Fondation Hardt, 1987.

Räisänen, Heikki. *Paul and the Law*. Vol. 29. 2nd ed. Tübingen: J. C. B. Mohr (Paul Siebeck), 1987.

Rasimus, Tuomas, Troels Engberg-Pedersen, and Ismo Dunderberg, eds. *Stoicism in Early Christianity*. Grand Rapids: Baker, 2010.

Rawson, Beryl. "Marriages, Families, Households." In *The Cambridge Companion to Ancient Rome*, edited by Paul Erdkamp, xx, 625. New York: Cambridge University Press, 2013.

Reasoner, Mark. "Romans 9–11 Moves from Margin to Center, from Rejection to Salvation: Four Grids for Recent English-Language Exegesis." In *Between Gospel and Election: Explorations in the Interpretation of Romans 9–11*, edited by Florian Wilk, J. Ross Wagner, and Frank Schleritt, 73–90. Tübingen: Mohr Siebeck, 2010.

Reasoner, Mark. *The Strong and the Weak: Romans 14.1–15.13 in Context*. New York: Cambridge University Press, 1999.

Reasoner, Mark. "The Theology of Romans 12:1–15:13." In *Pauline Theology*, edited by David M. Hay and E. Elizabeth Johnson. Minneapolis: Fortress, 1995.

Reichert, Angelika. *Der RöMerbrief Als Gratwanderung: Eine Untersuchung Zur Abfassungsproblematik*. Göttingen: Vandenhoeck & Ruprecht, 2001.

Rhyne, Thomas C. "Nomos Dikaiosynēs and the Meaning of Romans 10:4." *CBQ* 47 (1985): 486–99.

Rich, J. W. "Treaties, Allies, and the Roman Conquest of Italy." In *War and Peace in Ancient and Medieval History*, edited by Philip De Souza and John France, xi, 247. New York: Cambridge University Press, 2008.

Richardson, J. S. *Augustan Rome 44 BC to AD 14: The Restoration of the Republic and the Establishment of the Empire*. Edinburgh: Edinburgh University Press, 2012.

Richardson, Lawrence. *A New Topographical Dictionary of Ancient Rome*. Baltimore: Johns Hopkins University Press, 1992.

Ridley, Ronald T. "The Historian's Silences: What Livy Did Not Know—or Chose Not to Tell." *JAH* 1 (2013): 27–52.

Riggsby, Andrew. "Rhetoric." In *The Oxford Handbook of Roman Studies*, edited by Alessandro Barchiesi and Walter Scheidel. New York: Oxford University Press, 2010.

Robinson, O. F. *The Sources of Roman Law: Problems and Methods for Ancient Historians*. New York: Routledge, 1997.

Röhser, Günter. "Paulus Und Die Herrschaft Der Sünde." *ZNW* 103 (2012): 84–110.

Roller, Matthew. "On the Intersignification of Monuments in Augustan Rome." *AJP* 134 (2013): 119–31.

Rosner, Brian S. *Paul and the Law: Keeping the Commandments of God*. Downers Grove: IVP, 2013.

Rosner, Brian S. *Paul, Scripture, and Ethics: A Study of 1 Corinthians 5–7*. Grand Rapids: Baker, 1999.

Rowe, Greg. *Princes and Political Cultures: The New Tiberian Senatorial Decrees*. Ann Arbor: University of Michigan Press, 2002.

Rudich, Vasily. *Dissidence and Literature under Nero: The Price of Rhetoricization*. New York: Routledge, 1997.

Rudich, Vasily. *Political Dissidence under Nero: The Price of Dissimulation*. New York: Routledge, 1993.

Ruiz, Jean-Pierre. "Of Walls and Words: Twenty-First Century Empire and New Testament Studies." *USQR* 59 (2005): 122–30.

Rutgers, Leonard Victor. "Roman Policy towards the Jews: Expulsions from the City of Rome during the First Century C.E." In *Judaism and Christianity in First-Century Rome*, edited by Karl P. Donfried and Peter Richardson. Grand Rapids: Eerdmans, 1998.

Sabin, Philip A. G., Hans van Wees, and Michael Whitby, eds. *The Cambridge History of Greek and Roman Warfare: Greece, the Hellenistic World, and the Rise of Rome*. New York: Cambridge University Press, 2007.
Said, Edward W. *Beginnings: Intention and Method*. New York: Columbia University Press, 1985.
Said, Edward W. *Orientalism*. 1st ed. New York: Pantheon Books, 1978.
Sanday, William, and Arthur C. Headlam. *The Epistle to the Romans*. Edinburgh: T&T Clark, 1902.
Sanders, E. P. *Paul and Palestinian Judaism*. Minneapolis: Fortress, 1977.
Sanders, E. P. *Paul, the Law, and the Jewish People*. Philadelphia: Fortress, 1983.
Sandmel, Samuel. "Parallelomania." *JBL* 1962 (1962): 1–13.
Sandnes, Karl Olav. *Paul, One of the Prophets?: A Contribution to the Apostle's Self-Understanding*. Tübingen: J. C. B. Mohr (Paul Siebeck), 1991.
Schellenberg, Ryan S. "Does Paul Call Adam a 'Type' of Christ? An Exegetical Note on Romans 5, 14." *ZNW* 105 (2014): 54–63.
Schleritt, Frank. "Das Gesetz Der Gerechtigkeit. Zur Auslegung Von Römer 9,30-33." In *Between Gospel and Election: Explorations in the Interpretation of Romans 9–11*, edited by Florian Wilk, J. Ross Wagner, and Frank Schleritt, 271–98. Tübingen: Mohr Siebeck, 2010.
Schnelle, Udo. *The Letter to the Romans*. Leuven: Peeters, 2009.
Schofield, Malcolm. "Aristotle: An Introduction." In *The Cambridge History of Greek and Roman Political Thought*, edited by Christopher Rowe and Malcolm Schofield. New York: Cambridge University Press, 2006.
Schreiner, Thomas R. *The Law and Its Fulfillment: A Pauline Theology of Law*. Grand Rapids: Baker, 1993.
Schreiner, Thomas R. *Romans*. Grand Rapids: Baker, 1998.
Schröter, Jens. "Der Heilstod Jesu—Deutungen Im Neuen Testament." *Luther* 84 (2013): 139–58.
Schumacher, Leonhard. "Slaves in Roman Society." In *The Oxford Handbook of Social Relations in the Roman World*, edited by Michael Peachin, 589–608. New York: Oxford University Press, 2011.
Schumacher, Thomas. "Der Begriff [Pistis] Im Paulinischen Sprachgebrauch: Beobachtungen Zum VerhäLtnis Von Christlicher Und Profangriechischer Semantik." In *The Letter to the Romans*, edited by Udo Schnelle, 487–502. Leuven: Peeters, 2009.
Schweitzer, Albert. *The Mysticism of Paul the Apostle*. Baltimore: Johns Hopkins University Press, 1998.
Schwindt, Rainer. "Mehr Wurzel Als Stamm Und Krone: Zur Bildrede Vom Ölbaum in Röm 11,16-24." *Bib* 88 (2007): 64–91.
Scott, James C. *Domination and the Arts of Resistance: Hidden Transcripts*. New Haven: Yale University Press, 1990.
Scott, James M. *Paul and the Nations: The Old Testament and Jewish Background of Paul's Mission to the Nations with Special Reference to the Destination of Galatians*. Tübingen: J. C. B. Mohr (Paul Siebeck), 1995.
Segalla, G. "L' 'Obbedienza Di Fede' (Rm 1,5; 16,26) Tema Della Lettera Ai Romani?" *Rivista Biblica* 36 (1988): 329–42.
Sherwin-White, A. N. *Roman Society and Roman Law in the New Testament*. Oxford: Clarendon, 1963.

Shotter, David. *Nero*. New York: Routledge, 1997.
Smallwood, E. Mary. *Documents Illustrating the Principates of Gaius, Claudius and Nero*. London: Cambridge University Press, 1967.
Smith, R. R. R. "Simulacra Gentium: The Ethne from the Sebasteion at Aphrodisias." *JRS* 78 (1988): 50–77.
Snodgrass, Klyne R. "Justification by Grace—to the Doers: An Analysis of the Place of Romans 2 in the Theology of Paul." *NTS* 32, no. 1 (1986): 72–93.
Söding, Thomas. "Verheißung Und Erfülling Im Lichte Paulinischer Theologie." *NTS* 48 (2001): 146–70.
Stambaugh, John E., and David L. Balch. *The New Testament in Its Social Environment*. Edited by Wayne A. Meeks. Philadelphia: Westminster, 1986.
Stanley, Christopher D. *Arguing with Scripture: The Rhetoric of Quotations in the Letters of Paul*. New York: T&T International, 2004.
Stanley, Christopher D. *The Colonized Apostle: Paul through Postcolonial Eyes*. Minneapolis: Fortress, 2011.
Stanley, Christopher D. *Paul and the Language of Scripture: Citation Technique in the Pauline Epistles and Contemporary Literature*. Cambridge: Cambridge University Press, 1992.
Staples, Jason A. "What Do the Gentiles Have to Do with 'All Israel'? A Fresh Look at Romans 11:25-27." *JBL* 130 (2011): 371–90.
Starling, David I. *Not My People: Gentiles as Exiles in Pauline Hermeneutics*. Berlin: De Gruyter, 2011.
Steel, Catherine. "Divisions of Speech." In *The Cambridge Companion to Ancient Rhetoric*, edited by Erik Gunderson, 77–91. New York: Cambridge University Press, 2009.
Steel, Catherine. *The End of the Roman Republic, 146 to 444 BC: Conquest and Crisis*. Edinburgh: Edinburgh University Press, 2013.
Steel, C. E. W., ed. *The Cambridge Companion to Cicero*. New York: Cambridge University Press, 2013.
Steel, C. E. W. *Cicero, Rhetoric, and Empire*. New York: Oxford University Press, 2001.
Stegemann, Ekkehard W. "'Set Apart for the Gospel' (Rom 1:1): Paul's Self-Introduction in the Letter to the Romans. Different Readings of Romans." In *Celebrating Paul: Festschrift in Honor of Jerome Murphy-O'connor, O.P., and Joseph A. Fitzmyer, S.J.*, edited by Peter Spitaler, 189–209. Washington, DC: Catholic Biblical Association of America, 2011.
Stendahl, Krister. "The Apostle Paul and the Introspective Conscience of the West." *HTR* 56 (1963): 199–215.
Stendahl, Krister. *Paul among Jews and Gentiles: And Other Essays*. Minneapolis: Fortress, 1976.
Stenschke, Christoph. "Römer 9–11 Als Teil Des Römerbriefs." In *Between Gospel and Election: Explorations in the Interpretation of Romans 9–11*, edited by Florian Wilk, J. Ross Wagner, and Frank Schleritt, 197–226. Tübingen: Mohr Siebeck, 2010.
Stenschke, Christoph. "Your Obedience Is Known to All (Rom 16:19): Paul's References to Other Christians and Their Function in Paul's Letter to the Romans." *NovT* 57 (2015): 251–74.
Stowers, Stanley K. *A Rereading of Romans: Justice, Jews, and Gentiles*. New Haven: Yale University Press, 1997.
Strabo, and Duane W. Roller. *The Geography of Strabo*. New York: Cambridge University Press, 2014.

Stuhlmacher, Peter. *Paul's Letter to the Romans: A Commentary.* Translated by S. J. Hafemann. Louisville: Westminster John Knox, 1994.
Sumney, Jerry L. *Reading Paul's Letter to the Romans.* Atlanta: SBL, 2012.
Talbert, Charles H. *Romans.* Macon: Smyth & Helwys, 2002.
Talbott, Rick F. *Jesus, Paul, and Power: Rhetoric, Ritual, and Metaphor in Ancient Mediterranean Christianity.* Eugene: Cascade, 2010.
Tan, Andrew Kimseng. *The Rhetoric of Abraham's Faith in Romans 4.* Atlanta: SBL, 2018.
Taubes, Jacob. *The Political Theology of Paul.* Translated by Dana Hollander. Stanford: Stanford University Press, 2004.
Taussig, Hal. "Prologue: A Door Thrown Open." *USQR* 59 (2005): 1–5.
Theobald, Michael. *Der Römerbrief.* Vol. 1. Stuttgart: Katholisches Bibelwerk, 1992.
Theobald, Michael. *Studien Zum RöMerbrief Wissenschaftliche Untersuchungen Zum Neuen Testament.* Tübingen: Mohr Siebeck, 2001.
Thielman, Frank. *Paul & the Law: A Contextual Approach.* Downers Grove: IVP, 1995.
Thiessen, Jacob. "Paulinische Versus Jüdische Und Hellenistische Anthropologie? Zur Frage Nach Dem Verständnis Von Römer 7,7-25." *EuroJTh* 21 (2012): 17–34.
Thiessen, Matthew. *Paul and the Gentile Problem.* New York: Oxford University Press, 2016.
Thompson, James W. *Moral Formation According to Paul: The Context and Coherence of Pauline Ethics.* Grand Rapids: Baker, 2011.
Thompson, Michael. *Clothed with Christ: The Example and Teaching of Jesus in Romans 12:1–15:13.* Eugene: Wipf & Stock, 2011.
Thornton, John. "Polybius in Context: The Political Dimension of the *Histories*." In *Polybius and His World: Essays in Memory of F. W. Walbank*, edited by Bruce Gibson and Thomas Harrison, 496. New York: Oxford University Press, 2013.
Thorsteinsson, Runar M. "Paul's Interlocutor in Romans 2: Function and Identity in the Context of Ancient Epistolography." Originally presented as thesis (doctoral), Almqvist & Wiksell International, Lund University, 2003.
Thorsteinsson, Runar M. *Roman Christianity and Roman Stoicism.* New York: Oxford University Press, 2010.
Thorsteinsson, Runar M. "Stoicism as a Key to Pauline Ethics in Romans." In *Stoicism in Early Christianity*, edited by Tuomas Rasimus, Troels Engberg-Pedersen, and Ismo Dunderberg. Grand Rapids: Baker, 2010.
Thurén, Lauri. *Derhetorizing Paul: A Dynamic Perspective on Pauline Theology and the Law.* Vol. 124 Wunt. Tübingen: Mohr Siebeck, 2000.
Tobin, Thomas H. *Paul's Rhetoric in Its Contexts: The Argument of Romans.* Grand Rapids: Baker, 2005.
Toit, A. B. Du. "Faith and Obedience in Paul." *Neot* 25 (1991): 65–74.
Toit, A. B. Du. "Persuasion in Romans 1:1-17." *BZ* 33 (1989): 192–209.
Towner, Philip P. "Romans 13:1-7 and Paul's Missiological Perspective." In *Romans and the People of God: Essays in Honor of Gordon D. Fee on the Occasion of His 65th Birthday*, edited by Sven K. Soderlund and N. T. Wright. Grand Rapids: Eerdmans, 1999.
Tränkle, H. "Livy and Polybius." In *Oxford Readings in Classical Studies: Livy*, edited by Jane D. Chaplin and Christina Shuttleworth Kraus. New York: Oxford University Press, 2009.
Trapp, Michael. *Philosophy in the Roman Empire: Ethics, Politics, and Society.* Burlington: Ashgate, 2007.

Tuckett, Christopher M. "Paul, Scripture and Ethics. Some Reflections." *JSOT* 46 (2000): 403–24.
Ulrichs, Karl Friedrich. *Christusglaube: Studien Zum Syntagma Pistis Christou Und Zum Paulinischen Verständnis Von Glaube Und Rechtfertigung*. Tübingen: Mohr Siebeck, 2007.
Vanhoye, Albert. *L'apôTre Paul: Personnalité, Style Et Conception Du MinistèRe*. Bibliotheca Ephemeridum Theologicarum Lovaniensium. Leuven: Leuven University Press, 1986.
Viard, Jean-Sébastien. "Obéissance Ou Liberté? Redécouverte Structurelle De Rm 6,15-23." *ScEs* 54 (2002): 351–66.
W., Jackson. *Reading Romans with Eastern Eyes: Honor and Shame in Paul's Message and Mission*. Downers Grove: IVP, 2019.
Waetjen, Hermen C. *The Letter to the Romans: Salvation as Justice and the Deconstruction of the Law*. Sheffield: Sheffield Academic, 2011.
Wagner, J. Ross. *Heralds of the Good News: Isaiah and Paul "in Concert" in the Letter to the Romans*. Boston: Brill, 2002.
Wagner, J. Ross. "'Not from Jews Only, but Also from the Gentiles': Mercy to the Nations in Romans 9–11." In *Between Gospel and Election: Explorations in the Interpretation of Romans 9–11*, edited by Florian Wilk, J. Ross Wagner, and Frank Schleritt, 417–31. Tübingen: Mohr Siebeck, 2010.
Walbank, F. W. *Polybius*. Berkeley: University of California Press, 1972.
Wallace, Daniel B. *Greek Grammar: Beyond the Basics*. Grand Rapids: Zondervan, 1996.
Wallace, David R. *The Gospel of God: Romans as Paul's Aeneid*. Eugene: Pickwick, 2008.
Wallace-Hadrill, Andrew. "*Mutatas Formas:* The Augustan Transformation of Roman Knowledge." In *The Cambridge Companion to the Age of Augustus*, edited by Karl Galinsky, 55–84. New York: Cambridge University Press, 2005.
Wasserman, Emma. "The Death of the Soul in Romans 7: Revisiting Paul's Anthropology in Light of Hellenistic Moral Psychology." *JBL* 126 (2007): 793–816.
Wasserman, Emma. *The Death of the Soul in Romans 7: Sin, Death, and the Law in Light of Hellenistic Moral Psychology*. Tübingen: Mohr Siebeck, 2008.
Watson, Duane F. *The Rhetoric of the New Testament*. Blandford Forum: Deo, 2006.
Watson, Francis. *Paul, Judaism, and the Gentiles: A Sociological Approach*. New York: Cambridge University Press, 1986.
Watson, Francis. *Paul, Judaism, and the Gentiles: Beyond the New Perspective*. Grand Rapids: Eerdmans, 2007.
Wedderburn, A. J. M. *The Reasons for Romans*. Edinburgh: T&T Clark, 1988.
Wilk, Florian. "Rahmen Und Aufbau Von Römer 9–11." In *Between Gospel and Election: Explorations in the Interpretation of Romans 9–11*, edited by Florian Wilk, J. Ross Wagner, and Frank Schleritt, 73–90. Tübingen: Mohr Siebeck, 2010.
Wilk, Florian, J. Ross Wagner, and Frank Schleritt. *Between Gospel and Election: Explorations in the Interpretation of Romans 9–11*. Tübingen: Mohr Siebeck, 2010.
Wilson, Walter T. *Love without Pretense: Romans 12.9-21 and Hellenistic-Jewish Wisdom Literature*. Tübingen: J. C. B. Mohr, 1991.
Winger, Michael. *By What Law? The Meaning of Νόμος in the Letters of Paul*. SBL Diss. Atlanta: Scholars Press, 1991.
Winger, Michael. "Meaning and Law." *JBL* 117 (1998): 105–10.
Wink, Walter. *Naming the Powers: The Language of Power in the New Testament*. Philadelphia: Fortress, 1984.

Winter, Bruce W. "The Public Honouring of Christian Benefactors: Romans 13:3-4 and 1 Peter 2:14-15." *JSNT* 34, no. 1 (1988): 87–103.
Wischmeyer, Oda. "Römer 2.1-24 Als Teil Der Gerichtsrede Des Paulus Gegen Die Menschheit." *NTS* 52 (2006): 356–76.
Witherington, Ben. *The Indelible Image: The Theological and Ethical Thought World of the New Testament*. 2 vols. Downers Grove: IVP, 2009.
Witherington, Ben. *New Testament Rhetoric*. Eugene: Cascade, 2009.
Witherington, Ben. "Not So Idle Thoughts about Eidoluthuton." *TynB* 44 (1993): 237–54.
Witherington, Ben. *Paul's Letter to the Romans: A Socio-Rhetorical Commentary*. Grand Rapids: Eerdmans, 2004.
Witherington, Ben. *Paul's Narrative Thought World: The Tapestry of Tragedy and Triumph*. 1st ed. Louisville: Westminster John Knox, 1994.
Witherington, Ben, and Jason A. Myers. *Voices and Views on Paul: Exploring Scholarly Trends*. Downers Grove: IVP, 2020.
Wolter, Michael. "Apokalyptik Als Redeform Im Neuen Testament." *NTS* 51 (2005): 171–91.
Woolf, Greg. *Becoming Roman: The Origins of Provincial Civilization in Gaul*. New York: Cambridge University Press, 1998.
Woyke, Johannes. "'Einst' Und 'Jetzt' in Röm 1-3? Zur Bedeutung Von Nyni De in Röm 3,21." *ZNW* 92 (2001): 185–206.
Wright, N. T. *The Climax of the Covenant: Christ and the Law in Pauline Theology*. Philadelphia: Fortress, 1991.
Wright, N. T. "The Law in Romans 2." In *Paul and the Mosaic Law*, edited by James D. G. Dunn, 131–50. Grand Rapids: Eerdmans, 2001.
Wright, N. T. "The Messiah and the People of God: A Study in Pauline Theology with Particular Reference to the Argument of the Epistle to the Romans." PhD dissertation, Oxford University, 1980.
Wright, N. T. *Justification: God's Plan & Paul's Vision*. Downers Grove: IVP, 2009.
Wright, N. T. *The New Testament and the People of God*. Minneapolis: Fortress, 1992.
Wright, N. T. *Paul: In Fresh Perspective*. Minneapolis: Fortress, 2005.
Wright, N. T. *Paul and the Faithfulness of God*. 2 vols. Minneapolis: Fortress, 2013.
Wright, N. T. "Paul's Gospel and Caesar's Empire." In *Paul and Politics: Ekklesia, Israel, Imperium, Interpretation*, edited by Richard A. Horsley, 160–83. Harrisburg: Trinity Press International, 2000.
Wright, N. T. "Romans." In *The New Interpreter's Bible*, 754. Nashville: Abingdon, 2002.
Wright, N. T. "Romans and the Theology of Paul." In *Pauline Theology*, edited by David M. Hay and E. Elizabeth Johnson, 3, 30–67. Minneapolis: Fortress, 1995.
Wright, N. T. *What Saint Paul Really Said: Was Paul of Tarsus the Real Founder of Christianity?* Grand Rapids: Eerdmans, 1997.
Wuellner, Wilhelm. "Paul's Rhetoric of Argumentation in Romans: An Alternative to the Donfried-Karris Debate over Romans." In *The Romans Debate: Revised and Expanded Edition*, edited by Karl P. Donfried, 75–99. Peabody: Hendrickson, 1991.
Yarrow, Liv Mariah. "Book Review (Review of Polybius: The Histories Books 28–39. Translated by W. R. Paton. Revised by F. W. Walbank and Christian Habicht)." *Histos* 7 (2013): 1–5.
Yeung, Maureen W. *Faith in Jesus and Paul: A Comparison with Special Reference to "Faith That Can Remove Mountains" and "Your Faith Has Healed/Saved You"*. Wissenschaftliche Untersuchungen Zum Neuen Testament 2 Reihe. Tübingen: Mohr Siebeck, 2002.

Yinger, Kent L. *Paul, Judaism, and Judgment According to Deeds*. Sheffield: JSOT Press, 2007.
Yinger, Kent L. "Romans 12:14-21 and Nonretaliation in Second Temple Judaism: Addressing Persecution within the Community." *CBQ* 60 (1998): 74–96.
Young, Stephen L. "Romans 1.1-5 and Paul's Christological Use of Hab. 2.4 in Rom. 1.17: An Underutilized Consideration in the Debate." *JSNT* 34 (2012): 277–85.
Zanker, Paul. *The Power of Images in the Age of Augustus*. Translated by Alan Shapiro. Ann Arbor: University of Michigan Press, 1988.
Zeller, Dieiter. "Pauline Paraenesis in Romans 12 and Greek Gnomic Wisdom." In *Greco-Roman Culture and the New Testament: Studies Commemorating the Centennial of the Pontifical Biblical Institute*, edited by Frederick E. Brenk and David Aune, 73–86. Leiden: Brill, 2012.
Ziesler, J. A. *Paul's Letter to the Romans*. Philadelphia: Trinity International, 1989.
Zoccali, Christopher. "'And So All Israel Will Be Saved': Competing Interpretations of Romans 11.26 in Pauline Scholarship." *JSNT* 30 (2008): 289–318.

Subject Index

(Note: Modern authors and Biblical entries at the end.)

Abraham 136, 139–42, 160, 164, 192
Achaeans 31–2
Adam 7, 75, 94–5, 151, 151 n.92,
    183–4, 186
  descendants 160
  disobedience 145, 154
  epoch of 170
  Paul's discussion of 136, 146–7, 153–4,
    156, 172
  synkrisis 130, 145, 192
Aemilianus, Scipio 32
Aeneid (Virgil) 2–3, 5 n.17
Aequinians 65
Aetolians 37–8, 38 n.23, 133, 148–9
Agesilaus 91
Agrippina/Agrippa 50 n.57, 76, 77 n.35,
    110 n.25, 177
Alexander the Great 25, 32 n.6, 59
anti-imperial
  empire criticism 20, 21, 27
  hidden transcripts 26–7, 78
  investigations of New Testament 23
  movement 27 n.62
  Paul's call for obedience 121, 176
  readings 19–21, 26, 176 n.219
  resistance literature 175
anti-Jewish
  polemic 132 n.15
  sentiment 16
Antony 47, 49
Apollo 23
Apostle. *See* Paul (the Apostle)
Ara Pacis/Ara Pacis Augustae 105, 111,
    113–14, 149, 157
Archelaus 59
Archidamus 91
Arch of Cottius 106 n.11
Aristotle 178
  describing δικαίωμα 155

epilogos and *exordium* 119
frustration at inability of persons 153
Nicomachean Ethics 155 n.15
obedience in 84–7, 87 n.11
Rhetoric to Alexander 87
Atilius, Aulus 68
Atrebatians 49 n.56
Atreus 27
audience 117, 119
  Gentiles 10, 17–19, 55, 57, 115, 121, 133,
    139, 141–2, 144–5, 147,
    150, 163, 167, 169–70, 173,
    178, 181
  non-Jewish, familiarity with concept of
    obedience 2
  of Paul 5, 12 n.50, 13, 25, 30, 38, 42, 57,
    100, 102, 115, 129, 131, 139, 142–3,
    147–51, 158, 167, 173, 178, 180–1,
    183, 187, 195
  of Romans 17–19, 36, 64, 72, 83, 88–9,
    93, 96, 111, 114, 116, 121, 144, 146,
    149, 153, 183
Augustan Empire 22
Augustus 24–6, 46, 52 n.63, 54, 104–6, 108
  ability to lead 73
  death 71–2
  marriage laws 57
  Res Gestae 25, 50
  speech of 50–1
Augustus, Tiberius Caesar 108–9
Aviola, Silius 78 n.39

Blaesus, Junius 72
Boiocalus 75
Boudica 56
Britannia 56–8, 75–6, 163

Caesar, Caius 49, 74, 76
Caesar, Gaius 107

Caesar, Julius 21, 24, 26, 47, 47 n.52, 61, 73, 142
  death of 49
  usage of metaphors by 48
Caesar, Lucius 107
Campanians 64–5
Campus Martius 103–4, 106, 121, 175, 183
  obedience in the 110–14
Carthage/Carthaginians 39 n.27–8, 67
  destruction of 32
  Romans treaty with 38
  Third Punic War between Rome and 38–9, 39 n.28
Cato, Marcus 76
Cerilias 80
Christian Gentiles 1, 14, 124, 161, 169, 186, 195
Christianity 21, 50 n.57
  anti-imperial readings of the NT 31
  Early Christian discourse 11
  Paul's theological scope and aim for his congregation(s) 3
  pre-Christian literature 4
Cicero 24–5, 94–9, 117, 178
  De Legibus 95
  De Republica 94, 111
  Tusculan Disputations 96, 135
civic peace 37
Claudius, Gaius 16, 23–4, 23 n.42, 44
Claudius, Tiberius 54–5, 54 n.68, 55 n.69, 56, 69 n.13
common approaches 3
Connolly, Serena 108
Corcyreans 36
Cossutianus, Capito 76
Cranfield, C. E. B. 157 n.123, 158, 161
Crassus 46, 66, 69
Cyzicus 23

digression 34–6
Dio, Cassius 27, 47 n.52, 49 n.56, 50 n.58, 52 n.63
  about Mamercus Scaurus 27
  on barbarians 53–4
  on obedience 46–58
  record of conquering of Britannia 163
  subversive intentions 51
  on war between Rome and Britannia 56

Dionysius of Halicarnassus 40–6, 41 n.33, 131, 135, 179–80
Discourses 87, 90
disobedience 13 n.54, 122. *See also* obedience
  gentile 130–1
  Israel 160–1, 167–71
  of Jew and Gentile 131–4
  Jewish 134–6
  obedience and 51, 151–3
dissension 43, 72
  and disloyalty of legions 73
  and disobedience 47
  internal 44
  and offenses 127
  suppression of 79
Domitian 70, 83
doxology 126 n.38, 127, 127 n.46
duress 34–5, 42, 64, 67, 80

Eclogue (Siculus) 76
Epaphroditus 83
Ephesus 23–4
Ephizephyrian Locri 67
Epictetus 83–4, 87–90, 100–2, 148, 151, 178–9, 180, 194
Epizephyrian Locri 35
exordium 15–16, 117–19
  obedience 120–4

faith of the Romans 35, 36–9, 40, 61, 68, 106, 122, 143
fetiales 41 n.33
Fidenates 42–3
First Punic War 41
friendships *(amicitia)* 34–5, 64, 105

Gaius Arch 107
Galba 70, 77–8
Gallio 101
Gentiles/*Gentiles* 6, 12, 14, 20, 43, 57, 112, 125, 139–42
  audience 10, 17–19, 55, 57, 115, 121, 133, 139, 141–2, 144–5, 147, 150, 163, 167, 169–70, 173, 178, 181
  Christians 1, 14, 124, 161, 169, 186, 195
  disobedience 130–1
  Jews relations with 20, 136–9, 151

reading 2
salvation of 3 n.8
Germanicus 54 n.68, 71, 113 n.48
   death of 55
   oath of allegiance 72
   speech 73
grace and faith 143–7
Greco-Roman 1–2, 3, 4, 9–10, 11, 13, 14, 25, 29–31, 47, 64, 95, 120, 122, 142, 148, 156, 159, 173–4, 191, 194, 195

Homer 93
Horace 25
Hordeonius 79
Horologium Augusti 105, 113

imperial cult 21–6
imperialism, Roman 16
imperial theology 23
Israel
   disobedience 160–1, 167–71, 193
   and the Gentiles 162
   ignorance of the righteousness 163
   opportunity 127
   Paul's description of God's mercy 54
   pursuit of righteousness 186
   righteous standards 164
   in Rom. 10:16 123
   story of disobedience 159, 160–1
   unfaithfulness 137, 158–9

Jesus Christ 3, 5, 10, 13–14, 147, 154
   Christians allowed to show obedience to 75
   faithfulness 184
   faith not linked in Greco-Roman literature 10
   gospels of 21, 176
   Paul's call for obedience 59, 162, 181, 183, 192
   Paul's discussion of Adam and 136, 145–6, 157
Jewish/Jews 6 n.18, 10, 110, 134
   Christians 17, 124, 127, 172 n.202, 186
   disobedience 134–6
   Judaism 10
   relations with Gentiles 20, 136–9, 151, 191–2

King Ptolemy II 173 n.207
King Theopompus 60
kyriarchical family 10
Kyrios language 8 n.28

Lacedaemonians 59–60, 91
Larcius, Titus 44
Lex Iulia de maritandis ordinibus 52
Ligurians 68, 68 n.10
Livia 24, 52 n.63
Livy 122
   Books from the Foundation of the City 63–4
   on obedience 63–70
Lower Rhine 72–3
Lucius 107, 109 n.21
Lycia 69 n.13
Lycurgus 59, 91

Macedonians 31, 41, 59, 180
marriage law 57, 151 n.92
Maximus, Pontifex 114
Metaphysics 86
Mithridates (King of Pontus) 46–7

Nero 70–1, 75–7, 77 n.35, 83, 92, 99, 112, 115, 177–85
New Testament (NT) 21, 34
   anti-imperial readings of 21
   critique of empire 24
   and the Roman Empire 19, 25
Numidians 67

oath of allegiance *(iuravere)* 71–2, 76, 78, 109, 109 n.24
obedience 1, 8–11. *See also* Paul (the Apostle)
   in Campus Martius 110–14
   defined 45
   and disobedience 51, 151–3
   failure to exercise 161–7
   familiarity of non-Jewish audience with 2
   by grace 153–8
   in inscriptions and monuments 106–7
   language 33 n.9
obedience, philosophizing on 83–102
   in Aristotle 84–7
   in Cicero 94–9

in Epictetus 87–90
philosophical reflections on 101–2
in Plutarch 90–4
in Seneca the Younger 99–101
obedience, sculpting 103–14
   in the Campus Martius 110–14
   in inscriptions and monuments 106–7
   oath to the emperor 108–10
   Pisan decrees of 2 and 4 CE 107–8
   Res Gestae Divi Augusti (RG) 104–6
   Roman audience 114
obedience in argumentation 129–90
   Abraham 139–42
   disobedience of Jew and Gentile 131–4
   failure to exercise obedience 161–7
   gentile disobedience 130–1
   Gentiles 139–42
   grace and faith 143–7
   Israel's disobedience 160–1, 167–71
   Jew and Gentile 136–9
   Jewish disobedience 134–6
   Nero 177–85
   obedience and disobedience 151–3
   obedience by grace 153–8
   obedience of faith 172–6, 185–90
   power of the spirit 153–8
   propositio in 1:16-17 129–30
   Rom. 9:1–11:36 158–9
   Rom. 12:1-15:13 171
   sin and death 143–51
obedience in Greek literature 29–61
   Cassius Dio on 46–58
   Dionysius of Halicarnassus 40–6
   foundations of 31–9
   perspectives on 45–6, 60–1
   Polybius 31–40
   rhetoric of 40–5
   Strabo's *Geography* 58–60
   theme of 57–8
obedience in Latin literature 63–81
   in aftermath of chaos 70–80
   foundations of 63–9
   The Histories 77–80
   importance of 70
   perspectives on 81
   reflections in Tacitus 80–1
obedience of faith 1 6, 8, 9 n.34, 10, 172–6, 173 n.206, 185–90

Octavian 40
Old Testament 17, 138, 144, 159, 189

pacification 37, 51, 143
Paetus, Thrasea 75, 76
Paradox Stoicorum 97
parallelomania 21, 21 n.30, 81
Pauline/Paulinus 56–7
   anti-imperial readings of 20
   conception of obedience in Romans 144
   creation 9
   ethics 4
   evidence 12
   mission 182
   scholarship 5
   theology 4
   unrighteousness 91
   vocation 132 n.16
Pax Romana 36, 143–4, 175, 192
peroration/peroratio 15–16, 119–20
   obedience 124–7
Perseus 68–70
Persia 41, 61, 180
Persis (16:12) 18, 147
Philip of Macedon 68, 145
   relationship with Rome 36
Philus 111
Phraates 74
Pisan decrees of 2 and 4 CE 107–8
Piso, Cnaeus Calpurnius 73
pistis (fides) 9, 35, 38 n.25, 104 n.3, 123, 165, 186 n.272, 195
pistis Christou 9
Plato 92, 152, 152 n.57
   Republic 94
plebeians 43–4
Pliny 106
Plutarch 59–60, 90–4
Polybius 3, 31–40, 32 n.6, 32 n.7, 36, 38 n.25, 39, 39 n.27, 70, 77–80, 122
Pompey the Great 25, 46, 46 n.48, 47
   installation of Archelaus 59
Popilius, Marcus 67–8, 68 n.10
Portico of Nations 121
power of the spirit 153–8
Praetorian Guard 56
pragmatism 66

priestly/cultic setting of sacrifice 174
propositio in 1:16-17 129–30

Quinquennium 88
quinquennium Neronis 92, 177

Rectus, Lucius Aemilius 110
Res Gestae (Augustus) 25, 50
Res Gestae Divi Augusti (RG) 104–6
rhetoric 15–16, 116, 128
   anti-imperial readings 19–21
   empire criticism 21
   hidden transcripts 26–7
   imperial cult 21–6
   of obedience in Greek literature 40–5
   reading Romans against Rome
      19–21
   reading Romans as a Roman 17–19
   Romans 117, 118
   at Rome 16
Rhetorica Ad Herennium 117
Rhodians 69–70
Roman Antiquities (RA) 41–2, 180
Roman Christians 94, 172
Roman Empire 1, 3, 5, 11, 19, 20, 25,
      29, 32, 34, 40, 41, 55, 56, 63, 77,
      83, 90, 95, 99, 101, 104, 105–7,
      110, 123, 150, 176, 180, 181,
      193, 194
Romans/Rome 54, 141
   attack and defeat of Carthage 39 n.28
   audience 114
   citizens 44
   communities 16, 18
   conditions for obedience 45
   congregation(s) 19
   disobedience 44, 57
   enemies 44
   faith 36–9, 38 n.24
   Gentile Christians in 14
   house churches in 17
   immigration 61
   imperialism 16
   internal conflicts 43
   obedient territories 44
   origin to 9 BCE 63
   physical transformation 46
   relationship with Philip of
      Macedon 36
   rhetorical situation at 16
   theology 4
   treaty with Carthaginians 38
   war between Britannia and 56
Romulus 42, 74 n.30
Rufus, Musonius 83

Samnite Wars 45, 64
Scaurus, Mamercus Aemilius 27
Scipio, Cornelius 32 n.6, 67
Second Punic War 67
Seneca the Younger 99–101, 178
   Apocolocyntosis 55
   De Clementia 99
   De Vita Beata 101
Siagu 78 n.39
Siculus, Calpurnius 76
sin and death 143–51
Society for Ancient Mediterranean
      Religions 23
Spain 2, 16, 49, 105, 113, 125, 141
Sparta 60, 91–2
Spurinna, Vestricius 79
Strabo 58–60, 59 n.78
strife
   civil 71
   eradication of 50 n.57
Sulla 61, 109 n.21
surrender *(deditio)* 35 n.16, 39 n.28, 56,
      107, 114, 149
   Campanians 65
   defined 34 n.12
   digression on 34–6
   duress 64, 67
   obedience of 68
   treaty with Rome 37
   unconditional 42

Tabula Siarensis 55 n.71
Tacitus 80–1, 174, 177
   The Annals 70, 77 n.35
   on obedience 70–81
Theater of Pompey 111–12
Third Punic War 38, 39 n.28
Tiberius 58, 70, 74, 109
Timarchus, Claudius 75
Tiridates 74–5
Trajan 47 n.53
Tyrrhenians 44

Varus, Quintilius 53–4
Veientes 42
Veno 66
Venus Victrix (Victory) 112
Victoria 157, 175
Virgil 25, 99 n.55
   Aeneid 2–3, 5 n.17

Vitellius, Lucius 74, 79
Volscians 43, 65–6

Zanker, Paul 113
Zeus 23–4, 108, 159

Index of Modern Authors

Barclay, John 5 n.16, 12, 176 n.219, 186, 186 n.272
Baronowski, Donald 32 n.6, 39 n.28
Barrett, C. K. 6 n.19, 147, 153 n.102, 171 n.99
Barth, Karl 16, 168 n.185
Bates, Matthew 12
Beard, Mary 23, 112
Bersot, Jonathan 143 n.58
Billows, Richard 35
Bjerkelund, Carl 173 n.207
Bryan, Christopher 180
Burton, Paul J. 34, 34 n.12

Cohick, Lynn H. 24

Donaldson, Terence L. 4 n.9
Donfried, Karl P. 2 n.3, 15 n.2, 15 n.5, 17 n.13, 116 n.4
Dunn, James D. G. 125, 135, 147, 147 n.76, 170, 172 n.200, 186
Dyson, Stephen 112

Eastman, Susan 152
Elliott, Neil 2 n.4, 152, 159, 180 n.238
Engberg-Pedersen, Troels 84 n.3, 178
Esler, Phillip F. 172 n.202

Fitzmyer, Joseph A. 138

Galinsky, Karl 23, 24, 25, 51, 104, 113
Gamble, Harry Y. 126, 126 n.38
Garlington, Don 4, 9, 9 n.32, 9 n.34, 10, 145
Gathercole, Simon 132 n.15, 134
Gaventa, Beverly Roberts 12 n.50, 161 n.144
Georgi, Dieter 21 n.30
Glabrio, Manius Acilius 37–8
Gorman, Michael J. 4–5, 149
Gupta, Nijay 12

Hanes, Holly 77
Harrison, James 114
Holdsworth, Ben 18
Horsley, Richard 20–1
Howard, George 164
Hurtado, Larry 3 n.8

Jewett, Robert 7, 7 n.22, 131, 144
Jipp, Joshua 4 n.8, 132 n.16
Johnson, Timothy 141, 181

Keener, Craig 180 n.236, 185 n.296, 188
Kittredge, Cynthia 10
Kittredge, Cynthia Briggs 179

Lavan, Myles 50 n.58
Lendon, J. E. 7 n.22

McKnight, Scot 13
Michael, O. 9
Miles, Richard 39
Miller, James C. 9 n.32
Minear, Paul S. 8, 10
Morgan, Teresa 11, 104 n.3, 123

Nanos, Mark D. 9 n.34
Noreña, Carlos 37
North, John A. 23

Oakes, Lampe 2
Oakes, Peter 2, 2 n.6, 18, 129
O'Brien, Peter T. 4, 6 n.18
Olson, Stanley N. 124 n.30
Osgood, Josiah 56

Paton, W.R. 38
Peerbolte, Bert-Jan 186 n.270
Porter, Stanley 14 n.55
Price, S. R. F. 21–2, 23

Reasoner, Mark 2 n.4
Rich, J. 34 n.12

Roller, Matthew 104
Rosner, Brian 165
Rowe, C. Kavin 84 n.3
Rowe, Greg 84, 107

Said, Edward W. 2 n.4
Sandmel, Samuel 21 n.30
Schleritt, Contra 162 n.151
Scott, James C. 26–7
Spencer, Cole 24

Steele, C. E. W. 98
Stendahl, Krister 19–20, 20 n.26
Stuhlmacher, Peter 158

Thiessen, Matthew 150
Thurén, Melanie 16
Toit, A. B. du 7 n.25

Viard, Sébastian 149 n.82

Wagner, J. Ross 159, 167, 170 n.193
Walbank, F. W. 38 n.25
Wallace, David R. 5 n.17
Wasserman, Emma 152, 152 n.97
Wiedemann, T. E. J. 54, 72, 73 n.26, 109
Wilk, Florian 160
Wischmeyer, Oda 132 n.15
Witherington, Ben 116, 126, 136, 148 n.79, 173
Wright, N. T. 7, 8, 8 n.28, 154

Index of Biblical and Other Ancient Sources

Old Testament

Genesis
17:9-14   135 n.28

Leviticus
18:5   164 n.158

Deuteronomy
30:11-14   165
32:21   166
32:43   189 n.287
32:43 (15:10) 188, 189 n.287

Psalms
17   189
17:50   188
17:50 (LXX)   189
18 MT   188
117:1   189 n.287
117:1 (15:9, 11) 188

Ecclesiastes
7:20   138

Isaiah
10:22-23   161
11 (LXX)   189
11:10   189
11:10 (15:12) 188
40:1-2   167
45:23   185
65:1   166
65:1-2   167

Apocrypha or Deutero-Canonical Books

1 Maccabees
1:48   135 n.28
2:46   135 n.28

2 Maccabees
6:10   135 n.28

New Testament

1 Corinthians
9:27   93
12:12   93

Ephesians
3:7   181 n.248

Colossians
1:25   181 n.248

1 Thessalonians
4–5   171 n.197
5:3   21

1 Peter
2:13-17   50 n.57
2:14-15   181 n.246

Romans
1   3, 121
1: 17-18   7 n.21
1-7   10
1–11   184
1–16   115
1:1   157, 160
1:1, 6-7   157
1:1-4   6
1:1-5   130 n.3, 191
1:1-12   115–28
1:1-15   15, 15 n.4
1:1–11:36   16
1:1–17 +
15:14–16:24   16 n.5
1:2-15   127
1:3-4   132
1:5   1, 3–6, 5 n.13, 5 n.17, 6,
               7 n.25, 8–9, 9 n.34, 11,
               11 n.41, 12, 13, 19, 25,
               26–7, 29, 30, 33, 39, 43, 57,
               61, 67, 70, 74, 75, 78–9, 81,
               91, 109, 111, 113, 114, 119,

	120–3, 125, 129, 131, 132, 135, 142, 146, 164, 166, 167, 170, 172, 175, 186, 190, 191, 195	2:6-9	48
		2:7	73
		2:7; 5:10, 17–18, 21	156 n.119
1:5, 3:1	73	2:7-10	132
1:5, 13	142 n.54	2:8	13, 30, 90, 137 n.33
1:5, 13:1	76	2:8-9	42
1:5; 16:26	140	2:8-11	133
1:5-6	161	2:10	156 n.119
1:5-7	17	2:11	133
1:6-7	157	2:12	133
1:7	17 n.10, 156 n.119, 166, 170	2:12-27	152
		2:13	134
1:8	126	2:13-16	137
1:8-15	16, 123	2:13-27	135
1:8-17	131 n.12	2:14, 24	142 n.54
1:16	14 n.55	2:14-15	13 n.54, 134
1:16-17	6–7, 129–30, 133, 138, 139, 146, 160, 162, 166, 188, 192	2:15	155 n.18
		2:17-5:11	160 n.141
		2:17-29	17, 134–6
1:17	130, 171	2:21-23	134, 135
1:18	139	2:25	43
1:18, 2:5, 8	90	2:25-27	43, 135
1:18, 29	137 n.33	2:26	30 n.3, 155 n.18
1:18-32	42, 57, 80, 87, 91, 110, 130–1, 131 n.12, 134, 140, 146, 148, 161 n.44, 162, 171 n.197, 188, 192	2:27	43, 135, 155 n.18
		2:555–6	168 n.185
		2:654	168 n.185
		2:728–9	186 n.271
1:18–2:27	135	2:856	125 n.36
1:18–3:20	139	2:901	127 n.45
1:18–3:23	139	3	136
1:19-20	89	3-4	7
1:27	90	3-4, 9-10	7
1:30	86	3:1	136
1:32	155, 155 n.18, 156 n.119	3:1-20	136–9, 192
1:123	135 n.29	3:1-31	192
1:343–4	150 n.83	3:2	137, 155 n.18
1.1-5	14 n.55	3:3	136–7, 138
1.1.3	32	3:5	137, 137 n.33, 138
1.1.5	32	3:5; 5:9	90
1.5	14 n.55	3:5-18	137
1.8	7 n.23	3:10	138 n.37
1.16	14 n.55	3:10-12	138
1.16–17	7	3:10-18	138
2	7	3:12	138 n.37
2:1-3	96	3:13-18	138
2:1-3, 17-23	96	3:17; 5:1	156 n.119
2:1-16	136–9, 191	3:21-24	139
2:4-5	49	3:21-31	136, 192

3:22, 26	140	6:1-15	142
3:23	13, 90	6:1-21	38
3:29	142 n.54, 164	6:1-23	130, 142, 145, 146, 172, 186, 192
3.3.9	33		
3.4	91 n.23	6:3-5, 9, 16, 21, 23	156 n.119
3.4.2-3	33	6:4, 22-23	156 n.119
3.4.7	33	6:12	30, 86
3.12.5-6	36	6:12-13	43, 93
4	135	6:12-13, 6:19	93
4:1-8	13	6:12-17	13
4:1-15	13 n.54	6:12–17	7
4:1-25	139, 139 n.42, 192	6:13	137 n.33, 148
4:11, 16	140	6:13, 17-19	90
4:13	141	6:13-16	183
4:13-14, 16, 20	188	6:13-19	174
4:13-25	140	6:13b	148
4:16	140	6:14	149
4:17-18	140, 142 n.54	6:15-23	151
4:17-18, 1:5	140	6:16	30, 130, 140, 142, 150, 164, 186 n.270, 192
5	7, 143		
5-8	25, 97	6:16; 13:1	92
5–6	42, 72, 100	6:16-23	97
5–8	25, 97, 139	6:17	5, 123
5:1	19, 114, 162, 172	6:18	89, 150, 162
5:1-11	143 n.58	6:19	93
5:1-12	95	6:20-23	36, 150
5:1-17	142	6:22	89
5:1-21	142, 143–51, 192	7	13
5:1–6:23	156, 184, 192, 193, 195	7 (23/74)	152 n.95
5:1–6:25	160	7:1-25	151, 152, 153, 154, 192–3
5:1–8:39	151, 170, 173, 184, 192	7:5	93
5:3-11	51	7:5, 10, 13, 24	156 n.119
5:3–11	144	7:7-25	151–2, 153, 162
5:6-10	190	7:10	156 n.119
5:8	54	7:10; 8:2, 6, 10, 38	156 n.119
5:9	5, 143		
5:10, 12, 14, 17, 21	156 n.119	7:14-20	97
5:10-11	144	7:23	153
5:12-18	145	8	7
5:12-21	145, 154	8:1-3	89
5:14	13	8:1-4	10, 13 n.54, 153, 183
5:15-21	93, 145	8:1-11	156
5:18	30	8:1-39	145, 151, 153–5, 157, 193
5:18; 8:1	157	8:2, 6, 38	156 n.119
5:19	4–5, 7, 30, 140, 142, 144, 145, 146	8:4	13, 154, 155, 155 n.18
		8:6	156, 156 n.119
6	7, 19	8:7, 20	156 n.120
6:1	38	8:8	89

Index of Biblical and Other Ancient Sources   233

8:28	157	11:13	17, 169
8:37	157	11:13-31	100
8:38	30	11:15	156 n.119
9-10	7	11:27	88 n.14
9-11	73	11:30-31	100
9–11	17, 127, 136	11:30-32	57, 170
9:1-3	88	11:32	57
9:1-5	160	11.23	7 n.23
9:1-29	160–1, 162	11.26	170 n.193
9:1-33	162, 164	12-13	178 n.228
9:1–11:36	158–9, 171, 172, 193, 195	12-15	184
9:4	88 n.14	12-16	123
9:4, 8-9	188	12–13	171 n.197, 172 n.202
9:7-8	160	12–15	16, 50 n.57, 148, 171 n.196
9:13-18	68, 161	12:1	57, 100, 172, 173
9:14	137 n.33	12:1-13:15	172–6
9:15-16	100	12:1-15:13	171
9:15-16, 18, 23	100	12:1-21	173
9:16	163	12:1–15:13	171, 172, 173, 174, 193
9:22, 12:19	90	12:1–15:21	172
9:24, 30	142 n.54	12:1–15:33	123, 126, 170
9:24-26	161	12:3	125
9:27-29	161	12:3-21	174
9:30	162	12:3–15:13	175
9:30-10:21	161–7	12:4	93
9:30-33	161 n.48, 162, 163	13	13
9:30–10:4	164	13:1	10, 25, 26, 44, 47 n.52, 50 n.57, 54, 60, 68, 75, 78, 89, 90, 91 n.26, 93, 96, 97, 100, 101, 109, 113, 121, 180
10:1-4	163		
10:1-21	167		
10:3	156 n.120, 163		
10:4	10, 127, 164, 165		
10:5	182	13:1, 5	156 n.120
10:5-13	164, 164 n.161	13:1-4	92
10:6, 8-11, 14, 16-17	165 n.165	13:1-7	26–7, 43, 50 n.57, 87, 88, 121, 175, 176, 176 n.216, 176 n.217, 177, 178 n.229, 179, 181, 182, 194
10:6-17	165		
10:14	5 n.15		
10:16	5, 30, 123, 130, 165, 166	13:1-14	184
10:16-17	13	13:2	181
10:18-19	167	13:2-4	181
10:18-21	168, 188	13:3	88, 92, 177
10:19	142 n.54	13:3-4	101
10:19-20	166	13:4	110, 181 n.248
10:21	167	13:7	96
10.16	7 n.23	13:8	187
11:1-2	167	13:8-10	13, 183
11:1-36	167–71	13:8-14	184
11:3-5	54, 168	13:10	96
11:11-13, 25	142 n.54	13:12	43

Index of Biblical and Other Ancient Sources

14-15	13	17-21	124
14:1	124, 186	17-23	96, 142
14:1-15:13	185–90	17–18	7 n.23
14:1-23	185	18	100
14:1–15:13	94, 126, 148, 185–90	19	13, 30
14:1–15:33	127	19-21	142
14:4, 6, 8, 11, 14	185	21	13, 165
14:14	30	23	100
14:17, 19	156 n.119	25	13
15	13	26	13, 30
15:1	136, 186	27	13
15:1-2	187	30-31	7 n.23
15:7-29	128, 187	31	13
15:8	181 n.248, 188	33–6	7 n.23
15:9	100, 189	47–57	117 n.9
15:9-12	188	49–50	135 n.28
15:9-12, 16, 18, 27	142 n.54	252–3	127 n.44
		267	186 n.271
15:10-12	189	319–20	186 n.271
15:12	189	375–6	120 n.19
15:13, 33	156 n.119	378–80	186 n.271
15:14	30	678–9	169 n.188
15:14-16	124–8	872	186 n.271
15:14-16:23	115–28		
15:14-21	120, 124		
15:14-33	15		

Other Ancient Sources

15:14–16:27	128
15:15	125, 175
15:17-29	187
15:18	7, 7 n.23, 13, 30
15:19	7
15:23-33	16
15:31	136
15:33	126
16	5 n.15, 124, 126, 127
16-17	30, 67
16:1	111
16:1-7	124
16:1-25	126
16:4	17
16:4, 26	142 n.54
16:10-11	103 n.1
16:12	18
16:19	7, 13, 30, 120
16:20	156 n.119
16:25-27	127
16:26	127, 128, 142
16:27.3	36
16:34.4	36

1–2 Aristog.
1.20.8	58 n.76
2.25. 2	58 n.76
21.2	58 n.76
26.1, 27.1	58 n.76

1[2] Boeot.
13.9	58 n.76
1[2] Boeot. 13.9	58 n.76

ad Aen
8.721	112 n.43

Adul. amic.
25F	92

Aem.
3.7.3	59 n.80

Aen
6.852	3

Ages.
1.2	92 n.31
1.2.3, 28.3	59 n.80

2.1	91 n.27	*Ant. rom.*	
4.2	91 n.23	1.9.2, 35.1	43 n.37
6.4.6	58 n.76	1.20.2; 2.26.3	42 n.34
15.4	91	1.23.4	42 n.34
		2.3.6, 8	42 n.34
Amat.		3.3.4, 34.3	42 n.34
753E	59 n.80	3.4.1, 23.9	43 n.37
761F	92 n.31	3.34.1	42 n.34
		3.51.1-3	42 n.34
Anab.		4.5.3, 45.2,	
1.3.6, 9.5	58 n.76	70.5; 5.54.2	42 n.34
6.6.20	58 n.76	4.9.2	43 n.37
		5.59.1-75.3	44 n.39
Ann.		5.63.1, 71.1-3	42 n.34
1.19, 21, 28,		6.18.2, 19.4	43 n.37
35, 40, 65	72 n.24	6.23.2-3, 35.1,	
1.84	72 n.25	56.5, 91.4	44 n.39
2.43	72 n.25	6.89.4	42 n.34
2.55	72 n.24	7.14.5, 23.1, 56.4	42 n.34
3.12	72 n.24	7.19.2, 27.1, 46.4	44 n.39
3.40	80 n.42	8.16.2, 35.2,	
3.50	72 n.25	81.3	42 n.34
3.55, 75	76 n.34	8.36.4, 68.2	42 n.34
3.65	64 n.7, 71 n.21	8.68.3, 70.2,	
3.72	112 n.37	77.2, 3	43 n.37
4.18	72 n.24	8.87.3	44 n.39
4.20	71 n.21	9.3.2	44 n.39
4.46, 72	71 n.22	9.5.2, 59.5, 6, 69.3	43 n.37
5.3	71 n.21	9.37.2, 41.1, 60.1	42 n.34
6.10-11	71 n.21	10.4.4, 33.3, 43.2	44 n.39
6.44	72 n.24	10.5.3, 18.3	42 n.34
11.24	74 n.30, 80 n.42	10.21.8	43 n.37
12.11	71 n.22	11.4.2	42 n.34
12.47	76 n.34	11.45.2	44 n.39
12.54	71 n.22	11.56.1-2	42 n.34
13.54	71 n.22	12.13.2	42 n.34
14.13	76 n.34	15.5.1, 2, 7.5, 8.4	43 n.37
14.24	71 n.22	15.7.2	42 n.34
15.6	72 n.24	16.4.1	42 n.34
15.25	72 n.25	19.10.2	43 n.37
16.21	77 n.35	20.13.3	42 n.34
		32.1, 43.2	42 n.34
An seni		40.1; 3.23.3	42 n.34
797D	92 n.34	75.3, 76.1, 91.4	43 n.37
Ant.		*Apol.*	
9.55	181 n.248	20.2	58 n.76
13.257-8	135 n.28		
34.3	91 n.23	*[Apoph. lac.]*	
40.5, 61.2	59 n.80	219A	59 n.80

Index of Biblical and Other Ancient Sources 237

236E	59 n.80, 92 n.34	10:203	55 n.69
Arat.		10:229	55 n.72
9.5-6	59 n.80	10:888	52 n.61
11.1	91 n.27	10:889	52 n.62
Arch.		*Cal.*	
5.9.1	112 n.40	21	112 n.37
Arist.		*Cam.*	
5.2.5	59 n.80	17.4	92 n.31
Art.		*Cat.*	
26.5, 35.5	91 n.23	4.22	97 n.49
Att.		*Cat. Min.*	
6.3	126 n.39	1.4-5	59 n.80
293	96 n.44	8.2	92 n.31
Aug.		*Cato. Maj.*	
31	112 n.37	12.1-2	59 n.80
Bell. civ.		*Cic.*	
1.5.42, 11.101	58 n.75	21.5.5; 36.2.1	59 n.80
2.4.33	58 n.75	Cicero, *Inv.* 2.66	7 n.22
2.4.33; 3.8.63,		*Cim.*	
11.82	58 n.75	1.3	91 n.26
3.8.63, 11.82	58 n.75	*Claud.*	
5.3.21, 6.57	58 n.75	21	112 n.37
Ben.		*Clem.*	
2.18.5	100 n.56	4.2-3	91 n.28
3.21.2	100 n.58	24.2	100 n.57
3.38.2	100 n.56, 131 n.10	*Clu.*	
4.2.1	100 n.56	53.146	96 n.43
5.9.1	100 n.56	58.159	97 n.47
Brut.		*Coheb. ira*	
29.4	92 n.31	453C	92 n.32
Caecin.		*Cohib. ira*	
18.52	96 n.45	455B	59 n.80, 93 n.35
Cael.		*Comm. not.*	
400B	86 n.10	1060D	59 n.80
401A	86 n.10	*Comp. Ag. Cleom. cum Ti. Gracch.*	
Caes.		9.3 (2x)	92 n.31
15.2	59 n.80	*Comp. Eum. Sert.*	
33.2	91 n.23	1.1	91 n.23
CAH.		*Comp. Lys. Num.*	
10:198-209	54 n.68	2.3.11	59 n.80

Index of Biblical and Other Ancient Sources

Con. 1.2 — 131 n.10

[Cons. Apoll.]
111E — 92 n.31

Cor.
16.3 — 91 n.25
16.4-5; 18.1 — 59 n.80
167.7 — 58 n.76

Cry.
1.1.2-3, 8, 6.13-14, 20-22, 26, 42 — 58 n.76
2.2.8, 3.8, 4.22 — 58 n.76
3.1.18, 20, 3.9, 70 — 58 n.76
4.1.3, 4.8 — 58 n.76
5.1.11, 3.6 — 58 n.76
7.5.69, 70 — 58 n.76
8.1.3-4, 29, 3.6, 6.2 — 58 n.76

Curios.
13 — 92 n.32

De Constantia
2.1.1 — 100 n.56

De Invention
1.18.26 — 117

De Ira
20.5 — 100 n.57

Demetr.
15.1 — 59 n.80, 91 n.23
38.8 — 59 n.80

De Providentia
5.9 — 100 n.56

De Repub
1.4 — 146

Diatr.
1.25.14 — 89 n.17
1.29.29 — 90 n.18
2.10.6-8 — 90 n.18
2.16.45 — 90
3.1.16-18 — 90 n.18
3.12.13, 24.43 — 89 n.17
3.24.95-97 — 90 n.18
3.24.107 — 90 n.19
3.24.111 — 90 n.18
3.26.29 — 90 n.18
4.1.15 — 89 n.16
4.3.10 — 90 n.18
4.4.32 — 89 n.17
4.7.1 — 88 n.15
4.7.30-33 (31) — 88 n.15
4.12.12 — 89 n.17

Dion.
10.1 — 91 n.23

Dionysius of Halicarnassus
6.35 — 47 n.52
11:54 — 47 n.52

Disc.
1.14.16-18 — 180
2.14.11-13 — 148
3.1.37 — 90
3.11.1 — 131 n.11

Disobey Fort.
570D — 92 n.31

Div.
1.53 — 95 n.40
2.33 — 97 n.48

EN
1.13 — 85
10.14-15 — 86

Ench.
31.1 — 89 n.16

Ep.
8.5 — 100 n.56
16.5, 76.4 — 100 n.56
59.7 — 99 n.54
67.16 — 100 n.56
76.4 — 100 n.56
90.5 — 99 n.54
90.5 (2x) — 100 n.56
91.5 — 100 n.56
93.2 (2x) — 100 n.56
94.38 — 100 n.56
94.44 — 100 n.56
96.2 — 100 n.56
99.21 — 100 n.56
107.9 — 100 n.56
114.2 — 91 n.28, 99 n.55

Ep. Brut.
17.4 — 98 n.51

Index of Biblical and Other Ancient Sources

Eth. nic.
1.7.13-14   86 n.6
1.13.18-9,
3.12.16-7, 9.2,
10.12   86 n.9

Fab.
4.2   91 n.23
4.3.3   59 n.80

Fam.
9.25.2   97 n.49
15.1.5, 4.10   97 n.49

Fat.
8   112 n.40
11.25   97 n.47

Fin.
3.22   101 n.59

Flam.
12.11.1   59 n.80

Fort. Rom.
322F   92 n.30
322F; 325D-E   59 n.80

Frat. amor.
487C   92 n.33
elders (2x)   92 n.33
Gal. 1   3
Gal. 3:28   17

Galb.
4.2   91 n.26
22.3-4   92 n.29
22.4, 22.8   91 n.23

Garr.
503C   93 n.36

Gen. Socr.
578B   92 n.31
581F   59 n.80
591E   93 n.36
592C   59 n.80
595B   91 n.23

Geog.
4.6.6-9   106 n.10

Geogr.
3.4.13   59 n.78
4.1.5   59 n.79

4.2   91 n.28, 99
4.6.6   59 n.78
5.1.9   59 n.78
5.3.2 (2x), 4.1.12   58 n.78
5.3.4   58 n.78
6.1.13, 2.10, 4.2   58 n.78
6.3.9   59 n.78
6.4.2   59 n.79
7.1.4, 4.3 (2x), 4.4   58 n.78
8.4.1   58 n.78
8.9   58 n.78
9.1.20, 5.5   58 n.78
9.3.12   59 n.78
10.2.13, 4.11, 5.19   58 n.78
11.2.3, 10-11 (2x)   58 n.78
12.3.28   58 n.78
12.3.34, 6.2, 7.3   58 n.78
15.2.7, 3.12   58 n.78
15.3.23-24   59 n.79
16.1.18, 24, 2.14, 4.21   58-9 n.78

Hell.
1.6.6, 8   58 n.76
2.2.22, 3.34   58 n.76
2.4.23   58 n.76
3.1.13   58 n.76
6.1.1   58 n.76
7.1.8, 5.19   58 n.76

Her. mal.
863D   59 n.80

Herodotus
1.13   183
7.218   183

Hist.
1.2.3   3
1.10.5   33 n.8
1.24.11, 126.4-5   58 n.76
1.35.3   58 n.76
1.80, 82, 83-4   79 n.40
1.141.1   58 n.76
2.1.7   33 n.8
2.11   36
2.18.1   33 n.8
2.23.11-14   33 n.9
2.27, 97   79 n.40
2.58.7   33 n.9
3.15, 50   79 n.40
3.18.6-7   36 n.19

3.22.12	33 n.8	23.3.3	33 n.9
3.24.1-6	33 n.9	23.11.4	33 n.9
3.30.1	36 n.19	24.8.4	33 n.9
3.46.7; 12.4.5	33 n.9	24.8.4, 9.1	33 n.9
3.73.10	58 n.76	24.9.9	33 n.9
4.15.15-16, 137.4	58 n.76	24.9.14	33 n.9
4.19, 56, 72	79 n.40	24.12.1-4	33 n.9
4.22.4	33 n.9	25.2.11	33 n.9
4.71	80 n.42	29.27.13	33 n.9
5.2.10	33 n.9	30.8.1, 30.3	33 n.9
5.29.2 -5.30.1,		30.9.18	33 n.9
33.4, 91.3, 98.10	58 n.76	30.13.9, 23.2-3,	
5.30.1	33 n.9	31.8, 31.20	33 n.9
6, 9.2	33 n.9	31.1.1	33 n.8
6.4.4-5	33 n.9	32.8	33 n.9
6.12.2	33 n.9	32.8.6	33 n.9
6.12.4, 20, 35.		33.17.2	33 n.9
13, 41.15	58 n.76	36.4.6	33 n.9
6.22.1	58 n.76	36.9.1-17	39
6.57.8	33 n.9	36.9.7-8	39
7.5.1	33 n.9	36.9.16-17	33 n.9
7.8.9	33 n.9	36.11.2, 4	33 n.9
7.9.5, 7	33 n.8	36.19.17	39
7.16.6	58 n.76	54.2	33 n.9
7.20.2, 57.4	58 n.76	56	168

History of the Peloponnesian War

5.9.9	58 n.76
7.73	58 n.76

8.35.1	33 n.9	
8.64.1, 5	58 n.76	
8.69.10, 110.4	58 n.76	
9.4	33 n.9	
9.34.3	33 n.8	
9.53.6	58 n.76	

Histos 8

146–79	37 n.22

10.4.7	33 n.8
10.34.6	36 n.19
10.40.2	36 n.19
11.34.14	33 n.9

Il.

1.274, 295	58 n.76

15.1.2, 4.1-3,	
25.13	33 n.9

ILS

91	114 n.53
103	114 n.53
139	107 n.13
140	107 n.15, 107 n.16

15.2.2	33 n.9
15.5.13	33 n.8
15.20.7	33 n.9
16.27.3, 34.7	36 n.20
18.38.5	36 n.19
18.53.6	33 n.9

Inim. util.

90C	92 n.32

20.4.4-5	33 n.9

Inst.

4.1.5	117 n.12

20.9.10-12	133
21.22.8	33 n.9

Inst. Lac.

237D	92 n.33
237E	92 n.34

22.4.10	33 n.9
22.10.8	33 n.9
22.12.3	33 n.9

Inst. Or.
3.8.61-36	154 n.11
3.9.1	119 n.15
4.4.2-4	117 n.9
6.1	120 n.17

Inv.
1.2.3	98
1.14.19	117 n.10
1.15.6-7	117 n.13
1.38	96 n.43
1.52.98	124
1.55-6	120 n.17

Ira
9.4	99 n.54
13.6	100 n.56
17.2	100 n.56
18.6	99 n.54

J.W.
4.626	181 n.248

Leg.
1.7	95
2.8 (2x of priests)	97 n.48
3.1	96, 96 n.42
3.2	95
3.3	95, 96
3.4, 7, 19	95 n.41
3.8, 13	96 n.43

Leg. man.
15.48	97 n.49

[Lib. ed.]
7E	92 n.31

The Library of History
1.27.2	58 n.76
2.21.5	58 n.76
3.6.3, 49.3	58 n.76
4.11.1.4, 16.2, 31.5	58 n.76
5.8.2	58 n.76
7.12.2	58 n.76
11.65.2	58 n.76
12.16.3, 26.3, 29.2	58 n.76
14.6.2	58 n.76
16.8.1	58 n.76
17.5.4, 65.4,104.4	58 n.76
18.59.3, 63.3	58 n.76
19.61.3, 84.6	58 n.76
20.57.2, 5, 111.1-2, 4	58 n.76
21.21.11; 29.22.1	58 n.76
39.5	58 n.76

Libya
240.4	58 n.75

Lig.
7.20 (4x) 22	95 n.41

Livy
1.35.5	68 n.11
3.38.13–3.39.1	68 n.10
4.5.5	68 n.10
5.12.13	68 n.10
6.4.-5	66 n.8
6.6.8, 18	68 n.10
8.13.16-18	66 n.8
8.32.3	68 n.10
9.4.15-16	68 n.10
9.34.24	68 n.10
9.36.7	66 n.8
26.36.3	68 n.10
27.10.10	66 n.9
28.16.11	66 n.8
29.15.2-3	66 n.8
32.8.8-10	66 n.9
36.16.9	68 n.11
38.16.10	66 n.8
38.31.5-6, 34.1-4	66 n.8
38.43.1-6	66 n.8
39.25.12-15	68 n.11
39.42.16	66 n.8
39.53.11	66 n.8
40.21.8	68 n.11
41.10.7-8	68 n.10
44.10.1	68 n.11
45.31.9-10	66 n.8

Luc.
29.6	59 n.80

Lyc.
2.3; 16.4-6 (3x)	91 n.23
3.7	91 n.27
15.2	59 n.80
Lycg 15.2	92 n.31

Lycurgus
30.2	91

Lys.
10.5; 23.2	91 n.23

[Macart.]
6.5; 72.10	58 n.76

[Mag. mor.]
2.3.13	86 n.7
2.6.18	86

Mar.
14.2	59 n.80
14.4	91 n.23
29.4, 42.3	92 n.31

Marc.
3.4	91 n.23

Meg.
23.6	58 n.76

Mem.
1.2.34	58 n.76
2.2.11	58 n.76
3.3.8-10	58 n.76
3.9.11	58 n.76
4.4.13-17	58 n.76

Mem. Deeds.
4.3.3	72 n.25

Metaph.
1.2.3	87 n.12

Nat.
2.59.8	100 n.56
7.98	112 n.45
36.39	112 n.43
d. 2.3.8	97 n.48

Num.
6.2, 20.1, 3, 8	59 n.80

OCD
478	41 n31
877–8	63 n.2
928–9	151 n.92
1209	32 n.6
1447	58 n.77
1469	70 n.18

[Octavia]
458	99 n.54
840, 863	100 n.57

Od.
2.27	58 n.76
19.210-12	93
20.23	93 n.36

Oec.
5.15	58 n.76
13.5-10	58 n.76
21.4-5	58 n.76

Off.
1.23, 28, 29 (3x)	97 n.47
2.7	95 n.41

[Olymp.]
27.4	58 n.76

On the Accession of Alexander
14.2	58 n.76
17.1	58 n.76

Orat.
1.13.5	58 n.75
2.75-76	58 n.75
2.77.1	58 n.75
2.80	119 n.15
3.5.6, 40.5	58 n.75
6.51.3	58 n.75
14.8.4	58 n.75
23.12	58 n.75
35.14.6	58 n.75
56.6.1, 10.2	58 n.75
57.1-3	58 n.75
62.4.4, 5.3	58 n.75
76.5.4	58 n.75
80.3.2	58 n.75

Oth.
4.4	91 n.23

Parad.
5.33	97 n.46
5.35	151

Pel.
9.4	91 n.23

Per.
29.6.2	59 n.80

Phil.
2–4	171 n.197
2:5	188

Index of Biblical and Other Ancient Sources 243

3 4.8-9	97 n.49	*Publ.*	
4.9	95 n.41	11.4	59 n.80
4.14; 9.26	95 n.41		
5 11.29-30	97 n.49	*Quaest conv.*	
6, 3.5, 9 (2x)	95 n.41	618C	59 n.80
6 2.4 (3x)	97 n.49	620B	59 n.80
7, 1.2	95 n.41	655D	92 n.31
9, 3.6	97 n.49	708A	59 n.80
9.8	91 n.23		
13, 3.7	94 n.38	*Quaest. plat.*	
13, 6.14	95 n.41	1008B	92 n.32
Phoc.		*Quaest. rom.*	
10.5	91 n.23	55	92 n.31
24.3	59 n.80		
		Rab. Perd. (to orders)	
Pol.		8.22	97 n.49
2.5.14	153		
4.9.4	86 n.6	*Rect. rat. aud.*	
		26E	92 n.32
[Poly.]			
65.9	58 n.76	*[Reg. imp. apophth.]*	
		192D-F	59 n.80
Pomp.			
6.2.2	59 n.80	*Rep.*	
12.4.1	59 n.80	1.34	186
13.2	59 n.80	3.15	111
31.1	59 n.80		
41.1	59 n.80	*Resp.*	
41.1, 59.2	91 n.23	1.36, 40	95 n.41
45.2	112 n.42	1.39	97 n.49
54.4 59.2.1	59 n.80	2.1.	97 n.48
65.1.4	59 n.80	3.11 (3x)	96 n.43
70.1-3	59 n.80	3.15	94 n.38
75.2	59 n.80	3.29	97 n.49
		6.11	97 n.49
P. Oxy.			
114.16-18	126 n.39	*R G*	
1296.9-19	126 n.39	(20.1)	112 n.43
		13	144
		26.1	51
Praec. ger. rei publ.			
20	91 n.27	*R.H.*	
815E	92 n.34	10:94	52 n.64
		36.36.4, 47.2	47 n.51
Princ. iner.		36.46.2	47 n.54
779A	59 n.80	37.25.4	47 n.51
780B-C, F	59 n.80	38.10.1, 41.5	47 n.51
780e	164 n.156	38.35.3	47 n.52
		38.47.1; 40.5.3	47 n.54
Prov. cons.		39.60.1	51 n.59
10.25	95 n.41	40.30.2	47 n.51

40.43.1-3	49 n.56	*Rhet. Ad. Herr.*	
40.62.4	47 n.54	1.3.4	117 n.10
40.65.4	51 n.59	*Rhet. Her.*	
41.11.2	51 n.59	4.26.35	142 n.55
41.55.2, 57.3, 59.4	47 n.51		
42.3.4, 20.4, 44.1	47 n.51	*SEG*	
43.9.2	47 n.51	18 578	109 n.22
44.44.2, 45.2	47 n.51		
45.9.2	47 n.51	*Sera*	
46.50.6	47 n.54	550B	59 n.80
47.13.2	51 n.59	*Sert.*	
47.22.3, 24.2, 39.3	47 n.51	3.2	59 n.80, 91 n.23
47.39.2; 52:42.1-3	47 n.54		
48.2.4	51 n.59	*Sest.*	
48.49.1	47 n.51	63.143	95 n.41
50.16.1	47 n.51		
50.17.5	51 n.59	*Sol.*	
50.33.2	47 n.51	8.3	91 n.23
51.18.1	47 n.51	8.3.4	59 n.80
52.5.4, 19.2-3,5			
21.8, 27.1	47 n.51	*Soph. elench.*	
53.1.13	51 n.59	12.2, 15.40	86 n.9
53.5.4, 10.5,		*Sull.*	
19.5, 26.3, 32.5	47 n.51	16.4	59 n.80
54.9.1, 32.1	47 n.51		
54.19.2	51 n.59	*[Theocr.]*	
55.17.3	52 n.63	49.5	58 n.76
55.34.5	47 n.51		
56.19.1	47 n.54	*Ti. C. Gracch.*	
56.25.6, 33.4,		3.1; 10.8	59 n.80
41.4	47 n.51	17.4	91 n.23
57.15.8	47 n.54		
58.25.1	47 n.51	*Tim.*	
59.21.3	47 n.51	10.1	59 n.80, 91 n.23
60.6.7	51 n.59	*Top.*	
60.9.5	47 n.51	1.14.20	86 n.9
60.22.4	47 n.54	25.98-99	120 n.17
68.14.3, 5, 23.1	47 n.51	97-98	119 n.15
69.5.3	47 n.51		
69.22.2	47 n.54	*Tranq.*	
70.30.1	47 n.51	9.1.3, 10	100 n.56
		Tranq. an.	
Rhet.		472C	92 n.31
1.25.21-3	87 n.11		
2.12.3	86 n.9	*Tu. san.*	
2.18	116 n.2	123C	93 n.36
3.13	119 n.15		
427	117 n.11	*Tusc.*	
		1.49	95 n.40

2.20	97 n.47	[Virt. vit.]	
4.9	96 n.43	7.1–5	87
4.9, 17	97 n.47	Vit. beat.	
Tusc. Disp.		11.3	100 n.56
2.4	135	13.2	100 n.56
		15.4	100 n.56
Verum I\mp.			
2.6.	126 n.39	Vit. pud.	
		529E	59 n.80
Virt. mor.		534E	92 n.31
442D	93 n.36		
445B	92 n.32		

www.ingramcontent.com/pod-product-compliance
Lightning Source LLC
Chambersburg PA
CBHW062132300426
44115CB00012BA/1890